Tyndale New Testament Commentaries

Volume 20

Series Editor: Eckhard J. Schnabel
Consulting Editor: Nicholas Perrin

Revelation

An Introduction and Commentary

Ian Paul

IVP Academic
An imprint of InterVarsity Press
Downers Grove, Illinois

Inter-Varsity Press, England
36 Causton Street, London SW1P 4ST, England
Website: www.ivpbooks.com
Email: ivp@ivpbooks.com

InterVarsity Press, USA
P.O. Box 1400, Downers Grove, IL 60515, USA
Website: www.ivpress.com
Email: email@ivpress.com

Inter-Varsity Press, England, publishes Christian books that are true to the Bible and that
communicate the gospel, develop discipleship and strengthen the church for its mission in the world.

IVP originated within the Inter-Varsity Fellowship, now the Universities and Colleges Christian
Fellowship, a student movement connecting Christian Unions in universities and colleges throughout
Great Britain, and a member movement of the International Fellowship of Evangelical Students.
That historic association is maintained, and all senior IVP staff and committee members subscribe
to the UCCF Basis of Faith. Website: www.uccf.org.uk.

InterVarsity Press®, USA, is the book-publishing division of InterVarsity Christian Fellowship/
USA® and a member movement of the International Fellowship of Evangelical Students.
Website: www.intervarsity.org.

Unless otherwise stated, Scripture quotations are from the HOLY BIBLE, TODAY'S
NEW INTERNATIONAL VERSION.

First published 2018

Set in Garamond 11/13pt
Typeset in Great Britain by CRB Associates, Potterhanworth, Lincolnshire

UK ISBN: 978–1–78359–344–6 (print)
UK ISBN: 978–1–78359–345–3 (digital)

US ISBN: 978–0–8308–4300–8 (print)
US ISBN: 978–0–8308–7385–2 (digital)

British Library Cataloguing-in-Publication Data
A catalogue record for this book is available from the British Library.

Library of Congress Cataloging-in-Publication Data
A catalog record for this book is available from the Library of Congress.

TYNDALE NEW TESTAMENT COMMENTARIES

VOLUME 20

REVELATION

CONTENTS

General preface   vii
Author's preface   ix
Chief abbreviations   xi
Select bibliography   xiii

Introduction   1

1. Approaching Revelation   1
2. Who was John?   7
3. The date of Revelation   11
4. The social and historical context   16
5. Did John actually have a vision?   22
6. What kind of text is Revelation?   25
7. Reading Revelation's imagery   30
8. Revelation's use of numbers   34
9. Revelation's use of the Old Testament   39
10. The structure of Revelation   41
11. Revelation's main theological themes   45
12. Approaches to its interpretation   48

Analysis   53

Commentary   57

GENERAL PREFACE

The Tyndale Commentaries have been a flagship series for evangelical readers of the Bible for over sixty years. Both the original New Testament volumes (1956–1974) as well as the new commentaries (1983–2003) rightly established themselves as a point of first reference for those who wanted more than is usually offered in a one-volume Bible commentary, without requiring the technical skills in Greek and in Jewish and Greco-Roman studies of the more detailed series, with the advantage of being shorter than the volumes of intermediate commentary series. The appearance of new popular commentary series demonstrates that there is a continuing demand for commentaries that appeal to Bible study leaders in churches and at universities. The publisher, editors and authors of the Tyndale Commentaries believe that the series continues to meet an important need in the Christian community, not least in what we call today the Global South, with its immense growth of churches and the corresponding need for a thorough understanding of the Bible by Christian believers.

In the light of new knowledge, new critical questions, new revisions of Bible translations, and the need to provide specific guidance on the literary context and the theological emphases of the individual passage, it was time to publish new commentaries in the series. Four authors will revise their commentary that appeared in the second series. The original aim remains. The new commentaries are neither too short nor unduly long. They are exegetical and thus root the interpretation of the text in its historical context. They do not aim to solve all critical questions, but they are written with an awareness of major scholarly debates which may be treated in the Introduction, in Additional Notes or in the commentary itself. While not specifically homiletic in aim, they want to help readers to understand the passage under consideration in such a way that they begin to see points of relevance and application, even though the commentary does not explicitly offer these. The authors base their exegesis on the Greek text, but they write for readers who do not know Greek; Hebrew and Greek terms that are discussed are transliterated. The English translation used for the first series was the Authorized (King James) Version, while the volumes of the second series mostly used the Revised Standard Version; the volumes of the third series use either the New International Version (2011) or the New Revised Standard Version as primary versions, unless otherwise indicated by the author.

An immense debt of gratitude for the first and second series of the Tyndale Commentaries was owed to R. V. G. Tasker and L. Morris, who each wrote four of the commentaries themselves. The recruitment of new authors for the third series proved to be effortless, as colleagues responded enthusiastically to be involved in this project, a testimony both to the larger number of New Testament scholars capable and willing to write commentaries, to the wider ethnic identity of contributors, and to the role that the Tyndale Commentaries have played in the church worldwide. It continues to be the hope of all those concerned with this series that God will graciously use the new commentaries to help readers understand as fully and clearly as possible the meaning of the New Testament.

Eckhard J. Schnabel, Series Editor
Nicholas Perrin, Consulting Editor

AUTHOR'S PREFACE

No scholarship is ever done in isolation; it is always the work of a community, whether that is real or virtual. I am indebted to all who have gone before me, in particular to Richard Bauckham, whose monumental collection of essays was published while I was doing my PhD, and who helped me enormously to think through issues of numerology, composition and context. I have greatly valued David Mathewson's meticulous work on the text of Revelation, Craig Keener's remarkable catalogue of primary sources in his commentary, Gordon Fee's lively observations and Craig Koester's exemplary scholarship and review of options, even at points where we disagree. I appreciated Steve Moyise's chairing of the British New Testament Conference Revelation seminar group for seven years, and his invitation to me to chair following him (which I did for ten years), and all the members of the group who contributed much stimulating discussion. Thanks go to Joel Green and Anthony Thiselton for various encouraging conversations, to Paula Gooder for friendship in the task of writing, to Richard Briggs for helpful interaction at various stages, and to Eckhard Schnabel for his thorough and helpful editorial comments. I am indebted to Christopher Rowland and Stephen Travis as my PhD supervisors many years ago, and to Stephen for going above and beyond the call of duty in proofreading the first draft of this text – a very generous gift, much appreciated. I am indebted to Michael Wilcock, whose volume in The Bible Speaks Today series was my first introduction to Revelation while a teenager; to Steve Walton, who was my PhD examiner and is a continuing friend and conversation partner; and to the late Dick (R. T.) France, an inspiration both in person and in writing for his clarity, insight and integrity in his reading of the Scriptures.

Scholarship never happens without the support of friends, and I am so grateful to Simon and Glenda Devlin, who invited me and my wife to join them in France for what became for me a very fruitful writing week that helped this work on its way to completion. Thanks too to the Westlife Missional Community, my clergy colleague Amanda Digman, and my in-laws Ray and Pam Fardon, who have all been constant supports in prayer, and the staff of Froth, the Waffle House and Coffee Shop, where a good deal of this was written. Thank you to Lizzi, Ben and Becca, who have tolerated for many years the theological eccentricities of their father (and especially to Lizzi for proofreading some sections of the text); to Barney for constant companionship; and last but by no means least to my wife Maggie. Your love, support, understanding, humour and encouragement have been like a pearl without price – you are a 'suitable companion' in more ways than you can imagine. Thank you.

Ian Paul

CHIEF ABBREVIATIONS

AB	Anchor Bible
AT	Author's translation
BNTC	Black's New Testament Commentaries
ICC	International Critical Commentary
JSNTSup	Journal for the Study of the New Testament Supplement Series
NIGTC	New International Greek Testament Commentary
NovTSup	Novum Testamentum Supplement Series
NT	New Testament
OT	Old Testament
WBC	Word Biblical Commentary
WUNT	Wissenschaftliche Untersuchungen zum Neuen Testament

Bible versions

SELECT BIBLIOGRAPHY

Commentaries on Revelation

Aune, David E. (1997–8), *Revelation*, WBC, 3 vols. (Dallas: Word;
Nashville: Thomas Nelson).

Beale, G. K. (1999), *Revelation*, NIGTC (Grand Rapids:
Eerdmans).

Boesak, Allan (1987), *Comfort and Protest: Reflections on the
Apocalypse of John of Patmos* (Edinburgh: St Andrew Press).

Caird, G. B. (1966), *A Commentary on the Revelation of St John the
Divine*, BNTC (London: A. & C. Black).

Charles, R. H. (1920), *A Critical and Exegetical Commentary
on the Revelation of St John*, ICC, 2 vols. (Edinburgh: T&T
Clark).

Fee, Gordon D. (2010), *Revelation*, New Covenant Commentary
(Eugene: Wipf and Stock).

Keener, Craig S. (2000), *Revelation*, NIV Application Commentary
(Grand Rapids: Zondervan).

Koester, Craig R. (1) (2001), *Revelation and the End of All Things*
(Grand Rapids: Eerdmans).

—— (2) (2014), *Revelation: A New Translation with Introduction
and Commentary*, AB (New Haven: Yale University Press).

Kovacs, Judith and Christopher Rowland (2004), *Revelation:
The Apocalypse to Jesus Christ* (Oxford: Blackwell).

Mathewson, David (2016), *Revelation* (Waco: Baylor University
Press).

Osborne, Grant R. (2002), *Revelation* (Grand Rapids: Baker Academic).

Rowland, Christopher (1993), *Revelation* (London: Epworth Press).

Smalley, Stephen (2005), *The Revelation to John* (London: SPCK).

Swete, Henry Barclay (1906), *The Apocalypse of St John: The Greek Text* (London: Macmillan).

Thomas, John Christopher and Frank D. Macchia (2016), *Revelation* (Grand Rapids: Eerdmans).

Wall, Robert W. (1995), *Revelation* (Peabody: Hendrickson).

Witherington III, Ben (2003), *Revelation* (Cambridge: Cambridge University Press).

Other works

Allen, Garrick, Ian Paul and Simon Woodman (eds.) (2015), *The Book of Revelation: Currents in British Research on the Apocalypse*, WUNT 2/411 (Tübingen: Mohr Siebeck).

Aune, David E. (2008), *Apocalypticism, Prophecy, and Magic in Early Christianity: Collected Essays* (Grand Rapids: Baker Academic).

Bauckham, Richard (1993), *The Climax of Prophecy: Studies on the Book of Revelation* (Edinburgh: T&T Clark).

—— (1993), *The Theology of the Book of Revelation*, New Testament Theology (Cambridge: Cambridge University Press).

—— (1997), *The Gospel for All Christians: Rethinking the Gospel Audiences* (Edinburgh: T&T Clark).

—— (2007), *The Testimony of the Beloved Disciple: Narrative, History, and Theology in the Gospel of John* (Grand Rapids: Baker Academic).

Bullinger, E. W. (2011), *Figures of Speech Used in the Bible Explained and Illustrated* (Eastford, CT: Martino Fine Books; facsimile reprint of 1898 edn).

Burridge, Richard (2004), *What Are the Gospels? A Comparison with Graeco-Roman Biography*, 2nd edn (Grand Rapids: Eerdmans).

Collins, John J. (2016), *The Apocalyptic Imagination: An Introduction to Jewish Apocalyptic Literature*, 3rd edn (Grand Rapids: Eerdmans).

Fee, Gordon D. and Douglas Stuart (2014), *How to Read the Bible for All Its Worth* (Grand Rapids: Zondervan).

Friesen, Steven J. (1993), *Twice Neokoros: Ephesus, Asia and the Cult of the Flavian Imperial Family* (Leiden: Brill).

—— (2001), *Imperial Cults and the Apocalypse of John: Reading Revelation in the Ruins* (Oxford/New York: Oxford University Press).

Gamble, Harry Y. (1995), *Books and Readers in the Early Church: A History of Early Christian Texts* (New Haven: Yale University Press).

Gentry, Kenneth L., Sam Hamstra, C. Marvin Pate and Robert L. Thomas (1998), *Four Views on the Book of Revelation* (Grand Rapids: Zondervan).

Gorman, Michael J. (2011), *Reading Revelation Responsibly: Uncivil Worship and Witness; Following the Lamb into the New Creation* (Eugene: Cascade).

Green, Joel B. (1997), *The Gospel of Luke* (Grand Rapids: Eerdmans).

Heil, John Paul (2014), *The Book of Revelation: Worship for Life in the Spirit of Prophecy* (Eugene: Cascade).

Hemer, Colin (1989), *The Letters to the Seven Churches of Asia in Their Local Setting*, JSNTSup 11 (Sheffield: Sheffield Academic Press).

Howard-Brook, Wes and Anthony Gwyther (1999), *Unveiling Empire: Reading Revelation Then and Now* (Maryknoll: Orbis).

Kraus, Thomas J. and Michael Sommer (eds.) (2016), *Book of Seven Seals: The Peculiarity of Revelation, Its Manuscripts, Attestation, and Transmission*, WUNT 363 (Tübingen: Mohr Siebeck).

Lincoln, Andrew T. (2001), *Truth on Trial: The Lawsuit Motif in the Fourth Gospel* (Peabody: Hendrickson).

Longenecker, Bruce (2010), *Remember the Poor: Paul, Poverty, and the Greco-Roman World* (Cambridge/Grand Rapids: Eerdmans).

Maier, Harry O. (2002), *Apocalypse Recalled: The Book of Revelation after Christendom* (Minneapolis: Augsburg Fortress).

Menken, Maarten J. J. (1985), *Numerical Literary Techniques in John: The Fourth Evangelist's Use of Numbers of Words and Syllables*, NovTSup 55 (Leiden: Brill).

Millard, Alan (1964), *Reading and Writing in the Time of Jesus* (Edinburgh: T&T Clark).

Moyise, Steve (ed.) (2000), *Old Testament in the New Testament: Essays in Honour of J. L. North* (Sheffield: Continuum).

—— (ed.) (2002), *Studies in the Book of Revelation* (Edinburgh: T&T Clark).

Murphy, Kelly J. and Justin Jeffcoat Schedtler (eds.) (2016), *Apocalypses in Context: Apocalyptic Currents Through History* (Minneapolis: Fortress).

O'Hear, Natasha and Anthony O'Hear (2015), *Picturing the Apocalypse: The Book of Revelation in the Arts over Two Millennia* (New York/Oxford: Oxford University Press).

Palmer, James (2014), *The Apocalypse in the Early Middle Ages* (Cambridge: Cambridge University Press).

Parcak, Sarah H. (2009), *Satellite Remote Sensing for Archaeology* (London/New York: Routledge).

Ramsay, Sir William Mitchell (1994), *The Letters to the Seven Churches*, rev. edn by Mark W. Wilson (Peabody: Hendrickson).

Rudwick, M. J. S. and E. M. B. Green (1957), 'The Laodicean Lukewarmness', *Expository Times* 69, pp. 176–178.

Stark, Rodney (1997), *The Rise of Christianity* (San Francisco: HarperCollins).

Stiver, Dan. R. (2001), *Theology after Ricoeur: New Directions in Hermeneutical Theology* (Louisville: Westminster John Knox).

Thompson, Leonard L. (1996), *The Book of Revelation: Apocalypse and Empire*, rev. edn (New York: Oxford University Press).

Walton, Steve, Paul Trebilco and David W. J. Gill (eds.) (2017), *The Urban World and the First Christians* (Grand Rapids: Eerdmans).

Winter, Bruce W. (2015), *Divine Honours for the Caesars: The First Christians' Responses* (Grand Rapids: Eerdmans).

Witherington III, Ben (2008), *The Letters to Philemon, the Colossians, and the Ephesians: A Socio-Rhetorical Commentary on the Captivity Epistles* (Grand Rapids: Eerdmans).

INTRODUCTION

1. Approaching Revelation

The book of Revelation is the most remarkable text you will ever read. Setting aside any claims that we might want to make about it as a result of its being part of the canonical Scriptures of the Christian faith, it is one of the most extraordinary pieces of literature ever written by a human being, and it ought to feature in any university course on world literature. Its engagement with the canonical Old Testament Scriptures, its use of contemporary first-century culture and mythology, its elaborate structure and multiple echoes, interweaving, repetition and development of themes, its extraordinarily sophisticated use of numerology in three different ways, and the sheer power of its rhetoric and impact of its imagery – all these make it a remarkable and endlessly fascinating text. Outside of the Christian Scriptures, there really is nothing in all of human literature to compare with it.

The nature of this text is reflected in the impact that it has had on human history, belief and culture. At a popular level, it is hard to escape the pervasive influence of its imagery, all of which is unique in the New Testament. There is hardly a day that goes by without some mention of Armageddon (16:16) as a metaphor for a cataclysmic event involving conflict, and the first word of the text, 'apocalypse', has not only become the descriptor for a whole genre of literature from the period, but serves as common expression for any kind of impending disaster. Images of people seated on clouds and playing harps (14:2, 14) have entered the popular consciousness, becoming a visual metaphor for anything thought to be 'heavenly', even in television advertisements. Disasters that include warfare, famine or disease are identified with the 'four horsemen of the apocalypse' (6:1–8);[1] we all know that to enter heaven we must pass St Peter who is standing at the 'pearly gates' (21:21); and everyone is wary of the 'number of the beast' (13:18). We might then add 'Jezebel' (2:20), being 'lukewarm' (3:16), the 'grapes of wrath' (14:19), a 'scarlet woman' (17:3) and 'streets paved with gold' (21:21) – the list goes on![2]

But Revelation has shaped the world at a more serious level too. Through the school of interpretation know as Dispensational Premillennialism, which originated with J. N. Darby around 1830 and was popularized by the Scofield Reference Bible in 1909, the book of Revelation has had a direct impact on significant world leaders, and through them shaped international politics.[3] Many people influenced by this approach ask the question: 'If God is going to destroy and remake the world, do we really need to care for it, or is this a distraction from more important things?' (We will see, as we read the text itself, that this is a mistaken interpretation of what Revelation actually says.) Revelation was an important text in shaping the religious imagination, especially in Europe around the year 1000

---

1. Francis Ford Coppola's 1979 film about the Vietnam War, *Apocalypse Now*, had four helicopters crossing a sunset sky on its promotional poster.

2. For a thorough review of the influence of apocalyptic ideas on contemporary culture, see the third part of Murphy and Schedtler, *Apocalypses in Context*.

3. A very different reading of the contemporary political importance of Revelation can be found in Howard-Brook and Gwyther, *Unveiling Empire*.

since this was thought to be connected to the millennium in Revelation 20.[4] It induced a significant crisis around the year 1260 thanks to the influence of the teaching of Joachim of Fiore, who equated the 1,260 days of Revelation 12:6 with the 1,260 years that had passed since Jesus was born so that many expected the ideal 'kingdom of the Spirit' to break into history. The conflict between the beast and the true people of God shaped Martin Luther's outlook, and he was happy to identify the false belief of the Roman Catholic Church with the great prostitute of Revelation 17.[5] More positively, Revelation has been a text that has provided profound comfort and encouragement to many generations of Christians under pressure or persecution for their faith,[6] and a new generation of readers is discovering its personal, social and political significance.[7]

Revelation has also been uniquely influential in Christian art and worship. The use of the Hebrew term 'Hallelujah' in Christian worship derives from its use in the hymns in Revelation (the term occurs nowhere else in the NT).[8] We are accustomed to think of

---

4. See the study by Palmer, *Apocalypse in the Early Middle Ages*, which demonstrates the close interweaving between apocalyptic ideas and political action in the period.

5. One of the illustrations in Luther's translation of the Bible depicts the prostitute riding the beast wearing what is very clearly a Papal tiara. The compliment was returned by Catholic theologian Peter Bungus, who showed that Martin Luther's name added up to 666!

6. An engaging example from a modern context is Boesak, *Comfort and Protest*, written after an angelic visitation to Boesak when he was imprisoned by the apartheid regime in South Africa.

7. Maier, *Apocalypse Recalled* offers a reading rooted in the text but engaging with the contemporary relevance to a post-Christendom culture.

8. 'Hallelujah' is an approximate transliteration of the Hebrew term that introduces or occurs in many of the Psalms. But normal translational practice is to render this in English as 'praise the Lord', which is what it means. Where Hebrew terms are transliterated (rather than translated) in the Greek New Testament – such as 'Amen', 'Abba' and 'Hallelujah' in Revelation – it is normal to transliterate them into English and thereby they enter the English language.

God and Jesus as the 'Alpha and the Omega', of Jesus 'coming quickly' and (perhaps slightly less often) of Jesus 'having the keys to death and Hades'. These ideas come from Revelation, and (somewhat ironically) are ones that John has appropriated from pagan magical cults (principally that of the underworld goddess Hekate) and refashioned as claims about God and Jesus as a way of denying the reality of those cults. The same is true of the importance of the colour white in Christian worship down the ages, deriving from the repeated descriptions of God's people worshipping in white (3:4; 6:11; 7:9; 19:8). It has been estimated that nearly 50% of all Christian art over two millennia has been influenced by Revelation, not least because, apart from Jesus' parables, it offers the richest supply of visual descriptions. Perhaps the most extravagant example of this is the series of tapestries that can be seen at Château d'Angers in the Loire Valley in France; it originally comprised ninety scenes in six sections that were each 78 ft wide and 20 ft long. On a smaller scale, scenes from Revelation can be found in almost every church or cathedral in the West that contains stained glass.[9]

Revelation has been equally important in its contribution to Christian theology, having the most developed trinitarian theology of any New Testament book. It identifies Jesus and God by depicting them sharing the same throne, ruling as equal sovereigns, sharing the same titles, and even at key points in the text together sharing singular verbs and pronouns (11:15; 14:1; 21:22; 22:3–4). The Spirit is also closely identified with Jesus, particularly in the image of the seven spirits of God which are the eyes of the Lamb in 5:6. Revelation was one of the earliest texts given wide attestation as part of the early Christian canon of Scripture, largely because it was believed to be written by the apostle John, but its authorship was later disputed, so that it did not have the influence on patristic debates about the status of Jesus and the nature of God that it might have had – John's Gospel instead being the most influential.[10]

---

9. For a comprehensive overview of Revelation in artistic expression, see O'Hear and O'Hear, *Picturing the Apocalypse*.

10. See Michael Kruger, 'The Reception of the Book of Revelation in the Early Church', pp. 159–174, in Kraus and Sommer, *Book of Seven Seals*.

Despite the importance of this text, it remains widely neglected. In many churches it is rarely preached on; many ordinary Christians do not know what to do with it; some deliberately avoid it, perhaps because of strange or unnerving encounters they experienced in the past. But contemporary Christians need to engage responsibly with this text more than ever, for at least two reasons. First, Revelation is the book that above all others tests our ability to read Scripture well. People who might agree on the meaning and significance of other texts in the New Testament or other parts of the Bible suddenly find themselves at odds when it comes to making sense of this one. It demands that we pay attention and listen well, and that we allow the text to be 'other' than us without us imposing our own assumptions on it, and it calls us to be rooted in its canonical context as part of Scripture. There is no more urgent need for God's people than to recover both confidence and competence in our reading of Scripture (all our current disagreements are symptoms of this), and reading Revelation provokes us to address this.

Second, Revelation is the most developed example of a writer in Scripture wrestling with the ideological implications of the gospel, and engaging with an opposing ideological system in the light of what God has done for us in Jesus, as shaped by the inspiration of the Spirit. The near-universal decline in church attendance in the West is a sign that, like the Christians in Sardis, Western Christians have been caught napping: the ideological climate has shifted dramatically in the last generation or two, and we have been so complacent and content with a 'Christendom' model of society that we haven't known how to respond. Whilst Christians in other parts of the world have not experienced this, globalization and the spread of economic wealth could see the same thing happen elsewhere in the next generation. Revelation shows us very clearly how to be alert to the context we are in and how to both engage with and stand up to the pressure of ideology, and it gives us the resources to live courageously in an inhospitable climate.

My approach to this text includes four emphases. The first is a disciplined attention to the text itself. It is surprising how many approaches to Revelation, even some quite sophisticated and scholarly ones, do not pay sufficient attention to the actual text. Although John reports a vision, what he gives us is a text, and there are several places where he emphasizes that we need to attend to the actual words he uses. In this regard, he sits within a Jewish rabbinical tradition of carefully studying each and every word – and one thing that recent scholarship has been very clear on is the importance of John's actual words. A theory of structure or meaning that does not account for John's precise wording (e.g. in discussing the 'three woes' of 8:13) will not be able to offer a satisfying explanation of what John is saying. I have worked on the Greek text, but this commentary is for readers of the English text, so I have been careful to explain any observations in English terms. I have mostly cited the text of the TNIV, but I have quite often used my own translation to make the connections between texts clear. When reading Revelation, to see more clearly the words John uses, it is always best to use a translation that is more word for word than a dynamic equivalent or paraphrase.

Second, I pay careful attention to the way John draws on the Old Testament and the way that he uses and reuses such words and ideas. I have therefore frequently commented on how the text relates to other parts of Scripture, which Old Testament texts John appears to be drawing on, and the parallels we find in other parts of the New Testament.[11]

Third, it is also vital that we understand how John's message will have communicated to, and been understood by, his original audience in the first century, so I have included observations from first-century culture and understandings where they inform our reading.

Lastly, I myself am someone who preaches week in and week out to a local congregation, so I am acutely aware of the demands of making connections between the text and our contemporary world. I have therefore included, within the comments on the texts as well as in summary paragraphs, language and ideas that I hope will be useful to preachers and spark ideas for contemporary reflections.

---

11. The question of John's use of the OT, including how we even
    determine whether there is an allusion, has been the subject
    of much scholarly debate. On detecting and classifying allusions,
    see my 'The Use of the Old Testament in Revelation 12', in Moyise,
    Old Testament in the New.

My hope and prayer is that this commentary will inform, enlighten, enrich and inspire its readers, and through them many others, and equip God's people to be faithful witnesses to the testimony of Jesus and the Word of God.

2. Who was John?

The author of Revelation names himself as 'John' four times in the text, three at the beginning (1:1, 4, 9) and once near the end (22:8). He makes a strong claim to identify with his audience, addressing them directly in the epistolary opening (1:4) and describing himself as 'brother and companion' (1:9). This claim seems very well supported by the local detail that is found in Revelation 2 – 3, where numerous aspects of the messages appear to make particular sense of local features of the cities that are addressed here and their culture.[12] It is also evident in several parts of the text that John had a well-developed knowledge of the workings of the Roman Empire, particularly expressed in the details of the twenty-eight cargoes that the merchants of the earth mourn they will never again be able to trade in 18:11–13.[13]

The immediate question that then arises is whether this John is the same as John the Apostle. Irenaeus (AD 130–202) states that Revelation was written 'no long time ago, but almost in our own day, towards the end of Domitian's reign'.[14] He also states that the author was 'John the disciple of our Lord', or simply 'John', and in this he

---

12. The work which highlighted this more than any other, and which commentators frequently draw on, is Hemer, *Letters to the Seven Churches*. Hemer based his approach on the earlier work of William Ramsay, available in a modern edition as Ramsay, *Letters to the Seven Churches*. For a critique of the over-interpretation that Hemer and Ramsay are sometimes guilty of, see my 'Cities in Revelation' in Walton, Trebilco and Gill, *Urban World and the First Christians*.

13. See the comprehensive assessment of this in the chapter 'The Economic Critique of Rome in Revelation 18', in Bauckham, *Climax of Prophecy*, pp. 338–383, as well as the detailed comment on pp. 702–707 in Koester (1).

14. Irenaeus, *Against Heresies* 5.30.3. Domitian was emperor from AD 81 to 96.

appears to be following the belief of Justin Martyr (AD 100–165).[15] It is evident at this early stage that Revelation was accepted as an authoritative part of the early collections of Christian Scripture[16] because its apostolic authorship was assumed. Questions about its authorship appear to have arisen as a means of questioning its status out of concerns for the content of its message, and particularly its use in support of chiliasm. This was an early form of millennialism which interpreted Revelation 20 as predicting a literal thousand-year reign of Christ, and was probably taught by Melito of Sardis (died *c.*180). Eusebius of Caesarea (*c.*260–340) was a vocal opponent of chiliasm, and he cites Papias (*c.*60–130), bishop of Hierapolis, whose work we have only in citations by others, to suggest that there were *two* Johns in Ephesus: John the Apostle and another, otherwise unknown figure, John the Elder.[17] Eusebius is probably misreading Papias here, since Papias refers to the Twelve as 'elders' and 'apostles' as well as 'disciples of the Lord', but it suited Eusebius to distance Revelation from apostolic authorship. The external historical evidence, on balance, supports the identification of both the Gospel of John and the book of Revelation as being written by the apostle – and this was relatively unquestioned by scholarship until the nineteenth century.

Do Revelation and the Gospel of John look as though they could have been written by the same person? The two texts have many features and ideas in common, including the understanding of Jesus as the Word of God (John 1:1; Rev. 19:13), the importance of light (and the accompanying contrast with darkness), a focus on 'living water' derived from Ezekiel's vision of the stream coming from the restored temple (John 7:38; Rev. 22:1), Jesus as the lamb (John 1:29; Rev. 5:6) and the notion of Jesus and his followers winning the

---

15. Justin Martyr, *Dialogue with Trypho* 81.4. Apostolic authorship was also supported by Clement of Alexandria, Tertullian, Cyprian and Hippolytus, but disputed by Dionysius of Alexandria, Cyril of Jerusalem, Gregory Nazianzen and John Chrysostom.

16. See Kruger, 'The Reception of the Book of Revelation in the Early Church', in Kraus and Sommer, *Book of Seven Seals*, pp. 159–174.

17. Eusebius, *History of the Church*, Book III, ch. 39.

victory by faithful suffering. The Gospel of John's description of Jesus' death is much more theological than that of the other Gospels, and his theology of the atonement is highly 'exemplary'; Jesus sacrifices himself as a servant as an example for his disciples to follow (John 13:15). In a similar way, the language of 'faithful witness' and the close parallel between the 'blood [i.e. death] of the Lamb' and 'not shrinking from death' in Revelation 12:11 offer a highly exemplary understanding of the atonement. Added to that, both the Gospel and Revelation see Jesus' death and resurrection in what we might call 'Christus Victor' terms: in being raised up on the cross, he dethrones the power of 'the ruler of this world' (John 12:31, AT; Rev. 12:10). Both the Gospel and Revelation have a central emphasis on the importance of testimony, and this contributes to the sense of a theological trial where the truth is at stake.[18] As part of this, John ends Revelation with the characteristically Johannine phrase 'heard and seen' to underline his reliability as an eyewitness, a pairing found both in 1 John 1:3 and in John's testimony when on trial with Peter in Acts 4:20.

Against that, Revelation and the Gospel of John use different language, and where they use similar language they use it in a different way. The most striking example of this is in their contrasting descriptions of Jesus as 'lamb': John 1:29 uses *amnos*, but throughout Revelation uses *arnion*, which the Gospel uses only once (John 21:15) and then to refer to believers, not Jesus. In the Gospel, light imagery focuses on Jesus in his ministry and relationships, and the metaphor appears to derive from texts in Genesis 1; Psalms 27:1; 36:9; and Isaiah 42:6; 49:6. In Revelation, light is mentioned in relation to God and the lamb in the New Jerusalem, and imagery derives from Isaiah 60:3, 19; and Zechariah 14:7. There is phraseology in common, such as 'preparing a place' (John 14:2–3; Rev. 12:6), 'doing truth/falsehood' (John 3:21; Rev. 22:15) and 'having a share' (John 13:8; Rev. 20:6), but there are also numerous words and constructions, some of them quite common, which occur in the Gospel but are absent from Revelation.[19]

---

18. For the proposal that John's Gospel is essentially an extended trial narrative, see Lincoln, *Truth on Trial*.

19. For a full list, see pp. 80–83 in Koester (1).

Perhaps the most significant difference in theology is what appears to be a highly 'realized' eschatology in the Gospel, expressed in the phrase 'eternal life' (in contrast to the 'kingdom of God' in the Synoptic Gospels), contrasted with the very much future, as yet 'unrealized' eschatology of Revelation.[20] The most significant linguistic difference is that the entire register of the Greek used in Revelation is different; the Gospel is written in a grammatical Greek style, while the peculiarities and grammatical anomalies of Revelation continue to be the subject of much debate.

Whether we think the two texts were written by the same person will depend on the extent to which we expect an author to use a common style in different documents, written at different times, in different genres for different purposes.[21] This is a key issue behind the debates about Pauline authorship of Ephesians, Colossians and the Pastoral Epistles, where (as with Revelation and the Gospel of John) there are both changes of theological emphasis and differences in vocabulary and style. In relation to Ephesians, it is worth bearing in mind the argument of Ben Witherington, that Ephesians is written in the style of 'Asiatic epideictic rhetoric', a lofty style distinctive to the region which accounts for some of the key differences between this letter and others which are widely thought to be by Paul (see 'Theology' section following 1:8).[22] If Paul can write so

---

20. The future emphasis of Revelation's eschatology should not, however, be overestimated. In 12:10 the 'salvation and the power and the kingdom' have come 'now', at the time of Jesus' death, resurrection and exaltation, and of the seven occurrences of Jesus saying 'I am coming' (AT), two are local and in the near future, not at the end (2:5, 16).

21. The term for the features that you would expect to find in different documents by the same person is 'author invariants'.

22. Witherington, *Letters to Philemon, the Colossians, and the Ephesians*, pp. 7–10. Jermo van Ness has used statistical regression analysis on sections of the whole Pauline corpus to demonstrate that the differences between the Pastorals and the epistles viewed widely as 'authentically Pauline' are not, in fact, statistically significant; see 'Pauline Language and the Pastoral Epistles: A Study of the Linguistic Variation in the Corpus Paulinum' (PhD diss., April 2017, Leuven, Belgium).

differently for different audiences, why cannot John also be doing so in his Gospel and his apocalypse, adapting his language to relate to the region? We might also wonder whether someone who knew Jesus personally could describe him in the terms that we find in Revelation – though the descriptions in the accounts of the Transfiguration in the Synoptic Gospels (Matt. 17:1–8; Mark 9:2–8; Luke 9:28–36) have things in common with the vision in Revelation 1, and it is notable that his company is 'Elijah and Moses' (Mark 9:4) who are clearly alluded to in the ministry of the two witnesses in Revelation 11:6.

It is striking that John does not describe himself as an 'apostle' – though of course Paul does not do so in all his letters either.[23] However, John does describe himself as part of a chain of transmission in which each person is 'sent' (*apostellō*) by God (1:1; 22:6); he claims that what he passes on is no less than the 'revelation of Jesus Christ'. And, quite remarkably, in the closing of his letter he appears to claim to be the amanuensis for a letter which is really by Jesus himself and, in line with conventional understandings of the significance of letters in the ancient world, that what he writes to the assemblies in the seven cities represents the presence and words of Jesus to them (see comment on 22:16–21). The reading I offer in this commentary puts Revelation quite clearly within the theological outlook of the rest of the New Testament, and John invites us to judge the authority of what he writes on the basis of its content and claims, not on an appeal to external evidence of authority.

3. The date of Revelation

It is important to have an idea when a text was written and circulated, in order to take seriously its context. But we need to be careful of three things. The first is the projection of our own assumptions and

---

23. Paul describes himself as an 'apostle' in the openings of Romans, 1 and 2 Corinthians, Galatians, Ephesians and Colossians, as well as in the Pastorals, but not in Philippians or 1 and 2 Thessalonians. In these last three letters, Paul mentions being an apostle only once, in 1 Thess. 2:6.

experience of writing and publication on the first-century context. For us, writing and publication is a more or less instant process; if I want to write something, I can reach for pen and paper or turn on my electronic device and start writing. In the ancient world, formal writing was expensive and laborious, and to be a scribe was a specialist and elite occupation.[24] It is also clear that, like John's Gospel, the book of Revelation is the fruit of extended reflection and careful composition. We therefore need to set aside notions of 'the' date of a text as if the moment of production was at a single instant or even a narrow and defined period of time, as it often is in modern writing.[25]

The second thing to be careful of is constructing too detailed an argument which pins the writing down to a very specific date. Arguments which do this have to make a long list of assumptions, and texts cannot easily be dated unless they make specific reference to particular events that we have external sources for dating. This is related to a third danger – that of circular arguments. There is a real possibility of arguing that something in the text points to an event in history that we know of, dating the text in relation to that event, and then, when it comes to our interpretation, pointing out that this must be the relevant event because of the date of the text![26] For that reason, the most reliable information that we can look to in deciding

---

24. Though it is possible to overstate this. The discovery of the Vindolanda tablets at Hadrian's Wall from 1973 (more tablets continue to be found) demonstrates the casual and everyday use of writing notes and short messages.

25. The most detailed exploration of writing and reading in early Christianity is Gamble, *Books and Readers in the Early Church*. On this area, see also the earlier and very good Millard, *Reading and Writing in the Time of Jesus*.

26. This kind of circularity has been a major failing in much scholarship of the Gospels, where an issue in Jesus' teaching has been used to construct an imagined situation in the reading community, and the Gospel is then seen to offer a wonderful engagement with the concerns of that constructed community. The problems here are tackled head-on by Stephen Barton in his chapter 'Can We Identify the Gospel Audiences?', in Bauckham, *Gospel for All Christians*, pp. 173–194.

Revelation's date is external testimony, and there is not very much of it.

The evidence we have for dating Revelation is of three kinds: the external testimony of Irenaeus; textual details which might be thought to correlate with historical events; and historical considerations about the context of Revelation.

a. The evidence of Irenaeus

Irenaeus, who lived during the second century and was bishop of Lugdunum in Gaul, comments in his major work *Against Heresies* 5.30.3:

> We will not, however, incur the risk of pronouncing positively as to the name of Antichrist; for if it were necessary that his name should be distinctly revealed in this present time, it would have been announced by him who beheld the apocalyptic vision. *For that was seen no very long time since, but almost in our day, towards the end of Domitian's reign* [emphasis added].

Irenaeus also believed that the apostle John was the author, which was later contested (see above on 'Who was John?'), but those who questioned apostolic authorship did not do so on the basis of the date of the text, but on the basis of its content and the differences between Revelation and John's Gospel. Irenaeus' testimony is worth taking seriously, since he was probably born and raised in Smyrna and was a student of Polycarp, the bishop of Smyrna who was martyred at the age of eighty-six and claimed to have known John. Irenaeus does not deduce the timing from the idea of Domitian as a 'great persecutor', but simply records it as a chronological fact.

b. Textual details

Several details in the text of Revelation have been taken as pointers to historical incidents. In AD 92, Domitian issued an edict to remove half the vines in the provinces in order to grow more wheat because of grain shortages, and some commentators point to the declaration in 6:6 of shortages of grain 'but do not harm the oil and the wine' (AT) as fitting with this situation. It is difficult to make such a precise link, since grain shortages were common in the first century.

The description of the 'mountain, all ablaze', being 'thrown into the sea' (8:8) would have strong resonances with anyone aware of the eruption of Vesuvius in AD 79 which was widely reported. It is interesting to note that this image is distinctive in *not* drawing on any obvious Old Testament or Greco-Roman source – but it is going too far to suggest that this *must* be a reference to Vesuvius, given the general nature of the symbolism.

Commentators are divided between those who think that the mention of measuring the temple in 11:1–3 means that the temple must be standing and those who think the temple must have fallen. Some even suggest that Revelation must have been written *during* the siege of Jerusalem – but this is to read the text with a very odd literalism which ignores some compelling signs that this account should be read metaphorically. As I explore in the commentary, this is a theological image of God's people who (on the one hand) appear to experience 'trampling' by their opponents but who (on the other hand) are protected by God. This theme is repeated in several different ways in the following three chapters. It is worth noting that language about the temple as a theological symbol of Jesus and his people occurs in writing prior to the destruction of the Jerusalem temple (1 Cor. 3:16; 6:19; 2 Cor. 6:16) as well as after it (John 2:19). The symbolic sense of this passage tells us little about dating Revelation.

The passage that generates most discussion is the king list in Revelation 17:9–14. There are various ways in which the 'five [who] have fallen, one is, the other has not yet come' have been matched with the different emperors, starting at different points and including or excluding different individuals, as shown in table 1.

The external problems with such an approach are that none of them matches well what the text says, and there is no precedent elsewhere for counting emperors by starting with Julius Caesar or omitting the three short-lived emperors Galba, Otho and Vitellius. The internal problem is that this does not appear to be John's reason for writing these verses: he did not need to offer a coded way for his first audience to work out when he was writing! The seven heads of the beast also function with multiple significance, since they are not only seven kings but 'seven hills' (17:9). It is quite hard to make sense, in these terms, of the beast being one of his own heads (17:11),

Table 1: The numbered kings and the emperors of Rome

Emperors

Julius Caesar	1			
Augustus	2	1	1	
Tiberius	3	2	2	
Caligula	4	3	3	
Claudius	5	4	4	
Nero	6	5	5	1
Galba	(7)	6		2
Otho	(8)	(7)		3
Vitellius		(8)		4
Vespasian			6	5
Titus			(7)	6
Domitian			(8)	(7)

and no-one can offer a very clear explanation using a similar correspondence of the ten kings who are the horns (17:12). This text, too, offers little help in answering the question of date.

The use of 'Babylon' as a metaphorical name for Rome fits well with a date after the destruction of Jerusalem in AD 70, since Babylon is primarily known within the Scriptures as the destroyer of Jerusalem in 586 BC. The term also occurs in other Jewish literature as a reference to Rome, and is often linked with the destruction of Jerusalem. It is mentioned in 1 Peter 5:13, and most commentators think this is also a reference to Rome; whether this supports a post-70 date for Revelation depends on the question of dating and authorship of 1 Peter, as Peter himself was almost certainly executed during the reign of Nero in AD 67.

It is clear that ideas about Nero and his possible return (the 'Nero Redivivus' myth) play an important part in Revelation. Apart from the *gematria* of 13:18 as a reference to Nero (see comment on 13:18), there are echoes of the threat of his return leading a Parthian army in 9:14–15; 13:3, 15; and 17:8 (see comments on those verses). The beginnings of such a myth began shortly after Nero's death in AD 68, but speculation also reached fever-pitch in the late 80s, with pretenders claiming to be the returning Nero making their appearances all through this period. The Nero references cannot therefore determine Revelation's date.

c. Historical considerations

It is sometimes said that Revelation is a text written under persecution, and that it therefore 'must' have been written in this or that period. But the evidence for systematic persecution under Domitian is not clear (see comment under 'The social and historical context'); there are many signs that Revelation was written to challenge complacency as much as to offer comfort; and writers are not at liberty to survey past, present and future history in order to 'choose' a time to write in the way that such arguments often seem to assume.

There are some external details worth noting which do appear to support a later date of writing. Laodicea was destroyed by an earthquake in AD 60, and the message to the assembly there seems to assume that it is prosperous and well established, which could hardly have been the case if John was writing in the late 60s. Polycarp, bishop of Smyrna, says (*Philippians* 11) that the church in Smyrna did not exist in the time of Paul, which would imply a later date for Revelation. And Epiphanius, writing much later (in his *Panarion*), notes that it was believed there was no Christian community in Thyatira until late in the first century.

All this evidence does not offer us a decisive date for the writing and reception of Revelation – but neither does it offer any decisive reason to reject the only early external testimony that we have, that of Irenaeus. A date during the reign of Domitian fits well what we read in the text, and the text does not contradict this. It still allows for the possibility of apostolic authorship if John was in his teens during the ministry of Jesus and so would have been in his seventies during the reign of Domitian.

4. The social and historical context

Modern archaeology continues to discover more about the nature of the Roman Empire as every year passes, and these discoveries emphasize both the technological sophistication of the empire in comparison with its neighbours and the benefits that were brought to those who became part of the imperial system. Scientists are only just beginning to understand why Roman concrete continues to harden over the years, even when exposed to sea water, making concrete harbours permanent in contrast to modern concrete that disintegrates in a relatively short time. Almost two thousand years after it was built, the dome of the Pantheon in Rome is still the world's largest unreinforced concrete dome. New techniques of aerial and satellite surveying are revealing hidden elements of infrastructure that were previously unknown and which demonstrate the extent of the transformation that imperial power brought to different regions.[27] The vast hexagonal basin constructed at Portus, adjacent to the natural harbour at Ostia at the mouth of the Tiber, was served by a canal running all the way back to Rome adjacent to the Tiber in order to accommodate the enormous shipping fleet that served the needs of Rome, bringing goods there from around the empire. It has long been a puzzle as to why the Nabataeans of northern Arabia, with their capital at Petra, welcomed Roman imperial rule with its imposition of taxes on their extensive trading. Satellite surveying reveals a dense network of farming settlements in the region, showing it was rich and fertile – and an extensive Roman wall with regular outposts, showing how imperial allegiance offered protection from tribal raids by others. The empire provided protection and stability which led to security and greater prosperity.

Despite this technological progress, the empire as a whole was very poor in comparison with the modern world, with only the wealthiest region of Italia exceeding the equivalent per capita income of the poorest nations in the world today. Wealth was highly stratified and its distribution was very unequal. It is difficult to make accurate estimates of economic dynamics from this distance, but the best estimates suggest the pattern shown in table 2 overleaf.[28]

---

27. A pioneer in this area is the American archaeologist Sarah Parcak, who explains her methods in *Satellite Remote Sensing for Archaeology*.

28. The table is based on the intriguing analysis by Bruce Longenecker, adapting the work of Friesen in '"The Least of These": Scaling Poverty in the Greco-Roman World', in Longenecker, *Remember the Poor*, pp. 36–59.

Table 2: Economic stratification in the first-century empire

Economic group	Description	% of popn
Imperial, provincial and municipal elites	Extremely wealthy, probably controlling around 25% of the wealth of the empire	3
Enjoying moderate economic surplus	The most successful merchants and traders, including some freedpersons, artisans and military veterans	17
Stable subsistence level	Most merchants and traders, those with regular income, artisans, large shop owners, freedpersons, some farm families	25
At or below subsistence levels	Small farm families, labourers, artisans, most merchants and traders, small shop owners	30
Below subsistence	Poorer farm families, orphans, widows, beggars, the disabled, unskilled day labourers, prisoners	25

Add to that the 30–40% of the population in slavery, and we can see the extent of poverty and financial insecurity within the empire. (In passing, it is worth noting that the evidence we have suggests that the Christian faith attracted adherents from all these socio-economic groups.) This offers a vital background to some of the phrases we find in Revelation, particularly 'kings of the earth, the princes, the generals, the rich, the mighty, and everyone else, both slave and free' (6:15) and 'all people, great and small, rich and poor, free and slave' (13:16). There was also significant inequality between regions in the empire, with the provinces in the east generally wealthier because of greater natural resources and more fertile farmland, including north Africa, which was then extremely fertile; Italia outstripped them all in wealth as resources were drawn in to Rome and the regions around it. Military conquest often served the commercial needs of the empire. The coastal farmlands of the province of Africa (modern-day Libya) provided a quarter of the wheat needed in Rome; the conquest of Spain provided gold and silver from the mines there; and the Emperor Claudius's invasion of Britannia was probably motivated by the availability of copper and tin in

Cornwall and gold in Welsh mines, which the Romans developed extensively.

The empire was highly urbanized, much more so than Europe in later history until the modern period. Rome had a population of around 1 million in the first century; no city anywhere in the world would surpass this size until the nineteenth century.[29] It was served by a remarkable infrastructure, including eleven major underground aqueducts and a sewerage system which continues to serve the city to this day. But urban life was overcrowded, dangerous and disease-ridden. Rodney Stark has estimated that the population density of Antioch was 117 per acre, which compares with 100 for the contemporary Manhattan district of New York with its high-rise accommodation.[30] Tenement blocks were crowded, with poor families living in one room and cooking without ventilation, which often led to fatal fires. Buildings collapsed when cheaper rooms in the upper stories were subdivided making them top-heavy. Such buildings were particularly vulnerable when earthquakes struck, as they did often in the province of Asia. The overcrowding meant that diseases were endemic and hygiene was poor. This is the background to the language of fire, death and disease in Revelation, addressed primarily to urban Christians. Life expectancy was extremely poor by modern standards; the mortality rate below the age of five was around 50%, and life expectancy for those reaching the age of ten was less than fifty years of age. (See the introductory comments to each of the seven messages for details regarding the individual cities.)

The imperial cult – the veneration or worship of the emperor – was all-pervasive across the empire, but it took different forms in different regions, and it provoked different responses, being viewed with suspicion by many in the ruling elite in Rome. In the east of the empire, and especially in the province of Asia that John was

---

29. The only candidates here are Baghdad in the tenth century and the Chinese cities of Chang'an (modern Xi'an), Hangzhou and Beijing. These might have attained a size similar to Rome, but all are dwarfed by the size of modern urban development.

30. 'Urban Chaos and Crisis', in Stark, *Rise of Christianity*, pp. 147–162.

writing to, the cult was greeted with enthusiasm, and the veneration of the emperor was often elevated way beyond what would have been acceptable in Rome.[31] This approach goes all the way back to the time of Alexander, who was given enthusiastic divine honours when he conquered the region, and the example of excessive veneration in the Asian cities spread westwards, eventually becoming acceptable across the empire in later years. The cities in the region competed with one another to curry imperial favour by bidding for the title of 'temple guardian', or *neokoros*, by building imperial temples; the first was granted to Ephesus for its Temple of the Sebastoi, and of the thirty-seven *neokoros* titles eventually granted, almost all of them were in Asia.[32] Worship of the Roman gods and similar honouring of the emperor was the price to be paid for all the benefits of membership of the imperial 'family' – and the Romans were not impressed by the obstinacy of those who refused on the grounds that their own native god required exclusive allegiance.

A good example of the centrality of the imperial cult within the power structures of local government can still be seen in the ruins of Miletus, the important port city at the mouth of the Meander to the south of Ephesus. The council chamber (*bouleuterion*) is entered through a peristyle courtyard, that is, one bounded by colonnades. It would originally have been an open space, but some years later a massive structure was built at the centre. It was originally thought to be a tomb monument, but recent excavation has shown it to have been a massive imperial altar that dominated the courtyard. No-one taking part in the city's council could reach its meetings without navigating past that altar, and it would have provided a very practical test of loyalty to the empire and the imperial cult.[33]

The importance of the narrative of imperial triumph in the popular imagination is illustrated by a remarkable temple, the Sebasteion

---

31. The best survey of the dynamics of the imperial cult in Asia is Friesen, *Imperial Cults*. See also the outline of the cult in the eastern empire in Winter, *Divine Honours for the Caesars*, pp. 296–302.

32. Details of Ephesus's leading interest and status here is documented in Friesen, *Twice Neokoros*.

33. Friesen, *Imperial Cults*, pp. 65–71.

at Aphrodisias, situated west of Laodicea.[34] It consists of a double-height colonnade which was filled with statues and reliefs documenting the conquest of various nations by the emperor, using personifications of the subdued nations as women who have been humiliated and are pleading for mercy, with the figure of the emperor often accompanied by a figure of the goddess Roma. The representation of individual nations by figures in a tableau bears a remarkable resemblance to political cartoons of the modern era, and corresponds to the scenes described by John in Revelation where nations, peoples and empires are personified.

A major question of context is whether or not John and his contemporaries were experiencing 'persecution'.[35] In the past many commentaries have assumed this to have been the case; a classic example is H. B. Swete's commentary which assumes that Revelation was written during the reign of the Emperor Domitian, whom he assumes was the 'second great persecutor', and so provides a list of evidence to this effect.[36] But it has been recognized that much of the 'evidence' relating to Domitian's claims to divinity (including the evidence from the Roman historian Suetonius in his *Lives of the Twelve Caesars*) formed part of a *damnatio memoriae*, the damning of someone's reputation by later rulers. A good example of the difficulty with the evidence is that of the remains of the enormous monumental statue erected by Domitian in the temple to the Flavian dynasty at the top of the main street in Ephesus. It is universally described as being an 8-metre high statue of Domitian, and is labelled as such in the Ephesus museum, where the right arm and head are on display. But a quick comparison with other known

---

34. See Friesen, *Imperial Cults*, pp. 77–95, which includes photographs of many of the tableaux.

35. I put the term in inverted commas because there is no consensus on how to define the difference between persecution, a sense of antipathy or pressure, or a generally negative response in culture to the Christian message. In most historical contexts, persecution is often local and sporadic rather than widespread and systematic.

36. Swete, pp. lxxviii–xciii, under the heading 'Antichrist in the Province of Asia'.

statues demonstrates that it is in fact a statue of his older brother Titus and not of Domitian himself.[37] Domitian's concern appears to have had less to do with his own name, and more with the reputation of his family dynasty.

Leonard Thompson has offered a strong case that though Domitian did push the language of the imperial cult further than his predecessors, he was no instigator of persecution in the way that Nero had been.[38] There is no doubt that Christians in different cities and different provinces felt under various degrees of pressure and experienced different forms of opposition, and there is no reason to doubt John's record of (the otherwise unknown) Antipas who was martyred for his faith (2:13). Because of the importance of local government and local management of the cult, the situation of Christians will have varied depending on the view of provincial governors and local magistrates. The lack of a consistent policy is illustrated by the letter of Pliny the Younger, governor of Bithynia and Pontus, to the Emperor Trajan in AD 112.[39] And it is worth noting that, although John is clear that martyrdom might well be a possibility and that faithfulness even to the point of death is the test of whether we follow the example of Jesus, the seven messages in Revelation 2 – 3 do not suggest systematic persecution. Although there are comforts and encouragements, the messages also contain a good level of rebuke, some of it quite severe, suggesting that complacency and compromise with an accommodating culture was at least as much a problem as conflict and opposition. They are not messages that would have been sent to Christians under persecution!

5. Did John actually have a vision?

Most ordinary readers of Revelation assume that John had some sort of vision, and that what we have is a more or less straightforward description of what he saw as if he was describing a picture. But there are several reasons for qualifying this kind of understanding.

---

37. See Friesen, *Imperial Cults*, pp. 50, 53 (with Figure 3.7).

38. Thompson, *Book of Revelation*.

39. The correspondence can be read in Pliny, *Letters* 10.96–97.

The first relates to the nature of visions and spiritual auditory experiences. I have once had what I would describe as a 'vision', and several times experienced what might be called auditory revelations, including as recently as early 2017 (the year of writing this commentary). I could tell you what the content was – but it is less easy to be specific about what the experience entailed, how I felt I knew what I knew and how either experience related to normal experiences of seeing or hearing things in everyday life. (If you have not had an experience like this, ask someone who has.) The second reason is the recognition that there is an established form of literature known as 'vision report', particularly in texts similar to Revelation among Jewish apocalypses, and there is considerable debate as to whether the authors or their audiences necessarily assumed that the text originated with an actual visionary experience. To take a modern parallel: when Martin Luther King said, 'I have a dream', I do not think that anyone imagined that he was reporting to them something that he had experienced while he was asleep.

But even more important evidence comes from the text itself. John quite often describes things that make no literal sense, or are inconsistent or incomplete, and these indicate that he is more concerned with the meaning of the words he uses – and their symbolic significance in the light of Old Testament texts he is drawing on and contemporary Greco-Roman symbolism – than in writing a report about meaningful things that he has seen. It is not actually possible for a rainbow to 'have the appearance of an emerald' (4:3, AT); English translations often try to make sense of this by rendering it as 'shining like an emerald', but this is not the language that John uses. In his vision of the throne room, it is often not clear how the location of each group (living creatures, angels, elders) fits with the location of others, and the description develops through the text as John adds further details which are quite prominent (such as the altar before the throne) such that it is odd that he did not mention these previously if he was simply describing a scene. In his description of the New Jerusalem, he describes it as 'like a jasper, clear as crystal', when jasper is an opaque gem (21:11); the walls made of jasper, though the city is of gold (21:18); the foundations decorated with gems, then actually being gems (21:19); the walls being '144 cubits', but John does not tell us in which direction (so

English translations usually supply the missing detail, 21:17); and John does not really make clear the relationship between the central street, the river of the water of life and the (single) tree of life which appears to manage to grow on both sides of the river (22:1–2).

On the other hand, John's text is constructed with extraordinary attention to the details of the words he is using. John repeats key words with certain frequencies (see below on numerology). He carefully repeats a phrase but with consistent variation, such as the fourfold 'every tribe and language and people and nation' repeated seven times but never twice in the same way (see comment on 5:9) and similar repetition with variation in the seven mentions of the living creatures with the elders. And he reuses and reworks Old Testament texts and ideas from all over the canon of Scripture. These all point to a text that has been composed with extreme care over some time.

Perhaps the most telling feature is John's own focus on his words, rather than on the visions themselves (1:3; 19:9; 21:5). In the final affirmation, the angel almost appears to step out of the scroll and address John's audience directly, referring to all that John has written as 'trustworthy and true' (22:6). And at the end of the text, John finishes his letter with an ending in striking parallel to the ending of 1 Corinthians, where Paul takes the pen from his amanuensis to sign off the letter himself (1 Cor. 16:21–24). In the same way, John appears to 'hand his pen' to Jesus to allow him to sign himself off (in place of Paul's 'Come, Lord!' we have the first person 'I am coming soon', 22:20). For John, it is clear that it is the words he has written, more than anything else, which constitute what he has been given by God as the 'revelation of Jesus Christ' (1:1, AT), and it is to the words – and not to any speculative reconstruction of what his vision might have looked like – that we must attend.

Did John have a vision (or series of visions)?[40] If he did, he has reported it in a very careful way. We don't have a vision; we have a vision report, a text, and we should attend to it. John's aim is not to

---

40. The episodic nature of the text suggests that John might have had a series of visions. But the overarching presentation of what John writes offers the whole as a single visionary experience.

impress us with his visionary experience, nor (necessarily) to encourage us to have our own. Rather, John wants us to order our lives in the light of the truth about God that these vision reports reveal to us.[41]

6. What kind of text is Revelation?

In approaching any text and its interpretation, it is important to think about what kind of writing we are engaging with; to use a more technical term, what 'genre' is it? The reason that this is important becomes evident from the following example:

> The stars will fall from heaven, the sun will cease its shining;
> the moon will be turned to blood, and fire and hail will fall from heaven.
> The rest of the country will have sunny intervals with scattered showers.

Reading this usually brings a smile to one's face – but why? The language is in many ways similar; the vocabulary in all three lines describes cosmological phenomena; and there is even a shared two-part structure to each line. The answer is, of course, that we instantly recognize the first two lines as a different genre, or kind of writing, from the third line. This is not something we will probably have been taught (though some educational systems are now focusing on this question as part of a drive for improved literacy); most of us

---

41. There is an analogy here to the relationship between the events reported by the Gospel writers and the texts that they have written. There is a constant temptation to use the texts that we have as a window to reconstruct the events that they report and then make sense of them. But the Gospel writers have given us a record of their own understanding of the events and their interpretation of them. Though the events are of vital importance, a belief in the authority and reliability of Scripture implies that we need to attend to their understanding and interpretation of the events, at least as much as to the events themselves. This is an imperfect analogy with John's visions, but in both cases our focus needs to be on the words that we have been given and what they mean.

learn to recognize different kinds of writing simply by experience, by seeing different examples and noticing what they have in common. I do not remember ever being taught what a 'bank manager' letter looked like, and when I received my first one in a window envelope, it was a slightly odd experience. Fortunately I can recognize it instantly now – and, more importantly, distinguish it from personal letters from those who love me! Recognizing genre is vital for two main reasons:

1. Genre is shaped by the relationship between the author and the anticipated audience for what is written. Someone who does not know me well will choose a more formal letter- (or email-) writing style; a friend will write quite differently. Church leaders addressing a general audience will write a circular; leaders writing to those they pastor will write differently. We can even see these differences within the various letters written by Paul.

2. Genre tells us how to interpret what has been written.[42] Authors rarely write an accompanying explanatory note telling us how to interpret what has been written;[43] instead, they will choose (possibly unconsciously) a particular style in order for it to be interpreted in a particular way. Jesus did not need to tell his audience the name of the particular sower he had in mind (Mark 4:3–8) or the name of the pearl merchant (Matt. 13:45–46) or the address of the home the prodigal son returned to (Luke 15:11–32), because the audience recognized that such details were not needed in these kinds of stories.

---

42. Gordon Fee and Douglas Stuart go so far as to claim that recognizing genre is one of two key essentials for reading the Bible, the other being a knowledge of the whole story and the place of a text within that. See Fee and Stuart, *How to Read the Bible*.

43. In particular, authors almost never say, 'I am now being poetic'; so assuming that a text should be interpreted literally unless it explicitly says so (as some suggest) ignores the reality of the way that writers communicate.

The importance of genre gives us three particular challenges in reading the book of Revelation.

First, if we learn to recognize a genre and how to interpret it, we need to ask honestly how familiar we are with it. We might have come across Daniel 7 – 12, or the visions of Ezekiel and Zechariah, but this is hardly everyday reading for us. Not so for the first Christians, who were surrounded by and often immersed in apocalyptic texts. I have always found it striking that when Jesus starts to tell parables, his disciples are (by and large) baffled (Mark 4:10–13). But when Jesus goes all apocalyptic on them in Matthew 24 (and in a shorter form in Mark 13), they seem to think that he has answered their question (Matt. 24:3)! They, and John's audience, were familiar with the conventions of apocalyptic language, but we are not (and neither were the generations immediately following the apostolic era). We therefore need to learn some of the linguistic and cultural assumptions that make the apocalyptic writing in Revelation work – hence the following two sections on its poetic imagery and numerology respectively.[44]

The second challenge is working out what Revelation's apocalyptic language is all about. It is generally thought that there is a genre called 'apocalyptic' which includes Revelation, parts of the Old Testament (Daniel 7 – 12, Ezekiel and Zechariah, as well as some sections of Isaiah and some of the other prophets), some passages in the New Testament, and a whole raft of Jewish literature from the period of the Second (Herodian) Temple. John J. Collins led a project to classify this literature, and produced the following influential definition:

> An apocalypse is a genre of revelatory literature with a narrative framework, in which a revelation is mediated by an otherworldly being to a human recipient, disclosing a transcendent reality which is both

---

44. It was for a long time thought that the Gospels were a unique genre of literature, until it was demonstrated that, in every important respect, they look very much like a typical Roman 'life' (*vita*, Greek *bios*, 'biography') of a famous person. See Burridge, *What Are the Gospels?*

temporal, insofar as it envisages eschatological salvation, and spatial,
insofar as it involves another, supernatural world.[45]

The difficulty here is that, while this definition works quite well
for some Jewish apocalypses, there are significant differences with
the book of Revelation. John does appear to go on a journey,
but (as we will note as the commentary progresses) it is far from
clear whether he remains in a 'supernatural' realm, and much of
what happens would be better described as a poetic or symbolic
description of earthly events. Eschatology certainly features
strongly, but the timeline of events appears to repeat itself, with
anticipations of 'the End' then followed by a return to the present.
If I am right about John's understanding of the 'third woe' (see
comment on 11:14), then much of his text is about the present
situation of his audience, and only focuses on 'the End' from Revelation 17 onwards as part of his rhetorical strategy of motivating
his audience to respond to the challenges they face right now. This
is confirmed by John's reworking of the *future* time of 'tribulation'
in Daniel – the 'time, times and half a time' or forty-two months
or 1,260 days – into a theological description of the *present* period
between Jesus' exaltation and his return (see comment on 11:1–3
and 12:6 and 14).

Underlying this question of apocalyptic genre is the fact that
Revelation is quite distinct from other Jewish 'apocalypses'. It
is actually the only text to use the (Greek) word *apokalypsis*, and it is
unique in that the author, John, uses his own name (rather than
writing pseudonymously, using the name of a prophet or patriarch
from the past), writing to contemporaries in his immediate historical
context whom he knows personally. There is always a danger that
the notion of genre is treated too rigidly as a kind of 'formula',
when in fact it is simply an observation about texts that appear to
function in the same way and so are grouped together. It might be

---

45. Collins, *Apocalyptic Imagination*, p. 5. The first chapter of this volume,
    'The Apocalyptic Genre' (pp. 1–52), discusses how this definition was
    arrived at, and the range of serious questions raised about it since its
    first proposal.

that texts currently called 'apocalyptic' are a rather loose group which have as much that separates them as holds them together.[46]

The third challenge in reading Revelation is the way that John mixes genres, sometimes from one verse to the next. Consider the first few verses of Revelation 1 (see table 3), which overall I would consider to be an 'epistolary prologue'.

Table 3: Changes of genre in Revelation 1

Verse	Text	Genre
1	The revelation of Jesus Christ . . .	Apocalyptic
3	Blessed is the one who reads aloud the words of this prophecy . . .	Benediction
4	John, to the seven churches in the province of Asia . . .	Epistle
5–6	To him who loves us and has freed us from our sins . . . be glory and power for ever and ever! Amen	Doxology
7	Look, he is coming with the clouds . . .	Apocalyptic
8	'I am the Alpha and the Omega,' says the Lord God	Prophecy
9	I, John, your brother and companion . . .	Epistle

This is an extraordinary and rather bewildering sequence of rapid changes of what we might call 'microgenre'. It has the effect of making the hearer or listener wonder exactly what this text is, and so is very involving and makes us sit up and take notice of what is going on. It also communicates that this text is not quite like anything we have read before. And this effect continues, though not quite as intensely as in these opening verses, so that in the middle of a vision we might get an interjection of praise (16:5–7), or at times it might

---

46. For that reason Sean Michael Ryan argues that Revelation ought to be classified as a 'testimony' rather than an apocalypse. See '"The Testimony of Jesus" and "The Testimony of Enoch": An *Emic* Approach to the Genre of the Apocalypse', in Allen, Paul and Woodman, *Book of Revelation*, pp. 95–113.

seem that John is stepping out of 'vision report' mode and adding his own response alongside his audience (see comments on 18:14 and 20). Despite these changes of microgenre, this book makes its strongest claims to be three things.

First, it is an *apocalypse*, that is, a revelation from God. John is claiming to offer us a perspective on the world that we could not work out for ourselves, and so we need to pay attention, to look and listen. This is emphasized in his repeated interjection of 'Behold!' (twenty-six times, from 1:7 through to 22:12, AT). Such 'revelation' is in fact at the heart of the Christian faith, and the verb *apokalyptō* is used repeatedly by Paul to describe how the good news has come to us (Rom. 1:17; 8:18; 1 Cor. 2:10; Gal. 3:23; Eph. 3:5, and so on).

Second, what John writes is a *letter*, clearly communicated in the epistolary markers in Revelation 1 which offer close parallels to the style of Paul's letters, and the closing epistolary comments which also echo Paul. Letters are written to particular people living in a particular time and place, and taking Revelation seriously as a letter means reading it in its historical and cultural context just as we would any other letter in the New Testament. John knew his readers who lived in the province of Asia, and he appears to have expected them to understand what he wrote.

Third, Revelation claims to be a *prophecy*, a word used seven times in the book, five times emphatically describing what John has written (1:3; 22:7, 10, 18, 19). Prophecy is less concerned with predicting the future in any abstract sense than with communicating God's message and calling people to obedience, by highlighting the consequences of their actions and the new possibilities offered by repentance and obedience. Having made sense of Revelation by reading and listening carefully, we then need to respond to what John reveals about the world we live in by keeping faith with Jesus, the Word of God.

7. Reading Revelation's imagery

Revelation is often described as a 'symbolic' text that is full of 'images', but that is a rather careless use of terminology. Symbols and images are things that are present in the real world, and not in the worlds of text that are written with words. What we are confronted with in this book is a series of metaphors, and metaphors of a particular kind, often piled one on top of another. In the modern era, which has a liking for literal descriptive language and is often ambiguous about the poetic or metaphorical, we struggle to know how to interpret metaphors, and this is one of the major reasons why modern readers struggle to make sense of Revelation.

It is a challenge that we need to address, not least because much Christian theology is done with metaphors, and it is not actually possible to say anything about God without making use of metaphorical language. God is Creator – similar language to that used of the craftsman or potter. God is King and Judge and (particularly in the NT) Father. Jesus is our Redeemer, using language of someone offering manumission to a slave in the slave market. He is the good shepherd, the light of the world and the bread of life. The Spirit is a flame of fire, something poured out, and a downpayment or deposit to guarantee the future. Even doctrinal statements about God as Trinity, using terms like 'person' and 'substance', are essentially metaphorical. Metaphor is at the centre of all Christian theology, and in that sense Revelation is the most Christian text in the New Testament.

One of the most important thinkers about metaphorical language was the French philosopher Paul Ricoeur (1913–2005).[47] Ricoeur began as an existentialist, but found this outlook unsatisfactory because it did not take into account human fallibility and sin, and Ricoeur soon noticed that we try to make sense of this through narrative and metaphors. He observed several important things about metaphors. The first is that they make real claims about reality, and are essential in the way that we describe the world: metaphors cannot be reduced to propositions, but are necessary in our engagement with reality. Second, metaphors are also fundamental to the way that language works, functioning as the mechanism by which we move from what we know to what we do not know. Every time human knowledge expands into new areas, we describe what we have not known before by extending our language through the

---

47. One of the best short introductions to his thought can be found in Stiver, *Theology after Ricoeur.*

coining of new metaphors. Think of 'inflation' in economics, genes as 'packets' of information in biology, or the idea of 'surfing' the information 'super highway' and 'visiting' 'Web' 'sites'!

Third, metaphors make claims in a very different way from literal statements. They function by connecting two words from different parts of our world of thought, and in doing so they connect those two parts. And the assertion (predication) they make is only ever *partial* rather than *total*. When I say that my friend 'eats like a pig', I still set cutlery for him at the table; he eats like a pig only in certain ways (he eats a lot, or messily), and what I am claiming in the metaphor (in Ricoeur's terms the 'tenor' of the metaphor) depends on conventional understandings rather than the actual facts about pigs (who are actually very hygienic). Recognizing this is vital in our reading of the metaphors in Revelation. For example, it is said more than once that in the New Jerusalem 'there will be no more night'. We need to understand the particular cultural and biblical connotations of 'night' (that it is a time of danger, threat and fear) that this metaphor is working with, otherwise we might imagine that life in the holy city will be an unbearable time of constant daylight when we can get no rest or sleep!

There is also a particular distinctive in the metaphors of Revelation which not only accounts for the difficulties we have in reading it, but also explains both its impact and the huge diversity of interpretations and applications that exist. Metaphorical language can create a range of different ways that the subject (what the metaphor is about) and the vehicle (the metaphorical term) are related in order to create the tenor (the meaning) of the metaphor. In a simile, we might say, 'John [subject] is like a pig [vehicle]' to express that he is greedy [the tenor]. If we make the statement stronger, we might move to using a directly metaphorical assertion: 'John is a pig!' But immediately we need to know something of the context to understand whether this really is a metaphorical statement (in which case, John is only like a pig in certain regards) or a literal statement – I might live on a farm, and John might be the name of my prize boar! In this latter case, everything that is true of a pig is true of John – the predication is total rather than partial, as in the metaphorical statement. But the grammar is the same, so we always need to consider the kind of writing (or genre; see above) and the context to determine whether a text is literal or metaphorical; features of the text alone cannot always do this.[48]

Finally, there is a third kind of metaphor, which is both more powerful and more challenging to interpret. I could simply say, 'You pig!' If I do, the subject of the metaphor now becomes hidden: it is not clear who I am identifying with the pig, and in fact my phrase could be reused in different contexts and applied to different subjects without any change to the grammar. This kind of statement was labelled as 'hypocatastatic' – a Greek term meaning 'stands underneath' – metaphor by E. W. Bullinger, a 'hyper-dispensationalist' Bible teacher in the nineteenth century, who was also interested in biblical numerology.[49] Bullinger comments,

> As a figure, it differs from Metaphor, because in a metaphor the two nouns are both named and given; while, in Hypocatastasis, only one is named and the other is implied, or as it were, is put down underneath out of sight. Hence Hypocatastasis is implied resemblance or representation: i.e., an implied Simile or Metaphor. If Metaphor is more forcible than Simile, then Hypocatastasis is more forcible than Metaphor, and expresses as it were the superlative degree of resemblance.[50]

This accounts for the powerful rhetorical impact of Revelation when it is read or heard; it is very hard to remain unmoved by it. But it also accounts for the way that readers in every generation have read the text and thought, 'That describes the world I am living in!' and have therefore assumed that John *wrote about* their own context,

---

48. For further details, see my exploration of 'Image, Symbol, Metaphor' in Moyise, *Studies in the Book of Revelation*.

49. Bullinger's original text has been reprinted as a facsimile, most recently as Bullinger, *Figures of Speech Used in the Bible*. Bullinger claimed that this term originates with Greek teachers of rhetoric, but there is no evidence of this. The term 'hypocatastasis' is used in Beale, p. 57, though he does not mention Bullinger as the source of this term.

50. Text quoted from the online edition, 'Bullinger's Figures of Speech Used in the Bible', StudyLight.org, <http://www.studylight.org/lexicons/bullinger/hypocatastasis-or-implication.html>.

not about his own. When John describes a beast emerging from the sea (13:1), the (hidden) subject is Roman imperial power which has come across the Aegean Sea. But in using hypocatastatic metaphor, John is allowing us to identify in this metaphor all sorts of different empires – and his combining of Daniel's four beasts into this one, and bracketing its origin and its final judgment inside the origin and judgment of the primordial opponent of God, Satan, suggests this is an identification he is encouraging us to make.

Perhaps the most striking example of this is the threefold funeral dirge of fallen 'Babylon' in Revelation 18. Although there are clear connections made with the specific realities of Roman imperial power, the metaphorical description that John offers us provides a critique of all human imperial aspiration. Empires all through history have aggregated extreme wealth for an economic and political elite, have worked with client kingdoms, have developed networks of trade through conquest, often relying on sea power, and in doing so have exploited their subjects and drained them of resources. John's specific prophetic critique in his own context provides us, through the power of his metaphorical language, with a prophetic critique of human misuse of power in every age.[51]

8. Revelation's use of numbers

One of the most striking features of Revelation is its use of numerology. Two aspects of this are obvious to the casual reader (though are more sophisticated and complex than they seem at first), while two other aspects only become evident after careful analysis.

The most obvious way in which we encounter numbers is when they simply occur within the text. Thus we are told that there are seven assemblies[52] represented by seven lampstands in 1:20, and the structure of the text that follows (the messages to the seven

---

51. A more detailed exploration of the power and effect of hypocatastatic metaphor can be found in my chapter 'Cities in the Book of Revelation', in Walton, Trebilco and Gill, *Urban World and the First Christians*.

52. On the translation of *ekklēsia* by 'assembly' rather than the usual 'church', see comment on 1:11.

assemblies in Rev. 2 – 3) naturally follows this sevenfold structure. But we are immediately confronted with the symbolic (or, rather, metaphorical) meaning of this number 'seven' since we know that there were Christians living in other nearby cities in the region (most notably Miletus and Colossae) who are not included in this list. In the ancient world, seven suggested completeness, since there were seven days in the week, seven seas and seven known planets. We can see that the messages were clearly intended to be read by those in other cities as well as those to which they were addressed, and that John assumes a wider audience for his work, so we might confidently infer that these particular seven symbolized the whole of the early Christian movement and that the letter was relevant to them all.[53] Similarly, we notice that there are seven seals on the scroll which are opened (6:1–17; 8:1), seven trumpets that are sounded (8:2 – 9:21; 11:15) and seven bowls which are poured out (16:1–21) – and each of these shapes the structure of what follows. What we might not notice, though, is that John uses a sevenfold structure elsewhere, so there are seven characteristics of the 144,000 in 14:4–5, and seven unnumbered visions from 19:11 through to 21:1 (see comments on those passages).

This leads on to the second use of numbers by John – words occurring with particular frequencies in the text. There are seven blessings, seven 'sickles' in Revelation 14, seven times God is titled 'Lord God Almighty', seven occurrences of 'Christ', 'testimony of Jesus', 'prophecy', 'I am coming', 'sign', 'endurance' and 'cloud', and seven mentions of the elders and living creatures together. Jesus, the Spirit and the saints are all mentioned fourteen times, significant as 2×7, where two is the number of reliable witness according to Deuteronomy 17:6, so all three are connected with 'faithful witness'.[54] There continues to be debate about the significance of these, and

53. It is now clear that Christian communities across the Roman world communicated frequently with one another and that the writers of the NT were well aware of that. See Bauckham, *Gospel for All Christians*.

54. See 'Structure and Composition' in Bauckham, *Climax of Prophecy*, pp. 1–37.

there is more work to be done in exploring all the patterns here. But it offers strong evidence that Revelation is a very carefully composed text which uses more (but not less) than the meaning of its words to communicate its messages, also deploying the actual structure of the wording. It also points to the text being a carefully constructed whole, rather than a poorly edited amalgam of earlier texts, as some commentators have argued.[55] I mention these word frequencies when the relevant terms arise in the commentary.

The third way that Revelation uses numbers is in drawing on the mathematical significance of square, triangular and rectangular numbers. We are very familiar with what we call square numbers (products of a number multiplied by itself, such as $16 = 4 \times 4$), but perhaps do not realize that the term comes from the possibility of arranging this number of items in a square pattern. In an analogous way, other numbers are triangular if that number of items could be arranged in an equilateral triangle, like the fifteen red balls on a snooker table at the start of a frame. Numbers which are the product of successive integers, such as $4 \times 5 = 20$, can be arranged as a rectangle, and such numbers share some properties with square numbers (20 is the fourth square number plus 4) and with triangular numbers (20 is twice the fourth triangle, 10, which equals $1 + 2 + 3 + 4$). The ancient Greeks were fascinated by the properties of such numbers, not least because they lived in a world where numbers were concrete rather than abstract, so that arrays of objects had a particular interest.

But our interest is in the way Revelation makes use of these properties.[56] Because of the distinctive square shape of Hebrew altars in the Old Testament (in contrast with pagan altars which were rectangular or round) and the shape of the Holy of Holies as a cube (1 Kgs 6:20), John consistently uses the square and cubic numbers 144 and 1,000 to designate the things of God, in particular the

---

55. For detailed exploration of this, see my chapter 'Source, Structure and Composition in the Book of Revelation', in Allen, Paul and Woodman, *Book of Revelation*, pp. 41–54.

56. The definitive study of this remains chapter 11, 'Nero and the Beast', in Bauckham, *Climax of Prophecy*, pp. 384–452.

people of God. By contrast, he uses the triangular number 666 to designate the opponent of God, and in a fascinating conjunction of maths and theology, he uses triangular numbers (which have something in common with both squares and triangles) to designate that period of time when God's people are oppressed by their opponents and yet enjoy the protection of God – the forty-two months equal the 1,260 days of Revelation 11:2, 3; 12:6 (42 is the sixth rectangle, equally 6 × 7, and 1,260 is 35 × 36). This offers more evidence of the sophistication and integrity of this text, and also explains why John changes the description of time period of 'patient endurance' from Daniel's periods of 1,290 and 1,335 days (Dan. 12:11–12) to the single figure of 1,260 days. Once more, we see that Revelation is a thoroughly symbolic text.

The fourth way that Revelation uses numbers is perhaps the most notorious: the isopsephism (the Greek meaning 'same calculation') or *gematria* (the Hebrew adaptation of the Greek word for 'geometry') involved in calculating the number of the beast, 666, in 13:18. Although this number has been used speculatively by every generation of readers, if we take seriously John's claim to be writing a prophetic word for his own audience, and not for some distant time in the future (see comment on 22:10), then we need to follow a way of understanding such numbers that was familiar to John and his first audience. In a world where there was no separate number system, and letters were used for numbers, it was natural to calculate the numerical value of words and names by adding up the values of their letters, and we have evidence of this happening in a wide variety of first-century contexts.

In the ruins of Pompeii, it is possible to make out a graffito: 'I love her whose number is 545.' Presumably the person who was the object of affection here knew her own number, and so would have understood the message – but while it is easy to move from name to number, it is difficult to move in the other direction, which means that the lover's secret was safe. In the Christianized apocalyptic work the *Sibylline Oracles* 1:324–329, it is 'predicted' that the name of the Messiah would add up to 888, which the name Jesus does in Greek. The number 8 was associated with the overflow of blessing that would be the hallmark of the age to come. The Roman historian Suetonius refers to a ditty circulating in Rome in his chapter on Nero: 'A new calculation: Nero killed his own mother', which relies on the fact that the numerical value of the name 'Nero' in this scheme is 1005, the same as the numerical value of the phrase 'killed his own mother', suggesting that the statement was true. The numerical value of the Hebrew term for 'branch' in the messianic title 'branch of David' (derived from Jer. 23:5) is 138, the same as that of the name 'Menachem' meaning 'comforter', so there was an expectation that the Messiah would bring comfort to his people. John uses this approach to numerology both to identify the beast with Nero, and to associate the New Jerusalem with the angels (see comment on 13:18 and 21:17).

Observing these kinds of numerical composition in a text is a completely different exercise from the kinds of speculative observations made about the Bible as a whole – which are usually quite fanciful and designed to prove that God is the 'author' of the text as a whole, but which end up undermining the idea of human involvement in the writing of Scripture. Here we are observing phenomena which are part of the human author's culture and intellectual world, and in exploring them we are doing no more nor less than being responsible readers by reading the text in its cultural context. The late Maarten Menken did pioneering research on this early in his career,[57] and this has been popularized and developed by Richard Bauckham. Bauckham argues that the numbers of words and syllables in key parts of John's Gospel correspond to the *gematria* value of important terms within those passages, and the numbers also have mathematical significance.[58] Joel Green draws on Menken's other work in relation to Luke and Acts, noting that the verb 'to have compassion' comes at the numerical centre of the three passages in Luke where it occurs (at Luke 7:13; 10:33; and 15:20).[59]

57. Menken, *Numerical Literary Techniques in John*.

58. See the chapter 'The 153 Fish and the Unity of the Fourth Gospel',
    in Bauckham, *Testimony of the Beloved Disciple*, pp. 271–284.

59. Green, *Gospel of Luke*, p. 291. For a fuller discussion, see the article
    'Numerical Composition and Reading Luke', on my blog, *Psephizo*, 9
    May 2014, <https://www.psephizo.com/biblical-studies/secret-codes-
    in-the-bibleand-n-t-wright/> and <https://www.psephizo.com/
    biblical-studies/numerical-composition-and-reading-luke/>.

The first writers lived in a culture where copying was costly and payment to the scribe was made by the word or syllable, so they would have known the numbers of words and syllables in their texts – and of course there were far fewer texts for them to know about. The use of computer technology is now allowing us to explore something which they were well aware of but which we have previously ignored.

9. Revelation's use of the Old Testament

Another of Revelation's distinctive features is its extensive use of language, ideas and imagery from the Old Testament. While John never cites the Old Testament – in the sense of saying (for example), 'This is what the prophet Isaiah said . . .' (cf. Mark 1:2) or 'as it is written' (cf. Matt. 4:4; Rom. 2:24) – his text is saturated with allusions to the Old Testament.[60] The United Bible Society's edition of the Greek New Testament includes a list of Old Testament allusions in each of the New Testament books, and it lists 676 allusions in Revelation's 405 verses, meaning that we will be encountering (on average) one or two allusions in every verse. The allusions are most frequently to Isaiah (128 times), Psalms (99), Ezekiel (92), Daniel (82) and Exodus (53), indicating the relative importance of these Old Testament texts for John.[61]

Some commentators suggest that there is no deliberate design to John's use of Old Testament texts; this is just the mark of someone whose mind is saturated with biblical language.[62] Others take the view that the texts of the Old Testament retain their original meaning and significance even in their new context

---

60. For a detailed discussion of the methodology of detecting OT allusions and the way John uses them, see my essay 'The Use of the Old Testament in Rev 12', in Moyise, *Old Testament in the New*.

61. For a table of a similar listing of allusions from the Greek edition of Nestle-Aland 26, see Kovacs and Rowland, pp. 284–295.

62. So Rowland, pp. 24, 37, who comments that John 'wrote more than he ever fully understood' and so 'these other [Old Testament] texts cannot be determinative for the way I read'.

within Revelation.[63] Neither view makes the best sense of the way
that Old Testament allusions function within Revelation. On the
one hand, John appears to make frequent, detailed and systematic
use of Old Testament language. For example, the important
fourfold phrase 'from every tribe and language and people and
nation' and its six parallels draw on the language of Genesis 10:31
('tribes, tongues, territories and nations', AT) and Exodus 19:5 ('out
of all nations you will be my treasured possession'), which is echoed
in the restoration promise of Ezekiel 36:24 (see comment on
Rev. 5:9). And the unusual expression about Satan, 'nor was their
place found any longer in heaven' in 12:8 (AT), uses the language
of the destruction of the statue in Daniel 2:35 and the judgment of
the wicked in Psalm 37:36 (see comment on 12:8).

On the other hand, John appears to reinterpret and redeploy
images from the Old Testament in the light of the Christ event and
the future eschatological judgment. So, for example, his descriptions
of both the devil in Revelation 12 and the beast from the land in
Revelation 13 combine the imagery of the four beasts coming from
the sea in Daniel 7. Most of the main ideas and scenes in Revelation
are based on adaptation of Old Testament episodes and images:

- the vision of Jesus in Revelation 1 draws on the angel
  in Daniel 10 and the Ancient of Days in Daniel 7;
- the worship of God in Revelation 4 includes imagery from
  God's descent to Mount Sinai, as well as images from
  elsewhere in the Old Testament;
- the seals, trumpets and bowls sequences draw on the plagues
  of Egypt in Exodus 7 – 10;
- the sealing of the saints in Revelation 7 draws on Ezekiel 8;
- John's eating of the scroll in Revelation 10 draws on Ezekiel 3;
- the two witnesses in Revelation 11 use imagery from the
  accounts of Moses and Elijah;
- the figures in Revelation 12 draw on images from Psalm 2;
  Isaiah 66; Micah 4 and 6, and elsewhere;
- the beasts are described using imagery from Daniel 7;

---

63. So Beale, pp. 76–99.

- the judgment of the great prostitute draws on imagery from the judgment of Tyre in Ezekiel 27;
- the vision of the New Jerusalem makes use of a wide range of Old Testament ideas and texts.

In making sense of these, we will need to attend both to the meaning of the language as it is in its Old Testament context as well as to the way that John reuses these images in the context of the narrative of Revelation.

10. The structure of Revelation

The challenge of understanding Revelation's structure is quite different from exploring this question for other books of the New Testament, because of four distinct features of the text.

The first is that Revelation has a very large number of explicit markers of structure, often making use of the number seven. Most obviously, there are seven messages to the Christian assemblies (*ekklēsiai*) in Revelation 2 – 3, seven seals that are opened in Revelation 6 (concluding after an interlude in 8:1), seven trumpets that are blown in Revelation 8 – 9 and seven bowls that are poured out in Revelation 16. In addition, there are patterns of seven within the text which are not explicitly signalled or counted, such as the seven occurrences of the term 'sickle' in Revelation 14, and the seven unnumbered visions in Revelation 19 – 21 (see introductory comment at 19:11). These features serve to bind together different sections of the text into unified blocks. Complementary to that is the use made by John of particular phrases which appear to signal the introduction of a new focus or the arrival of a new character, the most common being 'and I saw' (*kai eidon*) which occurs frequently at the beginning of major sections as well as at the start of subsections within them. John also makes use of noticeable changes in his style of writing: the vision of Jesus in Revelation 1 takes the form of a vision report, but Revelation 2 – 3 has its own distinctive style and structure (see comment introducing this section); the language shifts again at 4:1; then again at 6:1; there is a change of focus at 7:1; and so on. The most noticeable break (observed by all commentators) comes at 12:1, where John uses the language of a 'sign appeared' instead of 'and I saw'; what is less often noticed is that the preceding section in Revelation 11 is the only section of the text cast in the future tense.

Altogether, these markers indicate a clear set of major units that make up the text as a whole:

1:1–8	Revelatory-epistolary prologue
1:9–20	John's commission and vision of Jesus
2:1 – 3:22	Messages to the assemblies in the seven cities
4:1 – 5:14	Worship in heaven
6:1–17	The opening of the seven seals of the scroll (completed in 8:1)
7:1–17	Interlude: a twofold vision of the people of God
8:2 – 9:21	The blowing of the seven trumpets (completed in 11:15–19)
10:1 – 11:14	Interlude: the prophetic task of John and God's people
12:1–17	The woman, the dragon and the male child
13:1–18	The beast from the sea and the beast from the land
14:1–20	The 144,000 and the visions of harvest
15:1 – 16:21	The pouring out of the seven bowls
17:1 – 19:10	The great prostitute and the scarlet beast
19:11 – 20:15	Visions of God's eschatological victory
21:1 – 22:5	The ultimate vision: the New Jerusalem
22:6–21	Revelatory-epistolary epilogue

This leads to the second observation: within each of these larger units there is a clear microstructure. It is these smaller units of text that form the structure of the Analysis below. Some of these structural elements are clearly signalled, such as the shared structure of the seven messages, while others are less obviously signalled but are evident nonetheless, such as the fourfold structure of Revelation 12, as it moves from the narrative of the woman and the dragon, to the account of heavenly angelic warfare, to the hymn of praise, and back to the opening narrative of the woman and the dragon. Many of these are indicated in English translations by means of paragraph breaks. There are other structuring features which are evident only on a close reading of the text, such as the six angels in two sets of three that give structure to the harvest visions in Revelation 14. All these are noted in the commentary on the text.

The third feature of Revelation's structure, which is only evident when looking at the text as a whole, is the striking discontinuity between different units. This is drawn to our attention by the various abrupt changes in language and in the changes of *dramatis personae* from one unit to another, as is evident when we look at the characters themselves. At first there appears to be little in common between the six main descriptions of Jesus – in the epistolary greeting, the vision in 1:12 that follows, the image of the lamb on the throne, the male child in Revelation 12, the one like a son of man in Revelation 14 and the rider on the white horse in Revelation 19. The angels of the seven assemblies quickly disappear from view, as do most of the angels that we meet, however splendid they appear – and the revealing angel mentioned in 1:1 and 22:16 never appears at all! The beast from the land abruptly changes into the false prophet (16:13) and the beast from the land then becomes the scarlet beast ridden by the great prostitute (17:3). Other characters in the drama disappear without trace, most notably the woman clothed with the sun, whom we last see waiting in the desert, protected by God. This discontinuity led an earlier commentator, R. H. Charles, to argue that Revelation was originally a series of separate units that was edited together by a series of clumsy and ignorant editors, and a similar theory of multiple composition was again proposed by David Aune.[64]

The main problem with these theories is that they do not adequately take into account the fourth feature of Revelation's structure: the widespread occurrence of links and connections between different sections. The most obvious of these occur in the messages to the seven assemblies in Revelation 2 – 3, in each of which the opening greeting links back to the first vision of the exalted Jesus, and whose closing comments include an anticipation of the New Jerusalem in Revelation 21. Connections can be seen

---

64. Charles, I, pp. l–lv; Aune, I, pp. cxviii–cxxxiv.

too in the hymns at the end of Revelation 7 and 11 which also anticipate the final vision of the new creation. Some sections do not
obviously belong to one larger section or another, but function to
link one to another. For example, 1:9–11 looks like a continuation
of John's epistolary greeting from verse 4, but it also looks back to
the opening verses in reiterating John's commission, and then leads
into the vision of the exalted Jesus. In 11:1, John is 'told' as he was
in 10:11, so these verses look like a continuation of the encounter
with the mighty angel of 10:1, but they lead directly into the account
of the two witnesses which continues to 11:13. And the 'woes'
announced by the eagle in 8:13 are not completed until 12:12, and
have some connection with the 'woes' of 18:10, 16, 19.

But there are other, more subtle connections throughout the text.
Although in other ways Revelation 11 and 12 are quite distinct, not
only in the characters featured but also in the style of John's writing,
they are linked together by the use of the threefold time period
described as 'time, times and half a time', '42 months' and '1,260
days' (11:2, 3, 9, 11; 12:6, 14) which are used only in these two
chapters. The words occurring with special frequencies mentioned
above under 'Revelation's use of numbers' occur throughout the
text; there are no units which avoid occurrences of at least some
of these terms.[65] In the detailed commentary I note the various
connections across the text whenever they occur.

It is unclear whether there is one overarching structure to the
book that will somehow unlock its meaning for us. Some have
proposed a detailed chiastic structure, where the whole book is
arranged in a 'concentric' pattern of A-B-C-D-E-E'-D'-C'-B'-A'
with the same pattern echoed within each section,[66] but the data of
the text simply does not match this. Craig Koester suggests a more
general structure of six cycles, covering the message of Christ to
the assemblies; the seven seals; the seven trumpets; the dragon, the
beasts and the faithful (up to 15:4); the seven bowls and the fall of

---

65. I include a detailed analysis of the distribution of these terms in 'Source,
    Structure and Composition in the Book of Revelation', in Allen, Paul
    and Woodman, *Book of Revelation*, pp. 41–54.

66. Heil, *Book of Revelation*, pp. 2–9.

Babylon; and the beast's demise and the New Jerusalem.[67] It is not clear to me that this puts all the major divisions in the right place, and we need to distinguish between structures that are there in the text and structures which we use in order to help us make sense of it.

What we have in Revelation is a finely woven cloth, with major patterns that are discernible as well as subtle threads that link different parts together. In our reading and interpretation of this fascinating and intricate text, we need to attend to both.

11. Revelation's main theological themes

The central focus of Revelation is given to us from the opening words of the very first verse: this is a revelation 'of Jesus Christ' (AT). The fully human Jesus ('someone like a son of man') was in fact God's anointed one who, in his death and resurrection, fulfilled all the things promised to the people of God over the years of their being called and formed as a people – being freed from slavery, travelling through the wilderness and entering the Promised Land, and then being once more delivered from exile to live in freedom and to the praise of God as a light to the world. Jesus' death atoned for his people's sins, and has bought them and set them apart to fulfil God's original aspiration that they should be a priestly people, mediating God's presence to a rebellious world. But the grace of God in Jesus has transformed this age-old hope, so that this people are no longer from one ethnic group but from all the peoples of earth, offering testimony of God's love and faithfulness to every corner of God's world.

The distinct visions of Jesus' presence and action throughout Revelation each communicate a different aspect of this theological understanding. In Revelation 1, Jesus shares divine identity but also (in being described using the features of an angel from Daniel 10) functions as the one who communicates the message from God; he brings both the awesome power of divine presence as well as mediation between the human and the divine. In Revelation 5, the

---

67. Koester (2), pp. ix–xii.

central image (here and throughout the rest of the book) is of Jesus as the slain lamb, standing: the one who has exercised his power by giving up his life, but has now conquered death and shares the throne with God his Father. His death has achieved victory over every force that opposes the purposes of God – but this has been achieved only by his faithfulness to the point of death. He therefore offers his followers the gift of life and the promise of victory, but also an example of the pattern of victorious life for them to emulate. Revelation's implicit theology of atonement has strong elements of both 'Christus Victor', Jesus' triumph over sin and evil, as well as a strong exemplary focus.

This christological focus takes its place alongside a focus on the centrality of God. Jesus shares many of the titles with God (who is once described as his 'Father' in 1:6) and most strikingly shares the throne which sits at the visual centre of the heavenly scenes in the book. As the narrative develops, Jesus and God the Father even come to share singular verbs, indicating their close relationship. Yet they are also always distinguished, making Revelation one of the most important resources for reflecting on God as Trinity, with the diversity of 'persons' held within an essential unity. God is consistently portrayed as the all-powerful one (*pantokratōr*), so that all other claims to power, human and spiritual, are either pale imitations of his splendour or usurp what rightly belongs only to God. God's might is particularly expressed in his actions as Creator and the one who cherishes the created order. This means that the end of all things must involve the destruction of all forces of destruction (11:18) and the restoration and cleansing of the cosmos, so that heavenly reality comes down to a renewed earth, rather than the other way around (earth being taken up into the heavens). As part of this, the forces of chaos and judgment, while under God's sovereign control, are given permissive rather than directive authority; John is consistently reticent to attribute damage and destruction directly to God's intention, even though he will not surrender the notion of God's sovereignty over all. As becomes clear as God's judgments unfold, the principle of *lex talionis* is central to all God's judgments: he gives to people only what they have given to others, and his judgment is testimony to his justice and equity. This repeatedly sits alongside his grace and the free offer of forgiveness and life; God only gives to people what they deserve if they have refused the gift that they do not deserve.

John's theology of the Spirit is more implicit and diverse than his theology of Jesus and God, but also weaves throughout the narrative in the different expressions of John being 'in the Spirit', the 'seven spirits before [the] throne' and the Spirit as an explicit voice who carries the words of Jesus to the Christians in the seven cities of Asia and beyond. It might even be that in the image of the 'river of the water of life' we find a metaphor for the Spirit's life-giving presence within the new creation, in line with a broader Johannine theology of the Spirit as the water of life (see John 7:38).

Eschatology looms large throughout Revelation, as is fitting for the book which finds itself at the end of the New Testament canon. But Revelation's eschatological focus is more complex and nuanced than many traditions of reading have allowed, reflected in its complex configuration of both space and time. Jesus is consistently described as the 'coming' one (and his coming expresses the future of God as the one who 'is, and was, and is to come'), and yet that 'coming' happens in the present and locally as well as in the future and cosmically. Although the events accompanying the opening of the seals and the blowing of the trumpets have often been read as future, a proper understanding of John's structuring of time makes it clear that they describe things that happen in the present age, which John's first readers are already experiencing. These events create a crisis of understanding when those who are faithful cry, 'How long?' and have to wait patiently for God's intermediate and final interventions in the world. Within the overall structure of Revelation, the judgment on the particular system of defiant human power found in the Roman Empire sits within a wider narrative of cosmic judgment over all human defiance. God's particular verdict is an expression and an anticipation of God's universal verdict which we still await. And John is clear from the very beginning that both he and his readers are located within the 'end times' tribulation' (*thlipsis*, 1:9) experienced by all those who follow Jesus and seek his kingdom (Acts 14:22).

The rhetorical goal of John's writing – for his first readers as well as for subsequent generations – is that they should be motivated and equipped to live as mature disciples of Jesus. The central element of this is to be a 'faithful witness' as Jesus was, living a life of 'patient endurance' (1:9) in the face of opposition and difficulty, but motivated by a clearer understanding of the 'kingdom' that is ours in Jesus. It is this 'quietist' approach, involving non-violent resistance to the forces of imperial conformity, which constitutes true victory, trusting as it does in God's ultimate power and justice for vindication. This is a life that is lived in constant anticipation, always looking forwards to the promised end, so that the present becomes shaped by the hope of the future. As in Paul's understanding (seen, for example, in his description of baptism and resurrection in Romans 6), the saints are already beginning to live the resurrection life – they are already casting their crowns before the throne of God since they are already 'dwellers in heaven' – and this is to be lived out in their various contexts on earth until the final and definitive visitation of God's presence in the form of the holy city that descends from heaven. In Revelation, being a disciple is about living in the 'now' as well as the 'not yet' of expectation, with the former decisively shaped by the latter.

12. Approaches to its interpretation

Within the history of interpretation of Revelation, there have been four major distinctive approaches:[68]

- *Idealist.* This sees the text as describing timeless spiritual truths about the nature and purposes of God, and the relationship between the church and the world. Some of the earliest allegorical interpretations of Revelation were of this sort, but this approach has more recent exponents too.
- *Futurist.* A rival school of early interpreters saw in Revelation the prediction of an imminent end and the advent of the millennial age. Joachim of Fiore in the twelfth century understood it as predicting the end in his time, and there was a strong revival of this approach in the twentieth century.

---

68. For a full exploration of these four approaches, see Gentry et al., *Four Views.*

- *Church historical.* As the centuries passed, it became increasingly attractive to see Revelation as having some historical references, but not to the 'end times' only. Berengaud in the ninth century was the first to suggest that Revelation described events through history to the writer's day.
- *Contemporary historical (or preterist).* The rise of biblical criticism and the rediscovery of the historical context of Revelation's writing have made it possible to argue that Revelation is primarily speaking to its own day, and only secondarily (and derivatively) to later readers. A particular variant of this approach sees the whole of the text as referring to events prior to the destruction of Jerusalem (which is interpreted as 'the great city' and 'Babylon') and the End as fulfilled in Jerusalem's destruction.

These four approaches are often closely related to different interpretations of the millennium of Revelation 20. The four dominant understandings of the millennium (which do not correspond directly to the four approaches above) are as follows:

- *Premillennialism.* This approach understands the thousand years as a literal period which follows the return of Jesus to earth (the 'pre-' relates to when Jesus' return takes place, i.e. it will be before, 'pre-', the millennium). This was the most common reading of Revelation 20 in the early church and can be dated back as far as Papias of Hierapolis who died in 130. It was followed by Justin Martyr and Irenaeus, but began to be opposed in the early third century. The difficulty with this reading is that it takes the number 1,000 as literal alone among all the numbers in Revelation, and it is hard to make sense of the release of Satan as a chronological description.
- *Amillennialism.* In the third century there was a move to understand the millennium 'spiritually' rather than literally, and Tyconius was the first to propose that the millennium was another way of describing the period between Jesus' exaltation and his return, a view that was followed by

Augustine and remained influential for centuries. The
difficulty with this reading is that John already has numbers
to describe this period – three and a half years, forty-two
months and 1,260 days – and it seems impossible to
reconcile the binding of Satan with Satan and the beasts'
trampling of the saints, even within the narrative of the
book. The thousand-year reign also *follows* the judgment
sequences, so would be completely out of narrative
order.

- *Postmillennialism*. In the medieval period, the idea developed
  that the millennium describes a period of future history, so
  that the return of Jesus will follow (is 'post-') the millennium.
  Joachim of Fiore in the twelfth century proposed that
  the kingdom of the Spirit would arrive in the year 1260,
  following the (then) present age of the Son. Postmillennial
  thinking was revived under the philosophical influence of
  Hegel and the social optimism of the nineteenth century,
  but disappeared in Western thinking after the catastrophe
  of the Great War. The difficulty of this reading is in making
  sense of the placing of the millennium *after* the coming of
  Jesus riding the white horse in Revelation 19.
- *Dispensational Premillennialism*. Renewal of a belief in a literal
  thousand years came with the complex dispensational
  schemes created by John Nelson Derby around 1830, one
  of the founders of the movement known as the Plymouth
  Brethren. This approach takes a strictly futurist view of
  Revelation, and within it there are different schemes to relate
  the seven-year period of 'tribulation', the rapture of the
  saints (in effect, a secret first coming of Jesus involving
  believers being taken up to heaven), which might come
  at the beginning, in the middle or at the end of the seven
  years, and the final return of Jesus. The difficulty with this
  reading is that it does not attend to John's use of the
  language of 'tribulation' (suffering), it attempts to take the
  text literally but often reads it allegorically, and it imports
  misreadings of Paul (in the form of the 'rapture') into
  Revelation's text. It is, nevertheless, one of the most
  widespread approaches within Protestantism globally.

Although these eight approaches (four to Revelation as a whole and four to the millennium) are usually presented as interpretative strategies, they are in fact interpretative *conclusions*. Revelation should be approached as any other letter in the New Testament which claims to offer prophetic insight into spiritual reality. We need to attend carefully to what the text actually says; understand what the writer and first audience might have thought it meant in their own context; and from that discern what God through his Spirit might be saying to us in the situations and challenges that we face. In that sense, we are making use of aspects of each of the four approaches. Clearly, Revelation is speaking to first-century Christians, and we need to know as much as we can about them to make sense of it (contemporary historical). But Revelation makes sense of their present situation in the light of the ultimate destiny of the world, and we need to do the same for our situation (futurist). We might even see ways in which God's promise and judgment have been worked out in history (church historical), and all these things will teach us truths about the nature of God and his relation to the world (idealist).

ANALYSIS

1. EPISTOLARY PROLOGUE (1:1–8)
A. Prologue (1:1–3)
B. Epistolary introduction (1:4–8)

2. JESUS THE ANGELIC SON OF MAN SPEAKS TO THE ASSEMBLIES (1:9 – 3:22)
A. John's commission (1:9–11)
B. The vision of Jesus (1:12–20)
C. The messages to the seven assemblies (2:1 – 3:22)
 i. Message to the assembly in Ephesus (2:1–7)
 ii. Message to the assembly in Smyrna (2:8–11)
 iii. Message to the assembly in Pergamum (2:12–17)
 iv. Message to the assembly in Thyatira (2:18–29)
 v. Message to the assembly in Sardis (3:1–6)
 vi. Message to the assembly in Philadelphia (3:7–13)
 vii. Message to the assembly in Laodicea (3:14–22)

3. JOHN IN THE HEAVENLY THRONE ROOM (4:1 – 5:14)
A. John's encounter with the heavenly throne (4:1–6a)

B. John's encounter with the heavenly worship (4:6b–11)
C. John sees the scroll and the lamb (5:1–7)
D. The worship of the lamb (5:8–14)

4. THE OPENING OF THE SEVEN SEALS (6:1–17)
A. The first four seals are broken: the four horsemen (6:1–8)
B. The fifth and sixth seals: the martyrs and the wrath of the lamb (6:9–17)

5. INTERLUDE: THE VISION OF GOD'S PEOPLE, AND THE FINAL SEAL (7:1 – 8:1)
A. The sealing of the 144,000 (7:1–8)
B. The great multitude in praise and the seventh seal (7:9 – 8:1)

6. THE SOUNDING OF THE SEVEN TRUMPETS (8:2 – 9:21)
A. The seven angels and the prayer of the saints (8:2–5)
B. The first four trumpets are sounded (8:6–13)
C. The fifth trumpet (9:1–12)
D. The sixth trumpet (9:13–21)

7. INTERLUDE: THE PROPHETIC TASK OF TESTIMONY OF JOHN AND GOD'S PEOPLE (10:1 – 11:19)
A. John's (re)commissioning to prophesy (10:1–11)
    i. The great angel and the seven thunders (10:1–7)
    ii. The command to eat the little scroll (10:8–11)
B. The people of God as the two prophetic witnesses (11:1–14)
    i. Measuring the temple (11:1–2)
    ii. The ministry of the two witnesses (11:3–6)
    iii. The two witnesses are killed and raised to life (11:7–14)
C. The seventh angel sounds his trumpet (11:15–19)

8. THE WOMAN CLOTHED WITH THE SUN, THE CHILD AND THE DRAGON (12:1–17)
A. The woman, the dragon and the child (12:1–6)
B. War in heaven (12:7–9)

C. The hymn of praise (12:10–12)

D. The dragon pursues the woman (12:13–17)

9. THE BEASTS FROM THE SEA AND THE LAND (13:1–18)

A. The beast from the sea (13:1–10)

B. The beast from the land (13:11–15)

C. The mark of the beast (13:16–18)

10. THE 144,000 ON MOUNT ZION AND THE HARVEST OF THE SON OF MAN (14:1–20)

A. The vision of the lamb and the 144,000 on Mount Zion (14:1–5)

B. Three angels announcing the gospel and judgment (14:6–13)

C. The harvest of the Son of Man (14:14–20)

11. THE POURING OUT OF THE SEVEN BOWLS (15:1 – 16:21)

A. Introductory vision and the song of Moses (15:1–8)

B. The first five bowls (16:1–11)

C. The sixth and seventh bowls (16:12–21)

12. THE GREAT PROSTITUTE AND THE SCARLET BEAST (17:1 – 19:10)

A. The vision in the wilderness (17:1–6)

B. The interpretation of the beast (17:7–11)

C. The interpretation of the horns and the woman (17:12–18)

D. The judgment of Babylon (18:1–8)

E. The mourning of the kings, merchants and seafarers (18:9–20)

F. The declaration of the mighty angel (18:21–24)

G. Celebration in heaven (19:1–10)

13. SEVEN UNNUMBERED VISIONS OF THE END (19:11 – 20:15)

A. The rider on the white horse (19:11–16)

B. The beast and the kings of the earth, and the last battle (19:17–21)

C. Satan chained for a thousand years (20:1–3)
D. The reign of the martyrs and the destruction of Satan
   (20:4–10)
E. The final judgment before the great white throne (20:11–15)

14. THE NEW JERUSALEM (21:1 – 22:5)
A. The appearance of the holy city (21:1–8)
B. The description of the holy city (21:9–21)
C. The glory of the holy city (21:22–27)
D. The river of the water of life and the tree of life (22:1–5)

15. EPILOGUE TO THE VISION REPORT AND THE LETTER (22:6–21)

COMMENTARY

1. EPISTOLARY PROLOGUE (1:1–8)

Context

In most letters we read in everyday life, the address and opening greeting tell us little, though the format might warn us whether to expect a formal demand from our bank manager or the warm greetings of a friend when we open it. But, as with Paul's letters, the opening of Revelation is part of the text, not simply something written on the outside, and so gives us much information about what is to follow – and here John packs in many more key ideas than Paul ever does.

John is writing to specific people he knows pastorally, so we should not be surprised to find from verse 4 that he writes in the style we find in Christian adaptations of the usual letter-writing styles of the first-century world. What is more surprising is to find this letter style wrapped around (at the beginning here and the end in Rev. 22) with the language of 'revelation' from which the book gets its common name – 'revelation', which elsewhere in the New Testament contains the good news of God's grace in Jesus, is a work of the Spirit in the believing community and will one day disclose Jesus to the world when he returns (see comment on v. 1).

The opening verses and the epistolary greeting which follows are both rich in important theological terms which shape all that follows. The most significant of these are found in the threefold greeting by John from God, the seven spirits (the Holy Spirit) and Jesus, which turn out to form the clearest and most exalted articulation of God as Trinity anywhere in the New Testament. In each of these, John draws on and adapts Old Testament terms and ideas, and expresses them in a way which presents a direct challenge to the dominant narratives in his day, starting the process of raising the stakes for his audience as they consider everyday questions of life and loyalty as a small minority in a vast and powerful empire.

The range and density of ideas are expressed through rapid change of genre (kind of writing) as John moves from revelatory language, through the epistolary, prophetic and doxological, and back to epistolary (see Introduction, 'What kind of text is Revelation?'). This has the effect of disorienting us, as we struggle to make sense of what kind of text we are reading. But this also has the effect of drawing us in as we engage for ourselves in the revelation that John experienced and consider what it might mean for us as we face similar questions of life and similar challenges to our loyalty.

A. Prologue (1:1–3)

In the opening verses of this book, the writer identifies himself as 'John', and makes a powerful claim about the significance of what he has written. The focus is first on the origins of this text, and looks upwards, at John's relationship with God, Jesus and the angel as he describes the transmission of what becomes his writing. He introduces some key ideas (revelation, testimony, blessing, obedience and urgency) which will be repeated and revisited through the book.

Comment

1–2. The text appears to start quite abruptly, with an authoritative claim to what it is and where it has come from. The phrase *revelation of Jesus Christ* (AT) is not preceded by 'the' in Greek (i.e. it has no article) but this is not unusual (the same is true in Matt. 1:1 and

Mark 1:1). The opening word *apokalypsis* (*revelation*) lends its name both to this book of the Bible as well as to a whole genre of literature in Second Temple Judaism, though in fact the word occurs only here and not in that literature, and there are questions as to whether this book actually belongs in that genre (see Introduction, 'What kind of text is Revelation?'). That we should only know God's will and purposes by 'revelation', that is, by God's own disclosure (*to show his servants*), is characteristic of both Jewish and Christian theology. Paul describes his understanding of the gospel in these terms (Gal. 1:12), but bringing revelation is also the work of the Spirit, both in the process of maturing discipleship (Eph. 1:17) and as one of the 'charismatic' gifts in the Christian assembly (1 Cor. 14:6, 26). These anticipate the final revelation of Jesus at his return (1 Cor. 1:7; 2 Thess. 1:7; 1 Pet. 1:7, 13). John, too, is a *servant*; the term occurs fourteen times in Revelation, matching the occurrence of *hagioi*, 'saints', another designation for God's people. These things must *soon* take place, but the emphasis here is not so much on the immediate nature of the events (the meaning of *tachys* in Matt. 5:25; Luke 15:22; and John 11:29) but on their suddenness when they come (*en tachei*; cf. Acts 12:7; Rom. 16:20).

It is not clear whether *of Jesus Christ* (AT) is an objective or subjective genitive – that is, whether the revelation comes *from* Jesus or is a revelation *about* Jesus that discloses him. The words that immediately follow suggest the former, since the message comes to John by the angel from Jesus. But the second half of this chapter suggests the latter – John actually sees a revelation of Jesus. John might be intending us to understand both; the revelation that Jesus offers is a renewed vision of who he is and what it means to follow him. He is both the sender and the centre of the message we need to hear.

Jesus occurs fourteen times within the book (and *Christ* seven times),[1] signifying the importance of the name and connecting with his distinctive characterization as the 'faithful witness' (see below on v. 5). John's ministry in writing this book parallels that of Jesus,

---

1. The term *Christos* (usually translated 'Christ', though occasionally as 'Messiah' in English versions) is the Greek translation of the Hebrew *māšîaḥ*. Both derive from the respective verbs meaning 'to anoint'.

in that he *testifies* to what he sees. But immediately, John breaks down the distinction between seeing and hearing, since he 'sees' a 'word': *the word of God and the testimony of Jesus Christ.* The first of these appears to have the 'subjective' sense, in that the word comes from God (rather than being about him), but the second shares the ambiguity that we saw in *the revelation.* What John shares is both a trustworthy testimony *from* Jesus, the true witness, but also a trustworthy testimony from John *about* Jesus.

3. The invocation of a blessing comes at the beginning and end of this book (see 22:7 and 14), and *blessed* comes seven times in total. In the ancient world, reading would normally be out loud, and the singular (*the one who reads*) evokes the idea of a lector reading to a congregation, which comprises *those who hear.* This 'revelation' which is a 'testimony' is also a *prophecy*; the writing style draws on the whole range of biblical genres, and John is keeping us on our toes as readers and hearers.

The parallel between hearing and *keeping* (AT) follows the assumption of the Old Testament, that true hearing means obedient action in response ('Hear, O Israel . . .', Deut. 6:4; cf. Jas 1:22). The importance of responding is because *the time is near,* but John here uses *kairos,* suggesting moment, opportunity, rather than *chronos,* which has days and hours more in view. The phrase here is reminiscent of Jesus' early preaching that 'The time [*kairos*] has come, and the kingdom of God is near' [*engizō,* from the same root as the word 'near' here], Mark 1:15, AT). In Aristotle's theory of rhetoric, *kairos* referred to the moment when the speaker could persuade the listener and win him or her over. As you hear these words being read out, today, this is the day to respond (cf. Heb. 3:13).

John presents himself here as the person who is not the originator of his message (even if the style of it bears the marks of his own personality, context and experience) but a recipient, who passes on faithfully what he himself has received. In this way, he makes similar claims to St Paul, who passed on to the Christians in Corinth (and others) the 'tradition that was passed on to me' (1 Cor. 15:3, AT). But John adds two other dimensions to this. First, he stands close to Jesus, in mimicking his example of faithful witness; as Jesus has been faithful, so John is faithful, and his message will encourage his readers to that same kind of enduring, patient faithfulness in the face of pressure. But in other ways he stands closer to his listeners, in that he has been someone watching and listening carefully, and he is near the end of the chain of revelation (God – Jesus – angel – John – readers/hearers). He is a servant just as his listeners are also servants of God.

John will give many clues to the kind of experience that he has had, but from the beginning he undermines the idea that this is a straightforward vision report, since he 'sees' what can only be 'heard'. This is a 'revelation', a 'testimony' and a 'prophecy' and, as we will soon see, a whole range of other things besides. The revelation of God is already pushing the boundaries of human categorization.

B. Epistolary introduction (1:4–8)

John continues from the startling opening of his work to offer a second striking introduction. Whereas the opening prologue appears to focus on the 'vertical' dimension, highlighting the origin of his writing in God's revelation, this second introduction appears at first to focus on the 'horizontal' dimension, emphasizing his communication with his anticipated recipients. But he quickly returns the focus to the 'vertical', as he brings greetings from God, and immediately moves into both doxology to Jesus for what he has achieved for us, and prophetic utterance from God, the Almighty.

4–5a. Having told us that this is a revelation, testimony and prophecy, *John* now adopts the style of a first-century letter, following the usual format of author, recipient and greeting. Unlike Paul, he does not introduce himself beyond his name; we must assume that he knows and is known by those to whom he writes. There were significant *churches* in the Roman province of *Asia* (western Turkey) other than the ones he names, so, in the light of John's symbolic use of numbers, we must assume that his message relates both to the particular situation of these seven and to the Christians as a whole in the region and elsewhere in the empire.

John follows Paul's adaptation of the standard letter format which changes the opening 'greetings' (*chairein*) to the similar but distinctively Christian *Grace* (*charis*) and adds the equivalent of the Jewish greeting *shalom*, *peace*. This double greeting points to the 'vertical' and 'horizontal' dimensions of Christian faith: the gracious gift of

God's love and forgiveness in Jesus leads to transformed relationships of peace within his people. As with Paul, the usual wish of blessing from the gods is replaced by identifying the source of grace and peace, God and Jesus. But, uniquely in the New Testament, John's greeting here has a trinitarian shape by including symbolic reference to the Spirit.

The threefold formula for God, *[he] who is, and who was, and who is to come*, is in the nominative case (rather than using the expected genitive) which indicates that John is using it as a fixed title. It derives from God's revelation to Moses at the burning bush (Exod. 3:14), 'I AM WHO I AM', or 'I will be who I will be', which gives rise to the Old Testament name for God, YHWH (the so-called Tetragrammaton, often written as the name Yahweh and rendered in most English translations by the form 'LORD'). The order of terms is slightly odd; we might expect the past tense to have come first, but this order emphasizes God's living presence. Instead of an open future ('who will be'), the last term links the future of God to the expected return of Jesus – the one *who is to come*.

The insertion of the *seven spirits* between the references to God and Jesus makes it impossible to understand it as anything other than a symbolic description of the Spirit as the third person of the Trinity. In this phrase, which comes four times in total (3:1; 4:5; 5:6), John combines the description of the anointing of the Davidic Messiah in Isaiah 11:2 (the six qualities in the Hebrew text become a description of the sevenfold Spirit of God in the Greek Septuagint which John and his readers knew) with the seven lamps on the golden lampstand in Zechariah 4:2 which are associated with the seven 'eyes of Yahweh' (Zech. 4:10).

The threefold description of *Jesus Christ* derives from Psalm 89, which combines praise of God's faithfulness, delight in the Davidic kingship and lament over its failure. Like the ideal David, Jesus is a *faithful witness* reflecting the permanence of the moon (Ps. 89:37); 'faithful' should be taken as an attributive of 'witness' rather than as a separate term. He, too, is the *firstborn* (Ps. 89:27a), but his resurrection *from the dead* makes him not only pre-eminent, but also the pioneer and guarantor of the hope of new life for all who trust in him, the 'firstfruits of those who have fallen asleep' (1 Cor. 15:20). And it is he, not Caesar, who is the true *ruler of the kings of the earth*

(Ps. 89:27b); though the kings do not yet recognize his rule, 'committing adultery' with the great prostitute (Rev. 17:2) and fighting on the side of the beast (19:19), at the end they 'bring their glory' into the New Jerusalem (21:24, AT).

5b–6. John now moves into a doxology; praise and worship will punctuate every episode of the text. It is striking that the first part of this is directed to Jesus, rather than to God (made clear by reference to *his blood*). What God has done for us in Jesus was indeed the act of Jesus himself, and not simply as an instrument of the Father's will. Though the act that *freed us* was in the past, his *lov[ing] us* continues into the present. The language of *sins* occurs only here and in 18:4–5. In Revelation, Jesus' death is portrayed more as example and victory than as ransom for forgiveness. The language of *kingdom* and *priests* comes from God's words to Moses on Sinai in Exodus 19:6; together with the language of freedom, these words introduce the exodus motif found throughout Revelation, but here combine it with the typically Pauline ascription of the *God and Father* of Jesus. To give Jesus *glory and praise* (AT) is to offer to him what rightly belongs only to God (4:11).

7. The style changes again, drawing on the apocalyptic texts in Daniel 7:13 and Zechariah 12:10. Most commentators think that *coming with the clouds* refers to expectation of Jesus' return; but everywhere else in the New Testament, Daniel 7:13 is used to describe Jesus' victorious ascent to the right hand of the Father. In Matthew 24:30–31, the same two verses are combined, and Jesus then declares solemnly, 'This generation will not pass away until all these things take place' (Matt. 24:34, AT). In Mark 14:62, Jesus quotes Daniel 7:13 to tell the high priest what he will witness. And Stephen's final vision, before his martyrdom, is a vision of the ascended Jesus, described using the 'Son of Man' terminology from Daniel 7:13 (Acts 7:55–56). Those who *pierced* Jesus have indeed mourned (Acts 2:37), and many have seen the truth about Jesus. John reconfigures the context of Zechariah 12 from being Jerusalem to the whole of the known world, where Jesus has been 'publicly attested as crucified' (Gal. 3:1, AT).[2]

---

2. For a fuller exploration of this meaning of 'coming with the clouds', see my article 'When Is God "Coming on the Clouds"?', *Psephizo* (blog),

Such a reading fits perfectly with the preceding verses: the acclamation here is of God and Jesus as the ones who are enthroned with power, setting the stage for the displacement of imperial authority as the one that rightly commands our allegiance. The Greek 'Yes' corresponds to the Hebrew affirmative *Amen*, emphasizing the mixed Jewish–Gentile nature of the recipients.

8. John returns to the prophetic tradition as he quotes the words of the Lord that have come to him. *I am* connects with Johannine tradition which makes use of the name of God from Exodus 3:14, which is repeated here. *The Alpha and the O* (AT; spelling out the letter omega did not occur until the sixth or seventh century) re-expresses God's eternity, past and future in terms borrowed from Greek and Roman magical cults, which would have been widely known among the Gentile Christians to whom John was writing.[3] The Greek transliteration of God's name Yahweh was written IAO. It is striking that the emphasis on God alone having power, *Almighty*, follows on immediately from the explicit trinitarian language, thus holding together the paradox of the three-in-one.

Theology
John continues to keep us on our toes as we are trying to work out what kind of book we are reading, with sudden shifts between the epistolary, doxological, apocalyptic and prophetic. The result is a kind of interpretative vertigo – if you are beginning to feel dizzy, don't panic! It is beginning to look as though Revelation will defy easy categorization, and it is no wonder that it has been described as the 'climax' of biblical prophecy.[4] If John is drawing together all the different strands of earlier biblical writings, then it is fitting that this book stands as the conclusion to the canon of the New Testament. Like the prologue of John's Gospel, this prologue continues to introduce both characters and ideas which will be significant in

---

(note 2 *cont.*) 5 October 2016, <https://www.psephizo.com/biblical-studies/when-is-god-coming-on-the-clouds/>.

3. For detailed exploration of this, see 'The Apocalypse of John and Graeco-Roman Magic', in Aune, *Apocalypticism*, pp. 347–367.

4. The title of the major work by Bauckham, *The Climax of Prophecy*.

the main body of the text. But, whereas in the Gospel the language is repeated and developed, in Revelation the development often happens using quite different vocabulary and imagery.

The elaborate expansion of the epistolary greetings follows Paul's example in Ephesians, where he too launches into an extended praise of God (Eph. 1:3–14) before returning to the letter form. In this regard, Revelation follows the style of lofty rhetorical speech which might well have been common to the culture of the area.[5] He does this primarily by drawing on the Scriptures (OT), which in fact saturate his writing in almost every verse. But he is also happy to adapt and revise these references in the light of his understanding of what God has done for us in Jesus – where the outpouring of God's grace breaks any ethnic and national boundaries and is offered not just to his covenant people who trace their origins to Abraham, but to all the sons and daughters of Adam. John therefore also draws on pagan symbols and imagery, in this instance from magical cults; the God and Father of our Lord Jesus is almighty over all principalities and powers, and all rulers must submit to him, regardless of their origin or sphere of influence.

---

5. Witherington III, *Letters to Philemon, the Colossians, and the Ephesians*, p. 2.

2. JESUS THE ANGELIC SON OF MAN SPEAKS TO THE ASSEMBLIES (1:9 – 3:22)

As happens frequently in Revelation, the next few verses do not mark the beginning of a new section so much as provide a bridge from one section to another. John resumes his epistolary style, which immediately moves into a recapitulation of his commission to write and then blends into an account of his vision of the exalted Jesus.

The vision itself draws heavily on imagery from Daniel's description of an angelic figure in Daniel 10, but incorporates aspects of Daniel's earlier vision of the Ancient of Days, so that John sees Jesus both as divine and as the messenger of the divine. Many aspects of this opening vision are revisited in the introduction to each of the royal pronouncement messages that Jesus speaks by the Spirit to John for him to pass on to all the assemblies in the region by means of this written record. The distribution of these titles among the seven messages is not straightforward, but they have some correspondence with the situation of each community to which John is writing. The visionary description of Jesus is not very obviously connected with later visionary language, particularly the depiction of Jesus as the lamb who appears to be slain from

Revelation 5 onwards; the connections are to be found at the level of theology rather than at the level of words and language.

It is not often noted that, although John's recorded experience is frequently described as a 'vision', most of what follows is in fact an 'audition' – something John hears rather than something he sees. This is true of large parts of the text, including the hymns of praise that punctuate the narrative at key moments, most of Revelation 17 – 18, and the beginning of 19 as well as Revelation 2 – 3. The interrelation between John's seeing and hearing does important work – for example, in our reading of the two halves of Revelation 7. The messages themselves include some clear connections with the specific situation of John's first audience, though these have sometimes been over-interpreted, and elements of the opening vision and their Old Testament antecedents remain important. The seven messages are often treated as quite detached from the main body of the book, but in fact the two parts need to be read in connection with each other. The real pressures and dilemmas faced by these early Christian communities, as John outlines them in these royal proclamations, are ultimately addressed by the imagery and narrative that follow from Revelation 4 onwards.

A. John's commission (1:9–11)

Context
Following the acclamations of praise, John returns to an epistolary style to address his recipients and locate himself in relation to them. But there is quickly another change of style – to vision report. In response to the command to 'write', he begins to recount his visionary experience.

Comment
9. Despite having apostolic status by virtue of being the bearer of a testimony from Jesus, *John* here emphasizes his similarity with his recipients. Echoing Jesus' language of disciples-as-family in Matthew 12:49, he is both *brother* and *companion* – one who is a partner, sharing in a common experience. This includes *suffering* or (in older translations) 'tribulation'; the word *thlipsis* is used frequently by Paul to describe the common lot of those seeking to be disciples

of Jesus in a hostile world (Acts 14:22; Rom. 5:3; 2 Cor. 4:17; 1 Thess. 1:6), and echoes the teaching of Jesus himself (Mark 4:17; John 16:33). But it also includes experience of the *kingdom* of God – God's just and holy reign which is ours in Jesus – a better alternative to the kingdom (or empire; the word is the same) of Caesar. But to live with the future hope of God's reign as well as the present reality of trouble, we need to develop *patient endurance*, another key term, coming seven times in Revelation and also in the teaching of Jesus (Luke 8:15; Rom. 5:3–5). All three of these – suffering, kingdom and endurance – are ours *in Jesus*.

John was on *Patmos*, a rocky island in the Aegean about 8 miles long and 5 miles wide (13 by 8 km), and about 40 miles (64 km) south-east of Ephesus. It is usually inferred from the comment that he was there *because of the word of God and the testimony of Jesus* that John had been exiled as punishment for his faith, but we have no conclusive evidence that Patmos was used as a penal colony or even that it was populated at this time.

10. This is the first of four times John mentions being *in the Spirit* (4:2; 17:3; 21:10), and is reminiscent of the role of the Spirit in Ezekiel's visions (Ezek. 2:2; 3:24; 11:24 and elsewhere). The *Lord's Day* does not use a possessive noun but an adjective derived from 'Lord' which came to be used to designate Sunday as the day of Christian worship, celebrating the resurrection, as distinct from the Jewish Sabbath. (It also designated Christian buildings, and gives us our words 'kirk' and 'church'.) In the Old Testament, the *trumpet* (a shofar, rather than the modern instrument) signalled a call to action, either to war or to worship. But on Sinai, it also describes the powerful voice of God as he reveals his commandments (Exod. 19:16, 19; 20:18). In John's unexpected grammar, he describes the *great voice* as sounding like a *trumpet speaking* (AT).

11. John will not only *see* but also hear things, and will *write* (the first of twelve such commands) both on a *scroll* – the proper meaning of *biblos* in this context, before the widespread use of the 'codex' form with which we are familiar. The *seven churches*, already mentioned in 1:4, are now listed. 'Church' is not the best translation of the word *ekklēsia*, since it has institutional and organizational overtones that are not present for John and his readers. The term is used in the Greek Old Testament (the Septuagint) for the 'congregation of

Israel', meaning God's people gathered, as well as referring to the gathering of the citizens in Greek culture in order to make decisions about the running of the city – so 'assembly' is perhaps a better term. The seven cities listed were not the only ones in the province of Asia, nor the seven most important; but these cities were linked by road and, in this order, sit in a semicircular arc, moving north from *Ephesus* to *Smyrna* and *Pergamum*, then east to *Thyatira*, south-east to *Sardis* and *Philadelphia*, and ending in *Laodicea*, the most easterly. For detailed comments on these cities see Revelation 2 – 3.

Theology

In these verses, John repeatedly uses 'in' to locate himself in three important ways, all of which we need to consider in reading what follows.

First, he locates himself theologically and eschatologically. He is in the overlap of the ages ('suffering and kingdom', 1:9), between this age (which will pass away) and the age to come of the kingdom of God, which has broken into this world through Jesus' ministry, his death, resurrection and ascension, and the gift of the Spirit at Pentecost. This sense of overlap, and the competing claims on the loyalty of John's audience, forms the context for John's challenge to keep faith in Jesus after the example of Jesus. If this age, along with its rulers, is passing away, why remain loyal to it, rather than to the one who will reign for ever in the age to come? This decision to be faithful to Jesus will result in difficult times ahead, 'tribulation', but it is lived out in the light of a sure and certain hope of what is to come.

Second, John locates himself in a particular time and place ('on the island of Patmos', 1:9). Whatever the implications for us (as those still living in the same theological time as John, between the ages), his message is first of all for the followers of Jesus living on the mainland that, on a fine day, he can see from his island home. Whether he is there because of God's direction or as a result of persecution, he remains connected to his audience by close bonds of fellowship and mutual understanding. If we are to hear what he is saying to us through this text, we must first attend to what John believed God was saying to his first audience.

Third, John locates himself personally and spiritually. The revelation he has been given has been received 'in the Spirit' and in the context of worship 'on the Lord's Day' (1:10), so perhaps we should not be surprised that the text is peppered with phrases of praise and worship all the way through. What John passes on is intended to evoke in us a response of worship – not just in acts of praise, but in lives lived in the faith of Jesus in our own particular contexts.

B. The vision of Jesus (1:12–20)

Context
We encounter here the first 'other-worldly' vision of the apocalypse, with the dense, rich and multilayered symbolism that characterizes the visions of the body of the book.

At first reading (or hearing), this is a breathless account in which the images tumble out on top of one another in a kaleidoscope of colour and sensation which threaten to overwhelm us just as they overwhelmed John ('I fell . . . as though dead', 1:17). The introduction to the vision in verses 12 and 13 is a single sentence, as is the central description in verses 14–16 – the characteristics are piled up one on top of another with hardly a pause. But like John, we should not be afraid as we approach this text. On second reading, we can see that it is very carefully built together, drawing on imagery from the Old Testament, particularly from Exodus and the visions of Daniel 7 and 10, as well as incorporating elements from pagan deities.

In one sense, John is describing a vision of that which cannot be seen; it is not possible to look on the 'sun shining in full strength' (AT), as it is more than human sight can bear. But he does share a vision which is refracted through the lens of Old Testament theology, particularly the uniqueness of the God of Israel which Jesus now shares, and pagan worship which should now be directed to Jesus alone.

Comment
12. John turns to *see the voice*, which is literally impossible; the phrase continues John's interplay between the senses, and introduces a dynamic he returns to at key moments – the relationship between what he sees and what he hears. The *seven golden lampstands* are often depicted in art as separate from one another (probably to enable the figure of Christ to be in their *midst* [AT]), but, in the light of the

language about the 'seven spirits/sevenfold Spirit' and the importance of Zechariah 4:2, it is possible that he is referring to a seven-branched menorah similar to the one in front of the tabernacle and temple (Exod. 25:31–40). This would connect John's understanding with Pauline language of the Christian community as God's temple (1 Cor. 3:16), explain further why John is writing to only seven congregations and suggest an essential interdependence between them. The symmetry of the menorah would both correspond to the literary symmetry of the messages to the seven congregations and connect with the seven lamps (spirits) before the throne (Rev. 4:5); the word 'lampstand' (*lychnia*) occurs seven times in the text. *Gold* is consistently the colour and material of spiritual power and majesty, and in particular the heavenly realms. But Revelation's distinction between the heavenly and the earthly is less about different places, and more about different aspects of reality, allegiance and ways of living.

13. John's description of the risen Jesus combines elements from the Old Testament depictions of Israel, God, angels and the high priest with imagery from pagan cults. John uses the term *someone/something like* twenty-one times in total, emphasizing the symbolic significance of his descriptions. Here and in 14:14, the one *like a son of man* draws on the imagery of Daniel 7:13. The term is originally an idiom for 'human', possibly emphasizing human fragility (as in Ezek. 2:1 and throughout the book), but in Daniel it comes to symbolize the nation of Israel personified, oppressed by the powers, awaiting God's deliverance and vindication, and exalted to the presence of God himself. It is Jesus' favourite term of self-designation in the Gospels, and the language of 'the coming of the Son of Man' depends on Daniel 7 and refers to Jesus' exaltation to the right hand of God (see on v. 7 above).

The *robe reaching down to his feet* recalls the attire of Aaron and the other priests (the word is the one used in the Greek OT of Exod. 28:4 and Zech. 3:4) and in art is assumed to be of white linen like that of the high priest (Lev. 16:4) which is also worn by angelic figures. He has a *belt of gold* (AT) not round his waist (like the angel in Dan. 10:5) nor round his *chest* (like the angels in Rev. 15:6), but round his *mastoi*, translated 'breasts' in Luke 11:27 and 23:29 and rendered as 'paps' in the KJV. We find similar imagery (which seems equally odd to modern ears) in Isaiah 60:16: 'You will suck the milk of nations and suck the breasts of kings' (AT), and 1 Peter 2:2 talks of the 'spiritual milk' we find in Jesus. Goddesses in the ancient world were often depicted as having a belt around their breasts; throughout Revelation Jesus is consistently depicted as taking the place of other spiritual powers and being the true source of the benefits they claim to offer.

14–15. The next three verses form one sentence describing seven aspects of this figure (head/hair, eyes, feet, voice, right hand, mouth and face) each connected with 'and'. The description of his *head and hair* as *white as snow and wool* (AT) echoes the description of the Ancient of Days in Daniel 7:9; in a culture which valued the wisdom of old age (see Prov. 16:31 and 20:29) and the enduring power of ancient beliefs, this evokes veneration and respect. The appearance of his *eyes*, feet, voice and face echo parts of the description of the angel in Daniel 10:5–6. His eyes being of *flames of fire* (AT) suggests divine power of vision and understanding, a common motif in pagan depictions of deities. The word *chalkolibanon* is otherwise completely unknown, but related to the term *chalkos*, meaning *bronze*, and so usually translated by the same term; it parallels the 'arms and legs' of the angel in Daniel 10:6, and so suggests a contrast with the vulnerable 'feet of iron and clay' of the statue seen earlier in Daniel 2:33. The *voice* that was like a trumpet is now described as *like the sound of rushing waters*, using the language of Ezekiel 1:24 for the voice of God.

16. The idea of holding the *seven stars* has no Old Testament precedent, but borrows imagery from pagan astrology where the stars and the planets ('wandering stars') determined the fortunes of humanity. The *two-edged sword* (AT) that comes from his mouth is an image of the words that he speaks, borrowing from Isaiah 49:2, and with a parallel in Hebrews 4:12. Such a sword can (we might say) cut both ways; as we will see in the messages that follow, Christ's words bring comfort and salvation as well as warning and judgment. That his face *was shining like the sun* (AT) looks back to Moses on Sinai, where his face shone from being in the presence of God, and forwards to the New Jerusalem, which does not need the sun because 'the glory of God . . . and the Lamb' provide its light (Rev. 21:23).

17–18. John's reaction and Christ's response remind us of similar reactions of Isaiah (Isa. 6:5), Ezekiel (Ezek. 1:28) and particularly

Daniel (Dan. 10:7–10) to their encounters with God. It is Christ's *right hand*, which holds the stars, that reaches out to John and assures him in terms that identify Jesus with God. The *First and the Last* comes from Isaiah 44:6 where it denotes the uniqueness of God; it parallels the earlier 'Alpha and Omega', and the two phrases converge in 21:6 and 22:13 as a description of God and Jesus. The language of *living . . . for ever* and the contrast with death also borrows Old Testament terms describing God's uniqueness, here from Deuteronomy 32:39–40, expressed with reference to Jesus' death and resurrection. 'Christ once raised from the dead dies no more; death has no more dominion over him' (Rom. 6:9, AT). This is re-expressed as Jesus having the *keys to death and Hades* (AT), language stolen from the magical cult of Hekate, the goddess of death and the underworld.

19–20. The reiteration of the command to *write* (which first caught John's attention in v. 11) has sometimes been taken as an interpretative key to the book, referring to past, present and future. But it is more convincing to understand the second and third as explanatory of what John sees – both how things are now and how they will be in the future of God's kingdom come to earth. The *mystery* is perhaps better translated as 'secret', since it is now disclosed and passed on. The *angels* of the churches are unlikely to be human messengers, despite their role in receiving the messages that follow, since angels are so prominent in Revelation and are consistently heavenly. Neither should they be taken as standing for the 'spirit' of the churches in terms of their character. The most likely background is that of Daniel, where angels represent the earthly reality of nations and peoples in the heavenly realms (Dan. 10:12; 12:1), so Jesus holding the stars/angels signifies his hold on the church communities themselves.

Theology
As we read through Revelation, we will find there are features of the text which could not be evident from a cursory reading or hearing, but become evident only with careful study. This includes the way that John draws on a wide range of ideas from the Old Testament and from the surrounding culture (as well as his careful structuring of what he writes) and integrates the different elements together.

In much Christian art drawing on this opening chapter, the figure of Christ is depicted as a more or less human being with some minor modifications, typically the sword coming from his mouth and stars held in his right hand. But despite being of 'someone like a son of man', what we have here is not a literal description of a vision of a human person, but a composite symbolic picture, telling us key theological truths about the person of Jesus.

Part of this picture is of Jesus as High Priest, the one who mediates for us before God (cf. Heb. 4:14), and this idea is reinforced by the absence of anyone resembling a priest in the visions of worship in Revelation 4 – 5. Second, much of his appearance makes him resemble the Ancient of Days, God himself on his throne; he is the 'image of the invisible God' (Col. 1:15) and the 'exact representation of his being' (Heb. 1:3). Third, he resembles an angel, a messenger from God, the one who communicates to us through his life, words and actions the revelation of God that we need to hear. Fourth, he displaces all counterfeits that we might find in other religions; it is he, and no other, who nourishes us and holds the keys to the most vital questions of life and death. While human empires rise and fall, his kingdom is everlasting for he is trustworthy and true. It is his words which cut through to the truth, confirming what is right and refuting what is false. The light of his countenance offers us the light of life.

This multisensory and overwhelming picture is at one level incomprehensible, but is given to communicate the reality of Jesus. At the same time as being unapproachable – how can we look on the sun or come close to bronze as it glows in the furnace, without being consumed ourselves? – he yet comes close to John to reassure him and is present among his people as he walks in the midst of the lampstands.

There is surely nowhere else in the New Testament such a comprehensive and exalted depiction of Jesus as one with the Father.

C. The messages to the seven assemblies (2:1 – 3:22)

What follows in Revelation 2 – 3 are frequently called 'letters to the seven churches' but, in terms of form, they look more like royal pronouncements than letters,[1] since they have no formal epistolary features, and the whole of Revelation is a letter (see on 1:4). They appear to be the least 'apocalyptic' section of Revelation, since they are not expressed as a vision report but have much in common with prophetic utterances from the Old Testament, not only in the form of introduction ('thus says the Lord') and the description of divine knowledge, but also in the call to repent and change to avert the possibility of coming judgment.

The seven messages are striking in their consistent structure of seven main elements, including opening and closing phrases which are repeated word for word:

1. To the angel of the church in (place name) write:
2. Thus says he who (appellation drawn from the vision of Rev. 1)
3. I know your (attributes and actions, varying considerably from one message to another) . . .
4. But this I have against you . . .
5. (Command to respond, including the requirement to repent)
6. Whoever has ears, let them hear what the Spirit says to the churches
7. To those who are conquering (promise drawn from the vision of the New Jerusalem)

The messages vary considerably from one to another, the longest being to the assembly at Thyatira (222 words in Greek) and the shortest to the assembly at Smyrna (90 words). The variation in length arises from the differences in the content of elements 3 and 4, the affirmations and rebukes. The final message, to Laodicea, includes no affirmation, and both the second and second last, to Smyrna and Philadelphia respectively, include no rebuke, which lends the seven a degree of symmetry. The final two elements of the

---

1. See similar royal pronouncements by King Solomon of Israel (1 Kgs 2:30), King Cyrus of Persia (2 Chr. 36:23; both of these use the same formula *tade legei*) and the Emperor Tiberius (Josephus, *Antiquities of the Jews* 19.280).

messages, 'whoever has ears' and 'to those conquering', switch their order from the fourth message to Thyatira onwards, and this gives the seven a structure of 3 + 4 – though it is not very clear what the significance of this change is.

My comments on the shared features of the messages are included in the discussion of the first message to Ephesus, and will need to be referred to when studying the other six messages.

i. Message to the assembly in Ephesus (2:1–7)
Context

At the end of the first century, Ephesus (whose ruins are near modern Selçuk in Turkey) was the largest city in the region and one of the five largest in the empire. Although there was an earlier settlement in the area, it moved to its first-century site three hundred years previously when it was fortified. Its importance was due to its situation on the coast with a large harbour, and its later decline was hastened by the silting up of the harbour, which has meant that the current ruins are some way from the modern coast. It was also helped by having good inland communications to the important centres of population further north and inland, and its population was ethnically very mixed, including Greeks, Romans and Jews, and people from both around Anatolia as well as further afield – the Greek islands and northern Africa. It grew to be larger than its ancient rivals, Smyrna and Pergamum, and Rome moved its centre of administration for the province from Pergamum to Ephesus.

Under imperial administration the city flourished and developed. There was considerable building work, including two new aqueducts to the city built under Augustus. The imperial cult also flourished; a temple to Nero was planned but never built, but one of the most prominent buildings, at the head of the main street, was the Temple of the Sebastoi dedicated to the Flavian dynasty of Vespasian and his two sons Titus and Domitian. This included a colossal statue of Titus, erected by his younger brother Domitian, in a military pose (see comment in 'The social and historical context' in the Introduction); it was Titus who succeeded his father as commander in Judea during the Jewish War of AD 66–70, and the one who besieged and demolished Jerusalem and its temple in AD 70. Ephesus was the only city amongst the thirty-seven (most of them in Asia) that were awarded the honour of 'Imperial Temple Warden' to receive the honour twice, once in the 80s and again in the 130s. Local religions flourished as well, and worship of the emperor (called 'god' and 'son of god' from the time of Augustus) was seen to sit comfortably with traditional religions. The most notable among them was the cult of Artemis, sister of Apollo, and the Artemis temple was one of the seven wonders of the ancient world. The men and women who served in the priesthood of Artemis (and the other deities) were typically leading citizens who paid the costs of the regular festivals.

A Christian community was established in Ephesus in the 50s by Priscilla and Aquila, who had been left there by Paul on their journey from Corinth where they had met and ministered together (Acts 18:19). Paul then returned and spent two years there, enjoying a spectacular and fruitful ministry which saw the community grow but also provoked serious opposition. This resulted in a major protest, with two of Paul's companions enduring a terrifying ordeal as they were paraded in front of an enormous crowd in the city's theatre. This new religion of Jesus ('The Way') not only threatened the traditional religion of Artemis from which the city derived its reputation and splendour; it also challenged its economic status as a manufacturer of shrines and statues along with the associated trades. Christians in Ephesus knew the cost of following Jesus and the opposition it could provoke.

Comment

1. The first message begins with the formula that all other messages follow: the command to write to the *angel* of the *assembly* (AT) from the risen Christ, identifying him by characteristics drawn from the vision in Revelation 1. On the role of the angel, see the comment on 1:19; on the translation of *ekklēsia* as 'assembly', see the comment on 1:11.

The introduction formula *Thus says* (AT; *tade legei*) uses language frequently found in the Greek Old Testament on the lips of the prophets but which had fallen out of use by this time – so it would have had an 'antique ring' to it, as when someone today quotes the Authorized (King James) Version. (Compare the only other occurrence of the phrase in the NT beyond the seven here, in Acts 21:11.)

These are the words of Jesus, but a similar phrase has already been used by God (1:8), and these words will be claimed as the words of the Spirit (2:7) – part of John's effortless depiction of the persons of the Trinity. His *hold[ing]* the seven stars has changed from 'having' in 1:16 (AT) to 'grasping powerfully' in a word (*kraton*) which echoes God's self-description as 'Almighty' (*pantokratōr*) and sets the context for the challenge of 2:5.

2–3. That the risen Christ is able to see and *know* the situation of the assemblies accords with his having 'eyes . . . like blazing fire' in 1:14. In two of the messages he knows their situation (Smyrna) and location (Pergamum), but here and in the other four he knows *your works* (AT); as elsewhere in the New Testament, faith is not an interior state so much as something that shapes life and shows itself in action (Jas 2:17–18). The pronouns are singular throughout, since strictly speaking the messages are to the 'angels' of the assemblies, supporting the idea that they are in some sense representative.

The impressive list of seven virtues of the Ephesian Christians is identified in groups of two, two and three respectively in a single sentence running through the two verses. In other messages the 'works' or 'deeds' can be positive or negative, so here the two terms that follow should be taken as explanatory, making clear what the works are. The *hard labour* (AT; *kopos*) is frequently used elsewhere in the New Testament to refer to the work of discipleship and sharing the gospel (1 Cor. 3:8; 1 Thess. 3:5), and the related verb is used by Paul of those who shared his gospel ministry with him (Rom. 16:6, 12). In showing *patient endurance* (AT), they are exhibiting with John himself that quality needed to bridge the joy of the king-dom and the suffering of the present age as they look for the return of the Lord (see 1:9); these two qualities are also paired by Paul in 1 Thessalonians 1:3.

It is not clear whether *evil* (AT) has a general reference or refers to evil *people*, but the Ephesians' unwillingness to tolerate it is expressed in the strongest terms. The idea of *test[ing]* is often negative elsewhere in the New Testament, but here has the positive sense of discerning true from false (present both in Paul, 1 Cor. 12:10, and in the Johannine tradition, 1 John 4:1, though in both cases using different terminology). The *apostles* should sometimes be understood as the twelve appointed by Jesus (who are clearly in view in Rev. 21:14), but sometimes the term appears to have a wider meaning of those leaders who have a pioneering ministry in taking the proclamation of Jesus to new places (Rom. 16:7; 1 Cor. 12:28; Eph. 4:11). The concern with apostleship is whether their teaching is part of the shared tradition about Jesus passed on from eye-witnesses to his life, death and resurrection (1 Cor. 15:1–7). The final three virtues include a repetition of the *patient endurance* (AT); they have stayed with the cause of Jesus and reflected the character of Jesus (*because of my name*, AT) without growing *weary*.

4. All these impressive qualities make the sudden contrast of the rebuke that follows all the more startling. All the work in the world, it appears, is worth nothing without *love* at its heart. A Christian community was established there in the early 50s (Acts 18:19; 19:1–20), and if John is writing in the mid-90s (see Introduction), then the community will have been in existence for forty years, so it is quite possible that it has lost its *first* excitement and commitment (the sense is temporal). The *love* could be a sense of God's love for them (cf. Rom. 5:5), though this is unlikely because it is 'your love'. It could then either be their love for God, or their love for one another. Appeal to the text of Ephesians cannot decide this, not least because it is so much earlier, and the text here gives us no further clue one way or another. In any case, in the Johannine corpus the two are inseparable, since we cannot claim to love God without showing love to our brothers and sisters in Christ (1 John 4:20).

5. Although the command to *remember* (AT) is a present imperative in Greek, this is a simple instruction to bring the past to mind – not as nostalgia, but for reform and renewal. It is clear that there is no separation to be understood between love and *works* (AT); recapturing their first love will show itself in their doing their first works. The mention of *repent[ance]* not once but twice, and at the end of the sentence in the Greek, makes it emphatic. Though the etymology of the term suggests 'thinking again', this idea had fallen out of use by the first century, and in the New Testament it corresponds to the Hebrew *šûb* in the Old Testament, meaning 'turn from your sins'. The *com[ing]* of Jesus here is in the present, not in the distant future, and in judgment rather than deliverance. The seriousness of the situation is highlighted by the possibility of their *lampstand* being removed. To modern ears this might sound like a 'punishment' out of proportion to the 'crime', but it shows that the heart of Christian faith is not in the first instance ethical or institutional but relational – in relationship with Jesus and with one another as the body of Christ. Organization and action must flow from this, not take its place. And this threat must be read in the context of Christ grasping the stars firmly in his right hand; his first word here is assurance, and his last word is hope.

6. Only in this message of the seven do we find the adversive 'but' ('yet') in verse 4 followed by another adversive here – a reversal of the reversal. We might wonder whether this unique second affirmation reflects John's traditional association with Ephesus and his affection for the Christians there. Despite speculation from the second century onwards, we actually know nothing of the group John calls *the Nicolaitans* – or even whether there was such a group, rather than John coining the term as a rhetorical device (note that Balaam in 2:14 and Jezebel in 2:20 are not the actual names of the people referred to either). The collective term appears to derive from the name Nicolas (Greek *Nicolaus*), which occurs only in Acts 6:5 (though any link with this person is purely speculative), but is more often an honorific title meaning 'Conqueror of the People'. Given the importance of the term *nikaō* 'to conquer' in Revelation generally and in the messages in particular, it makes more sense to take this as a reference to some otherwise unknown group seeking to captivate the followers of Jesus and thwart their faithfulness to his call. The Ephesians' 'hatred' is not for the people, but for their actions; our battle is not with flesh and blood, but with principalities and powers (Eph. 6:12).

7. The first of two concluding phrases is repeated without variation at the end of each message, and echoes Jesus' use of a similar stock phrase in his parabolic teaching (Matt. 11:15; 13:9; Mark 4:9, 13; Luke 8:8; 14:35). Although the imperative *hear* is often translated as an invitation – 'Let them hear . . .' – the sense is of a strong command: 'Listen!' It is notable that the hearers are enjoined to listen to what the Spirit is saying to all the *churches* and not just to their own; even though the affirmations and rebukes are particular to each context, all the Christian communities must listen to and learn from what is said to all the others.

The final phrase is also repeated at the end of each message. The present tense of those *conquering* (AT) suggests a continued commitment to faithfulness reflected in the quality of patient endurance. Just as the opening appellation of Jesus draws from some aspect of the vision in Revelation 1, so these final promises anticipate some aspect of the vision of the New Jerusalem in Revelation 21 – 22, positioning these messages as suspended between 'what is' and 'what is to come'. The *tree of life* is an image that Revelation 22:2 draws from Genesis 2:9 and suggests a tree whose fruit gives life when eaten. The term *paradise* originates from the Persian idea of a walled garden in the king's palace, but 'paradise of God' is consistently used in the Greek Old Testament to refer to 'the garden of God' in Genesis 2, reinforcing the link between the New Jerusalem and the Garden of Eden. One of the things achieved by the victory of Jesus, in which his followers are to participate, is the restoration of the good creation of God before the entrance of disobedience into the world.[2]

Theology

The words of the risen Jesus to the assembly in Ephesus offer both reassurance and affirmation. He holds the stars tight in his right hand, and is present among his people. The affirmations for the qualities of the Christians in this city are extravagant and emphatic, and concern non-trivial attributes. They are exhibiting the patient endurance which John himself says is a necessary quality for living in both the world and the kingdom (Rev. 1:9), and are exercising the discernment required to differentiate between true and false teaching and claims to apostolicity. These are qualities that many of our churches could do with!

And yet the risen Jesus also offers words of stern rebuke. The Ephesians might be tough-minded, but it appears they have also become hard-hearted. Protecting themselves and others from error and exhaustion is only of value if they are protecting their relationship of love with their Lord and with one another. The consequences of

---

2. One of the themes often passed over in Revelation is the importance of creation. See comments below on 4:3, 6b; and 11:18.

judgment are serious ('I will remove your lampstand') but never without hope; it is reading too much into this phrase to interpret it as a loss of salvation for individuals. The presence of Jesus among his people is to offer once more the invitation to 'repent and believe' (Mark 1:15) – to turn again to their Lord in their midst, and trust afresh in him as he offers them a new vision of hope for the future. The purpose of the threat of judgment, in the context of Jesus' faithfulness, is once more to bring his people to newness of life.

ii. Message to the assembly in Smyrna (2:8–11)

Context

Smyrna lay about 50 miles (80 km) north of Ephesus and, being at the head of a deep gulf, also had an excellent harbour, but (in contrast to Ephesus) one which continues in use today as part of modern Izmir. The most important commodity traded was myrrh (Greek *smyrna*), from which Smyrna probably took its name. The ancient city was destroyed by the Lydians in around 600 BC, and it was refounded by the successors of Alexander the Great in 290 BC. As one of the principal cities of the Roman province of Asia, it vied with Ephesus and Pergamum for the title of 'First City', and because of its beauty called itself 'the crown of Asia' and included crowns on its coinage. It was famously loyal to Rome, even before becoming part of the empire, and was granted the title of 'Temple Guardian' when an imperial temple was built in AD 26.

Smyrna was the home of Polycarp, who became bishop there in the second century, and to whom Ignatius wrote a letter from Troas around AD 100. Polycarp was probably martyred in around 156, and the account of his death includes his comment that he has served Christ for eighty-six years. That would make him a young man in his twenties at the time of the writing of Revelation.

This message is the shortest of the seven, less than half the length of the longest (to Thyatira), and along with the message to Philadelphia it includes no rebuke from the risen Christ. It most clearly fits a context of pressure or persecution, the situation that most people associate with Revelation, but it is striking that this is not the case for many of the other messages, which focus more on offering a challenge to Christians who have compromised with their surrounding culture. It offers quite a stark message, rather than the kind of encouragement we might expect, setting out the serious challenges that those loyal to Jesus can expect to face.

Comment

8. Jesus' self-designation as *the First and the Last* is taken from the opening vision of Jesus and his words to John in 1:17. It parallels the epistolary title of God in 1:8, and both derive from the claim of God in Isaiah 44:6 to be not only the one God whom Israel worships, but the one to whom there is simply no equal – offering a sharp challenge to the city's devotion to the emperor and the empire. Jesus *died and came to life*, a reworking of the next words to John in 1:18, emphasizes the events of his death and resurrection (the verb 'came to life' is a past rather than present tense). This would have particular resonance with people living in a city which had itself 'died' in its destruction and 'come to life' in its refounding, but also with those (like the young Polycarp) who would one day face martyrdom because of their loyalty to the One who has conquered death.

9. With divine insight, Jesus *know[s]* the three challenges (rather than their 'works') facing the Christians in Smyrna – but he also knows their true status. First, in suffering *afflictions* or 'tribulation' (*thlipsis*), they are experiencing what John describes as part of our lot in this world as followers of Jesus (1:9; see also 7:14) which was the experience of the disciples at the time of Stephen's martyrdom (Acts 11:19). Smyrna was generous in granting citizenship to its inhabitants, so there is a good chance that some of the Christians would have been citizens, alongside those who were slaves, tenant farmers or labourers living at subsistence levels. Yet this new faith had particular appeal to those who, second, knew *poverty*, following a messiah who, as a 'Son of Man', had 'nowhere to lay his head' (Matt. 8:20) and who describes his followers as 'my brother[s] and sister[s]' who are often 'hungry', 'thirsty', 'naked', 'strangers', 'ill' and 'in prison' (Matt. 12:50; 25:36–40). Despite their outward appearance, they are in fact *rich* in faith (cf. Jas 2:5; Luke 6:20) because they have the treasure of the kingdom which is theirs in Jesus, in line with the inversion of human values in God's economy (1 Cor. 1:27) and in contrast to their wealthier fellow city dwellers (Rev. 3:17).

The third challenge is the *slander* or 'blasphemy' they are experiencing from the *Jews*. Revelation follows Paul's experience (Acts 9:4) and his theology (1 Cor. 12:27) in closely identifying God with God's people, so that an attack on the latter is an attack on the former. There seems to have been a significant Jewish community in Smyrna; some appear to have supported the martyrdom of Polycarp and also denounced Christians during the later persecution under Diocletian. At the date of Revelation, the two communities are still closely related; John is a Jew, as are many of his readers, and so tensions are less between two religious groups as between two related branches of the same group. To claim that the accusers *are not* true Jews is not about displacing them, but about following the tradition of the Old Testament and of Paul (Rom. 2:28–29; Gal. 6:16) that being part of the people of God is at heart about faith and obedience, not simply about ethnicity. To accuse the people of God as they faithfully follow Jesus is to take the side of the great Accuser (the root meaning of *Satan*) who has been defeated by the death and resurrection of Jesus (Rev. 12:10).

10–11. In the face of these challenges, Jesus offers the same encouragement that he gave John: *Do not be afraid!* The form here is either more emphatic or more specific: do not be afraid of these things you are *about to suffer*. If the accusations of others lead to them being *put . . . in prison* by the Roman authorities, then this too is the work of *the devil*. As we shall see from Revelation 13 onwards, this primeval opponent of God and his people does have real power, but 'his time is short' (Rev. 12:12) and his power strictly limited, which is the probable meaning of the *ten days* of their tribulation. The call to be *faithful, even to the point of death* is both a battle cry of a spiritual army, about which we will hear more in Revelation 7, and the imitation of the pattern of Jesus' own faithfulness (Phil. 2:8; cf. Rev. 12:11). This is a call to universal faithfulness, but not to universal martyrdom, since only *some* will suffer this.

The challenges facing the Smyrnans elicit a double promise from Jesus, both parts of which are related to his opening self-designation. The *crown* designates a wreath rather than a diadem, and although it has some military associations, its primary meaning is as the trophy given to the victor in the games. Those who stay faithful even in the face of threats from 'those who [can] kill the body' (Matt. 10:28) are crowned with the gift of *life*, won by Jesus' own resurrection and signified in the New Jerusalem by the tree on either side of the river in the midst of the city (Rev. 22:1–2). The second promise parallels this with a kind of double negative: those who *conquer* (AT), that is, who share in the victory of Jesus and who have already begun to walk in newness of resurrection life, will *not be harmed by the second death* (AT; Rev. 20:14; 21:8), that separation from God the source of life which follows physical death. The tense of the verb here (aorist rather than future) emphasizes the certainty of the promise.

Theology
The message to those in Smyrna is positive, in the sense that there is no rebuke as there is in all the other messages. But it is also somewhat austere, in that it does not promise the Smyrnan Christians any respite from the pressures that they will be experiencing in the near future. There is no sense here of 'Jesus has a wonderful plan for your life.'

The assurance is given to them that Jesus knows and understands their situation, not least because he has walked the same path that they now walk – the path of accusation, opposition and faithfulness to the point of death. They are not forgotten and they are not alone. The double hope that they are to hold to is set out in the (unique among the messages) correspondence between the characteristic of Jesus which opens the message and the future promise which closes it, both of which centre on the questions of life and death.

Their hope looks back to Jesus himself, whom death could not hold and whose resurrection signalled the final defeat of death itself, so the ending of the power of those who threaten and accuse. And their hope looks forward to the fruits of that victory being revealed – the ultimate gift of life, the only prize really worth winning, in the New Jerusalem in the presence of the King himself. Their hope is not in vain, since it is not a hope 'only for this life' (1 Cor. 15:19) but is focused on the promise of life to come. It is a promise that has sustained generations of Christians who have faced the same challenge to pay the ultimate price for their faith.

iii. Message to the assembly in Pergamum (2:12–17)
Context
Pergamum (in Greek 'Pergamos', often written 'Pergamon') was further north again from Smyrna, but about 15 miles (24 km) inland

from the Aegean. It was the third of these three cities vying for supremacy in the province of Asia, and unlike Smyrna and Ephesus was situated on an impressive rocky outcrop that dominates the adjacent plain; pictures are often taken overlooking the steep seating of the theatre (the steepest in the Roman world) and offering a panorama over the modern city of Bergama below.

Pergamum had been a significant city in the region for at least four centuries by the time of John's writing. It was the seat of the Attalid dynasty, the descendants of Alexander's general Lysimachus, who were key players in the region during the Greek and Roman eras, and who pledged early allegiance to Rome as the empire started to grow. It contained temples to the early Attalid kings (the *hērōon*), a massive altar to Zeus which is now housed in the Pergamon Museum in Berlin, and the later Temple of Trajan which has been partially reconstructed. Below the acropolis was the Asclepieion, the healing centre and temple dedicated to Asclepius, the god of healing; this sanctuary was second in importance only to the Asclepius temple in Corinth. The famous physician Galen was born in Pergamum in the early second century. Pergamum flourished under Roman rule, growing to around 200,000 in population – a similar size to Ephesus and probably the fifth-largest city in the empire. It was capital of the province of Asia for a short time before this was transferred to Ephesus, and had an extensive library with a collection second only to Alexandria.

The message to the assembly in Pergamum contains both reassurances and challenges, though (like the message to Smyrna) it starts with Jesus' knowledge not of their deeds but of their situation – in this case their physical situation, which suggests something of the pressures they faced. It also includes a number of details whose meaning is largely lost to us, and commentary on these features is often highly speculative.

Comment

12. On the form of the introduction to the message, see the comment on 1:11 and 2:1 The definite article introducing the *sharp, double-edged sword* points us back to its description at 1:16. Its mention seems to be particularly important, since uniquely among the seven messages it occurs at both the beginning and the end, in the description of Jesus and the warning of judgment in verse 16. In a context where emperor worship was such a dominant feature of local life, it serves as a counterpoint to the authority of the emperor, expressed in the *ius gladii*, the 'right of the sword', the exercise of the highest power over life and death. Jesus' power is depicted both as higher than it and as a contrast to it. His authority over spiritual life and death comes not through inflicting violence but through sacrifice – a metaphorical rather than a literal sword.

13. This is one of the most convoluted verses in the whole of Revelation, framed at the beginning and end by a reference to *Satan*, which most translations break into two or three sentences. In five of the messages, Jesus *know[s]* the recipients' works or deeds, but here (as in Smyrna), he knows their situation, in this case expressed as living *where Satan's throne is* (AT). Commentators are divided about what this refers to, suggesting the altar of Zeus (which is claimed unconvincingly to look like a giant throne), the general occurrence of pagan worship, the Asclepieion, or, more generally, Pergamum's importance as a centre of the imperial cult. But the parallel with *where Satan lives* at the end of the sentence suggests that the throne is a metonym for Satan's exercise of authority: 'where Satan is enthroned and holds court',[3] suggesting a combination of these factors.

Following his knowledge of their situation, Jesus also affirms two further virtues of the Christians in Pergamum. The first is that they *hold fast* (AT) to Jesus' name – the mirror of Jesus' holding fast to them as one of the stars (2:1) – which could mean that they continue both to trust in and reflect his character, but also that they have not been afraid to be known as 'Christians', as Jesus' followers have been known since the establishment of the church in Antioch (Acts 11:26; cf. 1 Pet. 4:16). The second virtue is that they *have not denied my faith* (AT), which could also be understood in either an objective or a subjective way – either the faith they have in Jesus, or their confidence in his faithfulness, despite what has happened. *Antipas* is a real (though not common) name, so likely refers to a real character rather than being symbolic as the other names in these chapters are;

---

3. Smalley, p. 68.

he is one of the earliest named martyrs, along with Stephen (Acts 7) and James (Acts 12:2), but the first for whom the word for 'witness' (*martys*) is associated with death. In being called *faithful witness* he is closely identified with Jesus himself (1:5; 3:14). Satan exercises power here, not least in the accusations against Jesus' followers (*śāṭān* means in Hebrew 'accuser'), but his power has been defeated (12:10; cf. Rom. 8:1) and the faith of Christians testifies to that.

14. Despite these virtues, Jesus still has a *few things* against them. The story of *Balaam* is mostly found in Numbers 22 to 24, where he is depicted positively as refusing to curse God's people against Balak's request, and utters a series of oracles blessing Israel. But he gets a brief, negative mention in Numbers 31:16 as having misled God's people, and is portrayed in first-century Jewish literature as a dangerous magician. The use here appears to be part of this later, negative view; the eating of *food offered to idols* (AT) was clearly a practical dilemma for Christians (see Paul's long discussion in 1 Cor. 8 – 10), but here appears to signify compromise with pagan culture. It is not clear whether the accusation of *sexual immorality* should be taken literally, since Revelation draws on the Old Testament tradition of using this as a metaphor for idolatry as a form of unfaithfulness to God, and the two issues are paired both here and in 2:20.

15. We know nothing of the *Nicolaitans* (see comment on 2:6), but the opening 'thus' of the verse, omitted in most translations and replaced by *likewise* from the end of the verse, suggests a close relationship between the two strands of misleading teaching. This fits with the general emphasis in the New Testament and the Apostolic Fathers on the importance of true and trustworthy teaching about the faith (see e.g. Rom. 6:17 and 16:17).

16. As in the message to Ephesus before, and Thyatira, Sardis and Laodicea after, the Christians in Pergamum are called to *repent*, to turn from their errors, their virtues notwithstanding. The phrase *en tachei* (1:1; 22:6; cf. Rom. 16:20) can mean 'quickly' in the sense of 'with suddenness' rather than 'within a short time', but the related adverb here (*tachy*) does carry a sense of imminence. But, as in 2:5, Jesus' *com[ing]* is in the near present, rather than the distant future, and is part of his active presence and refining of his people rather than his *parousia* (the term used in the New Testament for the return of Jesus understood as the visit of a king). The idea of *waging war*

(AT) against the false teachers is part of the military/conflict language which includes the terminology of being 'victorious'. But it is very clearly metaphorical (and so fitting that we derive our word 'polemical' from it) since the war is waged with the *sword of my mouth*, that is, the words of truth that Jesus speaks. It is also striking that the battle for the truth is not waged with the whole assembly, but only with *them*, that is, the ones who are in error.

17. The same refrain is repeated from the previous two letters, inviting attentive listening to what the *Spirit is saying* (AT) in the words of Jesus. But the language of warfare in the previous verse sharpens the impact of the language of *conquering* (AT). This is spiritual warfare, where conquest comes through patient obedience and responsiveness to the words of God. The promise to those who conquer is twofold. The *hidden manna* alludes to Israel's exodus journey from Egypt to the Promised Land (Exod. 16) and signifies God's provision to sustain his people while they live in the tension between the hope of the kingdom of God and the reality of the suffering world (Rev. 1:9) – sustenance that comes from Jesus himself (John 6:35).

The *white stone with a new name [written] on it* has been much debated. The local rock in Pergamum is black basalt, and the name of any benefactor inscribed on a building would need to have been made on a piece of imported white stone (usually marble) – though the word here signifies a small stone or pebble, rather than anything more general. Black and white stones were also used in voting, and in trials a black stone would signify a guilty verdict, while a white stone signified acquittal. Small stones or pebbles were also used for admission to festivals. The metaphor here is probably composite, suggesting that it is Jesus' intimate knowledge (*known only to the one who receives it*) and approval of those who keep the faith that is the only thing of ultimate importance, in contrast to the opinion of surrounding culture and society.

Theology

The followers of Jesus in Pergamum appear to understand the dynamics of royal power, and are aware of those who claim to have the power of life and death. They have demonstrated their steadfastness and endurance, even in the face of serious opposition that has led to one of their number paying the ultimate price. And yet they have not attained perfection, and have been vulnerable to the compromises that are manifest more clearly in the other assemblies. Jesus assures them that his power is the kind that really counts – not the power of violence or coercion, but the power of the truth of the word that he speaks (the 'sword of my mouth'). Those in Pergamum need to ensure that they really are allied to Jesus and not to those who would lead them astray. He is their true patron, the one who offers them a vote of acquittal and entry to the heavenly city.

iv. Message to the assembly in Thyatira (2:18–29)
Context
Thyatira lay some 50 miles (80 km) south-east of Pergamum, in a level area of no military importance. A few of its ruins can be seen in a square in the middle of modern Akhisar, but otherwise little remains. It was probably given its name as a variation on the Greek for 'daughter', *thygatēr*, by one of Alexander the Great's generals, Seleucus I Nicator, who founded the Seleucid Empire. Some commentators suggest it was insignificant as a city; in fact, it had several gymnasia, a theatre and a stoa (a roofed colonnade) like other Greek and Roman cities. But it certainly was not one of the 'big players' in the region like Pergamum or Ephesus, and it is striking that it merits the longest message, at 222 words.

The city lay on trade routes and had good communications; the roads to and from it were well maintained by both Vespasian and Domitian. As a result, it became the centre of the slave trade in the region, and also developed a large number of trading guilds, including those for dyers, wool merchants, linen workers, cloth cleaners, coppersmiths, potters, tanners, leather cutters and bakers. In a world without the modern separations between private, religious and civic life, these guilds would be places of religious devotion as well as practical association, and as such would pose a particular challenge for early Christians, as we can see elsewhere in the New Testament (e.g. Paul's discussion in 1 Cor. 8 – 10). Feasting and pagan worship were long associated with sexual immorality in Scripture; they are described together in the incident of the golden calf (Exod. 32:6) and again in Moab (Num. 25:1–2), and both these passages are

alluded to in Paul's discussion of eating meat offered to idols in
1 Corinthians 10:7–8.

Paul must have passed close to the city, which was on the border
between the regions of Lydia and Mysia, when he and his companions were prevented by the Spirit from heading either south into
Asia or north into Bithynia and so went to Troas on the north-west
coast (Acts 16:7–8). When they crossed over to Philippi, they met
Lydia, a merchant of purple cloth, from Thyatira (Acts 16:14). She
was a 'God-fearer', that is, associated with the Jewish faith though
not a full convert. We have no clear evidence that there was a Jewish
community in Thyatira. It is not known whether Lydia returned,
with her faith, to Thyatira, but there was a Christian community
there from the 80s until 1922, when the Greek Orthodox were
expelled by the Turkish authorities and the archbishop took up
residence in London.

Comment

18. This is the only time in Revelation when Jesus is described as
Son of God, and this title does not derive from the opening vision. It
acquires its significance from three contexts: Jewish, Christian and
imperial Roman. Its Jewish meaning derives from the description
of God's anointed king as being God's son by adoption. This was
promised to David (2 Sam. 7:13–14) and is expressed in the Davidic/
messianic Psalm 2: 'You are my son; today I have begotten you' (Ps.
2:7, AT). In a Christian context, this is developed further, as Jesus
is confirmed as Son of God 'in power' by the resurrection to
deathless life (Acts 13:33; Rom. 1:4), effects God's redemption in his
death (Gal. 2:20) and is in fact in pre-existent relationship with God
(John 1:14; Heb. 1:1–3), sharing his qualities and character –
something developed in a quite distinct way in Revelation through
the sharing of titles between Jesus and God. Though not included
in the 'victory' saying in this message, in the final vision of Revelation 21, whoever conquers will share in this status as a 'son' of
God (21:7, AT). In a Roman context, the term would have been an
especially pertinent challenge to the claims of imperial authority.
Inscriptions in Thyatira describe Domitian as emperor, high priest,
and son of the deified Vespasian. The following pair of epithets do
come from the opening vision, the *eyes like flames of fire* (AT) signifying

divine vision and insight, and the *feet . . . like . . . bronze* signifying permanence and trustworthiness in contrast with the feet of iron and clay of human power (Dan. 2:33).

19. The *works* (AT) known by Jesus should not be thought of in a narrow way, or contrasted (in the Pauline sense) with 'faith'; rather, this refers to the whole life that the Christians there are living, and the terms that follow explain what these 'works' are. Their *love* could be for God or for others, though (as in 2:4) the two are closely related and there is no need to choose one rather than the other. *Faith* is their trust and sense of allegiance to Jesus, the one who himself is faithful and worthy of trust; such steadfast commitment was esteemed as a virtue in Roman culture. These two dispositions express themselves in the two that follow. The word for *service* (*diakonia*) is used for menial tasks of practical support and is characteristic of Jesus' life (Mark 10:45), but also includes the giving of money, and is the term Paul (and Luke) uses for his apostolic ministry. This is the fourth of seven occurrences of *patient endurance* (AT; see comment on 1:9; 2:2–3), that quality of living faithfully in the tension between the experience of the age of the kingdom of God as it breaks into the present, and this age of suffering and trial which ultimately will not endure. The fact that their later works *are greater* (AT) than those they did at first shows that the Christians in Thyatira understand that they are on a path of discipleship in which they are to grow into maturity (cf. Eph. 4:15).

20. The strong commendation makes the abrupt change to rebuke even more startling to hear, just as were the same words spoken to those in Ephesus (2:4). But the problem here is the reverse of that in Ephesus; their love has grown stronger whereas the Ephesians had lost their first love, and yet where the Ephesians did not *tolerate* wicked people, the Christians here have tolerated *the woman Jezebel*, whose teaching *leads [some of] my people astray* (AT), a serious charge suggesting major error (Mark 12:24, 27) which in Revelation is characteristic of the work of the devil (12:9; 20:10). If sound doctrine without love is worthless, then love without right teaching is at best flaccid and at worse misleading. The name *Jezebel* is John's symbolic pseudonym (as are 'Balaam' in 2:14 and 'the Nicolaitans' in 2:6, 15), linking her to the wife of King Ahab who led Israel astray in opposition to the prophetic ministry of Elijah

(1 Kgs 16 – 2 Kgs 9); her name represents the call to Baal in worship, and she became associated with false prophecy.

As in 2:14, *sexual immorality* and *eating food offered to idols* (AT) are paired, so it remains unclear as to whether the former is literal or a metaphor for unfaithfulness to God. If John shares Paul's theology, then sharing in cultic meals, possibly in the context of a trade guild, suggests not only identification with the group of worshippers, but in some sense union with the pagan deity as well, when in fact believers are already united to Christ.

21–23. The response of Jesus to the false teaching has several aspects to it, but the first is surprising: a call on this person to *repent*. Revelation is often seen as a text of judgment, with sharp and irrevocable lines drawn between the faithful and the enemies of God, yet here it is not just her followers, but the false teacher herself who is called to faith again. The offer of life is hers to refuse, not God's to withdraw; the boundaries between salvation and damnation are (in this sense) neither hard nor fast, with repentance and faith always an option. The ball of destiny lies firmly in the court of human decision.

The second aspect is a process of discipline; God will (lit.) *throw her on a bed* (AT), which most translations take as a metaphor for 'inflict her with sickness'. Those *commit[ting] adultery with her* suggests those following her lead rather than those having immoral sexual relations with her, which in turn implies that the image is a metaphor for spiritual unfaithfulness. They too will experience *great suffering* (AT) – but once again the purpose is to bring to repentance, as it is later in Revelation. Regardless of whether she, the teacher, responds, those who follow *her ways* can themselves change direction and return to the truth.

The third aspect of Jesus' response is the most drastic: *strik[ing] her children dead*. But, given the context of the previous verses, this must refer to Jezebel's spiritual children, that is, those who have adopted her ways and refuse to repent, and it seems most likely that 'death' refers to being cut off spiritually from the source of life, a parallel to the Ephesians having their lampstand removed (2:5). If so, this fulfils the 'Gamaliel test' (Acts 5:38): that which is not of God will come to nothing – but it is worth remembering that Paul actually thought sickness and death could result from playing fast and loose with the truth about God (1 Cor. 11:30).

The final result of this process of judgment and the offer of repentance is that *all the assemblies* (AT) will be convinced of the insight that Jesus has into the true condition of his people. The reference to all the congregations is further evidence both that each of the seven were intended to read the messages to all the others, and presumably that the Christians in other places would also hear and understand the messages; the seven are representative of all, not exclusive of them. The *search[ing]* of Jesus harks back to the image of 'eyes like flames of fire' (AT) at the opening of the message. The terms translated *hearts and minds* are actually 'kidneys' and 'hearts'. In ancient physiology, the kidneys were understood to be closely related to the intestines and belly, and all three were the seats of desire, longing or emotion (so, in Phil. 1:8, Paul yearns for the Philippians 'in the bowels of Jesus Christ', KJV). The heart was understood to be the seat of decision (and not feeling), so Jesus is the one who knows both the desires and the longings that might pull us in different directions ('kidneys'), and the decisions and commitments we make in the light of these desires ('hearts'). Rewarding people *according to [their] deeds* is not about some kind of 'salvation by works', but (in line with all other teaching in the NT) the conviction that the grace of God in Jesus effects the transformation of a person's life, and so true faith in Jesus manifests in the kinds of qualities and actions that the Thyatirans are commended for at the start of the message.

24–25. Though the previous comments have been addressed to those in all the assemblies, Jesus' words turn back to *the rest . . . in Thyatira*, who have not been led astray. It is not immediately clear what is meant by the *so-called deep secrets* of Satan. It might be that, arguing that idols are nothing, 'Jezebel' has been teaching about the details of pagan cults, thinking they are harmless. But perhaps it is no more complex than some sort of 'higher teaching', presented as being true to the gospel, but, since they are leading people astray as Satan does, these are in fact satanic deceptions. To follow Jesus faithfully does not require esoteric knowledge or complex rituals; there is no great *burden* to be borne other than to continue 'to keep on keeping on', holding on to what they have, growing in maturity in the love, faith, service and perseverance that the believers are already living in – until Jesus comes to claim them as his own.

26–27. This is the only message in which the nature of *conquering* (AT) is explained by expansion: it involves *do[ing] my will till the end.* Since this might mean staying faithful even to the point of death (see 2:10), this builds a picture of spiritual warfare as passive and non-violent but determined resistance to the dominant ideology of the world around. The idea of *ruling the nations* (AT) comes from Psalm 2, widely understood to be not simply about Davidic kingship, but as a royal messianic psalm looking forwards prophetically. Verse 27 is very close to the wording of Psalm 2:9; the word 'rule' can be translated 'shepherd', in the sense of 'care and provide for', but the second half of the phrase suggests something less pastoral. The psalm is cited again in relation to Jesus in 12:5 and 19:15.

Sharing in the reign of God and Jesus over the nations occurs throughout Revelation; the word 'reign' occurs seven times, three with reference to God and/or Jesus (11:15, 17; 19:6) and four with reference to the people of God (5:10; 20:4, 6; 22:5). It is also reflected in the kings of the earth bringing their glory into the New Jerusalem (21:24), thus submitting to the rule of both God and the saints. It appears to be an extension of Jesus' promise to his disciples that in the age to come they will sit on thrones judging the twelve tribes of Israel (Matt. 19:28; Luke 22:30), as developed in the parable of the talents ('ruler over many things', Matt. 25:21, AT; 'have authority over ten cities', Luke 19:17, AT). The cascading of authority from God the Father, to Jesus, then to his followers reflects the father–son relationship between God and his anointed ruler in Psalm 2:8, and is also found in Jesus' commission of the disciples, implicitly in Matthew 28:18 ('All authority . . . has been given to me . . .') and explicitly in John 20:21 ('As the Father has sent me, so I send you', AT).

28. The *morning star* is understood in negative terms in Isaiah 14:12, where it refers to the fallen king of Babylon, but here the term probably alludes to the prophetic word in the oracle of Balaam in Numbers 24:17: 'A star will come out of Jacob; a sceptre will rise out of Israel.' The language of 'sceptre' or 'rod' is the same as that in Psalm 2:9, and the oracle also includes the imagery of ruling and crushing of enemies. In the context of Roman culture, the star signified divine status; so, for example, a 'wandering star' (comet) appeared after the death of Julius Caesar, believed to signify his deification, and a star appeared on imperial coins in association with Augustus and Tiberius. This double sense – of the anointed one of God in Jewish thought, and the divine ruler from Roman thought – mirrors the double significance of 'Son of God' at the beginning of the message. Just as those who are victorious in the life of faithful discipleship to the end share in being sons of God and participate in the eternal reign of Jesus, so they are given a share in the morning star. There is no doubt a primary relational aspect to this, since Jesus himself is described as the 'bright Morning Star' (22:16), heralding the dawn of the promised new creation of God. But even as Jesus gives himself to us, so he invites us to share in the authority that he has over his world.

29. See comment above on 2:7.

Theology
This middle message of the seven is the longest, though written to the assembly of Christians in a much less significant city than the first three. Jesus pays them at least as much attention regardless of how important this group is in the eyes of others. There is much that he wants to commend – their commitment to faith and love, and how these make themselves known in practical action. The followers of Jesus here continue to grow in maturity, not satisfied with what they are doing, but seeking to do more and better.

And yet they have something to learn from those in Ephesus. Despite the rebuke to that assembly, they had the virtue of not tolerating false teaching, something those in Thyatira need to imitate. There is, for Jesus' followers, a right intolerance – one born not out of lack of love, but out of a commitment to the truth of who Jesus is and the allegiance he calls us to. It is claimed that there is a new word from God, a new prophecy that allows them to compromise with key practices in the surrounding, dominant culture. But the true prophetic word is consistent with who Jesus was and is: from beginning to end, it is Jesus who is the true anointed King, the true divine ruler, anticipated in the past, vindicated in the present, and the one who will exercise his sovereign authority into the future. He is a sharp contrast to other rulers who would claim these titles – and so his followers are to live in sharp contrast with those over whom such rulers hold sway, in every aspect of life.

In the light of this, it makes no sense to follow the seductive teaching. The rebuke to God's people in Thyatira is milder than elsewhere; judgment will not come upon them, but only on those who stick to the misleading teaching, and then only if they refuse to repent. Jesus wants all to return to the truth, and continues to offer his compelling invitation. For those who have stayed true, there is nothing more they need to do other than to keep on keeping on. The faith of Jesus is not merely the excited sprint of enthusiasm of those new to faith, but the committed marathon of a long obedience in the same direction. For those who reach the finish line, the reward is relationship into eternity with the one who has loved them and given himself for them, and a share in all that he is and has.

v. Message to the assembly in Sardis (3:1–6)

Context

Both the history and the geography of Sardis have a significant bearing on the interpretation of this message. In terms of geography, the city lay around 40 miles (64 km) south of Thyatira and 50 miles (80 km) east of Smyrna, and was on important trade routes in several directions (reflected in the pattern of roads in and out of modern-day Sart). The name in Greek has a plural form, suggesting the city was always in two parts. The lower city was located on the south side of the fertile valley of the river Hermus (modern Gediz), while the upper city (acropolis) occupied the small summit on a lofty spur at the end of the mountain ridge that extended north from Mount Tmolus. The sides of the acropolis were sheer in every direction and composed of a crumbly rock, making it almost invincible as a stronghold; the site is strikingly dramatic to view even today.

Its history goes back at least as far as that of Troy, and it was the capital of the ancient kingdom of Lydia. Its most famous king was Croesus, proverbial for his wealth, who ruled Lydia in the sixth century BC until his defeat by Cyrus of Persia. His gold came from the Pactolus River, which flowed from Mount Tmolus through the city into the Hermus. Because of its situation, with good defences, communications and supplies of food and water, it enjoyed continuous occupation and a reputation for wealth and prestige. When it was seriously damaged in the catastrophic earthquake of AD 17, it was rebuilt with assistance from the emperor himself within a decade, and thereafter owed a particular loyalty to Rome. Many of the extensive remains have been reconstructed, including an impressive bathhouse and gymnasium, a sizeable synagogue of the wealthy and influential Jewish community there (the term 'Sephardic' probably comes from here), streets and shops, and the substantial temple dedicated to Artemis of Ephesus, of which two of the massive columns still stand.[4]

And yet all was not what it seemed. Sardis lost out to Smyrna in competing to host an imperial temple, because of emphasizing its past splendour rather than the present reality. And though the capturing of the acropolis became a byword for an impossible task, it was in fact taken by force – not once, but twice! When Cyrus attacked the city in the sixth century, his forces noticed the use of a trapdoor under the unguarded walls, and while the occupants slept, he entered to open the city gates. Three hundred years later, the Seleucid king Antiochus III the Great besieged the city, and apparently took it after reading of Cyrus's victory. The inhabitants were once again asleep instead of on guard.

Comment

1. On the identity and role of the *angel*, see the comment on 1:19. On the meaning of *ekklēsia*, 'assembly', see the comment on 1:11. On the significance of *Thus says* (AT), see the comment on 2:1.

The epithets of the risen Jesus have so far alternated between using verbal actions (in participle form) and using titles: 'the one who holds . . .'; 'the First and the Last'; 'the one who has . . .'; 'the Son of God'; and now 'the one who has' (AT).[5] The epithet in the first message revised the description from the opening vision to emphasize Jesus' power; rather than 'having' the seven stars, he 'grasped [them] firmly' (AT). Here, the description returns to the opening vision, as Jesus simply *has* (AT) the stars. At first sight, it

---

4. A number of the buildings date from later than the first century, but they nevertheless give an idea of the city's wealth.

5. Note that the final two messages combine titles and actions: 'the holy and true, who holds . . .'; 'the Amen, the faithful and true witness, who rules . . .' (AT).

seems odd to talk of Jesus also 'having' the *seven spirits of God*, if the seven spirits are the same as those we encountered in 1:4 as part of a trinitarian greeting formula, and thus a metaphor for the Holy Spirit. This has led some commentators to understand the phrase as referring to 'angelic beings that serve as attendants of God'.[6]

This is unlikely for several reasons. It would be odd to refer to angelic beings in a threefold greeting between the references to God and Jesus in 1:4–5, and the Old Testament background to the term does not allow this (see comment on 1:4). Within the wider context of the New Testament, Jesus is indeed the one who dispenses the Spirit: in John 14:16, Jesus is the one who asks the Father to send the Spirit; in Luke 24:49, it is Jesus who will send the 'promise' (i.e. the Spirit) to clothe the disciples with power and equip them for witness; in John 20:22, Jesus symbolically breathes the Holy Spirit on them; and in the three Synoptics, Jesus is anticipated as the one who 'baptise[s] . . . with the Holy Spirit' (Matt. 3:11; Mark 1:8; Luke 3:16). Within the Johannine tradition, the Spirit is particularly identified as the giver of life (John 6:63; cf. Rom. 8:2), and this will become significant when we see the situation of the Christians in Sardis.

In other messages, Jesus knows either their *works* (AT; Ephesus, Thyatira, Philadelphia and Laodicea) or their situation (Smyrna and Pergamum), and where there is affirmation or encouragement to be offered, it is offered here. Yet, in this message, affirmation and rebuke are reversed, with the stern rebuke coming immediately. Jesus knows their *name* (AT), that is, their reputation, for being something that they are not. Just as the city has a reputation for being illustrious that belongs in the past rather than the present, and just as it has become a byword for being impregnable though it has in fact fallen to its enemies twice at key moments in its history, so the Christian community has a reputation for being *alive* but is actually on the point of being spiritually *dead*.

2. Following the rebuke comes the command, the first being a linked pair in the triple command that comprises five terms ('wake up and strengthen', 'remember', 'keep and repent'). The form of

---

6. See e.g. Koester (2), p. 312.

the first is slightly unusual – literally 'be wakeful' – and there is a sense of purpose linking the one with the other: 'Wake up so that you might strengthen'. *What remains* must refer to the remnant of belief and practice, rather than a remnant of people; the community has been found to be *incomplete before* [i.e. in the sight of] *God* (AT), in terms which are reminiscent of the writing on the wall: 'You have been weighed on the scales and found wanting' (Dan. 5:27). Throughout the Scriptures, 'completion' refers to a wholehearted commitment to God and to obedience to his commands (Deut. 18:13). Paul could talk of 'completing' the missional task he had been given (Acts 12:25; 14:26; Rom. 15:19), and in Christian living the idea is connected to the command to be 'perfect' or 'mature' (*telos*) in response to the perfection and wholeness of God (Matt. 5:48; Eph. 4:13; Jas 1:4; 3:2).

3. The second command is to *remember*; it is a present imperative, but it is assuming too much to conclude that this means 'keep on remembering'. Unlike the nostalgic affection that Sardis has for its glorious past, this is about allowing what happened previously to shape the present (cf. the comment on 2:5). We might expect the following terms to be in the reverse order, in that *hear[ing]* must come first before a message can be *received*. But the reversal serves to emphasize the first term: just as Paul received the tradition of teaching that was handed on to him, so he passed it on to others (1 Cor. 15:3). The good news about Jesus comes as a gift to us, one which we must attend to carefully and faithfully. The third part of the command comes in a connected pair, again in the reverse order from what we might expect, giving an emphasis to the first term. The Christians in Sardis need to *repent*, to turn from death to life, in order that they might *keep* (AT) what they have heard – living in responsive obedience to the life-giving word of the good news of Jesus.

If they fail to wake from this sleep of death, Jesus will come as a *thief*, an image found in the Gospels (Matt. 24:43; Luke 12:39) and the letters (1 Thess. 5:2; 2 Pet. 3:10). The main idea is the sense of sudden unexpectedness of the coming of Jesus, but it perhaps also has overtones of the destructiveness of judgment, in line with Old Testament expectation of the 'day of the LORD' (see e.g. Amos 5:18). Although elsewhere it has a purely eschatological sense, referring to the final coming of Jesus and the end of the age, Jesus has already talked of his 'coming' to bring judgment in the immediate future within history (2:5, 16). The image of an unexpected break-in to a community who were asleep must surely have had historical resonance for the inhabitants of Sardis.

4. At last, we find some word of affirmation for this community. Jesus has *a few people* who have remained true; the term used is 'names', but here it refers to individuals as opposed to 'reputation' as in verse 1. It is striking that the contrast drawn here is not between the (spiritually) dying and the living, but between the dying and the *unpolluted* (AT); spiritual life involves purity of living, symbolized by unsoiled *garments* (AT). From Genesis onwards, *walk[ing]* with God signifies approval, friendship and obedience (Gen. 5:22); the purity of the garments now is an anticipation of the life of the age to come (6:11; 7:9, 13). Although the high priests in the Old Testament wear linen, *white* is predominantly the colour of pagan worship, signifying purity, holiness and honour in Greek and Roman culture.[7] Participation in the life of God and Jesus includes sharing in their qualities; just as God and the lamb are lauded as being *worthy* (4:11; 5:9), so those who remain faithful are the ones who have 'lived a life worthy of [their] calling' (Eph. 4:1).

5. The first part of the promise to those *conquering* (AT) has perhaps the most continuity with the body of the message: they will, in the same way, be *clothed in white* (AT), so that the life of the future is in continuity with a life of holiness in the present. The second part of the promise, *I will never blot out*, is an example of litotes in which a double negative or understatement is used to emphasize the positive ('Are you hungry?' 'Not half!' – 'not a little' here meaning 'a lot!'). The idea of the *book* [or scroll] *of life* has its roots in both the Old Testament and Roman culture. Psalm 69:28 uses near-identical language of the wicked being 'blotted out of the book of life', as does Moses in Exodus 32:32. Lists of citizens in a Roman

---

7. White is occasionally associated with purity in the OT (Isa. 1:18), and angelic beings are sometimes dressed in white in the NT (Matt. 28:3; Mark 16:5; John 20:12; Acts 1:10). The context here is in part ethical, but in anticipation of worship in the presence of God.

colony would be kept on a scroll or inscribed in stone, and anyone convicted of a capital crime would have his or her name removed from it.[8] In some Jewish traditions, to have one's name written in the book of life was a reward for a righteous life (see e.g. *Apocalypse of Zephaniah* 3:6–9). But Revelation shares the view of Jesus in Luke 10:20 that to have names written there was the decision of God and a gift of grace. Elsewhere in Revelation, it is described as 'the Lamb's book of life' (13:8; 21:27), so the names written in it are of those whom the lamb has purchased from 'every tribe and language and people and nation' (5:9). The promise here contrasts God's judgment with human judgment, and gives the assurance of divine preservation into eternity, whatever happens in this present life.

The third part of the promise, like the warning of coming as a thief, is also found in the Gospels and combines elements of Jesus' saying in Matthew 10:32 (*before my Father*) and Luke 12:8 (*and his angels*). Belonging to Christ involves reciprocal acknowledgment – by us of him before others, and by him of us before the throne of God.

6. On the final saying, see comment on 2:7.

Theology
Although there is a substantial Jewish community in the city, there do not appear to be the problems in relationships that were present at Smyrna and Philadelphia (2:9; 3:9), and while Sardis is as loyal to Rome as any city, compromise with the imperial cult or trade guilds does not appear to be an issue.

Instead, the risen Christ comes to a community living in a city which has been caught napping on more than one occasion, and has discovered the serious consequences of being asleep when they should have been awake. And this is a place with a reputation of worthiness and honour – but a reputation based on the past, and

---

8. Dio Chrysostom, *Discourses* 31.80–86, discusses the merits of this practice, and mentions 'chiselling out names', attesting to the use of inscriptions. See also Xenophon, *Hellenica* 2.3.51 for an earlier example of this practice.

no longer a reality in the present. Don't be like this, Jesus says to his people, because this sleep is the sleep of death! To allow your clothes to be soiled, that is, to compromise in the way you live, is not just unfortunate but fatal – fatal to spiritual life in the present, and threatening to extinguish confidence for the future.

But there is hope; all is not lost. There remain some green shoots of life in the midst of all that has died; there is a remnant of faith that can be strengthened again. And the really good news comes in the person who speaks this word of reproof. He is the one who can pour out again the Spirit of life on his people. He is the one who holds his people in his hands. He is the one who renders true judgment – it is he, and not the surrounding culture, who speaks the sure and trustworthy word over his people, and who can guarantee their security through this life and into the next, their citizenship of the heavenly Jerusalem. His coming might be like a thief in the night to those who sleep, but he wants to come to the wakeful as a friend in the day (1 Thess. 5:4) so that he might bring to completion the work he has begun (Phil. 1:6) in those he loves and for whom he has given himself (Rev. 1:5b).

vi. Message to the assembly in Philadelphia (3:7–13)
Context
Philadelphia lay 30 miles (48 km) east-south-east from Sardis, further along the fertile plain of one of the tributaries of the Hermus. It was the youngest of the seven cities, having been founded in the second century BC by Attalus II, the fifth king of Pergamum, as a way of extending Pergamene control over the area.

The city knew insecurity from both its physical and its economic situation. Physically, it sat on the fault line that was the cause of the devastating earthquake of AD 17, which also affected Sardis. Because of the destruction it was exempted from taxes by the Emperor Tiberius for five years. As a result of its vulnerability, many of its citizens lived on farms in the surrounding countryside rather than in the city itself. Economically, the city depended for its wealth on grapes grown in the fertile valley; when Domitian issued an edict in AD 92 requiring all viticulture to be halved across the empire (probably to encourage the growth of grain to feed his armies), it devastated the economy and drove many into poverty. This was particularly resented in Philadelphia, since it was loyally committed to the emperor, even changing its name to Neocaesarea for a time.

Like many other cities in Asia, it contained a Jewish community, and this was large enough to attract Gentiles as God-fearers, including, it seems, some Christians. Only a few years after John's message, Ignatius of Antioch (died AD 108) wrote to the Christians there warning them not to be drawn into Jewish belief: 'If any one preach the Jewish law unto you, listen not to him. For it is better to hearken to Christian doctrine from a man who has been circumcised [i.e. Jesus], than to Judaism from one uncircumcised' (*To the Philadelphians* 6:1).

The city continued to be occupied because of its agricultural prosperity, and the modern city of Alaşehir on the site is still synonymous with dried sultana raisins and known for its fresh fruit market. But it also continued to be affected by earthquakes, including the one that devastated Laodicea in AD 60; there are no ancient ruins to be seen today except some walls and arches from the large basilica of St John, built in 600. It continued as an important centre of Christian faith through the Byzantine period, and is today both a centre of Orthodox faith and a titular see (i.e. one without any actual geographical area attached to it) of the Roman Catholic Church.

The message to Philadelphia, at 194 words, is only a little shorter than the longest, to Thyatira, and (as part of the symmetry of the messages, like the second letter to Smyrna) it contains no rebuke.

Comment

7. On the opening command, see the comment on 2:1. Most English translations treat the qualities *holy and true* as adjectives, but in fact they are titles: the Holy One and the True One (introduced here and not part of the opening vision in Rev. 1). This takes up Old Testament language about God, who is characteristically 'the Holy One of Israel' in the prophet Isaiah (Isa. 1:4; 5:19; 43:3, and so on) as well as in other prophets (Jer. 50:29; Hos. 11:12; Hab. 3:3). John might have Isaiah 60:14 particularly in mind, since this also includes reference to God's enemies prostrating themselves at his feet. But the phrase 'Holy One and True' is also used of God in Revelation 6:10 (AT), part of the pattern of John using titles of Jesus and God interchangeably as part of his exalted Christology of Jesus as the one sharing the qualities, status and action of God.

Key[s] were significant in the ancient world, particularly as part of religious and magical cults (see comment on 1:18), but the phrase here about the *key[s] of David* is almost word for word from Isaiah 22:22, a prophecy about the authority of a successor to the Davidic throne. The one with the keys, the steward of the household, had authority both to allow and to prohibit admission to the house itself, and the issue of authority is emphasized here in the chiastic repetition ('open, shut, shut, open'). As the successor to the Davidic kingdom, Jesus has authority to give access, not to the physical Jerusalem, but to the New Jerusalem and the presence of God.

8. As with the messages to Ephesus, Thyatira and Sardis, Jesus *know[s]* their *deeds* – but any statement of their virtue has to wait till later, with the abrupt change of focus to the promise of Jesus. The idea of *an open door that no-one can shut* has a powerful suggestive force as a metaphor for opportunity; when we cannot do what we want, we feel that a 'door has shut' in our face, and when some alternative arises, we feel that a 'door has opened'. Yet, in the context both of the previous verse and of what follows (and the 'open door' in 4:1), this must be a reference, not to particular opportunities, but to entering the presence of God by means of the access Jesus has won for us by his death and resurrection. The following phrase is emphatic: the door stands open to God, and absolutely *no-one can shut* it (cf. Rom. 8:39, 'nothing will be able to separate us . . .', for a similar idea using a different metaphor).

Some translations repeat Jesus' 'I know' before the following phrase, and others link it with what follows. It actually follows on from the promise; Jesus wants to reassure the Philadelphians that the door to God's presence stands open because, like the fragility of the city in which they live, they know that they are *weak* (AT) and cannot in their own strength stand the shaking of their world that they are about to face. Obedience to Jesus' command and allegiance to Jesus' person belong together; they have both *kept [his] word* and not *denied* their association with him.

9. The abrupt *Behold!* (AT) at the beginning of this verse (in some translations 'Listen!' or 'Look!') draws attention to Jesus' promise in relation to the conflict with the Jewish community, and there is discontinuity in the grammar so that the promise of action is broken off and then repeated before being resolved. The language around the *synagogue of Satan* is a very close parallel with the language around the same phrase in the message to Smyrna (2:9), and these are the only two mentions of *Jews*. It is striking that in the two cities that receive no rebuke, both are living in tension with the Jewish community, indicating not their enmity so much as their closeness. If Jesus is the Jewish Messiah, coming first to the Jewish people and only secondarily to Gentiles (as reflected in much of Paul's missionary activity in which he goes to the synagogue first; Acts 14:1), faithful proclamation will lead to disagreement with those Jews who do not recognize his claims.

We also need to note that this word is one of reassurance to Jesus' followers, and not an invitation to take action; it is Jesus himself who will vindicate them, and they are invited to leave that to him (cf. Paul's teaching on how we treat our enemies – blessing them and leaving God to judge; Rom. 12:20). Such language can never offer a foundation for anti-Jewish thought or action, not least because the assembly in Philadelphia will have included Jewish followers of Jesus. Their vindication lies less in what they have done and more in what God has done – he has *loved* them and given the life of his Son for them.

10. The slightly unusual position of the reason for action, *Since you have kept*, lends it emphasis. The following phrase could be understood in one of three ways: the word of Jesus' own patient endurance; a particular word from Jesus asking for patient endurance; or the word about Jesus (i.e. the good news) which requires patient endurance from those who respond. Given the sevenfold repetition of the word, and its application to all the people of God including John himself (1:9; 13:10; 14:12), the last is the most likely – though of course this can never be detached from the example of Jesus himself (1 Pet. 2:21).

The *hour of testing* (AT) might appear to be a contrast with the 'ten days of suffering' (tribulation) faced by those in Smyrna, but in fact both terms signify a time period that is limited, and given both the general and the widespread nature of such *test[ing]* or suffering, should be understood as characteristic of this age in contrast to the age to come; elsewhere in Revelation it is designated by the time

period of three and a half days ('time, times and half a time') adapted
from Daniel. To be *[kept] . . . from* such a time of trial could, con-
ceivably, suggest being removed from this testing or protected from
it. But the language through the entire book about the suffering that
the people of God will experience (both in the messages and in the
main body of the text) makes such a reading impossible.

The word for *whole world* is neutral, and refers primary to humanity
rather than the non-human created order. But the term *inhabitants
of the earth* (AT) comes ten times (3:10; 6:10; 8:13; 11:10 twice; 13:8;
13:14 twice; 17:2, 8) and describes those who are deceived by the beast
and follow him and who are opposed to the people of God, that is,
those whose true dwelling is in the presence of God in heaven (13:6).
The testing and suffering that comes upon the world highlights the
difference between these two groups and their respective loyalties –
but not in the sense of fixed and unchanging division, since the
possibility of repentance, change and a switch of allegiance is always
in view.

11. This is one of five places where Jesus talks of *coming soon*.[9]
This might suggest that John (and his readers) have a misplaced
expectation that the return of Jesus will be in their lifetime. But it
needs to be placed alongside the emphasis, in related language, that
the important issue is the suddenness and swiftness that will come
unexpectedly (see comment on 1:1) and that the urgency is to
respond while we can (see comment on 1:3). We also need to locate
Revelation's sense of expectation within wider New Testament
thinking, where it is a common misreading to imagine that the first
Christians saw themselves as the last generation. This is confirmed
by the overall message of Revelation, where confidence in Jesus'
ultimate victory leads to a commitment to patient endurance and
faithful living, rather than constant 'cloud watching' for Jesus' return.

The only command given to the Philadelphians is similar to the
command given to those in Thyatira (2:25), to *keep what [they] have*
(AT). Just as they can be sure of the commitment of Jesus to them,
so they need to grasp firmly the hope that he has set before them, as

_____

9. The others are in 2:16; 22:7, 12, 20. The third woe is also described
   as 'coming soon' in 11:14; see comment there.

in fact they already are doing. The warning of others who might *take your crown* might strike us as odd, but in fact highlights that it is those around us, as much as our own decisions or weaknesses, that can throw us off the course of faith.

12. The promise to *the one conquering* (AT) has striking resonance for those living with the perpetual threat of earthquake damage. In the Jewish temple, the *pillar*s were more ornamental, with the main structure and roof held up with solid walls. But in Greek and Roman temples, the outer ring of pillars often constituted the main structural element holding the whole building together. When the pillars toppled as the earthquake struck, the whole edifice came tumbling down. But here Jesus promises that those who keep faith will be like secure pillars (proverbial for the sure and upright among the faithful; see Gal. 2:9) that will never be shaken, and in a place with permanent security which they will never have to *leave* to flee for safety. This is the place of true security.

It was common practice to inscribe the names of either benefactors or dedicated gods on pillars in Greek and Roman temples, but the promise to *write on them the name* is not so much John mixing his metaphors as coining another metaphor. The writing of a name generally suggests ownership or allegiance, and as Revelation unfolds, humanity is divided between those inscribed with the name of the beast (encoded in his number, 13:18) and those inscribed with the name of Jesus and the Father (14:1; 20:4). The *new Jerusalem*, we shall discover, is the place of both the dwelling of God's people and the temple presence of God himself, finally united with his people (21:3). The *new name* of Jesus is the secret name that he has written on his thigh in 19:12 and 16, his true identity as 'KING OF KINGS AND LORD OF LORDS'. It is secret only in the sense that it is not yet recognized by the whole world – but that truth will one day be seen and acknowledged by all (Phil. 2:9–11).

13. On the final encouragement to pay careful attention, see comment on 2:7.

Theology
This remarkable (and fairly lengthy) message of affirmation comes to a community who seem to be weak and suffering from serious opposition from those who most vehemently deny the message

about Jesus. The revelation of Jesus' message to them here is that their weakness is not the most important thing about them: they have obeyed Jesus' call to 'patient endurance', which is the primary quality of those who live in the world, but are not of it, as they wait to see their final redemption in the coming of Jesus. However much they feel hemmed in by their circumstances, what matters is the sovereignty of Jesus as the one who can 'open doors' for them – and in particular, the door that really matters and which leads into a place of peace, security and salvation in God's presence. Despite their weakness, God himself will make them strong, and turn them into the ones looked to by others as exemplary members of the people and temple of God.

vii. Message to the assembly in Laodicea (3:14–22)
Context
The final message, to Laodicea, is one of the best known and most misinterpreted. Although quite long among the seven, it is one of the simplest and most straightforward in terms of its grammar and structure.

In relation to the other six cities, Laodicea was at the end of the more or less semicircular clockwise route that the letter carrier would have travelled to reach each of the cities in turn. It lay around 60 miles (97 km) south-east of Philadelphia on the main interior route through Anatolia, and was situated in the Lycus Valley (as were Hierapolis and Colossae) and therefore was also on the east–west route that ended on the coast at Ephesus. It was thus at the crossroads of major communication routes and prospered accordingly. The city itself was on a plateau above the south side of the Lycus Valley, on a site just below the modern town of Denizli. In recent years it has been extensively excavated, with some of the main streets being reconstructed. From the site it is possible to see, across the Lycus Valley on the north side, the white 'cotton castle' terraces of travertine (calcium carbonate) deposited by the hot springs of Pamukkale, ancient Hierapolis, which were used for therapeutic bathing and continue to be an important tourist destination.

Laodicea was founded in the third century by the Seleucids and was named after Laodice, wife of Attalus II. It soon became a centre of banking, perhaps because of its good communications, and was a regional centre for the collection of the Jewish temple tax, as well as home to a significant Jewish community. Although not the richest city in comparison with the larger population centres at Ephesus and Pergamum, it was very wealthy for its size and had many wealthy benefactors. When it was damaged by an earthquake in AD 20, it received imperial aid, but after another quake in AD 60 that completely demolished the city, it refused assistance, the citizens drawing on the resources of its benefactors to rebuild the city themselves without outside help. Part its wealth came from farming the nearby valley, including raising sheep with a luxurious black wool which was woven into cloth and widely traded, and it was close to a renowned medical centre at the temple of Men Karrou, some 13 miles (21 km) away. The city was in good standing with Rome, and like Sardis it competed for the honour of building a temple to Tiberius in AD 23, both losing out to Smyrna.

There seems to have been a Christian community in Laodicea by the late 50s or early 60s, and Paul mentions it as one of the places, along with Colossae, that he had not personally visited (Col. 2:1). Congregations were probably established there and at Colossae and Hierapolis by Epaphras; 'working hard' is Paul's language for apostolic church-planting ministry (Col. 4:13). The 'letter from Laodicea' (Col. 4:16) is most likely what we call Ephesians, sent as a circular around various Christian communities in the region.

Comment

14. On the opening command to write, see comment on 2:1. The epithets of Jesus in the opening of this message are once again titular, as in the previous message, but are striking in that (unlike the epithets in the previous six messages) they are not drawn from the opening vision of Jesus in Revelation 1, but in part repeat titles in the epistolary introduction (1:5). *Amen* occurs seven times in Revelation as an acclamation,[10] but only here as a kind of title. It is in Greek a transliteration from Hebrew, and so appropriate simply to

---

10. In 1:6 and 1:7 spoken by John; in 5:14 spoken by the living creatures; twice in 7:12 spoken by all those around the throne; in 19:4 spoken by the elders and living creatures; and finally in 22:20 spoken by John again.

transliterate into English, meaning 'Yes' or 'So be it'. Used as a title for Jesus, it therefore comes close to Paul's description of Jesus as the 'Yes' to all God's promises (2 Cor. 1:20; cf. Isa. 65:16). Jesus as *the faithful . . . witness* (also in 19:11) is a major idea in Revelation and communicated in its structure. Two is the number of witness, since two witnesses need to agree for their testimony to be true (Deut. 17:6, a criterion appealed to by Jesus in John 5:31–38 and failed in Jesus' trial in Mark 14:56), and seven is the number of completeness or perfection (there are seven days in the week, planets in ancient understanding, continents and seas), so fourteen is the number signifying perfect witness. The name 'Jesus' occurs fourteen times in Revelation, as do the words for 'servant' and 'saint', those who are called to follow his example of true witness (testimony), and together the words for 'testify' and 'testimony'. The true witness of Jesus also affirms the truth of John's testimony about him; the words John faithfully records are also 'faithful and true' (AT; 21:5; 22:6).

The word *archē* can be understood to mean 'beginning' or *ruler of . . . creation*. Jesus is elsewhere in Revelation depicted in general terms as the 'Alpha' and the 'Beginning' along with God (1:8; 21:6; 22:13), and *archē* is here paired with *telos* ('end') as a contrast. But in the scenes of heavenly worship to come, it is the One on the throne who has 'created all things' (4:11), and the lamb is worshipped with him because of the redemption through his blood. So the phrase here should be read as recalling 1:5, where Jesus is 'ruler [*archē*] of the kings of the earth'. This fits with the context of this message, where the final promise offers a share in Jesus' divine authority as ruler.

15–16. As with the message to Sardis, Jesus' declaration that he *know[s]* their *deeds* is followed immediately and abruptly by rebuke, that they are neither *cold nor hot* – though unlike Sardis there is no later positive affirmation. The contrast between hot and cold, and so the meaning of *lukewarm*, continues to be misunderstood in popular readings, because of the natural sense of the metaphors, at least in English-speaking contexts: in relation to faith, 'cold' suggests indifference, unresponsiveness and even unbelief; 'hot' suggests passion, commitment and life, not least because of the image of the Spirit as flames of fire. 'Lukewarm' therefore means half-hearted and mediocre, neither one thing nor the other.

There are some immediate textual problems with such a reading. The major one is that the risen Jesus appears to see either state of hot or cold as desirable in preference to being lukewarm; although both terms are given relative preference to luke-warm in verse 16, they have been given absolute value in verse 15, and their equal value is highlighted by their reversal in order (oddly disguised in some English translations). It is not convincing to suggest that, even if being cold is a bad thing, at least it makes it clear where the community stands; the repeated emphasis in all the messages is the complete knowledge of the risen Jesus about his followers, so he does not need any help! The second textual issue is that 'hot', 'cold' and 'lukewarm' in this understanding are taken to refer to the inner life of a believer, his or her disposition towards God and faith. But, consistently with all the other messages, the focus here is on *deeds* as a metonym for the whole of life as it is lived out, that is, faith expressed in changed living and actions.

As is now widely recognized, there is also a contextual problem with this reading.[11] Being just above the Lycus Valley rather than on the valley floor, Laodicea did not have access to the cold springs which supplied Colossae some ten miles further along, but being lower on the south side of the escarpment than Hierapolis was on the north side, it was at some distance from its own hot springs. The water that came to the city via its aqueduct was therefore both lukewarm (unlike in Hierapolis, where it was hot) and (like in Hierapolis) laden with dissolved calcium carbonate and other minerals; both the remains of the aqueduct (visible in a neighbouring field) and the clay pipes found all over the excavated site are lined with calcium carbonate deposits – in some pipes so much so that there is barely any space left for the water to run. Hot water is good for something: healing and therapy. Cold water is, particularly in the hot summer climate, good for something: cooling and refreshing. Lukewarm water, especially laden with minerals, is in its present state good for nothing – and would make the drinker want to spit it out.

----

11. This was first observed and connected with the interpretation of this text by Rudwick and Green, 'Laodicean Lukewarmness'.

It was not the *state of their faith* that Jesus was criticizing, but the *lack of fruit* in their lives.[12]

The idea that Jesus might *spit you out of my mouth* is startling and dramatic; the verb *emeō* gives us our word 'emetic', and most English translations hold back from giving its full force as meaning 'vomit'. Yet in the Gospels, Jesus has particularly harsh words for those whose faith and actions do not line up with one another. He criticizes the Pharisees less for their beliefs or teaching than for their actions (or lack of them): 'So you must be careful to do everything they tell you. But do not do what they do, for they do not practise what they preach' (Matt. 23:3). Similarly, he has stern words for those who give the appearance of discipleship without matching this in their actions and living: 'Not everyone who says to me, "Lord, Lord," will enter the kingdom of heaven, but only those who do the will of my Father who is in heaven' (Matt. 7:21). This teaching, especially in the form found in Matthew, has close parallels in the letter of James, where the separation of faith and

---

12. Koester (2), p. 337 is unusual among recent commentators in rejecting this reading, on the basis that some ancient sources suggest there was nothing wrong with the water supply in Laodicea. I think that he is here over-interpreting Strabo's comment in *Geographica* 13.4.14, that the water in Laodicea is 'drinkable' whereas the water at Hierapolis is not, since Strabo clearly states that '[t]he changing of water into stone is said also to be the case with the rivers in Laodiceia' just as it is at Hierapolis. This comment, together with the clear evidence from the ancient pipework, shows that the water was warm and not cold when it arrived in the city, and was indeed heavy with dissolved mineral content. Koester suggests that the metaphor comes from the context of Roman dining, where emetic practice was common, connecting it with the promise of Jesus later in the message to 'come and dine' (3:20): either cold or hot drinks would be welcomed as an accompaniment to a meal, but not lukewarm drinks. Even with this different background, the correction of the popular, surface readings remains: both cold and hot here are seen as positive and connected with practical effects, and lukewarm alone is a negative contrast to both.

action is seen as impossible: 'I will show you my faith by what I do [lit: by my deeds]' (Jas 2:18).[13]

17. The attitude of the Christian community here reflects the attitude of the city in which they live; they emphatically claim to be *rich* and to have *become rich* (AT; the adjective and the verb have the same root *plout*, from which we get 'plutocracy'), and that they *need nothing* (AT), just as the city itself refused any outside assistance in its rebuilding because of its wealth and prosperity. The striking contrast between what they think and the truth that Jesus knows (but which they have not realized) is expressed with poetic force. The three virtues are countered by five failings, each ending with the same sound ('-os'), connected with the Greek *kai*: 'and . . . and . . . and . . . and . . .' The last three of these are both related to the situation of the city (*poor [and] blind [and] naked*; see 'Context' section above) and give the framework for the invitation and promise that follow.

18. Following such harsh judgment, it is again striking that the motivation is not judgment but reform. The revelation of their true state is immediately followed by invitation to remedy the situation – a remedy that leans completely on Jesus' gracious, free offer. There is some irony in the invitation *to buy* from Jesus, since buying is what the city was good at. But there is a strong echo here of the invitation in Isaiah 55:1: 'Come, buy . . . without money'. There is no need to find a specific parallel to the *gold* in the notion of Laodicea being a centre of gold trading; treasure in general is a metaphor in the New Testament for the invaluable news of the kingdom of God (Matt. 13:44 and also 25:14–30), and gold is often a metaphor for our welcoming the kingdom and our faith and trust in the King (1 Pet. 1:7). Being *refined by fire* (AT) suggests not eschatological judgment (as in 1 Cor. 3:13), but the testing through suffering that inevitably comes with being a faithful witness, both for Jesus and for his followers (cf. 2:13 and 12:11).

The *white clothes* would be particularly striking for those familiar with the clothing made from the black sheep's wool of the region –

---

13. James later goes on to use the metaphor of different kinds of spring water to illustrate the problem of inconsistency in the Christian life (Jas 3:12).

though the primary contrast is less in the colour and more with the nakedness that it replaces. In Greek culture, *nakedness* served to show off the glory of the human body, and participants in the games competed naked – hence our word 'gymnast' derives from the Greek for 'naked'. The associated *shame* is in line with Jewish rejection of public nakedness (and hence their objection to the games), but here relates to the Laodiceans' failure to 'put on' the way of living that is true to their faith (cf. Col. 3:9–14). On the significance of white clothing, see the comment on 3:4–5; as the distinctive apparel of the people of God and their representatives we will encounter this again in 4:4; 6:11; 7:9, 13; 19:14. To think of Laodicea as a renowned centre of ophthalmology goes beyond the historical evidence – but this is not necessary to see the relevance of the offer of an *[eye-]salve* to restore their sight, that is, their understanding both of their true state and of what is of true importance before God.

19. The reason for both the stern rebuke and the gracious offer is now reiterated. In an echo of Proverbs 3:11–12, Jesus is emphatic that it is his *love* for them which leads him (negatively) to *rebuke* and (more positively than the translation *discipline* suggests) to 'instruct', two of the four goals of the gift of Scripture for Paul (alongside 'teaching' and 'correcting', 2 Tim. 3:16). If their rebuke has been public and made before the other assemblies in this letter, so is the declaration of Jesus' love for them. Being *earnest* or 'zealous' can often have a negative sense (e.g. Acts 17:5; Rom. 10:2; 1 Cor. 13:4), but it can be used positively as here and in 1 Corinthians 14:1 with a sense of energetic commitment. As in all the messages which contain some rebuke, the appropriate response is to *repent*, to change direction in the light of what has been made clear.

20. The image of Jesus *stand[ing] at the door* has been made famous by Holman Hunt's painting *The Light of the World*, where a crowned and robed Jesus holds a lamp and stands outside a closed door, covered in ivy, with the handle on the inside so that it can be opened only by the person within. Although the messages are written to the assemblies as whole communities, there is a striking individual focus here: *if anyone hears my voice*, reflecting practice in the ancient world of both knocking on the door and calling out to announce one's presence and ask for hospitality. After the powerful assertion of Jesus' authority to 'open doors' in the previous message, it is striking that here Jesus waits patiently for the door to be opened for him. There is no need to see any specific allusion in *com[ing] in and eat[ing]*, whether to the Old Testament (Song 5:2), Jesus' parables (Luke 12:36–37), Roman meals or even early Christian celebration of the Lord's Supper. All derive from the common significance of sharing a meal as expressing friendship and enjoying mutual fellowship.

21. The final victory statement, the promise to *those conquering* (AT), is in some ways the most extravagant, in Jesus' offer to share in his *throne* as a metonym for sharing the exercise of his authority, mirroring the opening status as the 'ruler of . . . creation'. The promise is even more direct than the promise to the disciples to sit on twelve thrones (Matt. 19:28), since it is an offer to share in Jesus' own throne, just as Jesus shares his Father's throne rather than (as elsewhere) sitting at the Father's right hand (Rom. 8:34). This is the only time when the conquering of his followers is placed so directly in parallel with Jesus having *conquered* (AT), mirroring his opening title as the witness who was faithful even to the point of death.

22. See the comment on 2:7.

Theology
The ethos of a city which was proud, satisfied and self-sufficient has infected the followers of Jesus there who exhibit the same qualities. The risen Jesus comes to them in his authority and with his example to reveal to them their true state, which is quite the opposite of what they think. In the only message without specific affirmation, the rebuke is stern. But with the rebuke come three remarkable things. The first is the fresh invitation to receive his offer of grace anew – to discover in him true riches that will stand the test of time, right clothing that will cover their shame, and the restoration of real vision. The second is the affirmation of Jesus' love for his people; it is only because he cares for them that he longs that they should see themselves as they truly are and act accordingly. And the third is his remarkable patience; he stands and waits for them to respond, and will not force himself on them. And if they do respond, they will not only know his friendship and fellowship in the present; they will also come to share in his victory and authority as they learn to be faithful as he was.

Apart from the particular lessons we can learn from each of these seven messages, there are important things to learn from the seven together.

There are clearly different challenges that each community faces, and different virtues that they are each displaying. Yet the distinct communities are rooted in a shared reality – that they are accountable to the same Lord, Jesus who is 'ruler of the kings of the earth' and 'the firstborn from the dead' (1:5), the one who not only ushers in the resurrection life of the age to come, but who is the rightful ruler of the present age, though this is not yet acknowledged by the powers that be. He walks among all the lampstands equally (1:13) and promises that he holds each of the stars firmly in his right hand (1:16).

John further communicates this unity-in-diversity by means of the structure of the seven messages. They share a tightly structured common framework, particularly at the beginning and the end, where much of the wording is identical from one message to the next. And yet the central sections of the messages vary, not only in content but also in structure, and attempts to systematize them further are misguided. Whilst we sit with all other believers equally under the lordship and grace of Christ, his word to us varies as he sees the different challenges we face, and he knows the different exhortations that we need to hear in order to reach the maturity that he longs to work in us (Phil. 1:6). There are times when we – and the communities of faith of which we are a part – will need to hear words of praise and encouragement, or words of rebuke and reformation. Yet God has the same goal for all: that we might know the victory both now and at the End of remaining faithful under pressure, just as Jesus did. As we turn from the specifics of these messages to the cosmic vision of the worship of God in the next two chapters, we will begin to learn more about what victory in the example of Jesus really looks like.

3. JOHN IN THE HEAVENLY THRONE ROOM (4:1 – 5:14)

Context

Following the opening greetings and visionary experience of Revelation 1, the messages in Revelation 2 – 3 looked less apocalyptic and more recognizable as imperial edicts, though with clear connections with what had gone before and anticipations of what is to come later in Revelation. Now, at the start of Revelation 4, there is a dramatic change, and it begins to look like a fully-fledged apocalyptic vision, with John embarked on a heavenly journey and reporting what he sees.

There are obvious contrasts here with what has preceded in the messages. The particular circumstances in the messages give way to a picture painted in grand sweeps across a cosmic canvas. The specifics of time and place fade into the timelessness of God enthroned over all creation. And the variety of challenges and responses facing the different assemblies across the cities gives way to a united scene of praise from both God's people and God's creation.

Yet in other ways the vision that unfolds is the answer to all the questions and issues raised up till now, and the picture of the power and majesty of God sets the wider context that all the followers of Jesus need to see as their own. Why worry about temporary opposition, whether from Jews or pagans, if God is truly enthroned and all-powerful? Why compromise with surrounding culture when the patterns of authority there are just a shadow of the reality of God's authority? And why falter and stumble if this vision represents your inheritance and your destiny?

Despite the generalities of the vision, they are still expressed in particular language which has a background traceable in two major directions. The first is that of the Old Testament Scriptures; John hardly deploys an idea or an image that does not have some Old Testament background, at times from multiple parts of the canon of Scripture. But this is never done slavishly; the language and ideas are always interpreted and adapted to describe this unique and integrated visionary experience. The second source is that of Roman imperial honour and 'worship'; we will find that ideas and practices from the wider world are threaded in and out of the Old Testament language.

Together, this blending of ideas and language in John's description of his divine encounter creates a dazzling vision that fully engages the imagination to its limits.

A. John's encounter with the heavenly throne (4:1–6a)

Comment

1. The temporal marker *After this* does not refer to a sequence of historical events – not least because of the static, permanent sense of the language of Revelation 4 – but to the sequence of visions that John is experiencing 'on the Lord's Day' while he is 'in the Spirit' (1:10). The phrase *I looked* often indicates the start of a new vision or section or a change of focus. The Greek text includes *idou*, 'behold!', here and in verse 2 (not always translated in English versions), drawing attention to the startling and sudden change of focus. The *door standing open* echoes the declaration of Jesus in the message to Philadelphia (3:8); the door being *in heaven* suggests a parallel to Isaiah's vision of God enthroned within the temple (Isa. 6:1–6; (though a contrast with Ezekiel's vision of God enthroned in the open air, Ezek. 1), but is also reminiscent of a Roman imperial

throne room, as are many other details of the vision in these two chapters.

The *voice I had first heard* refers back to 1:10, so this is the voice of the risen Jesus rather than that of an angel. So although this section seems much more like other Jewish 'apocalyptic' texts, which often involved a spiritual journey into the heavenly realms accompanied by an angelical interpreter, John's vision does not consistently conform to this. Despite the mention of an angelic mediator in 1:1, it is Jesus himself who calls John into the heavenlies, and this vision remains uninterpreted. The invitation to *Come up here* suggests that Jesus is already in the throne room, despite also walking among the lampstands which are the assemblies (1:13). We need to read John's cosmic geography as offering metaphors for spiritual realities rather than giving us a cosmic map. The events to take place *after this* have a general temporal sense in that the ultimate horizon is the end of all things. But that does not force us into a purely 'futurist' reading, since the vision in Revelation 12 is a clear reference to the life and ministry of Jesus, which is in the past when John is writing.

2. The call of Jesus means that John is *in the Spirit*, again signalling the close relationship between Jesus and the Spirit that we saw in the giving of the messages. In Jewish apocalypses there are often multiple heavens or layers of heaven, but here the vision is more straightforward. The repeated phrase 'in the Spirit' signals a new phase of the visionary experience here and at 1:10; 17:3; and 21:10, just as it had done for Ezekiel (Ezek. 8:3; 11:5). As this chapter unfolds, we see that the *throne* is the controlling centre of this vision, the term occurring fourteen times in the chapter and all the other features being defined in relation to it ('encircled', 'before', 'around' 'from', and so forth). Despite the vividness of the other elements, and despite the prophetic tradition of both naming and describing God, John resolutely refuses to do either; God is simply the *one seated on the throne* (AT).

3. John consistently avoids offering any actual description of the appearance of God; the only concession he makes to this is to liken the one on the throne to *jasper and carnelian* (AT), two varieties of silica coloured by traces of iron oxide. Jasper could be a range of colours, but was most commonly a reddish-brown, and was a favourite semi-precious gem in antiquity. Carnelian (*sardion*, in some translations 'ruby') was also red in colour, so together they suggest a fiery appearance (cf. Ezek. 1:13, 27). They were the first and last gems on the ephod of the priest which represented the twelve tribes (Exod. 28:17–20) and they characterize the New Jerusalem, especially jasper (21:11, 18–19).

The *rainbow* is a reminder of God's commitment to his creation (Gen. 9:13), reiterated by the presence of the living creatures (see on 4:6 below), and God's judgment on those who 'destroy the earth' (11:18). But the rainbow appears to consist of *emerald*, suggesting its splendour but reminding us that this symbolic vision is literally impossible – rainbows do not look like emeralds!

4. The *twenty-four elders* seated on *thrones* provides one of the more complex images in Revelation; there are questions about their number, their title, their apparel and their action.

First, it is clear that (contrary to some commentators) these are not angelic figures, of which there are many in Revelation that are clearly described as such, but human. In the light of John's extensive use of Old Testament imagery, it is surprising that those doing obeisance in the presence of God are not priests. Yet it is clear that John is working with the original Exodus vision of God's people as a whole being a 'kingdom [of] priests' (Exod. 19:6; Rev. 1:6; 5:10; 20:6), a vision now restored in the new covenant in Jesus (1 Pet. 2:9).[1] The elders already enjoy notable elements of what has been promised to the faithful in the messages: they sit on thrones (3:21), are clothed in white (3:5) and wear wreaths or crowns (*stephanoi*, 2:10). At key points they are closely associated with the redeemed, joining with their praise (7:9–11), celebrating both the anticipation (11:15–18) and (in voices fused with those of all God's people) the realization (19:4–8) of God's final victory – though they are notably absent from the New Jerusalem. They are therefore best understood as the *representatives* of the people of God in the presence of God, in anticipation of the End when all the redeemed, raised from the dead,

---

1. It is interesting to note that, in sharp contrast to the letter to the Hebrews, the imagery of Jesus as priest is almost completely absent from Revelation – the exception being aspects of his appearance in the opening vision of chapter 1.

are themselves in God's presence in the New Jerusalem.[2] This interpretation is confirmed by noticing that the term 'elder' occurs twelve times in Revelation.[3]

Why, then, are there twenty-four? One suggestion is that God's people are now comprised of those represented by the twelve tribes whose names are written on the gates of the New Jerusalem (21:12) together with the twelve apostles whose names are written on the foundations (21:14), corresponding to the first covenant with God's Jewish people and the new covenant with (Gentile) humanity. This has two major problems: first, the apostles are themselves Jewish, so cannot represent in any sense the 'non-Jewish' people of God as distinct from the Jewish people of God;[4] and, second, throughout the New Testament, including in Revelation, Jews and Gentiles together form one single, united people of God, not a people in two halves (Eph. 2:14–18; see comments on Rev. 7:1 – 8:1). More convincing is their correspondence to the twenty-four divisions of the Levitical priesthood (1 Chr. 24:7–18) and the temple musicians (1 Chr. 25:9–31); while not forming a distinct caste of priests, the elders do exercise the priestly functions of the people of God, including offering up prayers (5:8; 8:3). But the number also corresponds to the number of attendants (*lictors*) who functioned as assistants and bodyguards to consuls and emperors, carrying the

---

2. If this interpretation is correct, then the line in the final verse of Charles Wesley's hymn 'Love Divine' needs revision. It suggests that we will 'cast our crowns before thee' at the End when 'in heaven we take our place'. Revelation 4 suggests that we join in doing this with the elders now, whenever we join in the heavenly praise of God.

3. In 4:4, 10; 5:5, 6, 8, 11, 14; 7:11, 13; 11:16; 14:3; and 19:4. The occurrences in 5:5 and 7:13 mention 'one of the elders'; the other ten references are to the elders as a group around the throne. In seven of these, the elders are paired with the living creatures (5:6, 8, 11, 14; 7:11; 14:3; and 19:4), though the pairing is never worded the same way twice – typical of John's style of repetition-with-variation.

4. Notice that Paul uses 'Israel' to refer to both Jewish and non-Jewish followers of Jesus quite clearly in Gal. 6:16 and (in my view) also in Rom. 11:26.

bundles of rods (*fasces*) which included an axe to symbolize the *ius gladii*, the emperor's power over life and death in the right to exercise capital punishment. Emperors were originally entitled to have twelve *lictors* attending them, but Domitian doubled that number to twenty-four.[5]

Although the apparel of angelic beings and, possibly, of the high priest in the Old Testament (who wore linen), being *dressed in white* is primarily a pagan habit for worship, white being associated with purity, holiness and honour (see comment on 3:4–5). In this eastern part of the empire, as far back as the time of Alexander the Great, we know of elders of cities, the leading and prominent citizens, coming as delegates before approaching rulers, dressed in white and wearing gold wreaths (crowns) and bowing, casting their crowns before them to symbolize the submission of their city to that ruler's power.

5. Having described the elders around the throne, John's attention turns to what issues *from the throne* – and his language shifts away from that of his culture back to biblical imagery. The *lightning, rumblings and peals of thunder* are exactly what accompanied God's fiery presence on Sinai in Exodus 19:16 (recalled in Ps. 77:18). The *seven lamps of fire* (AT) which burn before the throne are described as the *seven spirits of God*, the second of four occurrences of this phrase which must be a circumlocution for the Holy Spirit (see comment on 1:4). That they are lamps *of fire* (AT) connects with the Pentecost imagery of the Spirit as tongues of fire on the heads of the disciples (Acts 2:3) and the promise by John the Baptist that Jesus would

---

5. Domitian made this change early in his reign, changing from the tradition that emperors have twelve lictors and reverting to the previous practice of dictators who had twenty-four. This practice was continued by subsequent emperors who retained the twenty-four. There is no need to reject some correspondence here on the basis that the elders around the throne do not carry the equipment of the *lictors*. John characteristically fuses symbolism from different contexts, and it is perfectly possible that to John and his readers the twenty-four elders would have suggested *both* the Jewish priestly attendants in God's presence *and* the imperial bodyguards symbolizing might and majesty.

baptize 'with the Holy Spirit and fire' (Matt. 3:11; Luke 3:16). It perhaps also suggests the work of the Spirit as testing, refining and purifying. The image relates to the seven burning lamps that stood in front of the Holy of Holies in the wilderness tabernacle (Exod. 25:37; 27:21) and in the second temple; Revelation is here suggesting a theological interpretation of the temple symbolism.

6a. The presence of the *sea of glass* before the throne is at first surprising, since Revelation picks up from the Old Testament the negative connotations of the sea as symbolizing chaos and disorder and (sometimes symbolizing the nations of the world) a source of evil and opposition to God (see comment on 13:1). For that reason, at the End, 'there was no longer any sea' (21:1). The image here has some connection with the idea of the waters 'above the vault' that separated them from the waters below (Gen. 1:6–7), an idea alluded to in the clear blue 'pavement' beneath God's feet (Exod. 24:10) and the 'crystal vault' in Ezekiel's vision of the throne chariot (Ezek. 1:22). But a more direct allusion is to the bronze 'sea' that stood in front of Solomon's temple (1 Kgs 7:23–26; 2 Chr. 4:2–5). Revelation is again offering a theological interpretation of the symbolism of the temple: that the 'sea' represented heavenly reality which connected with both the creation narrative and the encounter with God at Sinai.

B. John's encounter with the heavenly worship (4:6b–11)

Having described the static elements which he sees on coming through the door in heaven, John now describes the activity that is happening there.

6b–8. Though it is halfway through the verse, most English translations note the change of focus here with a paragraph break. John's description has not been systematic, in that having described what was around the throne and in front of it, he now returns to what was *in the centre*. The language is difficult here, meaning literally 'in the midst of the throne and circling the throne', which is perhaps best understood as 'circling the throne at the very centre'. The *living creatures* (lit. 'living [ones]') allude in general to the creation account (Gen. 1:20, 24, 28) and so represent the created order, but in their details to Ezekiel's vision in Ezekiel 1:4–14. In John's vision, the Old Testament imagery is never simply incorporated, but is adapted and reconfigured. Here, the living creatures are around the throne rather than supporting it, and rather than being in human form but with four faces, they take the four forms mentioned in Ezekiel, of a *lion*, an *ox*, a *human* (AT) and a *flying eagle*. Some commentators suggest that these are zodiacal images, but the eagle does not fit with this. The four have traditionally been associated with the four Gospels, but there is no obvious connection in the text itself.

Rather, the variety of creatures suggests the different forms of life in the creation accounts, so together they represent the created world directed in praise to God (cf. Ps. 19:1). Their *six wings* alludes to the seraphim of Isaiah 6 rather than Ezekiel (whose living creatures have four wings), and having *eyes all round* suggests their constant alertness and complete vision of the world. They later not only continuously worship, but also enact the delegated authority of God in calling out the four horsemen (Rev. 6) and passing on the seven golden bowls (15:7). Here is all creation in both the praise and the service of God. They *never stop* (lit. 'have no rest from') saying or singing (the term *legontes* is used for both) the 'trisagion' from Isaiah 6:3, *Holy, holy, holy*, which quickly became a standard element of Christian liturgical worship. The title *Lord God Almighty* here is the second of seven occurrences in Revelation.[6] In the Old Testament, it combines the name of Israel's God ('Yahweh') with the title *ṣĕbā'ôt*, meaning 'commander of the armies [of heaven]'. God as a mighty warrior (or, perhaps, 'warrior-in-chief') serves as a metaphor for his power over all creation. The threefold *who was, and is, and is to come* is a change from the similar title in 1:4 emphasizing the extent of his power across time – from past, through the present, and into the future.

---

6. 1:8; 4:8; 11:17; 15:3; 16:7; 19:6; and 21:22. The first of these is less clear in English translations than in the Greek, where the additional title 'who is, who was, who is coming' (AT) is inserted in the middle of exactly the same phrase that occurs in the other six places; we might translate lit.: 'The Lord God (who is, who was, who is coming) Almighty'. The shorter phrase 'God Almighty' occurs twice, in 16:14 and 19:15.

9–11. Though translated in the present tense in English, the description of the praise of the living creatures *whenever [they] give* is in the future tense in Greek, which has led some to see this as eschatological. But there are so many pointers to the transcendence of time in this scene that this is not a plausible reading; the action should be interpreted as taking place as John is looking on. The giving of *glory, honour and thanks* belongs naturally together, but they are in fact distinct elements of praise. God's glory in the Old Testament is communicated with the metaphor of weight, substance and significance in the Hebrew term *kābôd*. The idea of *honour* suggests a right recognition of this, and has a parallel in the second line of the Lord's prayer, in which we pray that God's holiness might be recognized by others. And we offer *thanks* specifically in gratitude for what God has done for us in giving us life.

The expression of worship here offers several direct counterpoints to the honours given to the emperor. As noted on verse 4, to *cast their crowns* (AT) before a ruler was to signal recognition of that ruler's authority and a submission to the ruler; gold wreaths or crowns were even laid before imperial statues as a symbolic gesture.[7] The acclamation that God is *worthy* (*axios*) occurs nowhere else in biblical worship of God (where English translations describe God as 'worthy of praise', they use a different term), but belongs to acclamation of the emperor whenever his acts of beneficence match the power of his office. The double title *Lord and God* was one that many emperors were fond of, even though the senate did not allow the formal adoption of the title 'god' for emperors while they lived. Suetonius tells us that Domitian insisted on formal adoption of this double title in his lifetime, though this is not supported by any inscriptional or numismatic (coins) evidence. The use of the double title was more often an informal way for enthusiastic supporters to endear themselves to imperial power.[8] But of course the claim made for God far outstrips anything that any human ruler could claim. Even if an emperor could claim some

---

7. Detailed references to these practices can be found in Koester (2), p. 365, and Aune, *Apocalypticism*, p. 107.

8. See the (sarcastic?) examples in Martial, *Epigrams* 5.8 and 7.34.

kind of power to rule over the whole (known) world, none could claim to be the origin of that world. Revelation here reiterates the creation language of John 1, that all of creation came into being *by your will* and by the word of God's command. The Greek text has the odd word order *existed and were created* (AT), which most English translations change to its more logical reverse order – but this is just poetic expression rather than logical or sequential. It is not just the prosperity of the world that is owed to God as Lord, but its very existence.

Theology
John here offers a dazzling vision of God which pushes the boundaries of human imagination in its metaphorical description. John's own language reflects this; in contrast with what has gone before, he now repeatedly reaches for 'as' and 'was like' and 'had the appearance of'. As elsewhere in Scripture, literal description of God is not possible; God is unknowable even though he has graciously revealed himself to us. Even John's grammar appears to reflect this; the throne itself is described without using finite verbs, and all in the nominative case, but when John turns to the things around the throne, he moves into the accusative case. Even if some features of this heavenly scene can be described as objects that John can see and apprehend, the throne and the one seated there are not objects to be perceived and analysed.

Yet within this kaleidoscope of language, two threads are clearly woven into the visionary fabric. The first – the warp threads which give structure – is the Old Testament theology of God as the supreme Creator and the source of all there is. We see this in the image of the rainbow and in the living creatures, as well as in the acclamations of worship; Revelation stands in continuity with the scriptural understanding of God as Creator and the repeated re-emergence of that theme in the life of his people and their encounters with God in the different stages of their pilgrimage. This transforms not only our understanding of God, but also our understanding of the world. It is neither an accident of self-generation to be trivialized, nor a resource to be exploited, but an expression of the creative love of God which continually points to it source. And if God is Creator of the world, he is also the Creator of his own people, and so they owe him not only glory and honour but also gratitude and allegiance.

The second thread – the weft, woven in out of the warp threads – is the imagery of imperial obeisance. Whatever honours and acclaim are given to those with human power – whether it is the wearing of white, the prostration, the casting of crowns, the cry of 'worthy' – they really belong to God, since the power that is being recognized is God's power which he shares. Jesus' words to Pilate, 'You would have no power over me if it were not given to you from above' (John 19:11), are, refracted through this visionary lens, spoken to all human power. Power that demands allegiance over against or ahead of the God and Father of the Lord Jesus Christ is speaking a lie and based on deceit; if we are tempted to believe it, we need our eyes opened to the true source of all things. God alone is worthy of our unceasing praise, our unswerving loyalty and our profound gratitude.

C. John sees the scroll and the lamb (5:1–7)

Comment

1. The repeated phrase *Then I saw* (*kai eidon*) is a frequent marker of a new scene, new characters or new events within a vision. The mention of the *right hand* of the one on the throne is one of the very few anthropomorphisms of God in Revelation. In the Old Testament, the right hand stands for the authority to bless (Gen. 48:14), and signifies strength and conquering power (Exod. 15:6, 12); it is in his 'right hand' that Jesus holds the stars in Revelation 1 and with which he reaches out to John to reassure him (1:16–17). The scroll is *in* the right hand in most English translations, but the Greek uses *epi*, upon, suggesting that the scroll is offered in God's opened hand for someone to take.

The scroll has been written *on both sides*, literally 'within' and 'on the back'. Papyrus scrolls in the first century would normally have been written on one side only (*recto*), along the lines of the papyrus stems that formed that side of the document. A scroll written on both sides (*recto* and *verso*) could be an indication of the poverty of the writer who could not afford another or a longer scroll, or it could be to give a summary of the contents of the scroll prior to unsealing.

Neither of these is likely here; God is not poor, and the emphasis in the following narrative is that no-one can read the scroll until it is unsealed. The most likely allusion is to the scroll in Ezekiel 2:9–10 which is offered, unrolled, to Ezekiel, and 'on both sides of it were written words of lament and mourning and woe'. Although there is both judgment and woe in what follows in Revelation, there is no need to assume that what is written on this scroll matches that in Ezekiel, given the way that John adapts his Old Testament allusions.

The scroll being *sealed with seven seals* has been much debated. There is little evidence for the practice in the first century of sealing a scroll part way through rolling it so that the breaking of each seal reveals a section of the scroll – besides, it would then not be possible to see that there were seven seals, since all but the last would be wrapped in the scroll. But there is good attestation of the practice of sealing a rolled scroll with seven seals, often with the seals of seven independent witnesses, so that they can each testify that the scroll has not been previously opened. Examples of this are found in Roman wills, especially the wills of emperors (such as Augustus and Vespasian), but also important edicts, and in the sealing of Jewish magical papyri. There is no need to identify the scroll here with any one of these examples. The metaphorical import of the image is that the scroll is completely sealed and unreadable except by the proper authority. As the plot of Revelation unfolds, it becomes clear that the scroll reveals God's will (i.e. his intention) for the world, which includes both judgment and redemption – and it is poignant that this will can only be opened following death: the death of the lamb.

On the relation between this scroll and the 'little scroll' of Revelation 10, see the comment on 10:2.

2. *And I saw* introduces a new character, a *mighty angel* whom we have not previously met and who does not obviously appear again (the angels in 10:1 and 18:21 seem to be different characters). Given his might or strength, it is no surprise that he proclaims *in a loud voice*; his rhetorical question is characteristic of the book (cf. 6:17; 7:13; 13:4; 15:4), and such questions often lead to further revelation. The angel's question once more uses the Roman virtue of being *worthy* regarding who can open the seal; it is striking that, with witness or testimony such a consistent feature of Revelation, the idea does not occur here, suggesting there is no exact correlation with (for example) a Roman will, which would need witnesses to break its seals.

3-4. The lack of anyone *in heaven or on earth or under the earth* uses the traditional three-tiered view of the universe, not to be taken literally but to emphasize that there is no-one in all the cosmos who can open the scroll. Neither can anyone 'look at' or 'see' it, which we must take as meaning *look inside* it, that is, read what it says and disclose the contents. John is overcome with grief – he 'wept much', which we might colloquially take as meaning he *wept and wept* – because no-one is able to unlock the secrets of God's plan and intention for the world, so that humanity remains in ignorance. His repetition of the key ideas of *worthy*, *open[ing] the scroll* and *look[ing] inside* reinforce the dramatic crisis that the sealed scroll represents.

5. One of the elders here (and in 7:13–14) has a minor role as an accompanying interpreter for John, as do the angels in 19:9 and 21:9–10. But for most of Revelation and its visions, John is largely unaccompanied, in contrast to many contemporary Jewish apocalyptic texts. He no longer needs to *weep* out of frustration at the mystery of God's purposes, since there is one who is able to *open the scroll*. The lion features frequently in the Old Testament as a symbol of destructive power and aggression, as it tears its prey apart; the image of the *Lion of the tribe of Judah* seems to come from the messianic oracle of Moses to the tribe of Judah in Genesis 49:9–12, where Judah is like a fierce lion and the one who will rule over the nations. The oracle includes the mention of the donkey and colt, which become the signs of the Messiah in Zechariah 9:9 that the Gospel writers draw on at Palm Sunday, and of the ruler's 'robe[s] dipped in [the] blood [of grapes]', which John alludes to in Revelation 19:13. The *Root of David* is an adaptation of another messianic title from Isaiah 11:10, the 'Root of [David's father] Jesse', which has an international dimension as he not only draws the nations but also gathers God's people back from exile to their homeland. In another of Revelation's reversals of the expected order, he can *open the scroll and its seven seals*, that is, he can open the scroll *by* breaking the seals. This person is now able to understand God's purposes and make them known because he has *conquered* (AT) – he has already done what the readers of the seven messages were repeatedly encouraged to do.

6–7. In response to the elder's invitation to 'Look!' (AT) in the previous verse, John reports what he *saw* – the most significant and central image in the whole of the book of Revelation, and (arguably) in the whole New Testament. At a number of key moments, John 'hears' the symbolic significance of something, and then (turns and) sees its symbolic meaning. So in Revelation 1 he hears the 'loud voice' of God 'like a trumpet' and turns to see the one like a son of man, and in Revelation 7 he will hear God's people counted out and then turn to see an uncountable crowd. Here he has heard of the 'Lion of the tribe of Judah' and he sees that it is a *Lamb*.[9] The word order in Greek reinforces the importance of this figure: 'in the midst of the throne, and the four living creatures, and in the midst of the elders, a Lamb standing . . .' We will learn that, in fact, this figure stands at the centre of creation. Most English translations describe the lamb as 'in front of' or 'between' the throne and the living creatures, but John's language does not make the position clear; the lamb appears to be at the centre of the throne scene (cf. 7:17, 'in the centre of the throne', AT), and we later find that the throne is 'of God and of the Lamb' (22:3). This corresponds visually with the language of Jesus in 3:21: 'I have conquered and sat down with my Father on his throne' (AT).

It is startling that John has not mentioned this central figure previously, and even more startling is the contrast with the statement of the elder: the powerful figure of a lion is in stark contrast to the vulnerability of the lamb. The lamb appears *as if it had been slain*, not in the sense of mere pretence, but it actually bears the marks of having been slaughtered. This connects with three ideas from the Old Testament. First, the proverbial sense of the vulnerability of lambs as they are slaughtered finds particular expression in Isaiah 53:7, the suffering servant who is wounded for

---

9. The word John uses for 'lamb' here is a diminutive form *arnion*, found elsewhere only in John 21:15, rather than the more usual *arēn/arnos* or *amnos* (used in e.g. Luke 10:3 and John 1:36 respectively). There does not appear to be any particular significance to this, and the diminutive had lost its significance in Greek by now, so there is no reason to think it means 'little lamb'.

our healing – perhaps the most important text used by the writers of the New Testament for understanding Jesus' death. Second, the slaughtered lamb in the exodus (Exod. 12:6) protects God's people from death and enables them to be set free from slavery to live in the Promised Land. The exodus motif is repeated in the later image of being carried on eagles' wings (Rev. 12:14; Exod. 19:4) and in the redeemed singing the 'song of . . . Moses and of the Lamb' (Rev. 15:2–4; Exod. 15). Third, the image recalls the slaughtering of lambs (amongst other animals) in the sacrifice of atonement; the later language of 5:9–10 recalls the opening statement in 1:5–6. Jesus 'has freed us *from our sins* by his blood, and has made us to be a kingdom and priests to serve his God and Father' (emphasis added).

The contrast between strength and weakness is continued in the description that the lamb *had seven horns*. Horns were symbolic of strength and honour (Ps. 89:17, 24) and particularly associated with the Davidic king (1 Sam. 2:10) and hoped-for salvation (Luke 1:69). The lamb thus has the power to save, but has done this through the weakness of self-sacrifice. The *seven eyes* of the lamb recall the stone with seven eyes given to the high priest Joshua (in Greek 'Jesus') in Zechariah 3:9; the image suggests the ability to see all things, something attributed to God (2 Chr. 16:9) and earlier claimed by Jesus (Rev. 2:23). These eyes are also the *seven spirits of God* previously mentioned in 1:4; 3:1; and 4:5. Although also described as seven lamps in 4:5, this should be understood as a circumlocution for the Holy Spirit (see comment on 1:4). By identifying the Spirit with the eyes of the lamb that are *sent out into all the earth*, Revelation is agreeing with Jesus' teaching in John's Gospel (John 15:26) that the Spirit is sent by Jesus from the Father, is both the 'Spirit of God' and the 'Spirit of Jesus' (Acts 16:7; Phil. 1:19), and is now the presence of God and Jesus at work in the world.

The lamb now *[takes] the scroll* from the one on the throne who has held it out. The verb here is in the perfect tense rather than the usual aorist for past action, and the most likely reason is that John is pointing to this as the climax of the scene and its action. The lamb is worthy to take, and therefore to open, the scroll and reveal its contents, and the scene of praise which now follows both celebrates this and explains why it is the case.

Theology

If the previous scene in Revelation 4 was one of dazzling splendour, then its development so far in Revelation 5 is one of astonishing drama. The appearance of the scroll causes John to be overcome with grief and frustration. Here before him, it seems, is the mysterious will of God for his creation, and yet it remains a mystery – firmly and decisively sealed, so that no-one is able to read it and make sense of it. Yet almost immediately another figure appears in the drama, the lion who looks like a lamb. Nowhere in the text of Revelation is the lamb explicitly identified with the figure of Jesus (itself remarkable), but there is no doubting the identification from both the theological and the textual parallels. Here is the one who fulfils the hopes of God's people Israel, as the promised anointed Davidic king who was to come. Here is one who is fierce and powerful enough to conquer their enemies and tear them apart. And yet when John sees him, he is like a weak and vulnerable lamb who has been slaughtered, just like the Passover lamb eaten by the people, the suffering servant who was 'wounded for our transgressions' and the lamb offered as an atoning sacrifice. He is the one who *was* slain, but *now* stands, shares the throne with God and with him sends the Spirit to enact his will on earth. Here we have the most explicit (and perhaps the most complex) trinitarian statement in the whole New Testament. John expresses his theological understanding by the juxtaposition of a series of (sometimes sharply contrasting) images. How we relate and resolve these images – especially the contrast between the lion and the lamb, and the images of power and weakness, of victory and suffering – will be key to our reading of the whole book.

D. The worship of the lamb (5:8–14)

Comment

8. It is at the moment when he *took the scroll* (AT; rather than after it, as implied by some translations) that the chorus of praise breaks out. The *four living creatures* and the *elders*, who have previously been prostrate before the one seated on the throne, now offer exactly the same worship to *the Lamb*. It was customary in the first century to stand for prayer, both in Greco-Roman practice and for Jews and

Christians (Luke 18:11; 1 Tim. 2:8), so this prostration demonstrates extreme reverence or urgent supplication. Although unclear in some translations, it is the elders (and not the living creatures) who *each . . . had a harp*; the seven-stringed harp or *kithara* was widely used, but here the allusion is to the depiction of the Levites in 1 Chronicles 24 – 25 (see comment on 4:4). To hold and play harps and to hold the bowls of incense, all while prostrated, is impossible; the symbolic significance is of the elders performing priestly acts as representatives of the priestly people of God. *Bowls* were in common use in both Greco-Roman and Jewish worship, usually wide and shallow in form; they were used to hold wine, flour or incense. The most valuable were made of *gold*. The burning of *incense* was not part of early Christian worship and was explicitly rejected by some in the early second century, so we are here offered a metaphor about prayer, not an insight into early Christian devotional practice. The idea of prayer as metaphorical incense draws on Psalm 141:2, 'May my prayer be set before you like incense', and the *prayers of the saints* (AT) will come to include (but are not limited to) the cries for deliverance and justice in 6:9–11; the two are combined in 8:4–5. The term *saints* (AT; *hagioi*, 'holy ones') occurs fourteen times in Revelation,[10] as does the term 'servants', another designation for the people of God (see comment on 1:1–2).

9–10. The idea of *[singing] a new song* comes primarily from Psalm 96:1 and 98:1 (though it is also found in Pss 33:3; 144:9; 149:1; Isa. 42:10) and is found again on the lips of the redeemed in Revelation 14:3. This is not particularly a song of victory, but a fresh song of celebration of God's mighty deeds of salvation for his people, especially in the context of God as Lord over the whole earth. In the light of Revelation's extensive use of the Old Testament, it is reading too much into this phrase to suggest that the 'newness' relates to the new salvation in Jesus, the lamb; the God of Israel has constantly been giving of himself to his people, even as they have turned from him, and this finds its fullest expression in the self-giving of the lamb. It is not clear whether John hears a

---

10. *Hagioi* occurs in 5:8; 8:3, 4; 11:18; 13:7, 10; 14:10, 12; 16:6; 17:6; 18:20, 24; 19:8; and 20:9.

song, a chant or a said acclamation; the word translated *saying* (*legontes*) is used in Revelation to introduce direct speech of any kind.

Although key ideas in this praise come from the Old Testament, the language of *worthy* and the repetition of honorific terms are (as in Rev. 4) reminiscent of the acclamations given to the emperor. The praise now makes explicit the connection between the lamb being *slain* and his being worthy, and combines the language of the sacrificial system (*blood*) with the distinct election of God's people (Ps. 74:2, 'Remember the people you purchased long ago . . . whom you redeemed'). If God's saving action has been redefined in the sacrifice of the lamb, the extent of God's people has also been redefined. The fourfold phrase *[from] every tribe and language and people and nation* combines the language of the genealogy of the peoples of the world from Genesis 10:31 ('tribes, tongues, territories and nations' [AT]) with the language of distinct election of Israel from Exodus 19:5 ('out of all nations you will be my treasured possession') which is echoed in the restoration promise of Ezekiel 36:24. The people purchased by the blood of the lamb are to be distinct, but instead of being separated from all the other nations as one nation, they are now members of every nation on earth. This fourfold phrase is repeated seven times in Revelation, though never in exactly the same form twice (see table 4).

Table 4: The seven occurrences of the fourfold phrase

Verse	5:9	7:9	10:11	11:9	13:7	14:6	17:15
Form	tribe	nation	peoples	peoples	tribes	nation	peoples
	language	tribes	nations	tribes	people	tribe	multitudes
	people	peoples	languages	language	language	language	nations
	nation	languages	kings	nations	nation	people	languages

The three terms 'language(s)', 'people(s)' and 'nation(s)' are included each time, while the fourth term varies between 'tribe(s)' (five times), 'kings' (once) and 'multitudes' (once).

The song repeats the affirmation from 1:6 that Jesus, the lamb, has made the people to be *a kingdom and priests*, but adds the future promise that they will *reign on the earth*.[11] This fulfils the creation intention that humanity should exercise dominion over the earth (Gen. 1:26) and points to the final victory at the End. The verb 'to reign' is used seven times (5:10; 11:15, 17; 19:6; 20:4, 6; 22:5), always of God, the lamb and his followers, and anticipates their shared reign in the New Jerusalem.

11–12. Again, John combines the two senses as he *looked and heard* the song of the angels and of all creation. He gives the number of them as *myriads of myriads and thousands of thousands* (AT), once again in the reverse order from what we might have expected – but the significance of this number is, paradoxically, that there are too many to count. Once more, it is striking that the lamb is given the praise that was previously given to the one on the throne; the seven terms suggest a completeness or totality of affirmation, and they include within them the three terms (*glory* and *honour* and *power*, in reverse order this time) of acclamation given in 4:11. The significance of these terms rests not so much in their individual meaning as in their cumulative impact.

13–14. John's cosmic geography breaks down here, as what he now hears is what is happening not simply in one place or in one part of creation, but *in heaven and on earth and under the earth and on the sea*, reflecting the language of the creation narratives that refer to the sky (heavens), earth and sea as the three realms of the created order. To emphasize this comprehensiveness, John's phrase contains the redundancy of specifying *all that is within them* (AT) when he has already mentioned *every creature*. Having heard two stanzas of praise to the one on the throne and two stanzas of praise to the lamb, John now hears the two praised as one, with acclamation being given to *the one on the throne and to the Lamb* (AT), so that they are both distinct and yet indistinguishable. The four terms of acclamation echo the three terms addressed to God in Revelation 4, adding *praise*, one of the other four terms addressed to the lamb. As representatives of the creation, the living creatures simply add their *Amen* to what

---

11. Some manuscripts have this in the present tense, 'they are reigning on the earth', but that hardly fits with what the following chapters say about the present condition or the future hope of God's people.

the creation itself is affirming (the third of seven 'Amen's declared in the book), and as representatives of the people of God, the elders *[fall] down and worship.*

Theology

The language of worship here does a remarkable thing in identifying the lamb as equal with the one on the throne in deserving worship and adulation, in a text which implicitly refutes the claims of human figures to be deserving of such obeisance. Because of this, it is reasonable to claim that it offers us the highest possible christological understanding in the whole New Testament: what we can say of God in worship, we can say of Jesus. The two figures of the one seated on the throne and the lamb are thus characterized as God the Creator and God the Redeemer. These figures are never quite merged and remain distinct within the narrative of Revelation, and, unlike the association of the Word with the work of creation in John's Gospel, their roles also remain distinct. But in the final hymn of praise, the worship is given to the two as if they were one.

The placing of these scenes of heavenly worship following on from the royal proclamations to the assemblies in the seven cities has a powerful rhetorical impact. The followers of Jesus might be facing particular challenges and opportunities, located within their own cultural and physical contexts, yet the context for all their struggles is this cosmic vision of the praise of God and of the lamb. Where they might feel as though they are 'swimming against the tide' in terms of dissenting from the cultural norms of their society – in their non-participation in the trade guilds with their associated deities, in their moral stance and in their reluctance to participate in the imperial cult – the juxtaposition of Revelation 4 – 5 offers a startling reconfiguration of their world. All of creation is caught up, not in obeisance to the emperor, but in the worship of the God and Father of Jesus, and of the lamb, and any who are not taken up with this are, in fact, in the minority. It is an extraordinary cultural and spiritual counter-claim to the majority perception of reality. And in its emotive extravagance, this vision of worship is not offered as a rational fact, but as a compelling call for all readers to join in themselves.

It is also important to note that, while there are elements that look to the future restoration and recreation of the world, this is primarily a vision of how things are now, and a reality in which readers can participate now, as an anticipation of the reality that all will one day see clearly.

4. THE OPENING OF THE SEVEN SEALS
(6:1–17)

Context

The image of 'four horsemen of the apocalypse' offers a powerful symbol of global destruction and chaos, and the continued popularity of the idea in contemporary culture is testimony to the rhetorical force of Revelation's imagery and the grip it has on the imagination. The scenes we see unveiled in this chapter have often been interpreted as portraying events set in an 'end times' future, still yet to happen, when God unleashes his vengeance on a rebellious world. But we need to note some important features of this series of events.

The most obvious is the way that it correlates with the two other series of 'sevens', the seven trumpets introduced in 8:6 and the seven bowls introduced in 15:1 (see table 5 overleaf).

There are striking similarities between the three series, not least that each has a 4/3 structure, with the first four in each series being recounted using a consistent formula, while the last three items have more variation both within and between them. In some respects, the trumpets and the bowls are more similar, each including elements

Table 5: The three sequences of seven seals, trumpets and bowls

Seven seals (6:1–17 and 8:1)	Seven trumpets (8:6 – 9:21 and 11:15–19)	Seven bowls (15:1 – 16:21)
1. White horse	1. A third of earth scorched	1. Painful sores
2. Red horse	2. A third of the sea to blood	2. The sea turns to blood
3. Black horse	3. A third of the waters turn bitter	3. The rivers turn to blood (angelic interjection)
4. Pale horse	4. The sun a third darkened	4. The sun scorches
5. The martyrs under the throne	5. The locust plague	5. Total darkness
6. The great earthquake	6. The fiendish cavalry	6. Frog-like demons
Interlude: 144,000 sealed and a great multitude	Interlude: eating the scroll and the two witnesses	(Call to battle)
7. Silence in heaven	7. The kingdom has come	7. 'It is done': destruction of Babylon

from the plagues of Egypt in Exodus 7 – 11, and the bowls often describing a more severe version of what we saw in the respective trumpets. But the sequences of the seals and the trumpets share the feature of having a significant interlude between the sixth and the seventh in each series. Most significantly, each series finishes with a clear proclamation of the End – silence in the seals sequence, the kingdom of this world becoming the kingdom of God in the trumpets sequence, and the triumphal cry 'It is done!' in the bowls sequence.

We also need to note the way God's sovereignty is depicted in these series. After the exaltation of God's majesty in the praise scenes in Revelation 4 – 5, there is no doubt that Revelation sees God not only as sovereign, but as *the* sovereign. Yet that sovereignty is expressed in quite circumspect terms as the chaos is unleashed – John hears the living creatures (rather than God) give the command to 'Come!' to each of the four horsemen, and John uses the 'divine passive' ('there were given') to describe their powers. This is very far from a depiction of God vengefully inflicting punishment on the world in a deliberate and vindictive way. In order to see God's direct action and voice, we have to wait until Revelation 21; his word then is 'I am making everything new!', and his action is to wipe away tears (21:4–5).

A. The first four seals are broken: the four horsemen (6:1–8)

Comment

1. *And I saw* (AT) indicates a new stage in the vision, though not a major change of focus; John is still 'in the Spirit' in the heavenly throne room, watching as the *Lamb opened one* [AT; i.e. the first] *of the seven seals.*[1] The spatial contrast between 'heaven' and 'earth' is not so much about different locations as about different aspects of reality. It is not God, but *one of the . . . living creatures* who issues the command to *Come!*, though it speaks with the thunder associated with God and his throne. The command is to the horseman and not (as some early manuscripts have it) an invitation to John to 'come and see'.

2. As the interplay between John's hearing and looking continues, *And I saw . . .* (AT) once again introduces a new character, the first of the four *horse[s]* and their *rider[s].* The description of the four horses is closely related to the four horses of Zechariah 1:8–11 and 6:1–7. In the first text, they are described as 'the ones the LORD has sent to go throughout the earth' (Zech. 1:10) by the angel who accompanies them; in the second, they are drawing war chariots, and are described by the angel as 'the four spirits of heaven, going out from standing in the presence of the Lord of the whole world' (Zech. 6:5). The context in Zechariah is the early years of the return of the Jewish people from exile in Babylon, when God's people are searching for security in an uncertain world.

The white colour of the first horse immediately calls to mind the white garments of the saints and elders (3:4; 4:4) and the association

---

1. This phrase 'And I saw' is repeated at 6:12 (AT), before the more major change in focus introduced by 'After this I saw' in 7:1 and 7:9.

with both the vision of Jesus in Revelation 1 ('his hair was white like wool', 1:14, AT) and the image of the rider in Revelation 19. The language of 'conquering' has also been associated with both the lamb (5:5) and his followers. For this reason, many commentators in the past have considered this first rider to be a depiction of Jesus that contrasts with the three who follow.

Yet these four are clearly to be taken together, as is shown both by the use of imagery from Zechariah and the parallels between the seals, the trumpets and the bowls. Moreover, the *bow* is never associated with Jesus, but is the common symbol associated with Apollo, and the mythology of Apollo is an important background to the key passage of Revelation in chapter 12. If this rider suggests an Apollo-like figure, it stands for pagan religion as it captures the hearts and minds of the peoples of the world. An alternative possibility is seeing a connection with the Parthians; they were a constant threat to those who lived in the east of the empire, were known for their use of bows and always included sacred white horses in their cavalry. In this case, the first horse symbolizes warfare in general, and fits even more closely with the other three that follow. The 'divine passive', *he was given a crown*, makes it clear that whatever power this rider has is derivative, and whatever deception or havoc he unleashes, God remains sovereign.

3–4. Although included in English translations for clarity, *the Lamb* is not mentioned in the repeated formula introducing the next four seals: 'when he opened the [nth] seal'. Colours are used with a range of meanings in Revelation, and here the *fiery red* of the second horse suggests the bloodshed it brings with it. If the first horse symbolized conquest (either by a foreign religion or a foreign nation – the two went hand in hand), then the second symbolizes the means by which such conquest happens: warfare. Once again, the 'divine passive' is used as the horse's rider *is given* both the *power to remove peace* and *a great sword* (AT). Though peace (with God and others) is seen as a major blessing of both old and new covenants, false claims of peace are deceptive and must be unmasked. Paul's warning that 'destruction will come on' those who insist that all is well and at peace (1 Thess. 5:3) echoes Jeremiah's denunciation of those who say 'Peace, peace . . . when there is no peace' (Jer. 6:14). The Roman

Empire celebrated its gift of *Pax Romana* to the world, yet this was also criticized for being a false claim. 'To rob, to butcher, to plunder, they call empire, and where they make a desert they call it "peace"' (Tacitus, *Agricola* 30, writing in AD 98).

The language of *slay[ing] each other* cannot refer to oppression of Christians by others, but suggests war between nations, or perhaps even civil war and fighting within groups, which was seen as especially alarming as it threatened the stability of civil order. The province of Asia had known violent civil disturbance in 88 BC; more Jews were killed by other Jews than by Rome in the revolt of AD 66–70.

The two mentions of *a great sword* (AT) in the Old Testament (Isa. 27:1; Jer. 25:38) both depict the devastation of warfare as expressing God's judgment on Israel and the nations.

5–6. It is not clear that there is any significance as to which *living creature* calls forth which horse and rider; although the living creatures are described in turn in 4:7, when the first seal is opened John does not specify which of these four speaks first. *Black* is an ominous colour throughout Revelation, but this horse is no more ominous than the others, and the variety of colours is reminiscent of Zechariah's horses. The *scales* that the rider carries are the usual balance scales, suspended from a rod held in the hand, that were used widely in the ancient world. Though updated to measures of weight in many English translations, the quantities of *wheat* and *barley* are given in Greek as measures of volume (*choinix*, approximately equivalent to one quart or one litre), which would have been unusual, especially in a time of shortage – a reminder that John's language here is general rather than precise, and evokes the idea of famine rather than referring to a particular incident.

The announcement of the shortage comes from *a voice in the midst of the . . . living creatures* (AT), that is, from the throne, but John is doubly oblique about highlighting this, as a way of holding together the tension between the absolute authority of God and his permissive will in allowing these things to happen. A *denarius* (AT) was the typical wages for a manual worker for one day, and would normally buy about sixteen quarts of wheat, rather than the one quart here. This would be enough for only one individual, leaving no provision for his family. *Barley* was usually about half the price of wheat, and, being less nutritious, was the choice of the poor (see John 6:9).[2]

The command *not to harm the oil and the wine* (AT) has been understood in a variety of ways. If oil and wine were luxury items, this might suggest a famine which harmed the poor and not the wealthy – but in fact both items were consumed by all sectors in society. It was an accepted practice for invading armies, even if they devastated annual crops such as wheat and barley, to leave vines and olive trees unharmed, since they take much longer to regrow and their destruction would devalue the land that had been captured. But the protection of vines and olive trees allowed those who owned them to continue to make a profit, and the reduced capacity then to grow wheat led to frequent shortages of bread in cities, and was the main reason behind Domitian's edict in AD 92 to destroy half the vines across the empire (see the introductory comment on the message to Philadelphia). So the command 'not to harm' allows the economic imbalance that exists to have its full effect in creating uncertainty about food supply and a greater vulnerability to the effects of war and conflict.

7–8. The horse that emerges on the opening of the *fourth seal* is a pale, sickly green colour; the term *chloros* gives us the word 'chlorine' after the colour of the gas, and it was used to describe the complexion of someone who was sick, dying or terrified. This is indeed the most terrifying horse and rider, in some ways summing up all that has gone before: the rider is personified *Death*, and is followed by (also personified?) *Hades*, the abode of the dead in the Greco-Roman world, and equivalent to Sheol in Old Testament texts. The two are often personified together as those who have a relentless grip on human destiny (2 Sam. 22:6; Pss 18:5; 89:48; 116:3), and Hades was depicted in mythology either as a creature with a gaping mouth who consumed the dying, or as the god of the underworld. But their *power over a quarter of the world* (AT) signals not just the extent of the

---

2. For information on the price of these foods and the impact of shortages, see Cicero, *In Verrem* 2.3.81; Josephus, *Antiquities of the Jews* 14.28; and N. Lewis and M. Reinhold (eds.), *Roman Civilization* (3rd edn; New York: Columbia University Press, 1990), 2:250.

damage they inflict but the limits to it as well – a quarter, no more and no less. God remains sovereign even over death, to which Jesus alone holds the keys (1:18), and in the final scenes of the book death and Hades are thrown into the lake of fire (20:13): the ultimate powers of destruction are themselves destroyed.

The four ways that they *kill, by sword, famine and disease* [AT; lit. 'death', often used to mean dying of plague or pestilence], *and by the wild beasts,* looks like a partial summary of what has gone before, but in fact exactly matches the list of the means by which God will bring his judgment on Jerusalem in Ezekiel 14:21. As we will see again at the beginning of Revelation 7, John uses the language of God's judgment on Jerusalem and recasts it as judgment on the whole of humanity, within which what were the 'faithful remnant' become the followers of the lamb.

Theology
These vivid images of chaos and destruction have gripped the imagination of readers down all the generations, and have continued to shape contemporary culture. This is in part due to the nature of the language John uses, with its direct and powerful metaphors, but it is also because he is describing things which have relevance in every generation. There is a tradition of reading which sees John's vision as describing some future time of judgment and destruction, but that is only due to a failure to appreciate the biblical language John is using and a lack of awareness of the context within which he is writing. In seeking to understand this text, we need to look, not for things to which the images *refer,* as if this were a coded version of future history, but for the things which (as metaphors) the images *evoke,* both from the canon of Scripture and the context of John's world.

Although there is no hint of literary dependence, there are significant parallels between the things related in the opening of the seals and those related in Jesus 'eschatological discourse' recorded in Matthew 24:4–35 (and Mark 13:5–31; Luke 21:8–33), as shown in table 6 overleaf.

But Jesus makes clear that these are the things the disciples should expect to see within their lifetimes: 'Truly I tell you, this generation will certainly not pass away until all these things have happened'

Table 6: The seals and the eschatalogical discourse of Matthew 24

Theme	Jesus in Matt. 24	Seals sequence
False religion	Verse 5	First (white) horse?
War	Verse 6	Second (red) horse
Famine	Verse 7	Third (black) horse
Earthquakes	Verse 7	Sixth seal (Rev. 6:12)
Believers put to death	Verse 9	Fifth seal: saints under the altar (Rev. 6:9)
Fleeing to the mountains	Verse 16	Sixth seal (Rev. 6:15)
Sun and moon darkened; stars fall	Verse 29	Sixth seal (Rev. 6:12–13)

(Matt. 24:34; see comment above on Rev. 1:7). In other words, these kinds of events are to mark the 'end times' period between Jesus' ascension and his return.

For John's first readers, these verses describe a world they know and live in – a world marked by periodic famine and shortage, one of chronic disease and early death (especially in the often overcrowded cities of the empire), a world in which earthquakes bring sudden destruction and devastation. John is not yet disclosing to them an unknown future, but revealing the reality about the present. The imperial myth of peace and prosperity is exposed as just that – a myth. There is only one who is sovereign – the one by whose permission the horsemen are released to allow humanity to reap what it has sown – and this one is not the emperor. And it is he alone, not the emperor, who can offer answers to the crisis that faces humanity; he alone who can usher in the true age of peace and prosperity.

B. The fifth and sixth seals: the martyrs and the wrath of the lamb (6:9–17)

Comment

9. There is a change in pace and focus for the last three seals compared with the first four, providing the 4/3 division of the seven which is also found in the series of trumpets and bowls. John has not previously mentioned the *altar*, though it recurs seven further times, where it is described as 'golden' (8:3), contains fire (8:5; 14:18), has horns (9:13) and even testifies to God's true judgments (16:7). In this way it is depicted as the heavenly equivalent of the altar in front of the Jerusalem temple, in line with the Jewish understanding that the physical temple was an earthly representation of heavenly realities. John's reference to it reminds us that this is still part of the vision that began in 4:1, when John entered through the door into heaven.

The word used for *soul* (*psychē*) should not be understood as reference to a distinct, immortal part of the human being, separate from, or even trapped in, the physical body. The New Testament uses the word to mean a person's whole life, above and beyond but not separated from physical existence, and does not treat the 'soul' as immortal (Rev. 8:9 says lit., 'those have souls [*psychē*] died'). Other apocalyptic literature also envisages the dead as visible souls, and this at first seems difficult to reconcile with Paul's language of 'sleep' as the intermediate state between death and final bodily resurrection. But the martyrs are (v. 11) told to 'rest' (AT), and Revelation depicts the ultimate hope not as souls being reclothed in bodies, but as the dead being given life, raised to a new form of bodily existence (20:4).

The presence of the martyrs under the altar suggests that their death is seen as an acceptable sacrifice to God – not in the sense of adding to the atoning sacrifice of Jesus, but as the ultimate expression of a life lived faithfully to God as the true worship of a living sacrifice (Rom. 12:1). Like the lamb, they too have been *slain*; just as those in the assemblies in the seven cities have been invited to conquer as the lamb has conquered (5:5), so the means of victory also follows the pattern of the lamb, remaining faithful even to the point of death (12:11). The *word of God and [their] testimony* echoes John's description of what he has been given to write (1:2) and is the reason for his own exile (1:9). As elsewhere, the two terms are closely related; God's word to his world and his people is the truth that is revealed in Jesus, who achieves victory through suffering.

10. The title the martyrs use for God, *Sovereign Lord*, sounds very much like a title from the Old Testament, but the term (*despotēs*) is more commonly used of emperors. It is God, rather than the holder of imperial power, who is *holy and true*; where the empire has inflicted unjust punishment on Christians (especially under Nero), God is the one who will vindicate those who have suffered unjustly, as we see in 20:4. The *inhabitants of the earth* (the second of ten mentions in Revelation) are not simply those who physically live on earth, but those who are earth-bound in the sense of following the beast rather than the lamb; see comment on 3:10. The cry for vengeance sits uncomfortably with Jesus' teaching to 'love your enemies and pray for those who persecute you' (Matt. 5:44), but the call for justice on the part of the oppressed stands in a long tradition in the Old Testament, particularly in the Psalms, where God's just judgment of the world is celebrated (Ps. 96:13), an expectation continued into the New Testament (2 Thess. 1:6–10). Some modern readers of Revelation find this idea harder to identify with than those in other ages and with those in other nations today who are daily suffering oppression for their faith.

11. The term used for *white robe* (*stolē*) is different from that previously mentioned as the attire of those who conquer in 3:4, 5, 18 and of the elders in 4:4, but is used again in the following vision in 7:9, 13, 14. However, the idea is the same, with white signifying purity, holiness and honour. The martyrs are invited not just to *wait*, but to rest in God's presence: the same term is used in the invitation of Jesus in Matthew 11:28, and those who 'die in the Lord . . . rest from their labour' (Rev. 14:13). Although this rest will last *a little time* (AT), this indicates that the period is limited by the power of God, and will last from the resurrection of Jesus until his return, a period designated elsewhere as 'time, times and half a time', 1,260 days or forty-two months (see comment on 11:2–3). The *fulfilment* (AT) of others who will also suffer martyrdom is here a reference not to a predetermined number, as it appears to be in other apocalyptic texts, but to the completion of the task of witnessing to the world (cf. 3:2, where the faith of the Christians in Sardis is, by contrast, described as 'incomplete' [AT] using the same root word). The *fellow-servants* and *brothers [and sisters]* are two terms describing the same group of people: those who obey God find themselves in fraternal relationship with others who do the same, just as John himself is 'brother and companion' (1:9) to those to whom he writes, and all share both spiritual opposition and the victory won by the lamb (12:10).

12–13. We can see that the series of opening the seals is moving to a climax, since John changes his language from the repeated formula 'When he opened' to *And I saw when he opened . . .* (AT). John's readers were well aware of the practical terror of a *great earthquake*, living in an area prone to tremors which had devastated or damaged many of their cities (see introductory comments on Sardis, Philadelphia and Laodicea). Yet, as always, this also draws its meaning from the Old Testament, where earthquakes were depicted as signs of God's presence and his coming in judgment (Exod. 19:18; Ps. 99:1; Joel 2:10). Even in our scientific age, when we know something of the causes of earthquakes, they hold an existential terror for us as they symbolize the loss of all security and safety.

The sun turning *black like hairy sackcloth* (AT) perhaps hints at the call to repentance, since this is traditionally what people wore as a sign of turning from sin, but this is not made explicit until later in Revelation. The combination of the darkening of the sun, the *moon turn[ing] blood red* and the *stars falling from the sky* (AT) was seen as a portent of divine judgment in the Greco-Roman world, but in the Old Testament they together signal the coming of God in judgment on the Day of the Lord and the end of this age (Isa. 13:10; 50:3; Ezek. 32:7–8; Joel 2:31). Although the opening of the seals culminates in a depiction of the End, we should beware of taking these signs as literally signifying the destruction of the created order, in part because of the use of this language to signal the transition from this age to the age to come in the resurrection and ascension of Jesus (in Matt. 24:29; Mark 13:24–25; Acts 2:19–20), and in part because people could not hide in 'caves and . . . mountains' (v. 15) if these had already been 'removed from [their] place' (v. 14). The *fig-tree* was associated with eschatological hope of peace and prosperity (Mic. 4:4; John 1:50), but also the judgment of those who fail to show signs of repentance and faith in God; the unfruitful fig-tree was a symbol of the Jerusalem temple which failed to welcome Jesus as God's anointed one (Mark 11:20).[3]

---

3. This is the only occurrence in the NT of the term *olynthos*, meaning 'unripe' or 'late' fig.

14. The term used for the *sky disappeared* (AT) could mean 'split apart', but the metaphor of a *scroll being rolled up* (AT) does not appear to relate to this at all. The sense is rather that when a scroll has been rolled up for a long time, it needs to be weighted down to stay open, and if released, it suddenly rolls up again and the writing disappears from view. A modern equivalent might be a spring-loaded roller blind which suddenly snaps upwards when released. This sudden and dramatic disappearance is another expression of the end of the age in the prophetic tradition (Isa. 34:4) and occurs again at the end of Revelation (20:11). The moving of *mountain*s demonstrates the power of the presence of God, and *island*s symbolize distant lands at the ends of the earth (cf. Isa. 49:1): there is no place to escape the power and extent of God's judgment.

15. The sevenfold description of the peoples on earth covers the whole socio-economic spectrum, all the way from the powerful elite right down to the poorest slave. Roman society was highly stratified, with power concentrated in the hands of the few, and financial wealth, political power and military control often went hand in hand. The *kings of the earth* is an Old Testament phrase (Ps. 89:27b) which occurs seven further times in Revelation (1:5; 17:2, 18; 18:3, 9; 19:19; 21:24) to describe the rulers who 'commit adultery' with the great prostitute (17:2) and fight on the side of the beast (19:19), yet at the End 'bring their glory' (AT) into the New Jerusalem (21:24). The mention of *slave and free* is a Semitic idiom (using 'gradable antonyms', that is, two terms at the opposite ends of a spectrum, a form of merism) to signify everyone – developed further in 13:16 ('rich and poor, great and small, slave and free', AT) – to emphasize the universal implications of God's judgment.

16–17. The appeal to the *mountains* and *rocks* as personal agents who might come to the aid of those facing judgment makes no literal sense, since in verse 14 the mountains have just been 'removed from [their] place'. John is here adapting the language of Hosea 10:8 ('Then they will say to the mountains, "Cover us!" and to the hills, "Fall on us!"'), and by doing so is extending God's judgment of sinful Israel to the whole of humanity, as he did in his reuse of Ezekiel 14:21 in verse 8. Just as the *Lamb* has shared in the praise and worship offered to the *one seated on the throne* (AT) in Revelation 5, so now he also shares in God's work of judgment, something in the Old Testament attributed to God alone.

The language of *the great day* recalls Old Testament expectation of 'the great and terrible day of the Lord' when the God of Israel would come in judgment. In the earlier prophetic texts, God comes in events in history in order to vindicate his people and liberate them from oppression (Isa. 2:12), but because God's people themselves have sinned, they too will face sifting and judgment (Amos 5:18). In the later prophets, the 'day' has cosmic significance and is accompanied by the signs of verse 12 (Joel 2:31). In the New Testament, God is never described as being 'angry' (as a verb of action), but the noun 'wrath' (*orgē*) expresses his steadfast opposition to all that is sinful. Some early manuscripts have in verse 17 'the great day of *his* wrath', corresponding to the mention of the *wrath of the Lamb* in the previous verse. But the reading of the majority of manuscripts, *their wrath*, is to be preferred; both the lamb and the one seated on the throne enact judgment against sin. The chapter ends with the poignant question which the following chapter answers at length: *who is able to stand?* (AT). We find the answer not in the merit of a section of humanity, but in the gracious redemption that the lamb has gained by his own sacrifice.

Theology

If the opening of the first four seals reveals what the world is really like – not one of imperial peace and prosperity but one of experienced chaos and suffering – then the opening of the next two seals reveals where this world is heading and the consequences of living in it. In the brief sketch we are offered here – which is filled out in more detail as the book unfolds – we see that it is also a world of injustice, where dissenting voices of those who are loyal to a different sovereign are not tolerated. But such injustice will not have the last word; we are offered here the first glimpse of an alternative narrative which is set in motion by the lamb who was slain but now stands before the throne: that those who are themselves slain because of their faithful testimony will also stand before God.

And it is a world which, without the redemption that God offers, is hurtling towards destruction. It is vital that we read this chapter, not as a complete account of the world and God's will for it, but in its place within Revelation's narrative. This is the world that God made, sees and loves; the question of his ultimate will for it has not yet been answered, since all seven seals have not yet been opened, and we cannot know his will until they have. This is not a description of God's will for the world, but a description of the world about which God has a will. We see the first insights into this will in the interlude, prior to the seventh seal, which follows in Revelation 7.

5. INTERLUDE: THE VISION OF GOD'S PEOPLE, AND THE FINAL SEAL (7:1 – 8:1)

Context

We have already seen how the text of Revelation moves from one scene to another (quite contrasting) one at key moments: the change from the epistolary introduction to the dramatic vision of the exalted Christ in Revelation 1, the change of focus to the assemblies in Revelation 2 – 3, John's entry into heaven in Revelation 4 – 5, and the horsemen riding throughout the earth in Revelation 6. At the start of Revelation 7 we have another change of focus and ethos, though this is still described from John's vantage point in the heavenly throne room.

We need to read this chapter in the context of what comes before and after, and in view of its connections with other parts of the book. This section of John's vision has two parts to it, related by the 'seeing versus hearing' motif we have encountered before: John 'hears' the number of those counted (but does not see them); he then turns to 'see' an uncountable people, and these two descriptions interpret one another. They describe the 'servants of God' who are before his throne, and so this vision, as an interlude between the sixth and seventh seals, functions to answer the specific question at the end of Revelation 6, 'Who can stand?' But this interlude also begins to address the larger question of God's will for the world and what he will do about humanity that has gone astray from his creation intention and both inflicts and suffers from chaos, evil and death.

This section looks back to the throne scene, since we discover the 'great multitude' are also before the throne, along with the living creatures, elders and angels, and they join in with the worship of the one seated on the throne and the lamb as the others have done. But it also looks forward to the end of the book, anticipating the final scenes in the New Jerusalem, where they will drink from springs of the water of life (7:17; 21:6) and God 'will wipe every tear from their eyes' (21:4).

A. The sealing of the 144,000 (7:1–8)

Comment

1. John introduces the new focus for this part of his vision with the phrase *After this I saw* (or 'looked'), which came with the change in 4:1, and is repeated in the introduction to the second part of the vision in 7:9, as well as at 15:5 and 18:1. As previously, the temporal reference (*after*) relates to John's sequence of visions, not to any chronology of the events in the visions. The reference to the *four corners of the earth* draws on conventional language about the world; in the first century the world was thought of as circular (rather than having corners), though some believed that the earth was actually spherical. We might talk in contemporary parlance of 'the four points of the compass'.

The *four winds of the earth* could be drawing on Jewish and pagan ideas of four winds that bring harm, rather than good, but more likely it comes from the vision of the four horses in Zechariah 6, which are interpreted as being 'the four winds [or 'spirits', *rûḥôt* in Hebrew, *anemoi* in Greek] of heaven, going out from standing in the presence of the Lord of all the earth' (Zech. 6:5, AT). This is confirmed by the fact that when the winds blow, they will 'harm' the land, sea and trees (vv. 2–3), just as the four horsemen harm the earth and its inhabitants when they ride out. This vision therefore offers a fresh perspective on what we have already seen in the previous chapter, filling in more detail – something we will see repeatedly later in Revelation. In Zechariah, the winds are 'of heaven', but here they are *of the earth*; John sees God as sovereign, but is circumspect about God's direct command of the agents of harm (see introductory comment on Rev. 6).

2–3. John sees *another angel* coming *from the east* (lit. 'the rising of the sun'). Both winds and the sun were often thought to be under the command of gods or angelic beings, though John is clear here that all are under the command of God, so once more uses the 'divine passive' of the *angels who had been given power* that we saw in relation to the horsemen in the previous chapter. The fifth angel has *the seal of the living God*, that is, something like a signet ring or stamp which allows someone to leave his or her mark in soft wax. The idea of sealing God's faithful people to protect them from coming judgment has a close parallel in Ezekiel 9:3–6, where the man dressed in linen is commanded to 'put a mark on the foreheads' of the faithful remnant in Jerusalem before God's judgment comes on the city. As in the previous chapter, John is using the language of judgment of God's people and extending it to the whole earth, and the faithful remnant who escape the judgment then correspond to the followers of the lamb or servants of God.

In Ezekiel 9:4, the word for 'mark' in Hebrew is *tāw*, the name of the last letter of the Hebrew alphabet. The Greek equivalent is *tau*, which (as in English) looks a little like a cross, and this has led some commentators to suggest that it is the sign of the cross on the forehead which offers protection. But this connection is not made in the Greek Old Testament nor in the text of Revelation, so is unlikely. This seal is a counterpoint to the mark of the beast (which is placed on the foreheads of those who follow the beast, 13:16, and is both a number and a name, 13:18), but is also depicted as 'the name of the Lamb and his Father's name' in 14:1 (AT). The idea of a mark which offers protection from judgment has some parallels with the lamb's blood on the doorposts at the passing over of the angel of death (Exod. 12:12–13).

4. It is highly significant that John *heard* the number of those who were sealed, since in verse 9 he then 'looked', and this strongly suggests that the two groups are the same, just as in Revelation 1 he hears a voice and then turns to see it (1:12). What is the significance of the number *144,000*? Groups of 1,000 (as a round rather than an exact number) were the basis of organization for some armies at the time, so this is not an unrealistic number to take literally. But the key lies in observing John's use of numbers elsewhere.

John's writing to the assemblies in seven cities (when there were other important urban centres) and the intention that all should read all the messages points to the symbolic significance of the number 7 as representing the totality of all Christian groups. The references to 'ten days' (2:10) and 'hour of testing' (3:10, AT) both symbolize a short time. The Danielic time period 'time, times and half a time', calculated to be equal to 1,260 days or forty-two months, has particular symbolic significance (see comment on 11:2–3). And, most clearly connected with this number, the New Jerusalem in Revelation 21 is a cube, 12,000 stadia in each direction with its walls of 144 cubits (see comment on 21:16–17). The symbolic significance of the cube is that it has the shape of the Holy of Holies (1 Kgs 6:20) and so represents the place of God's presence.[1] The number must refer to the whole people of God, and not a remnant or elite within them, since they are referred to as 'the servants of . . . God' (v. 3; a term used elsewhere for the redeemed) and constitute the total number who are protected from coming judgment.

If twelve is the number associated with the people of God, ten is a natural number (not least because it is the base for our number system), a square suggests the completeness of God's people (the plan of the New Jerusalem) and a cube suggests the Holy of Holies and the presence of God, then the number 144,000 has a powerful symbolic meaning. It is the complete people of God, representing his holy presence in the world, a meaning which correlates with the idea of God's people as the body of Christ and as the temple in Pauline theology. In response to the vision of Revelation 6, it becomes clear that God is not distant or absent from his world and its sufferings, but present in the form of his faithful people.

---

1. For further exploration of Revelation's numerology, see comment on 13:18 and the Introduction.

5–8. The counting out of the people, tribe by tribe, raises two main questions: why the enumeration? And why this list of tribes?

The enumeration suggests some form of census, and while censuses were taken in the Roman world for the purposes of taxation (cf. Luke 2:1), in the Old Testament the purpose was often to ascertain the fighting strength of the conscription army, which could consist of all able-bodied adult males. At the beginning of Numbers, Moses is commanded to 'count according to their divisions all the men in Israel who are twenty years old or more and able to serve in the army' (Num. 1:3), and in 2 Samuel 24 David is stirred up to take a census to show his military strength. The enumeration therefore depicts God's people as a spiritual army, disciplined and ready to engage in holy warfare.

There are eighteen different listings of the tribes of Israel in the Old Testament – and this list matches none of them! Perhaps most surprising is that this list does not match the list in Ezekiel 48, which is an eschatological rather than a historical listing. The four main differences are:

1. The inclusion of *Levi* when he is usually omitted as the priestly tribe that inherits no land;
2. The inclusion of both *Joseph* and *Manasseh* but the omission of Ephraim, where in most lists Joseph's sons Manasseh and Ephraim are included instead of Joseph in order to make up the list to twelve with the omission of Levi;
3. The omission of Dan from the list;
4. The placing of *Judah* at the head and *Benjamin* at the end, the two southern tribes.

Some commentators argue that these details are unimportant since the focus is on the enumeration rather than on the specific names. But it is worth noting the significance of these changes and how they relate to other issues in Revelation.

The inclusion of Levi suggests that the list looks back to the time before the incident of the Golden Calf (Exod. 32), following which the priestly function of the people was delegated to the Levites, and all other tribes had to redeem their firstborn from priestly service. So the list is of all the tribes being a kingdom of priests (1:6; 5:10).

The inclusion of Joseph rather than Ephraim might simply be part of this looking back to the ideal nation; Joseph and Ephraim are closely identified together in Numbers 1:32 and Ezekiel 37:16, 19.

Dan was the tribe in the far north and so furthest from Jerusalem. The tribe was viewed negatively, starting with Jacob's 'blessing' of his sons: 'Dan will be a snake by the roadside, a viper along the path, that bites the horse's heels' (Gen. 49:17), a saying that associated Dan with Satan and with temptation. And in Judges 18:30 and 1 Kings 12:29 they set up an idol and then a high place for the worship of Baal, and so led people astray from the true worship of Israel's God.

The placing of the two southern tribes at the beginning and end of the list emphasizes their importance, along with the inclusion of the verb *were sealed* in both places (a symmetry that is not evident in most English translations), and connects back to the description of the lamb as the 'Lion of the tribe of Judah'. It was among these tribes that the Messiah was expected to arise.

The list therefore portrays God's people as a community of the Messiah who have kept themselves pure in worship and thus stayed true to their calling as a priestly nation equipped for the holy war that they are to face.

B. The great multitude in praise and the seventh seal (7:9 – 8:1)

9–10. *After this*, that is, John's hearing the enumeration of the people, he now *looked*, and what he sees is striking and surprising. The *great multitude that no-one could count, from every nation* sounds like the fulfilment of the promise to Abraham in Genesis 13:16; 15:5; and 17:4. John reminds us that his vision continues from his position in heaven, since this crowd is *before me* as they are *standing before the throne*. Lest we think that the scene around the throne is getting rather crowded, the point is more theological than geographical: here is the answer to the question 'Who can stand?' from 6:17. Rather than fleeing fearfully from God, here are people who stand with confidence, joy and praise in his presence. On the fourfold phrase *every nation, tribe, people and language*, see the comment on 5:9.

The crowd are wearing *white robes*, the apparel of those in Sardis who have kept faith (3:4) and promised to those who 'conquer' (3:5,

AT), and the clothing of those under the altar (6:11). We will learn in verse 14 how they have merited this sign of purity and honour. The *palm branches* which they hold could (along with their attire) simply suggest pagan acts of worship, but it is also an echo of Psalm 118:27, a psalm used in celebration of the feast of Tabernacles, when the people remembered the presence of God with them as they journeyed through the desert from slavery in Egypt to the Promised Land. But it is read through a distinctively Johannine lens; John's Gospel alone specifies that at Jesus' triumphal entry the branches were from the palm tree (John 12:13), and it is his account which gives us the name Palm Sunday. The crowd's praise here, *Salvation belongs to our God*, continues to echo Psalm 118 (v. 25) and recollects the Palm Sunday crowd's acknowledgment of Jesus as the coming King who brings God's salvation. Now, as then, it is *the Lamb* who saves as well as *the one seated on the throne* (AT); the high Christology of Revelation matches the high Christology of John's Gospel.

11–12. The uncountable host of *angels* that we met in 5:11 once more join in praise with *elders* and the *four living creatures* and provide a heavenly counterpart to the uncountable human crowd. But this time it is clear that they are completely aligned with the human worshippers, as they *fell down on their faces*, prostrating themselves before the throne just as the elders had done (5:14) – they are closer to humanity than to divinity (cf. 19:10). Their chorus of praise clearly echoes the praise in Revelation 4 – 5, as shown in table 7.

Table 7: Acclamations of God and the lamb in chapters 4, 5 and 7

4:11	5:12	5:13	7:12
glory	power	praise	praise
honour	wealth	honour	glory
power	wisdom	glory	wisdom
	strength	power	thanks
	honour		honour
	glory		power
	praise		strength

Although the cumulative impression is more important than the individual items, the terms in the sevenfold praise here match the sevenfold list in 5:12, with *thanks* in place of 'wealth'. It is striking that, where we might consider gratitude to be the province of the crowd of people who have themselves been saved, the angelic crowd is also in awe of God's saving power and its benefits. The mystery of the redemption that is ours in Jesus is a wonder that 'even angels long to peer into' (1 Pet. 1:12, AT).

13–14. The second half of John's vision in this interlude is itself in two parts; he turns from recounting what he has now seen to recounting his dialogue with *one of the elders*, which offers a further explanation of the scene before him. The introduction to the whole section (7:1–3) has linked this to the preceding vision of the four horsemen. The enumeration of the tribes has introduced the exodus desert theme also alluded to in the praise in 7:10. The praise of the angels has tied the scene back to the worship of Revelation 4 and 5. And these next verses draw on a range of Old Testament hopes to point forwards to the final vision of Revelation 21. The text is developing into a rich and interwoven tapestry where each part has threads connecting it to all other parts of the book.

Rhetorical questions feature in several Old Testament prophetic texts (Jer. 1:11, 13; 24:3; Amos 7:8; 8:2; Zech. 4:2; 5:2) and occur at 5:2 ('Who can open?', AT) and 17:7 ('Why are you amazed?', AT) as well as here. In each case they serve to move the plot along and lead to a new disclosure or explanation. The question posed by *one of the elders* to John elicits a confession of ignorance, so the elder then answers his own question. The mention of the *white robes* in the question emphasizes the importance of this as their distinctive feature, which comes to define them in the answer. And he asks not only who they are, but *where did they come from?*, picking up on John's surprised 'Behold' when he first turns to look in 7:9 (AT).

The fact that they have *come out of the great suffering* (AT) cannot mean 'They have been removed from the suffering and avoided it' (as the theory of 'the rapture' supposes, whereby Christians are removed to heaven before the 'tribulation'), partly because the grammar does not allow it, partly because John is already in 'suffering' (*thlipsis*, the word translated 'tribulation' in older English versions, 1:9), partly because of the teaching of the rest of the New Testament that Christians will suffer (Matt. 5:11; Acts 14:22; the latter also using *thlipsis*) and partly because of the close association between their suffering and the suffering of Jesus as the slain lamb. The servants of God are protected from the wrath and judgment we see in Revelation 6, but endure the tribulation that comes from being faithful – which means that these two things are quite distinct.

For Daniel, the 'great suffering' would be an intense time of distress immediately preceding the End and the resurrection of all the dead, through which those 'whose name is written in the book' would be delivered. But as we shall see clearly in Revelation 11 − 12, John reconfigures Daniel's understanding of this time; it now becomes the time from Jesus' death, resurrection and exaltation all the way until he returns again, so it is the time which John and his readers (and we) are already experiencing.

It is possible that having *washed their robes and made them white* signifies the salvation of this group by means of their own martyrdom, so that the *blood of the Lamb* is the virtue of having stayed faithful to death as Jesus has. But the promises they receive are the promises for all God's faithful people, and the wearing of white is granted to all, not just to those who are martyred. Besides, Revelation nowhere suggests that anyone stands before God by virtue of his or her own achievements; from the beginning it is Jesus' death ('blood') which forms us as a 'kingdom and priests' (1:5–6). Enduring suffering out of faithfulness to Jesus is the right and natural response to what he has done for us, not an attempt to win his favour.

Some suggest that the washing points to baptism, since it is described as a single action. But elsewhere this washing is referred to as a process (3:4; 22:14), and it would be better to understand the practice of baptism followed by being clothed in white as referring to this verse, rather than the other way around. The paradox of making something white by washing it in something red which would naturally cause staining captures the paradox of the cross: that something apparently shameful and unclean (Num. 35:33; Deut. 21:23) should bring honour and purity. It is the death of Jesus for us, and this alone, which gives us the purity, holiness and honour signified by the wearing of white and which allows us to stand in the presence of God himself.

15. The elder again repeats that those in white are *before the throne*, that is, in God's holy presence, but now he locates it (for the first time in Revelation) within a heavenly *temple*, continuing the line of thought we saw in the reference to the 'altar' in 6:9. The fact that they *serve him* uses the language of both worship and practical service both inside and outside the sanctuary (Exod. 3:12; Deut. 6:13), though this is distinctively the role of the priests (Heb. 8:5) and in the New Testament such priestly service describes the offering of our whole lives as a sacrifice to God (Rom. 12:1).

The mention of pitching his *tent* recalls both the dwelling of God with his people in the tabernacle in the wilderness and the reuse of this image to describe the incarnation in John's Gospel, where the phrase 'the word came and *dwelt* among us' (AT) could be rendered '*pitched his tent* among us' (John 1:14). Here, though, the tent is pitched *over them*, and, given the theme of protection through being marked with the seal at the start of the chapter, and in the verses that follow, this is the most likely meaning. The phrase is drawn from the promise in Ezekiel 37:27, but the goal there is that the nations will know that Israel is holy, whereas now it is people from the nations themselves who experience God's holy presence sanctifying them.

16–17. The promise that they will never *hunger* nor *thirst* has general significance in the light of the threat of famine and shortages in 6:5–6. These were also particular threats both in the wilderness wandering (Exod. 16:3; 17:3) and in times of war and oppression (Deut. 28:48). But the promise here has been adapted from the promise of restoration to Israel in Isaiah 49:10 and continues with the mention of *springs of living water*. In the Old Testament, God is the true *shepherd* of Israel, in contrast to the false and unfaithful leaders who neglect the people or lead them astray (Jer. 23:1–4; Ezek. 34:1–4), and Jesus both sees the people as 'sheep without a shepherd' (Matt. 9:36; Mark 6:34) and offers himself as the good shepherd (John 10:11, 14), fulfilling the promise of God and of his promised Davidic king (Ezek. 34:11, 23). In a wonderful Johannine inversion of imagery, Jesus is both the lamb (John 1:29) and the shepherd. In the Old Testament and here, shepherding can be a positive, pastoral thing (Ps. 23:1–2) or a challenging one (Ps. 2:9; Rev. 2:27; 12:5; 19:15).

The *springs of living water* (again from Isa. 49:10) are a typically Johannine motif; Jesus offers living water to the woman of Samaria (John 4:10) and to all who believe (John 7:38), in fulfilment of

Ezekiel's vision of the river of life flowing from the new temple (Ezek. 47:1–12). The metaphor is, in ordinary speech, the equivalent of the English 'running water' and so is the opposite of standing pools of water. But the fact that water brings life to plants and animals creates the additional metaphorical meaning – not just 'water that *has* life' but 'water that *brings* life'. The promise that God will *wipe away every tear from their eyes* comes from Isaiah 25:8 and is only fulfilled when not only grief but death itself, the cause of grief, is finally done away with (21:4).

All these hopes are fulfilled in the coming of the New Jerusalem from heaven to earth – but they are also transformed and surpassed by it. Here, those before the throne enjoy protection; but there, God's sheltering presence extends over the whole city (21:3). Here, the sun will not harm them; but there, there is no more sun, since God and the lamb provide all the light that is needed (21:23). Here, they are led to springs of living water; there, they live by the waters of the river of life.

8:1. After the long interlude of Revelation 7, the sequence from Revelation 6 resumes with the statement *When he opened*, which is nearly identical to the opening of the first five seals. After all the noise and clamour of worship in Revelation 4 – 5, then the chaos of Revelation 6 and the counting and praising of Revelation 7, the declaration of *silence* comes as a surprising disruption to the narrative and makes the reader or hearer pause. Silence could simply indicate that no-one knows what to do or how to react now that the seals are all opened. But within the narrative sequence of the seals, this is the end of the series of seven, which has been building to the climax of God's final judgment on the world, so the silence is best understood as a sign of the end of all things. The prospect of judgment should make all the world fall into silence (Zech. 2:13; Rom. 3:19), and there was a Jewish tradition that the age to come would be marked by a return to the primeval silence before God spoke the world into being (see *4 Ezra* 7:30).

Half an hour indicates a finite period of time, but it is also a split time, like the half-week of time, times and half a time. Splitting a period of time in half indicates a transition, a sudden change of direction or rescue in the middle; for example, the judgment of God comes on Egypt at 'half night' (Exod. 12:29), usually translated 'midnight'. We have glimpsed God's dealings with the world, and the End, but there is more yet to be seen and revealed. Within the sequence of John's visions, the silence creates space for hearing the prayers of the saints in verse 4; silence as a sign of reverence as prayers are offered was part of Greek, Roman and Jewish practice.

Theology
The interlude in Revelation 7, between the opening of the sixth and seventh seals, is clearly connected with the preceding six seals, and both fills in details from a fresh perspective and answers the question posed at the end of the sixth seal: 'Who can stand?' The four winds are closely connected with the four horsemen, and the focus here is less on the destructive chaos that is unleashed and more on God's act of protection of those who have remained faithful to him, using imagery from the destruction of Jerusalem that led to the exile.

John's vision here offers three pictures of the people of God which are interrelated. The first is of a people looking like an army ready for spiritual warfare as they endure the intermediate time between their release from slavery and their entry into the Promised Land, recast by John to refer to the period from Jesus' death, resurrection and exaltation to his return and the renewal of all things. The second is of this people Israel now drawn from all nations of the earth, 'out of every nation' in terms of having members from every nation rather than being a nation set apart by national and ethnic boundaries. They are a people caught up in the praise of the one on the throne and of the lamb that we encountered in Revelation 4 – 5. The third portrait is of this people having come through intense suffering – not the suffering brought about by God's wrath and judgment, but the 'tribulation' that comes from staying faithful to the testimony of the lamb who was slain in the face of relentless opposition. They are protected from divine judgment, but nevertheless endure suffering at the hands of human power; chapters 6 and 7 together function as a narrative exposition of Jesus' injunction in Matthew 10:28: 'do not fear those who harm the body, but God who can destroy the soul' (AT).

Together, these portraits give us a picture of a people in receipt of God's grace and responding to it. In contrast to those who, in desperation, cry to the rocks and mountains for protection (6:16), the servants of God wait for the gift of protection that comes from God's sealing of them. They stand in white before the throne because of the gift of the blood of the lamb by which they have been purchased as a kingdom of priests for God (5:9). And their response to this gift is to remain faithful, just as Jesus did, and to be ready to live disciplined lives of obedience. The holy warfare for which they are prepared is their non-violent witness to Jesus, even to the point of death.

6. THE SOUNDING OF THE SEVEN TRUMPETS (8:2 – 9:21)

Context

The pattern of the seven trumpets follows closely the pattern of the seven seals, being grouped as the first four in parallel with one another, followed by a more extended description of the fifth and sixth, with an interval before the seventh, which ushers in an anticipation of the End. But there is also a close similarity to the pattern of the seven bowls, which follow in Revelation 15 – 16. In these last two sequences we find some of the most disturbing images of violence and judgment in the book, and it is vital that we read these within Revelation's symbolic world, which is shaped both by its cultural context (in which signs and portents were viewed as indications of divine judgment and warning) and by Old Testament imagery.

The most important Old Testament image drawn on is the sequence of the ten plagues of Egypt, and Revelation is unusual in modelling God's acts of judgment on these plagues. Between them, the two sequences allude to seven of these ten plagues, but (as with Revelation's use of other OT imagery) the details are adapted. The most notable change is that, in both sequences, the impact of judgment is only partial, whereas it is total in the plague narratives in Exodus 7 – 12. In the trumpet sequence, the theme of repentance is also prominent, and in both the assumption is that God's people are protected from these judgments, having been sealed in the vision of Revelation 7.

A. The seven angels and the prayer of the saints (8:2–5)

Comment

2. John's statement *And I saw* indicates a new stage in his vision, so that 8:1 really belongs to the end of the previous section, while this verse marks the beginning of the next section. We have not met *the seven angels who stand before God* before; the angels that represent the seven assemblies are in Christ's right hand, not before the throne, and these angels should not be identified with the seven(-fold) spirit(s) in 1:4 and 4:5. Since John appears to assume his hearers will know who they are (since they are introduced with the article 'the'), they are likely to be the seven archangels of Jewish tradition named as Uriel, Raphael, Raguel, Michael, Sariel, Gabriel and Remiel (see the Jewish apocalyptic text *1 Enoch* 20). We encounter Gabriel as the interpreter of Daniel's visions in Daniel 8:16 and 9:21, and in Luke's account of the annunciation in Luke 1:19 and 1:26, but in Revelation we encounter only Michael as a named angel (12:7).

Trumpets[1] in the Old Testament were usually made from rams' horns (the shofar) or from metal, and were blown to call people to worship (Lev. 23:24; Num. 29:1), to signal an alarm or to rouse people for battle (Num. 10:9). Because they called for attention, they were associated with God's presence on Sinai (Exod. 19:16) and with the coming judgment of the Day of the Lord (Joel 2:1; Zeph. 1:16). In Ezekiel 33:1–6, the trumpet alerts the people to the coming judgment so that they might repent and save themselves. The angels *were*

---

1. A better translation for the Hebrew *šôpār* and the Greek *salpinx* might be 'horn' rather than 'trumpet'; the etymology of the Greek term suggests something that is blown, and the phrase in Revelation translated 'sounded his trumpet' simply uses the verb 'to blow'.

given the trumpets, another 'divine passive' signalling God's authority in a circumspect manner.

3–5. Previously we were told that the incense offered in golden bowls by elders were the prayers of the saints (5:8), but here *another angel* offers *incense* in a *golden censer* along with the *prayers of the saints* (AT). This suggests divine collaboration with the desire of God's people, not least because it is now an angel (rather than an elder) who performs the priestly task of offering up prayers and incense together. The Jerusalem temple had an altar for incense as well as an altar for sacrifice, but the heavenly scene appears to have only one altar – though it is looking increasingly like the counterpart to the temple, as was hinted at earlier (see on 6:9). Given that the sacrifice of the lamb who was slain has already been made, there is no longer any need for the altar of sacrifice, and so this one must be the altar for incense. The prayers of the saints might be for the coming of the kingdom (Matt. 6:10), a prayer which we see answered in the anticipations of the End in 11:15 and 12:10. Alternatively, they might be the cry for justice from under the throne in 6:9–10. Either way, the response is for the angel to combine the prayers and incense with *fire from the altar*, another sign of divine collaboration, to bring judgment on the earth. The accompanying signs (*peals of thunder*, and so on) repeat the elements from the Sinai theophany of Exodus 19 that we heard and saw in 4:5, but are presented in fuller form by the inclusion of the Sinai *earthquake*.

B. The first four trumpets are sounded (8:6–13)

6–7. The angels having *prepared themselves* (AT) to sound their trumpets, the first of them does so. *Hail and fire* were generally understood to be portents of divine judgment in the ancient world, the fire *hurled to earth* (AT) probably signifying lightning, and *blood* was a signal of coming war. Hail and lightning ('fire' in Hebrew) formed the seventh of the ten plagues against Egypt (Exod. 9:22–26) and were also a sign of God's power in battle (Josh. 10:11) and in future judgment (Isa. 30:30; Ezek. 38:22). Destruction now comes on the *earth* and *trees*; what was being held back in 7:3 is now being unleashed. Whereas the destruction in the plagues of Egypt was total (the 'hail struck everything', Exod. 9:25), and Ezekiel expects judgment to affect everyone (Ezek. 5:2, 12), here only *a third* of the longer-term resources of the earth are affected, though all the *grass* for feeding livestock is gone. Judgment here is only partial, and is a warning to repent.

8–9. The *mountain, all ablaze* might be reminiscent of the fire on Mount Sinai, but the image here (it is *something like* rather than exact, as with John's description of the heavenly scene in Rev. 4) depicts something quite different. Although heavenly stars are sometimes thought to resemble burning mountains (as in *1 Enoch* 18:13; 21:3), there is a reference to a falling star in verse 10, and this mountain is not said to be *thrown* from heaven but simply *into the sea*. If Revelation was written in the 80s or 90s (see Introduction), it is hard to imagine John and his audience failing to hear an echo of the eruption of Mount Vesuvius in AD 79, when pyroclastic and lava flows ran into the sea at Herculaneum and Pompeii. But that is not the *reference* of this description, so we should not expect it to be exact; it is only the 'vehicle' of the metaphor, and its 'tenor' or significance is as a sign of divine cosmic judgment and catastrophe. The *sea* turning to *blood* alludes to the first of the ten Egyptian plagues, but is not exactly like it, in that the judgment is partial rather than total. Such a phenomenon was generally thought to be a mysterious portent that encouraged people to seek out the divine will.

Fish was an important part of the diet for many in the Roman Empire, so the loss of *a third of the living creatures in the sea* would have been as serious a threat as the loss of one-third of the grass and livestock. With a population of at least one million, Rome was highly dependent on food imports brought by ship to its artificial harbour at Portus, and had historically won critical victories in battles at sea. So the loss of *a third of the ships* would have been a military and economic disaster – something revisited explicitly in Revelation 18.

10–11. When the *third angel* blows *his trumpet*, we do this time have a *great star* falling from *the sky* (or 'heaven'; the same word is used in Greek). Such a falling star would have been understood to be a meteor, and stars falling from the sky, symbolizing the fall of heavenly powers, were understood to correspond to events in the human realm – the deaths of many people, and the falling of great stars, the deaths of rulers and leaders. *Wormwood* (Greek *apsinthos*) is a bitter substance (Prov. 5:4; Lam. 3:15, 19) that was also thought to be poisonous (so that *people died* from drinking it). The polluting of water with bitterness was widely seen as a sign of divine judgment, since water is essential for life, and recalls both the bitter waters of Marah which God purified in the desert (Exod. 15:23) and the past life of sin (Deut. 29:18) and slavery (Exod. 12:8).

12. The events following the blowing of the fourth trumpet match very closely the events of the ninth of the ten plagues against Egypt in Exodus 10:21–23, though again the darkness that is created by the loss of the *third of the sun, moon* and *stars* is partial rather than total, and it appears to affect all people, whereas the people of Israel were exempt from the effects of the Egyptian plague. Greco-Roman writers saw the dimming of the sun and moon as portents of looming disaster, but in the Old Testament they were particularly associated with the 'messianic woes' of the coming Day of the Lord (Isa. 13:10, and in particular Joel 2:30–31, cited in Mark 13:24–25 and Acts 2:20; see comment on 6:12). It is not clear whether the phrase *a third of the day was without light* (lit. 'was darkened') suggests that the light of day was one-third less bright, or whether one-third of the day had no light (and similarly with *the night*). But the point here is less about the description and more about its significance as a sign of divine judgment.

13. Once more John *looked* (AT) and he *heard*. The word *aetos* could mean either *eagle* or 'vulture' (cf. Matt. 24:28; Luke 17:37), but its use in 4:7 and in 12:14 (where it is a sign of God's exodus rescue) implies the former. Eagles were communicators of divine will in Roman culture and formed the insignia for the Roman legions; in the Jewish exodus tradition, they are a metaphor for God's rescue and provision (Exod. 19:4; Isa. 40:31). The cry of *'Woe!'* is a declaration of God's judgment on the lips of prophets (Isa. 5:8–22; Jer. 23:1) and Jesus (Matt. 23:13–29). The term comes fourteen times in Revelation: seven times in this section in relation to the three woes that are the last three trumpets, once in 12:12 and six times in relation to the fall of Babylon in Revelation 18. The *inhabitants of the earth* are those opposed to God and his purposes and people; this is the third of ten occurrences of the phrase (see comment on 3:10).

Theology

John's readers lived in a violent, chaotic and frightening world, one in which the sometimes terrifying events that they saw around them were often interpreted as portents of doom and disaster. John's account of the first four trumpets effects a transformation in their understanding of what they see around them.

First, rather than being chaotic, these events are brought into some sort of order. If the events that are described here are like the screeching discords of an out-of-tune orchestra, there remains the steady background rhythm of the sovereignty of God. John continues to describe these events with the reticence that he has displayed in describing the opening of the seven seals, in that what happens is not *directed* by God (the events are summoned in the opening of the seals by a living creature, here by the trumpet blast of an angel) but *permitted* by him. God no more creates chaos and disaster than a candle creates the darkness of the shadows that are thrown. But none of this is *beyond* the sovereignty of God; this chaotic world is not simply spiralling out of his control.

This leads to the second observation: shelter from the storm of calamity is not found in the emperor's promise of 'peace and prosperity', but in turning to the living God who is the Creator of the world and the Redeemer of its people, and who sits on the throne of heaven. The theme of repentance will become more prominent as this series unfolds, but it is already hovering in the wings in these first four blasts of the angelic trumpets.

What is quite remarkable here is the suggestion that God's people themselves are contributing to this process. As they pray for the justice of God – for his kingdom to come and his will to be done – they are hastening this process of testing and sifting of humanity.

C. The fifth trumpet (9:1–12)

Context

With the opening of the fifth and sixth seals, we encounter perhaps the further reaches of John's apocalyptic imagination. These are challenging texts to make sense of, partly because we are introduced to several significant new characters and there are different interpretations of how they relate to one another as well as how they relate to other characters in the drama; and partly because we are also introduced to new realms in John's apocalyptic cosmic geography.

As previously, John is recounting his vision drawing on both vivid Old Testament texts and ideas of terror that were circulating in the first-century world. To read responsibly, we will need to pay careful attention to the pool of ideas in Scripture and culture that John draws on, as well as the way John adapts and uses these ideas in the text. Above all, we will need to consider the impact that John's account of his vision will have had on his first readers. John recounted his vision to elicit a response of faithful commitment and patient endurance in his first readers, and that is what the text should provoke in us too.

Comment

1. John introduces the blowing of the trumpet by the *fifth angel* using the same formula as before. As with the third angel's trumpet, he sees a *star*, but rather than see it falling, he sees that it *had fallen* (the verb is in the perfect tense rather than the aorist of v. 10). The star here is clearly an angelic being acting as a personal agent, since he is *given* a key and uses it to open *the shaft of the Abyss*. There are two main questions relating to the star: is this an envoy from God and under his authority, so that his 'falling' is simply a descent from heaven on a quest? Or is this an evil angelic being who has been expelled from heaven? If the latter, is the *star* the same character in the narrative as the 'angel of the Abyss' in verse 11?

The language of 'falling' has similarities with the 'fall' of the 'morning star' in Isaiah 14:12–17, originally referring to Cyrus of Persia but often read theologically as describing the primordial fall of Satan. And both have links with Jesus' declaration in Luke 10:18 that he saw 'Satan fall like lightning from heaven' at the proclamation by the disciples of the kingdom of God. In Revelation 12:9, Satan is also cast out of heaven and hurled to the earth, along with his angels, after his defeat by Michael and his angels. But against this reading, the falling of stars in 6:13 and 8:10 does not suggest any kind of judgment against the stars themselves (in contrast to 12:9); the focus is, instead, judgment upon the earth. The text makes no connection between this star and the angel of the abyss, and, in narrative terms, the star comes to the abyss from the outside, whereas the angel of the abyss (as the leader of the locust hordes) appears to come from inside. So, on balance, the star here appears to be a neutral character rather than a malevolent one – but the key point is that its fall and the unlocking of the abyss are done with divine permission. Although God is not the origin of evil, as elsewhere John uses the 'divine passive' (he *was given*) to communicate in a circumspect way the sovereignty of God. Evil is real, but it is neither autonomous nor unbounded.

This is the third *key* that we have encountered in the text. Jesus holds the 'key to death and Hades' in 1:18 (AT) as well as the 'key of David' which gives access to the presence of God in 3:7. We come across the 'key to the Abyss' again in 20:1, when Satan is for a time locked in there securely. It is important to note that *the Abyss* (mentioned seven times) is distinct from three other places associated with death and evil in Revelation:

1. The domain 'under the earth' (5:3, 13) appears to be home to natural creatures, and its inhabitants acknowledge and worship God.
2. 'Hades' (1:18; 6:8; 20:13–14) is thought of as the realm of the dead in Greco-Roman mythology and appears to correspond to the Old Testament realm of Sheol. Revelation does not describe it in the same terms, but it is viewed as a temporary abode of the dead until the final judgment.
3. The 'lake of fire' (20:14–15) is the place of final judgment and destruction, and corresponds in this regard to the realm of 'Gehenna' in the Gospels (e.g. Matt. 10:28; Mark 9:43; the only reference elsewhere is in Jas 3:6).
4. In the Old Testament, the 'abyss' (Hebrew *tĕhôm*; Greek *abyssos*, meaning 'bottomless') refers to the chaotic primeval waters from which God formed the seas (Gen. 1:2; Ps. 77:16) and so signifies the threat of chaos that threatens to overwhelm people as well as the source of rebellion against God. In Revelation, the abyss is the source of evil.

These four regions are conflated in different ways in other parts of the Bible and in Jewish apocalyptic, but in Revelation they are kept distinct.

2–4. *Smoke* indicates two quite opposite things in Revelation in its twelve occurrences. On the one hand, the smoke of the incense rises with the prayers of the saints before God (8:4) and (in an echo of the cloud that interrupted the ministry of the priests in 2 Chr. 5:14) the 'smoke from the glory of God' fills the heavenly temple (15:8). But here smoke signals the devastating evil of the locust swarm, and later signifies judgment of the followers of the beast (14:11) and the city of Babylon (18:9, 18; 19:3). Furnaces were used for smelting ore and for firing pottery in the ancient world; in the Old Testament both the smoke of the presence of God (Exod. 19:18) and the smoke of judgment (Gen. 19:28) are likened to *smoke from a . . . furnace.*

Locust swarms look very much like billowing clouds of smoke over the countryside as they move, so the connection here is not surprising. But their description in the following verses draws on three passages of the Old Testament. First, we are reminded of the eighth plague of Egypt (Exod. 10:12–15) when locusts devoured everything in the land. Here, though, the plague is reversed; these locusts harm people but not the *grass of the earth* (even though this was burned up in 8:7) *or any plant or tree.* This connects the work of the locusts with the vision of 7:3, when those who are faithful receive *the seal of God on their foreheads* which serves as a sign of protection, just as it did in Ezekiel 9:1–6. The locust army therefore executes judgment on those without the seal, just as the six men did in Jerusalem in Ezekiel's vision, and God's faithful people are protected as they are both in Ezekiel 9 and in the other Exodus plagues. This then connects with the third passage from the Old Testament: Joel 2:1–25. Joel here describes the coming 'day of the LORD' involving an invading army, a 'northern horde' (Joel 2:20), with God at its head (Joel 2:11), which will lay waste the country. The description includes reference to darkness and clouds (Joel 2:2) and the darkening of sun, moon and stars, as well as blood, fire and smoke (Joel 2:10, 30), and it draws on military imagery so consistently that the reader thinks this is actually about foreign troops until the interpretative key is offered in verse 25: 'I will repay you for the years the *locusts* have eaten' (emphasis added).

5–6. The warrior locusts do not have unlimited power, since they are *not allowed* to kill, but only to inflict pain. The *five months* corresponds to the typical duration of a locust swarm, but it also signifies a limited period (cf. Matt. 14:17; Luke 12:6; 1 Cor. 14:19), perhaps because five is the number of fingers counted on one hand. *Scorpion* stings were not usually thought to be fatal (which they usually are not) but intensely painful. In the ancient world, even more than now, *death* was considered preferable to a long, lingering illness, and was seen as a release from suffering; the repeated parallelism in verse 6 ('they will seek death, they will not find/they will long to die, it will elude them') emphasizes the inability to escape from the pain that is inflicted. The Greek once again personifies death as an active agent: literally it reads 'death flees from them'.

7–9. In the previous verses, John had begun to draw on Joel 2 which describes locusts in terms of a human army. Now John uses Joel's locusts-as-humans language to describe humans-as-locusts, offering eight characteristics of the locust cloud, many of which correspond to the northern barbarians who were seen as a major threat to the supposed peace and prosperity of the Roman Empire. The locusts resemble *horses prepared for battle*, a close parallel to Joel 2:4–5: 'They have the appearance of horses . . . drawn up for battle.' They wear *something like crowns of gold*, which suggests that they have already been awarded the prize of conquest – in other words, their triumph appears to be inevitable. But these are not actual crowns, only 'something like them'; blond hair, virtually unknown in the Mediterranean world and Near East, was much more common among the tribes to the north of the Roman Empire and could have looked crown-like when tied with a headband. They are *human-looking*, and, in contrast to the short hair worn by most Roman men and soldiers, their hair is long like *women's hair*. Having teeth *like lions' teeth* draws on Joel's earlier imagery in Joel 1:6: 'a mighty army . . . has teeth like a lion' (AT), and signifies the ability to injure and harm their human opponents. *Breastplates of iron* were worn by both soldiers and horses in first-century cavalry. The *sound of their wings* resembling *chariots rushing into battle* draws on Joel 2:5: 'a noise like that of chariots . . . drawn up for battle'.

10. The first description of this locust horde described both their power and the pain they inflicted as 'like that of . . . a scorpion' (vv. 3, 5), but in this repeated description John goes further, specifying that *they had tails with stings, like scorpions* before repeating the *five months* as the limited period of their power. By adding this detail (which has no obvious OT antecedent), John is describing this invading force as resembling the manticore, a mythical creature (though included in both Aristotle and Pliny the Elder's natural histories as real) with a human head, the body and teeth of a lion, and the tail of a scorpion.

11. Their *king* is described as *the angel of the Abyss*; although the star that has fallen from heaven and unlocks the abyss appears to be an angelic agent, these two do not appear to be the same within John's narrative, since there is no link made, and the star comes to the abyss from outside it, whereas the angel presumably ascends from the abyss as the leader of the locust horde. What is the connection between this angel and the figure of Satan? In the Dead Sea Scrolls, Belial (another name for Satan) is described as the 'angel of the pit and the spirit of destruction', and in the Gospels Jesus calls him the 'prince of demons' (Matt. 9:34; 12:24; Mark 3:22; Luke 11:15). In Revelation, described as the dragon, he wears diadems (12:3) and he exercises dominion over the beast from the sea who is elsewhere described as coming up from the abyss (11:7; 17:8).

But Satan is never called an angel, and is pictured as being the primordial opponent of God and his people, whereas this locust army is strictly limited in the time it exercises power. Moreover, Satan has already been mentioned five times in the messages of Revelation 2 – 3 (2:9; 2:13 twice; 2:24; 3:9), and no connection is made with those mentions. When he is named again in 12:9, four different names are gathered together and identified ('dragon', 'snake', 'devil', 'Satan'), and the omission of any reference here to the angel of the abyss makes it doubtful that John intended his readers to identify the two. It is best, therefore, to see the 'angel of the Abyss' as closely related to, but not identical with, Satan.

'Ăbaddōn is the Hebrew term for 'destruction'; in the Old Testament it designates a place rather than a person (Job 26:6; Ps. 88:11; Prov. 15:11), though it is also personified along with death (Job 28:22). *Apollyon* is the Greek term for 'destroyer' and is closely related to *apolleia*, the Greek translation of the Hebrew *'ăbaddōn*, but it is also connected with the god Apollo, who was famed for his destructive power and was a favourite identification of several

Roman emperors including Domitian. On the detailed association between Domitian and Apollo, see comment on 12:1–6.

12. The identification of the last three trumpets of the seven as three *woes* was made at 8:13; the fifth trumpet is here confirmed as the first woe, and the second woe to come *after this* (AT; a phrase used everywhere else in Revelation to describe not successive historical events, but successive scenes in John's vision) is clearly the sixth trumpet. But the third woe is never clearly identified; the seventh trumpet brings an anticipation of the End, but the next 'woe' comes only after the account of Jesus' ministry in Revelation 12, when Satan is cast down to earth, filled with fury at his heavenly rout (12:12). The mention of the woes therefore serves to bind the interlude of Revelation 10 – 11 and the central events of Revelation 12 into the trumpet sequence in some way.

D. The sixth trumpet (9:13–21)

13. When the *sixth angel* blows his trumpet, John hears a *voice* as he has done before, coming from near where God is seated on his throne but not, as part of his consistent circumlocution in relation to the sovereignty of God, from God directly. We continue to be provided with additional detail about the heavenly temple: the golden altar has *horns* on it – meaning angled projections, rather than animal horns – just like its earthly counterpart. They were part of the detailed instructions for building the tabernacle and its furniture in Exodus 27:2, and appeared to signify God's presence as a place of sanctuary and refuge; anyone who held on to the horns was granted asylum (1 Kgs 1:50–53).

14–16. In contrast to what happened when the previous five trumpets were blown, the sixth angel is now involved in the drama which his trumpet-blowing initiates, being commanded to *release the four angels who are bound at the great river Euphrates*. At first, it looks as though the angels themselves are agents of evil, since they are to *kill a third* of the population – but John immediately switches his focus to the *mounted troops* who are the real agents, suggesting that the angels are symbolic of what is unleashed. If we are correct in seeing connections between the locust army of the fifth seal and popular fears of invasion by barbarians from the north, then there is little doubt of the connection between this army and fears of a Parthian invasion from the east. The Euphrates was established as the border between the empire and the Parthians by Pompey in the first century BC, and that was still the case in John's day. Parthian kings were famous for their ferocity, and while Rome believed it had subdued its enemies in the north, south and west, it never believed it had conquered in the east. If Parthians crossed the Euphrates, it was to fight with Rome. From the 80s onwards, there was also a widespread rumour that Nero had not really died in AD 68, but had fled to the Parthians and from there would lead an attack on Rome; the so-called 'Nero Redivivus' legend is possibly alluded to in Revelation 13 – 17.

Despite the chaotic and devilish description of the massive army that follows, there is even clearer emphasis on God's sovereignty. The angels had been *kept ready for this very hour and day and month and year*, the repetition of time periods emphasizing in the strongest terms that this is neither unplanned nor unexpected. The language of preparation (the Greek verb *hetoimazō*) occurs seven times in Revelation and includes the preparation of a place of safety and refuge for the woman in 12:6 and the preparation of New Jerusalem as a bride in 21:2.[2] John once more *heard* and then (in the next verse) 'saw', the two senses acting together in building his description. The *number* is sometimes translated *two hundred million* or as 'twice ten thousand times ten thousand', which is closer to the Greek 'tens of thousands times ten thousand'. It is approximately the total world population in the first century, so is in fact communicating an enormous number, beyond actual counting. It contrasts with both the 144,000 that John heard in 7:4 and the unnumbered and uncountable multitude that he saw in 7:9.

17–19. This is the only time in the whole text when John explicitly describes what he is seeing as a *vision*. It is not immediately clear whether the description of the *breastplates* refers to the horses themselves or the riders mounted on them, but since the three colours of *fiery red, sapphire blue and sulphur yellow* (AT) correspond to the *three plagues* of *fire, smoke and sulphur* that come from the horses'

---

2. The other four occurrences are at 8:6; 9:7; 16:12; and 19:7.

mouths, we should perhaps assume that the breastplates are the riders'. The combination of the horses having *heads* resembling *the heads of lions* and *tails . . . like snakes* owes something to the mythical creature known as the chimaera, thought to originate from the region of Anatolia (modern-day Turkey), which breathed fire, had a lion's head, and whose tail ended with a snake's head. It also alludes to Parthian mounted archers, who had perfected the art of firing their arrows backwards, and had defeated Roman legions by retreating uphill and firing backwards at the advancing Roman soldiers who followed in pursuit.

20–21. These verses first appear to function as a summary statement in relation not just to the sixth trumpet, nor even only to the trumpets as a whole, but perhaps to the two sequences of seals and trumpets, since the phrase *these plagues* could refer to the three plagues from the horses' mouths in 9:18 or to all that has happened from 6:1, not least because of the points of similarity with the plagues of Egypt in both sequences. The fact that the *rest of the people* still remain, and the calamities affect only part of the population, shows that these judgments are temporal and not eternal. Natural disasters were commonly thought to be warning messages from the gods, calling on people to change their ways. It now becomes clear that one purpose of the events surrounding the opening of the seals and the sounding of the trumpets is to lead people to repent – but this will not happen without the ministry of the two witnesses, which leads people to 'give glory to God' in 11:13.

The work of their hands is an Old Testament phrase; for God's people, it is used to signify that God will bless and reward them in all they do in obedience to him (Deut. 14:29; Prov. 12:14; Isa. 65:22), but for those who are unfaithful, it is part of the prophetic critique of their idolatry, as they worship what they themselves have made, who are no gods at all (Isa. 2:8; 17:8; cf. the extended critique in Isa. 44:9–20). Expressed in this way, idolatry is actually the worship of the self, since obeisance is given to what they themselves have fashioned. John goes on to describe such idols in two contrasting ways. They are fashioned of different materials, but are powerless because they *cannot see or hear or walk*, an echo of the warnings in Deuteronomy 4:28 of 'gods of wood and stone made by human hands, which cannot see or hear or eat or smell'. And yet he also describes them as *demons*, following the Greek version of Psalm 96:5: 'all the gods of the nations are demons [Hebrew: 'idols']'. This double understanding matches Paul's discussion in 1 Corinthians 8 – 10, in which he asserts, on the one hand, that 'an idol is nothing' (1 Cor. 8:4, possibly quoting the Corinthians back to themselves, but also following Isa. 44:9), but, on the other, that sacrifices offered to idols are in fact being offered to demons (1 Cor. 10:20). The irony here is that, in rejecting the true God and his worship, they are actually worshipping the very things (demons) that are causing their misery (by means of the demonic armies of the fifth and sixth trumpets). The list of sins which goes with such idolatry includes the breaking of commandments six, seven and eight of the Ten Commandments, and possibly adds *magic arts*, 'sorceries' (*pharmaka*), because of their association with sexual immorality in texts like Nahum 3:4. Mentioning five commandments is a common and convenient way of summarizing the ten; echoing this, John lists five things to repent of (idol worship, murder, magic, sexual immorality, theft) and describes the idols as made of five things (gold, silver, bronze, stone and wood).[3]

Theology
However we make sense of these verses in the wider context of a theology of suffering and judgment drawing from the whole testimony of Scripture, we need to note two features of this vision sequence. The first is the reality of pain and suffering, which is emphasized by the repetition of violence both from one trumpet event to another, and within each of the fifth and sixth trumpet sections themselves. John communicates a real sense of dread and terror through his vivid and detailed description of this strange locust army. But alongside this reality, John's vision report also emphasizes the sovereignty of God and his limitation on what is permitted to take place. Evil is real, and does not have its origin in God any more than a shadow has its origin in the light that contrasts with it. The forces of evil are not sent from God (even if they bring

---

3. Compare the five listed in Hos. 4:2 and the five negative and one positive in Mark 10:19.

judgment which might further God's purposes), but they are not beyond God's control.

Significantly, though these terrors were felt keenly within the Roman Empire, it is not loyalty to that empire which is the answer to the quest for security; it is receiving the seal of the living God which offers the only meaningful security in the long term. These fantastical hybrid creatures of chaos contrast with the ordered and orderly living creatures who worship God around the throne. The forces of evil are nothing but destructive, but we will learn from the visions to follow that the chaotic origin of such powers also stands behind the human empire which claims to bring order out of this chaos.

Within this series, there is still time for repentance; the third sequence, of the bowls poured out by the seven angels in Revelation 16, no longer offers that possibility. Nevertheless, it is notable that suffering alone does not bring repentance; the interlude to come tells us that God has another, more effective way to bring this change to human hearts: through the people of his redemption.

7. INTERLUDE: THE PROPHETIC TASK OF TESTIMONY OF JOHN AND GOD'S PEOPLE (10:1 – 11:19)

A. John's (re)commissioning to prophesy (10:1–11)

Context
Chapter 9 has ended with a summary statement of the impact of the series of plagues, referring back to the three plagues brought by the chimaera horsemen in the sixth trumpet, the series of six trumpets, or even the series of trumpets and seals together, looking back to the beginning of Revelation 6. We might expect now to have an interlude between the sixth and seventh trumpets – as indeed we find in Revelation 10 – to match the interlude of Revelation 7 between the sixth and seventh seals.

Like the interlude in Revelation 7, this one is also in two parts, though the differences between the two are even more distinct. And as in Revelation 7, the focus seems to move away from what is happening in the world, and attention is given instead to the people of God and their ministry. The first part (which comprises Rev. 10 itself) is a vision of John's own ministry and what he is called to do, and is one of the occasional moments in the vision sequence when John himself becomes the central figure in what is happening. It is not clear, though, where John is locating himself; there is no explicit statement that he has left the heavenly throne room that he entered at 4:1, but his perspective seems now to be an earthly one, since the mighty angel 'com[es] down from heaven' to where he is.

The second part of the interlude, which comprises Revelation 11, also begins with John as the central character, but then moves on to a description of two witnesses (representing the people of God) and their experience. What is striking is a shift from the previous 'vision report' form in the past tense to a 'prophetic foretelling' in the future tense. Combined with the aside about the seven thunders, this appears to be signalling an important temporal shift in John's visions.

i. The great angel and the seven thunders (10:1–7)
Comment

1. *And I saw* (AT) introduces a new episode in John's visions using the characteristic phrase that he has deployed all through Revelation 5 – 9, although it does not now occur again until the vision of Revelation 13, setting out the next three chapters as distinct from what has gone before and what will come after in the sequence. The *mighty angel* he sees here has sometimes been identified with the 'mighty angel' in 5:2 since there are only three characters in the narrative described with this title (including in 18:21), and both these two call out in a 'loud voice' and are connected with a scroll. But there are important differences too, and if John is using his language carefully, we need to pay attention to this. The angel in 5:2 'proclaims' (*kēryssō*) in a loud voice, whereas this one 'cries out' (*krazō*, 10:3); the angel in 5:2 refers to the scroll that is held by the one seated on the throne, whereas this one is holding a scroll; and John describes this angel as *another* (*allos*) – someone similar, but a different character.

The angel has also been identified with the figure of Christ, since he is *robed in a cloud*, and clouds are associated with Christ as the Son of Man in the presence of God (1:7; 14:14), his *face was like the sun*, just like the face of the 'son of man' in 1:16, and his *legs* (actually 'feet', *podes*)¹ *were like pillars of fire* (AT), similar to the feet of the 'son of man' glowing like bronze in 1:15. But again there are differences: the angel's face is merely *like the sun*, with no mention of shining, and his feet are *like* a fire, rather than the bronze glowing in them. In addition, the angel has a *rainbow upon his head* (AT), echoing the rainbow around the throne in 4:3, and the cloud and fire together recall God's wilderness journeying with his people (Exod. 13:21–22). We therefore have a messenger from God, coming with authority and closely associated with both the son of man figure and the one seated on the throne. It is notable that he *com[es] down from heaven* rather than coming (or going) down to earth, suggesting that John's vantage point is now on the earth rather than in the heavenly throne room, even though there is no explicit mention of his change of location.

2. The angel is holding out in his hand a *little scroll*. There has been much debate about the relation of this scroll to the scroll that has been at the centre of the narrative since its first mention in 5:1, and the relation of both to the text of Revelation.

We need first to note that John uses three different words for scroll: *biblos*, used only of the 'book of life' in 3:5 and 20:15; the diminutive form *biblion*, used of John's scroll (1:11; 22:18), the scroll the lamb opens (5:1), the second mention of the small scroll (10:8), the book of life (20:12) and the heavens metaphorically (6:14); and the double diminutive *biblaridion*,² used only of the 'little scroll' in 10:2, 9, 10.³ Although *biblion* is used of the small scroll, and despite

---

1. John does not use the usual word for legs, *skelē* (see John 19:31–33), but the word for foot, *pous* (plural, *podes*), probably to make the connection with 1:15. But it is hard to envisage how feet might look like 'pillars', so many modern versions interpret this as meaning 'legs'.

2. It is a double diminutive in the sense that the diminutive is formed by adding either *-arion* or *-idion* to a word, but this term includes both endings together.

3. The data are complicated by a number of other variants in early manuscripts, particularly of the terms in chapter 10. But these are the occurrences in the best manuscripts. It might also be of significance that the three terms together occur twenty-eight times, which is 4×7, and the same as the number of cargoes in chapter 18 (see comment there).

diminutive forms losing their significance in the first century, the threefold repetition of *biblaridion* in Revelation 10 seems to be of significance. Within John's account, he is commanded to eat this second scroll, which suggests that it must be small, since a scroll of the usual size would be impossibly large to eat.[4]

We should also note the parallels between the two scrolls. The first was 'sealed' and this second is now 'opened' and available to be read. The first was 'in' the hand of the one on the throne, but in such a way as being offered to be taken; this second is now open in the hand of the angel. Both are heavenly, the first being in the throne room and this second having come down from heaven with the angel, but this second one is now on the earth. So there are strong parallels, but each one includes a slight difference, just as the angel who brings the scroll has similarities with the figure of Christ in Revelation 1 and the mighty angel in Revelation 5, but with differences. The best understanding of the little scroll, then, is that it is closely related to the first scroll, but distinct from it.

The angel having his *right foot on the sea* and his *left foot on the land* signifies his universal authority, since he is connected with all three domains (heaven, earth and sea) created by God in verse 6, and this becomes especially pertinent in Revelation 13, when we encounter both a beast from the sea and one from the land.[5]

3–4. The angel's *shout* is like the *roar of a lion*, which provides a minor allusion to the 'Lion of the tribe of Judah' in 5:5, but a

---

4. The height of a (papyrus) roll ranged from 15 cm to over 40 cm; a height of 20–30 cm was normal (see A. Bülow-Jacobsen, 'Writing Materials in the Ancient World', in R. S. Bagnall [ed.], *The Oxford Handbook of Papyrology* [Oxford: OUP, 2009], p. 21). It might be objected that this is a vision and so a metaphor, and John does not in real life actually eat the scroll; apart from anything else, parchment is indigestible. And the question of size does not appear to be an issue in the vision of Ezekiel 3 from which John draws both ideas and language, so there might be no reason to think it is here.

5. It is interesting to note that this orientation of the angel (right in the sea, left on the land) is what John would see looking north from Patmos up the coast towards the cities of Asia, assuming the angel was facing him.

stronger echo of God coming in both rescue and judgment for his people (Hos. 11:10; Amos 3:8). Using the definite article, John mentions *the seven thunders* as if we know what they are – but we do not. They function to complete the series of sevens in a systematic way, since by including the thunders we have four series of sevens (making twenty-eight in all), but more importantly they offer a temporal key to the visions. The *voice from heaven* (another circumlocution for the voice of God) commands John to *seal up* what the thunders have said. This is a clear allusion to Daniel 8:26 and 12:9, where Daniel is more fully commanded to both 'close' and 'seal' the scroll he has written on because the visions relate to the 'distant future' (i.e. the events of the second century BC when Daniel is depicted as writing in the sixth century BC). So, for John, the events spoken about by the thunders are for the future, *in contrast to* the events of the seals and trumpets, which by inference are set in the present. Commentators speculate on who or what the seven thunders signify, and on the content of what they spoke. Thunder is associated with God's own voice and often signifies judgment, so perhaps we do hear what they say when we reach the judgment scenes from chapter 18 onwards. But the primary rhetorical effect of this instruction is to focus our attention on what John *has* written which has *not* been sealed up.

5–7. John again emphasizes that he has seen the angel *standing on the sea and on the land*, repeating the sense of the angel's authority over all the earth. To *raise [the] right hand* was a traditional gesture when taking a solemn oath (cf. Deut. 32:40), the right hand signifying strength (see comment on 5:1). The angel *swore by him who lives for ever*, echoing the words of the angelic figure of Daniel 12:7 – but where the angel there promises that there will be a period of suffering, the angel here swears that *there will be no more delay!* The text literally says, 'time no longer will be', leading older translations to suggest that time itself will come to an end.[6] But John has used

---

6. The popular children's story of a previous generation, *Tom's Midnight Garden* by Philippa Pearce, makes use of it; the clock which strikes 13 at midnight and sends him back in time has this verse as 'Time no longer' inscribed on its face.

'time' (*chronos*) earlier to mean 'delay' (2:21; 6:11), as it is also used elsewhere (Heb. 10:37). In fact, he is not yet declaring that the End is here, since the seventh angel is *about to sound his trumpet* but has not done so yet. John redeploys Daniel's period of delay 'time, times and half a time' from Daniel 12:7 in the next chapter to describe the present time during which John and God's people must both endure suffering and testify faithfully.

In contrast to common pagan practice (and in conformity with Jesus' command in Matt. 5:34), the angel does not swear by heaven or earth, but by God as Creator (and therefore Ruler) of *the heavens . . . the earth* [the same word *gē* as 'land'] . . . *the sea* and all that is in them, highlighting in the words from Exodus 20:11 (echoed in Neh. 9:6; Ps. 146:6; Acts 4:24) the universal sovereignty of God whose authority this angel now exercises. The *mystery of God* has nothing to do with secret timetables, but the redemptive purposes of God in his offer of grace to unexpected people, something that human reason cannot understand on its own. It is one of Paul's favourite terms for God's plan of redemption in Jesus, occurring twenty-one times in his letters (see 1 Cor. 2:7; Col. 1:27). The phrase *will be accomplished* expresses this using the theologically rich term *teleō* (see John 19:30), which with its cognates expresses the completion or perfection of God's plans for individuals and for the cosmos. The tense here is puzzling; that the angel 'is about to blow' his trumpet makes clear that the completion is future, but the verb itself is aorist (past) tense, perhaps emphasizing its certainty, or perhaps reflecting the way in which tenses at this period increasingly communicated *type* of action rather than *time* of action.

The completion of this mysterious plan of salvation was *announced to his servants the prophets*. It is not clear whether these prophets are the Old Testament figures or those exercising prophecy among the Jewish and Gentile people of God under the new covenant – and in any case, John and other New Testament writers consistently see continuity between these two groups. The verb here is *euangolizomai*, used to announce the good news of military conquests (2 Sam. 18:19) and then more broadly of God's deliverance of his people from exile and oppression (Isa. 40:9–10) and so the arrival of the longed-for kingdom of God in the teaching of Jesus (Mark 1:14–15) and the message about Jesus the Messiah (Acts 8:12). It stands as a rival claim to the 'good news' announced by Roman emperors of their conquests and the peace and prosperity that they bring. The combination of 'mystery' with 'prophets' draws on Amos 3:7: 'Surely the Sovereign LORD does nothing without revealing his plan to his servants the prophets.' But the change of verb from 'reveal' to 'announce [good news]' implies that the mystery that the prophets sought to understand is revealed in the good news about Jesus (cf. 1 Pet. 1:12).

ii. The command to eat the little scroll (10:8–11)

8–10. The *voice that I had heard* refers back to the voice that authoritatively commanded the thunders to be sealed in verse 4. A third time the authority of the angel is reiterated with the (unnecessary) repetition that he is *standing on the sea and on the land*. The scroll is referred to in verse 8 as a *biblion*, but in verses 9–10 the double diminutive *biblaridion* is used once more. The commands to *Go, take* . . . and *Take it and eat it* complete the second half of the allusion to Ezekiel's vision in Ezekiel 2:9 – 3:3 which was begun in 5:1. Ezekiel is offered a scroll that is closed, which God then opens and commands him to eat; John sees a sealed scroll in 5:1 that is opened, and he is now offered a scroll which lies, already opened, in the hand of the angel. This adds to the sense that the two scrolls within Revelation are very closely related – but not enough to suggest that they are the same scroll. In 5:1, the parallel with Ezekiel is that the scroll is written on both sides, which is not mentioned here. John is commanded to eat the scroll here, which forms no part of the narrative in Revelation 5. It is characteristic of John in his use of Old Testament texts to allude to a single text in several different ways, giving a sense of unity to the diverse elements in his narrative without collapsing them into one.

The allusion to Ezekiel is both a development and a transformation of the text. The paradox in Ezekiel, that the writing on the scroll comprises 'words of lament and mourning and woe' (Ezek. 2:10) and yet tastes sweet in Ezekiel's mouth, is changed into a purely gustatory paradox for John. As we have found before, the two experiences of the scroll tasting *sour* in the *stomach* but as *sweet as honey* in John's *mouth* (using the exact phrase from the Greek of Ezek. 3:3) come in the reverse order in verse 9 from what we would expect (see on 3:3; 4:9; 5:11), but John's description of the experience in verse 10 reverses the order back again, so that the terms form a 'chiasm' (sour/sweet/sweet/sour). Ezekiel has a message which will be 'sour' to others, in that it is a message of woe, but it is 'sweet' to him, in that it brings comfort to him that God is still sovereign and has a plan for restoration of his faithful people. But for John, the message is both sweet and sour for him and his hearers. For him, the message brings the consolation of hope that God will fulfil his purposes, but it also brings the suffering (tribulation) of opposition that demands he exercises patient endurance (1:9). For his hearers, there is also both sweet and sour, in (on the one hand) the offer of redemption made freely available in the lamb who was slain, but (on the other) the suffering to be endured by the saints and the judgment that is sure to come on those who refuse to repent.

11. As with Ezekiel, so for John the eating of the scroll is a metaphor for receiving a message, which both must now *prophesy*. But the command to John is the exact reverse of the command given to Ezekiel; where Ezekiel is sent 'not to many peoples of obscure speech and strange language' (Ezek. 3:6), John is to prophesy *about many peoples, nations, languages and kings*. This is the third of the seven occurrences of this fourfold phrase (see comment on 5:9) in which 'kings' replaces the 'tribes' of the previous two lists, possibly because of the focus on the power of the leaders in the following chapters.

Several commentators argue that what follows in the succeeding chapters, particularly in Revelation 11 – 13, constitutes the contents of the little scroll that John has eaten and (if the scroll of 5:1 is to be identified with it) the contents of the scroll now opened by the lamb. But there are some serious objections to such a reading:

1. In the narrative of Ezekiel on which John draws in recounting his vision, there is no sense in which what Ezekiel then writes are the actual words on the scroll. In fact, God then commands him to 'listen carefully' to what he will say, which is what Ezekiel must prophesy to the house of Israel. The eating of the scroll is an enacted metaphor of a commission to prophetic ministry.
2. In a similar way, John does not now speak out what he has ingested, but continues to narrate the next stage of

his visionary experience (continuing to draw on Ezekiel). Though the language of Revelation 11 becomes future tense, and the introductions to the visions of Revelation 12 – 13 use different formulae, from Revelation 14 onwards John returns to the visionary language that he has deployed since Revelation 4: there is clear continuity between earlier and later episodes.

3. There are simply no indicators that John is reciting the text which he has ingested; the form of his writing continues as a vision report.

4. If eating the scroll formed the commission to write the text of Revelation, we might expect to find it near the beginning of the book, rather than here – as in fact it is in Ezekiel.

5. The revelation of God's prophetic word to his people and to the nations comprises the whole of the text of Revelation, which from the beginning is styled as both a 'revelation' and a 'prophecy' (1:1; 1:3). There are so many intertextual connections between different parts of the book, including from the beginning anticipations of the final chapters, that it is impossible to isolate one particular section as the content of the scroll.

So it is much more convincing to see this episode as an enacted metaphor (as it is in Ezekiel) of John's commission to prophesy regarding the nations, of which the text he has written is the supreme (though not necessarily only) example.

Theology

This chapter provides the first half of the interlude between the sixth and seventh trumpets, just as Revelation 7 provided an interlude between the sixth and seventh seals. After the hectic cascade of Revelation 8 – 9, the pace slows here through the repetition of both the description of the angel and the command to take and eat the scroll. This first part of the interlude performs two important functions. The first is temporal; the seven thunders (which, with the later bowls, would complete the four sets of seven judgments) are 'sealed', that is (in terms of the language borrowed from Dan. 12), they remain in the future. This implies that the three series of seven which we do hear about are *not* about the distant future, but about the present. These series do not depict a fearful future apocalyptic disaster, but offer an apocalyptic interpretation of the fearful present, which has disastrously rejected its Creator God and the redeeming lamb.

The second function of this interlude is to identify John's ministry in relation to the mystery of God's will. The first scroll was sealed with seven seals; the purposes of God are completely hidden from human eyes until God reveals them. And in fact they are made known not simply by the one who created the world and calls us to obedience, but by the one who has redeemed us in the world and calls us to fullness of life. The close relationship between the scroll of God's will in Revelation 5 and the little scroll consumed by John in Revelation 10 demonstrates the close relationship between God's revelation of himself and the ministry to which his prophetic people are called. We do not have a monopoly on truth, but we are those 'on whom the end of the ages has come' (1 Cor. 10:11, AT). To us has been revealed the mystery of God's plan of redemption for the world: Christ in us, the hope of glory (Col. 1:27), a mystery that not even God's people of the first covenant could fully grasp. John's ministry, and the ministry of all God's people, is now, through their prophetic proclamation, to make that mystery known to the world while there is still time to repent.

B. The people of God as the two prophetic witnesses (11:1–14)

Context

The second part of the interlude between the sixth and seventh trumpets continues with an account of John's experience as a central figure in the narrative, just as he was in the second half of Revelation 10. Like Ezekiel, he is commanded to measure the temple, but unlike Ezekiel, there is no indication that he actually does this. The instruction about measuring then blends into a prophetic narrative, uniquely written in the future tense, about the ministry of God's 'two witnesses'. This passage is particularly complex to make sense of because of the dense allusions to a series of Old Testament texts, including Zechariah, Daniel, Exodus and 1 Kings alongside Ezekiel, and because of the introduction of John's use of numerological symbolism derived from Daniel's visions.

This chapter is bound together with Revelation 12 – 13 by the three equivalent time periods of forty-two months (11:2; 13:5), 1,260 days (11:3; 12:6) and three and a half years or days (11:9, 11; 12:14) mentioned seven times in total, and only in these chapters. The form of the report by John is different in these three chapters from what we have read previously; his frequent signalling of a new episode or new characters with the phrase 'and I saw' is absent until it resumes again in Revelation 14. In contrast with what we have read so far of the plagues that have afflicted humankind, the ministry of the two witnesses does lead some to repentance, with survivors of the great earthquake '[giving] glory to God' (11:13). Chapter 11 ends with praise in heaven celebrating the End and the final victory of God, connecting it with both the end of the interlude in Revelation 7 and the worship in heaven that we encountered in Revelation 4.

i. Measuring the temple (11:1–2)

Comment

1. John's language shifts from that used in the previous narrative, where the angel gives him the scroll, to the (divine) passive *I was given*. The grammar becomes a little awkward, since the text literally says, 'it was given to me . . . saying'; the one addressing him could be either the angel or the 'voice from heaven' that spoke to him in 10:8. The command to *measure* with a *reed like a measuring rod* recalls the extended vision of Ezekiel, when he sees an angelic figure measuring the eschatological temple in Ezekiel 40 – 42, but there are some important differences in John's vision. The first is that it is John, rather than an angelic figure, who is commanded to do the measuring; second, John never actually does do any measuring; and third, the *reed* (*kalamos*) is *like a . . . rod* (*rhabdos*), which connects John with the messianic figure who will 'rule the nations with a rod [*rhabdos*] of iron' (2:27; 12:5; 19:15, referring to Ps. 2:9). So where the measuring in Ezekiel suggests precision and certainty in the execution of God's plan (which becomes evident in the measuring of the New Jerusalem in Rev. 21), the measuring here also suggests authority.

Many commentators have assumed either that the command to measure the *temple* means that it must be standing, so that Revelation must have been written before AD 70, or that this is a vision rather than anything literal, implying that the temple must no longer be standing and that Revelation was clearly written after the destruction of the temple in AD 70.[7] In fact, the temple has already been mentioned, in the eschatological promise in 3:12 and in the vision of the unnumbered multitude in 7:15. The altar has also been introduced previously, as the dwelling-place of the martyrs (6:9) and the place where the incense and prayers of the saints are offered (8:3, 5). More detail about the altar was added in 9:13, and the space 'before the throne' has gradually looked more and more like a spiritual version of the earthly temple. So this text tells us nothing, one way or another, about the Jerusalem temple. The *worshippers* are the multitude 'standing before the throne and in front of the Lamb' (7:9), that is, those who have been sealed, who have kept faith through the great suffering and have been redeemed by the lamb's death. John's measuring of the temple *with* its worshippers brings us close to the Johannine and Pauline understandings of Jesus and those who are the body of Christ as the true temple (John 2:19; 1 Cor. 3:16; Eph. 2:21).

2. The reference to the *outer court* that has been *given over to the Gentiles* (AT) makes a passing reference to the Jerusalem temple of the first century, since the outer court was known as the Court of the Gentiles. But this simple division between the temple and the outer court ignores the other regions of the Jerusalem temple (the Court of Women and the Court of Israel) which lie between the temple itself (including the Holy of Holies) and the outer court – another reason to understand this as a reference to the heavenly temple. The mention of Gentiles who *trample* uses the same language as Jesus' prediction of the destruction of Jerusalem in Luke 21:24: 'Jerusalem will be trampled on by the Gentiles until the times of the Gentiles are fulfilled.' The parallel passage in Matthew 24:15–16 connects this with the 'abomination of desolation' at the end of the half-week in Daniel 9:27:

---

7. For a full discussion of questions on dating the text, see Introduction.

So when you see standing in the holy place 'the abomination that causes desolation', spoken of through the prophet Daniel – let the reader understand – then let those who are in Judea flee to the mountains. (Matt. 24:15–16)

He will confirm a covenant with many for one 'seven'. In the middle of the 'seven' he will put an end to sacrifice and offering. And at the temple he will set up an abomination that causes desolation, until the end that is decreed is poured out on him. (Dan. 9:27)

John describes this 'time of the Gentiles' which Matthew connects with Daniel's time of desolation as *42 months*, which in a calendar of twelve months per year equates to three and a half years, or a 'half-week' of years (as in Dan. 7:25; 9:27; 12:7). The significance of the number 42 within the biblical canon is that it is the number of 'stations' or places where God's people camped during the journey through the wilderness according to the listing in Numbers 33.[8] John is therefore further identifying the 'time of the Gentiles' and their trampling not only with the suffering of the half-week of Daniel, but also with the time of the wilderness wanderings which followed the ten plagues of Egypt and deliverance of the Passover.

ii. The ministry of the two witnesses (11:3–6)

3. The introduction of the *two witnesses* seems to be quite abrupt, except that two is the number for true witness, since two witnesses need to agree for their testimony to be true (Deut. 17:6, a criterion appealed to by Jesus in John 5:31–38 and failed in Jesus' trial in Mark 14:56; see comment on 3:14). Witness or testimony (the two English

---

8. Although the number 42 is not mentioned in the listing of 'stations' in Num. 33, the number has been important in both Jewish and Christian traditions. The Italian medieval writer Dante modelled his poetic work *La Vita Nuova* on the stations in its forty-two chapters. The wilderness journey also lasted forty-two years (including the period prior to Kadesh Barnea, though this is usually rounded to forty years: see Deut. 8:2; Acts 13:18).

terms translate the same word *martyria* in Greek) is the distinctive characteristic of both Jesus and his people in Revelation. The juxtaposition of this term with mention of the 'temple ... and ... its worshippers' and the introduction of the witnesses in definite terms (lit. 'the two witnesses of me') suggest that the two witnesses are a metaphorical description of the people of God. The time during which they *prophesy*, which is *1,260 days*, also matches the forty-two months of trampling in an ideal calendar with thirty days in each month.[9]

John has previously used square and cubed numbers (144; 1,000) to signify the people of God, and will do so again in the vision of the New Jerusalem. He will use a 'triangular' number – one that can be represented by objects arranged in a triangle of equal sides, like the fifteen red balls at the start of a frame of snooker – to signify the arch-enemy of God's people in the number of the beast (666, the thirty-sixth triangular number). At the start of this apocalyptic, prophetic letter, he described himself as a subject *both* of the 'kingdom' *and* of the 'suffering' that comes from hostility to God's people, being in exile on Patmos (1:9). If the priestly kingdom of God and his people (1:6) is signified by *square* numbers, and the suffering arising from opposition by the forces of evil is signified by *triangular* numbers, it would fit if John is using *rectangular* numbers to signify the overlap of the two – numbers formed by multiplying not the same number by itself, but a number by its successor. Both 42 ($= 6 \times 7$) and 1,260 ($= 35 \times 36$)[10] are rectangles; rectangles look

---

9. Commentators who see the final text of Revelation as a (perhaps poorly) edited composition from different earlier written sources see the change from 42 months to 1,260 days as evidence of a 'literary seam', with each term originally belonging to a different source. This assumes that John is not in the habit of reusing ideas, and it ignores the numerological patterns which are evident in the text. And there is neither manuscript evidence for smaller original pieces nor any explicit textual evidence of editorial activity.

10. John has revised Daniel's calculation of the three and a half years from 1,290 days (Dan. 12:11) to 1,260 by omitting an intercalated month (one added to keep the year in line with the solar calendar) in order to fit this numerological pattern.

very much like squares, but are also closely related to triangles since each rectangle is double the corresponding triangle (42 is twice the sixth triangle 21, and 1,260 is twice the thirty-fifth triangle 630).[11]

The witnesses are clothed in *sackcloth*, the apparel of repentance which is the appropriate response to the reception of the coming kingdom of God (Mark 1:15). It is not clear where the direct speech to John ends and his own commentary begins; some think it ends at the end of verse 3, others at the end of verse 4, still others at the end of verse 8.

4. Having used images from Ezekiel and Daniel, interpreted through the traditions of Matthew and Luke, John now draws on the language of Zechariah 4 in his vision of the two witnesses.[12] The *two olive trees* of Zechariah 4:3−14 that *stand before the Lord of [all] the earth* represent the governor Zerubbabel and the priest Joshua, who were leaders of the first group of Jews to return from exile in Babylon in the late sixth century BC. They are pictured as providing the olive oil to feed the golden lampstands of the temple – that is, they are the ones who are maintaining the worship of God. At the beginning of Zechariah's vision, the olive trees are distinct from the lampstands and feed them with oil, but by the end of the vision (in Zech. 4:14), the two images appear to have coalesced into one, and John follows this by identifying the witnesses as olive trees with two lampstands – another image of the people of God in the presence of God, first introduced in 1:12 as signifying the Christian communities in the seven cities of Asia.

5. The idea of *fire com[ing] from their mouths* sounds alarming, and appears to add to the problem of violence in the text. But since we do not take the image of them being olive trees or lampstands as literal, it is difficult to see why we should take this literally either. Jeremiah is told that 'I will make my words in your mouth a fire and

---

11. For detailed study of square, triangular and rectangular numbers, their significance in John's world and their use in Revelation, see Bauckham, *Climax of Prophecy*, ch. 11, 'Nero and the Beast', pp. 384–452.

12. The previous chapter in Zechariah has supplied John with the image of the stone with seven eyes, and chapter 6 provides the image of the four horses of different colours.

these people the wood it consumes' (Jer. 5:14), and Elijah (who is
alluded to in the next verse) is described as a 'prophet like fire' whose
'word burned like a torch' in the second-century BC book of
Ecclesiasticus (Sirach 48:1). Fire as a metaphor for powerful speech
forms a parallel to the speech of Jesus, who conquers by the sword
of his mouth as a metaphor for his true speech (1:16; 2:16; 19:15,
21) and as a contrast to the spirit-frogs that come from the mouth
of the dragon, the beast and the false prophet, symbolizing their
deceptive speech (16:13). This is a war of words between Jesus'
adversaries and his followers, but a non-violent one for the latter.
Those who *harm* them will not be harmed in return, but convicted
by their prophetic speech, just as Jesus will slay the kings of the earth
with his speech in 19:21 – though they later enter the New Jerusalem
in 21:24.

6. The people of God are not only true witnesses and a royal
priesthood who continue true worship, but they now also exercise
the prophetic ministries of Elijah and Moses. Elijah *shut up the sky*
for three years to call the people back to the worship of God in
1 Kings 17:1 and 18:1, but Luke 4:25 and James 5:17 recount this as
a period of three and a half years, matching Daniel's half-week of
years and so also matching the time of the witnesses' prophesying.
In both Jewish (Deut. 11:16–17) and Greco-Roman traditions,
drought was seen as a sign of divine judgment which called for
repentance. Moses was able to *turn the waters into blood* in the first of
every kind of plague inflicted on the Egyptians in Exodus 7:14–21;
sharing in this Mosaic ministry connects the prophesying of the two
witnesses with the second trumpet in 8:8. In both Exodus and Revelation 8, the purpose of this plague was to warn of divine judgment
and invite repentance – something also believed in Greco-Roman
religion.

iii. The two witnesses are killed and raised to life (11:7–14)

7. The *finish[ing] of their testimony* is not simply a question of
ending, but of accomplishing or completing what they set out to
do; the word *teleō* was used of the 'accomplishing' of the 'mystery
of God' in 10:7. The *beast . . . from the Abyss* has not been mentioned
before, but need not be identified with the 'angel of the Abyss' in
9:11. John habitually mentions a character or an idea in brief earlier

on, only to develop or expand on this as the narrative unfolds (as with 'tribulation' or 'suffering' in 1:9, the victor sayings in the messages in Rev. 2 − 3 and the portrayal of the heavenly temple from Rev. 4 onwards). Because of the close association in the Old Testament between the abyss and the 'deep' or the sea, we should see this as the same as the 'beast from the sea' in 13:1, who is paired first with the 'beast from the land' in 13:11 which is renamed 'the false prophet' in 16:13 and 19:20.

The beast will *make war on them and conquer them and kill them* (AT), echoing the attack and apparent victory of the little horn over the saints in Daniel 7:21. This is surprising, given what has gone before, and appears to contradict the promise of God's protection of his people. But in fact it matches the pattern that we have seen before, where the faithful witness of Antipas has ended in martyrdom in 2:13, and the great multitude who worship God have come through (rather than avoided) great suffering in 7:14. Even closer parallels between the beast and the little horn are drawn in 13:7, where the language of making war and conquering God's people is repeated. But the conquering (*nikaō*) through violence stands in stark contrast to the conquest and victory that God's people are called to: a victory won through non-violent resistance and faithful witness, following the example of the slain lamb.

8. The *bodies* of the two witnesses (in fact, their dead corpses, *ptōma* not *sōma*) are left to lie in the open. Corpses would normally be removed from public spaces because of the risk of disease, but in certain contexts of war or crucifixion, corpses were left on display to act as both the final humiliation of those who had been killed and a warning to others. The place of display (*plateia*) could mean either main street or (as it is used today in modern Greece) the central square or plaza of a city.

The *great city* has sometimes been interpreted as Jerusalem because of the only mention in Revelation of Jesus being *crucified*. But it is later described as ruling over the kings of the earth (17:18), named as Babylon (18:10), and portrayed as a centre of luxury and wealth (18:16) and of global sea trade (18:19), all of which makes identification with Rome conclusive. The identification of Rome with Babylon (1 Pet. 5:13) became common after the fall of Jerusalem in AD 70, since both powers had destroyed the city and its temple.

Within the biblical tradition, *Sodom* was a byword not only for sexual immorality, but also for violence, injustice, arrogance, neglect of the poor and idolatry (Gen. 19:1–25; Isa. 1:9–10; Jer. 23:14; Ezek. 16:46–50) and as a supreme example of judgment, including the judgment that the city of Babylon would face (Isa. 13:19; Jer. 50:40). *Egypt* is consistently assumed to be the enemy of God, and is frequently the unreliable ally who should not be trusted for national salvation in preference to the call to trust in God (Isa. 31:1). Rome/ Babylon is identified with Sodom and Egypt *figuratively*, though the word *pneumatikos* can mean 'symbolically' or (perhaps better) 'spiritually', that is, by the insight of the Spirit who identifies what the spiritual or theological reality is. Rome is not the saviour people should look to, but violent and idolatrous, and an unreliable refuge. Neither is Rome unique; though hailed as 'great', perhaps even the 'greatest' ever (18:18), it shared the characteristics of other 'great' human empires. Although Jerusalem was the physical location of Jesus' crucifixion, the cultural location was that of Roman rule and collusion by the Jewish leaders with Roman authority, and crucifixion was a Roman (rather than Jewish) punishment. So it was in the great city's orbit that his death occurred.

9. The time period *three and a half days* could be understood as following (in the narrative) the period of three and a half years (forty-two months, 1,260 days), but could (paradoxically) also be understood as simultaneous with it. The reasons for thinking this are that, in the texts from which this time period is borrowed in Daniel, days and years are interchanged, and the time during which the beast blasphemes, makes war on and conquers the saints is the same time period in 12:14 and 13:5, which functions as an amplification of this episode. The idea that God's people are both testifying and protected by God, yet at the same time also trampled and appearing to be conquered corresponds both to John's simultaneous experience of 'kingdom' and 'suffering' (1:9) and to the vision of the temple being protected while the outer court is trampled. God's people are in reality kept secure even when they appear to be defeated.

The fourth of the seven occurrences of the fourfold phrase *every people, tribe, language and nation* (see comment on 5:9) refers to humanity in general who at times are deceived into following the beast (13:7), but might also be redeemed by the lamb (7:9). Not allowing their corpses to be *placed in a tomb* (AT) is the ultimate disgrace, to be imposed on those who mislead God's people with false prophecy (Jer. 14:16), but in fact experienced by God's people when the temple was destroyed by Babylon (Ps. 79:2–3). The word for 'tomb' gives rise to the English term 'mnemonic' and hints at the dead being forgotten, the final indignity in a culture where being remembered was the only tangible way of transcending the finality of death.

10. In this verse we have the fourth and fifth of ten occurrences of the phrase *the inhabitants of the earth*,[13] which (in contrast to the fourfold phrase in the previous verse) refers consistently to those who are deceived by the beast and are opposed to the people of God, forming an antonym to those 'dwelling [tabernacling] in heaven' (13:6, AT). The *sending* of *gifts* suggests the kind of celebration that took place at Saturnalia in December each year, when seven days of feasting were accompanied by the sending and receiving of gifts – though this is not a direct allusion. The identification of the two witnesses as *two prophets* makes the connection with the ministries of Elijah and Moses explicit, as well as with 'his servants the prophets' (10:7) more generally, and with the prophetic ministry of John himself in particular (cf. 22:6). The witnesses *tormented* those who did not receive their prophetic testimony, just as the demons were tormented by the threat of Jesus' deliverance (Mark 5:7).

11–12. If the celebrations were intended to last a symbolic week, the triumph was cut short by the *breath of life* entering the corpses of the witnesses and raising them from death. The language here is from the vision of Ezekiel 37, where the dry bones of God's people are covered in sinews, muscles and skin and then the 'breath [*pneuma*, wind or spirit] entered them' (Ezek. 37:10) and they become a 'vast army'. The phrase in Ezekiel (and so here) is based on the creation account in Genesis 2:7, where the *'ādām* who has been formed from the ground (the *'ădāmâ*) becomes a living being only when God

---

13. The repetition of the phrase at the beginning and end of the verse
    is obscured in some English translations by rendering the same Greek
    phrase by two different English ones.

breathes the 'breath of life' into him. Although initially a metaphor of the renewal of God's people and their hope (Ezek. 37:11), the language of (new) creation meant that this vision became the basis for the hope of post-mortem bodily resurrection in the age to come, fulfilled unexpectedly in the resurrection of Jesus. The raising of the witnesses *after the three and a half days* makes a direct connection with Jesus' resurrection 'on the third day' or 'after three days' (Matt. 16:21; 1 Cor. 15:4; cf. Matt. 27:63; Mark 8:31). Just as they have been faithful witnesses to the point of death like Jesus (1:5), so they too are raised to life by God as he was. If, in some sense, the three and a half days of their being slain by the beast is simultaneous with the three and a half years of their testifying, the true life of the witnesses is the resurrection life which is the gift of God; it is this which is being preserved in the temple even if the appearance (the outer court) seems to be trampled. This corresponds to the way Paul describes his own apostolic ministry: 'Though outwardly we are wasting away, yet inwardly we are being renewed day by day' (2 Cor. 4:16).

It is notable that, whereas after his resurrection Jesus was seen by only a few who were his followers, in this narrative the two witnesses are seen by all, publicly, who respond with *terror.* This introduces the theme of public vindication of God's people who have suffered persecution which is revisited more fully as one of the themes in the millennial reign of Revelation 20. The *loud voice from heaven* is of unspecified origin, but parallels the 'voice from heaven' in 10:4, 8, as well as the voice of Jesus which calls John into the heavenly throne room ('Come up here . . .') in 4:1. The *cloud* is (as elsewhere in Revelation) a sign of divine presence; the ascent in a cloud is reminiscent of Jesus' ascension, but has no obvious parallel with Paul's description of 'meet[ing] the Lord in the air' at the final resurrection in 1 Thessalonians 4:17, since the context of that meeting is 'the Lord com[ing] down from heaven' (1 Thess. 4:16), which is not mentioned here.

13. The *earthquake* has earlier been a sign of God's presence (8:5), but also of penultimate, temporal judgment (6:12). Such an earthquake as a sign of judgment occurs in Ezekiel 38:19 (i.e. following the vision of resurrection in Ezek. 37) in a passage which also includes mountains being overturned, plagues and bloodshed, hail and sulphur, and the giving of Gog, the enemy of God, and his people as food for carrion birds – all ideas found in Revelation. As with the series of seals and trumpets, where only part of the world is affected, here only part of the city collapses and only some of its citizens die. If the *seven thousand* represent the *tenth* part of the city, its population would have been only 70,000, which is nowhere near the population of the larger cities of the Roman Empire. It must, instead, be symbolic of the complete number of those who were to suffer death. Although repentance is not mentioned in relation to those who remain, *fear* (AT) is seen as an appropriate response to the revelation of God throughout the Scriptures, and the fact that they *gave glory to the God of heaven* suggests recognition of the truth of who he is. This is not clear enough to be interpreted as a final widespread repentance of the nations, but it contributes to Revelation's mixed vision in which there is a sharp distinction between those who believe and those who do not – and yet there is also a surprisingly open invitation to all to repent and respond.

14. The mention of the *second woe* is not unexpected, since we were alerted to the three woes (which appeared to be associated with the last three trumpets) in 8:13, and then informed that the first woe had passed in 9:12 with the fifth trumpet (see comments on these verses). But we are now left with two puzzles: what exactly was the second woe which is now past – was it the events associated with the sixth trumpet, or does it also include the events related in the interlude? And what is the *third woe* which is coming soon?

It is important to note the relation of the two interludes of Revelation 7 and Revelation 10 – 11 with the sequences in which they are located. Although they are presented in the sequence of John's visions, it is clear that the content of the visions should not be taken as a series of chronological events because of the connections between them and the repeated anticipation of the End. In both interludes, the structural repetition of the respective sequence is interrupted, and a different series of images is introduced using quite different language. But both interludes are completed with an anticipation of the End (7:15–17 and 11:11–13), and this then merges with the conclusion of the surrounding sequence, which when resumed also includes an anticipation of the End

(8:1 and 11:15–19). The first woe refers to the chaos unleashed with the blowing of the fifth trumpet, so it is natural to read the second woe as referring to the similar chaos of the sixth trumpet. This merges with the images of judgment at the end of the interlude, so these might be included in the second woe. But the main events of the interlude – John's commission to prophesy and God's people acting as the true prophetic witnesses – cannot themselves be included in the second woe.

Some commentators assume that the seventh trumpet with its anticipation of the End *must* be associated with the third woe, because that is what the earlier sequence might suggest. But if we are to take John's own language seriously here, we need to note both that John does *not* mention the third woe in relation to the seventh trumpet, and that he *does* later mention a 'woe' – when the devil is cast from heaven to earth as a result of Jesus' death (the 'blood of the Lamb', 12:11). The third woe therefore relates to the time period that John and his audience are living in, which began with Jesus' death and resurrection, reaches a climax in the downfall of Babylon, but does not end until the New Jerusalem descends.

Theology

Three of the most important theological questions to ask are: 'What time is it?', 'Where are we?' and 'Who am I?' In this second part of the second interlude, through complex allusions to a wide range of Old Testament texts, this part of John's vision report addresses these questions.

First, this is the 'time of the nations' or 'Gentiles', in that it appears as though God's people (as his temple, his dwelling-place on earth) are being trampled just as the Jerusalem temple was trampled by the power of Rome. Yet it is also a time of preservation and protection, since the inner part of the temple – the spiritual heart of God's people – enjoys his presence and assurance.

Second, this is a transitional time of journeying, since God's people are travelling from one station to another, having been set free from slavery (enslaved not by Egypt but by sin, Rev. 1:5), but not yet having entered the promised land of dwelling in the full presence of God, which is the constant hope on the horizon in every section of Revelation.

Third, by a clever numerical identification, this journeying of forty-two 'stages' is also the time of tribulation anticipated in the visions of Daniel.

This is a time for God's people to maintain the true worship of God by refusing to compromise their allegiance and instead fulfil their calling to be a kingdom of priests. It is a time to offer prophetic testimony to God, just as the prophets before them had done, even though they too had suffered oppression. It is a time in which the nations gloat over their failure and even death, and yet a time when they experience God's resurrection power. Although they are a small, vulnerable group, in their faithfulness they follow the example of their Lord and so experience both crucifixion and resurrection as he did. By delaying identification of the third woe, John is confirming that the first two woes (and the series of plagues in which they are embedded) are not a future scenario of judgment, but a reality that already exists. The third woe stretches from the present into the future, and includes the challenge of faithfulness that confronts God's people.

By contrast, the 'great city' representing Roman imperial power is not the 'eternal city' as was consistently claimed, but a human institution like all others that went before it – subject to the judgment of God as they had been. The true eternal city is the one that God's people are already beginning to inhabit, as yet hidden, but which will be revealed in the visions of Revelation 21 – 22.

C. The seventh angel sounds his trumpet (11:15–19)

Comment

15. Having been brought back to the trumpet series after the interlude by the proclamation of the second woe, the *seventh angel* now sounds his blast. Revelation is a noisy book; twenty times we read of a *loud voice* as if the 'war of words' on earth corresponds to a war of praise in heaven, with the loud praises of God and the declarations of his salvation drowning out all other, rival voices. 'Hark! the songs of peaceful Zion thunder like a mighty flood'.[14]

---

14. William Dix (1837–98), 'Alleluia! Sing to Jesus!'

The *world* (*kosmos*) is mentioned in Revelation only twice elsewhere, in 13:8 and 17:8 in relation to its creation. In John's Gospel, the *kosmos* is both the object of God's love (John 3:16), and the creation in rebellion against him and under the rule of Satan (John 15:18; 12:31). Revelation expresses a similar ambivalence, but primarily through the terminology of 'the inhabitants of the earth' and 'the rulers of the earth'.

The direction of travel of the *kingdom* of God is from heaven to earth, in that the heavenly kingdom is now realized in the world. This is more fully developed in the movement of the holy city, the New Jerusalem, 'coming down out of heaven from God' in Revelation 21:2, and answers the prayer of Jesus and his disciples that 'your kingdom come . . . on earth as it is in heaven' (Matt. 6:10). Elsewhere in the New Testament (and particularly in Paul), *Lord* (*kyrios*) refers to Jesus, but in Revelation it consistently refers to God, especially in the phrase 'Lord God Almighty' (1:8; 4:8; 11:17; and so on). This is made clear by reference to *his Messiah*; the term *Christos* meaning 'anointed one' which is translated 'Messiah' here in many English versions is rendered 'Christ' elsewhere, which obscures its occurrence: seven times in total (1:1, 2, 5; 11:15; 12:10; 20:4, 6). It is notable that the plural subject of 'the Lord and his Messiah' attracts the singular verb *he will reign* (the second of seven occurrences of this verb), reflecting the identification of the one on the throne with the lamb, who together share the throne (symbolizing their joint authority to rule) in Revelation 5.[15] Their eternal reign (*for ever and ever*) offers another counterpoint to claims of Rome to be the eternal city.

16–17. The *twenty-four elders* falling down in worship connects this scene back to the worship of Revelation 4 – 5, 7. This is the only occurrence of the verb to *give thanks*, undermining the idea that Revelation is a liturgical text which in some sense reflects the worship practices of the early church (see comment on incense in 5:8). The title for God, *Lord God Almighty . . . who is and who was*, echoes the same combination in 1:8 and 4:8 but with the omission of the

---

15. The use of a singular pronoun to denote both God and the lamb recurs in 22:3–4; see comment there.

third ascription 'who is to come', since this hymn of praise assumes God has now come and has *begun to reign*, confirming that (as with the end of the seals in 8:1) this is one of many summary anticipations of the End which is filled out in more detail in successive similar anticipations until the full vision of Revelation 21 – 22.

18. The language of the *nations* being *angry*, expressing the rebellion of humanity against God's rule, is close to the Greek of Psalm 2:1. The next verse in the psalm provides John with the phrases 'the LORD and his *christos*' as well as 'the kings of the earth', and 2:9 provides the image of the 'rod of iron' (see Rev. 2:27; 12:5; 19:15). The verb translated *were angry* and the noun *wrath* are cognates, that is, they come from the same root. But Revelation is consistent with the rest of the New Testament in never describing God as being 'angry', instead portraying God's wrath as his steadfast opposition to sin (see comment on 6:17). The word used here for *time* is *kairos* rather than *chronos*; the issue here is less about chronology or delay than seeing that, now that God is finally reigning, this is the moment for the expression of his just judgment of *the dead* (revisited in more detail in 20:11–15). This includes *rewarding* God's faithful people, in fulfilment of the promises in each of the messages in Revelation 2 – 3. It is not clear here whether *your servants the prophets* functions as a parallel description of *your people* or as a subgroup within them. The phrase *small and great* (AT) is another 'gradable antonym' (see comment on 6:15) functioning as a merism (a device in which two contrasting elements of something are used to describe the whole) to signify the universal appeal of the good news of redemption. The destruction of those *who destroy the earth* is a key idea which expresses God's commitment to the created order, previously expressed in the rainbow around the throne (reiterating God's post-flood promise to Noah not to destroy the earth again) and the presence of the four living creatures. However we construe the sovereignty of God in relation to the seals and trumpets, it is made clear here that God's purpose in the world is its redemption and renewal ('I am making everything new', 21:5) and not its destruction.

19. Some commentators treat this verse as the beginning of the next section and read it with 12:1, rather than taking the traditional approach of seeing this as the conclusion of the preceding verses. Various elements in this verse are connected with the End and so belong with the declarations in the previous verses, and the introduction of distinctive new terminology in 12:1 also supports the traditional reading. The anticipation of the End in this part of the text is still being expressed using the imagery of the visions John has reported so far; though in the New Jerusalem 'I saw no temple' (21:22, AT), here the *temple in heaven was opened*, expressing the final visibility and openness of the presence of God when he comes. With a further development of the detail of the heavenly temple, we see the *ark of [the] covenant*, which contained the two tablets of the Ten Commandments, manna from the desert and Aaron's staff, reminding us both of God's covenant faithfulness and of the covenant obligations on his people to live in holiness. The ark was lost after the Babylonian destruction of the temple in 586 BC, so its presence here is another confirmation that the temple in Revelation 11 is not a reference to the Jerusalem temple in the first century. The *lightning, thunder* and other phenomena form the third of four references to the appearance of God at Sinai, which increase in their drama and severity, the first occurrence in 4:5 being augmented with the earthquake in 8:5, a *great hailstorm* being added in this verse and the earthquake becoming the most severe ever in 16:18.

Theology

This section, opening with the seventh angel trumpeting, functions both to complete the trumpet series and also to bring to an end the double interval which has elucidated John's prophetic ministry (in chapter 10) and the prophetic testimony of the people of God, envisaged as the two witnesses (in the first part of chapter 11).

In doing so, this section looks forward to the final visions of chapter 21, when the city of God that contains the throne of God and the lamb descends from heaven, signifying both the presence and the reign of God on earth. The merging of the identities of God and the lamb in the singular verb 'he will reign' (11:15) anticipates the even closer merging in chapters 21 and 22. But it also looks back to the worship scenes of chapters 4 and 5 – it is the twenty-four elders from that scene who in praise look forward to the final scene, from which they themselves will be absent. From a textual point of view, this serves to unify and link together the text of Revelation as a whole; from a theological point of view, it reinforces what John has said from the beginning (in 1:9): that John's readers (then and now) are living in the 'in-between' times, in tension between the kingdom where God's will is done and which has broken in on this world, and the need for patient endurance as we look forward to the final triumph of that kingdom.

The praise of the elders emphasizes the tensions involved in living in this in-between period, by highlighting a series of contrasts. The first is between the nations of the earth who have resisted God's rule, and the judgment they will now face as his reign is enacted. The second contrast is between the judgment of humanity as they must give an account of themselves to God, and the reward that is given to those who have kept faith despite the pressures to compromise. The third contrast draws the first two together: those who are destructive, and who have brought both death and destruction to God's people and God's world, will receive back what they have given out. This is the first anticipation of the theme of *lex talionis*: the principle of God's justice in treating people as they have treated others, which is developed more fully in chapter 18. But it also connects the theology of God as Judge with the theology of God as Creator; at the End he will remake creation and exclude from it those who have wrought its destruction and in doing so failed to recognize him as its source.

8. THE WOMAN CLOTHED WITH THE SUN, THE CHILD AND THE DRAGON (12:1–17)

Context

We now come to what commentators universally agree is the central and pivotal chapter in the book. Although this chapter is not styled as an interlude to a series in the way chapters 7 and 10 – 11 are, it stands out as distinctive in style and language. A decisive break with the previous narrative is marked by the opening comment, not 'And I saw . . .', but 'And a great sign appeared in heaven . . .' (AT).

The shape of this chapter and of the one that follows is also distinctive. Together, Revelation 12 and 13 form the longest continuous narrative within the whole book. But Revelation 12 itself has perhaps the clearest structure of any section, dividing into four interconnected parts:

1. Opening narrative about the woman, the child and the dragon (vv. 1–6);
2. Short narrative about war in heaven (vv. 7–9);
3. Poetic hymn of praise (vv. 10–12);

4. Resumption of the opening narrative of woman, child and
   dragon (vv. 13–17).

As we shall see, sections 2 and 3 are epexegetical of each preceding
section, that is, they function to explain what has gone before, until
the original narrative is resumed after the hymn has made clear what
this whole episode is about. And explanation is needed because of
the unusual nature of the main narrative in verses 1–6 and 13–17,
which contains many ideas that are not found in the Old Testament
nor earlier in Revelation. We can recognize the characters easily
enough – the woman as the people of God awaiting deliverance,
the dragon as 'that ancient snake called the devil', the child who
is the anointed king in Psalm 2, Michael the great angelic prince of
Israel – but the plot is strange to us.

However, it would not have been strange to John nor to his
audience. It has clear connections to a myth that was widely circulated
from the third century BC to the second century AD in a variety of
forms, the best known being the story of Leto, Python and Apollo.
Python, a huge dragon, was warned by an oracle that he would be
destroyed by one of Leto's children. Leto was a lover of Zeus who
was married to Hera. When Hera learned that Leto was pregnant,
she banished her; Leto gave birth to her twins, Artemis and Apollo,
on the island of Delos (about 40 miles [70 km] due west of Patmos).
Python pursued her in order to destroy her offspring, but she was
carried away by Aquilo (Latin for the north wind) and protected by
Poseidon with waves. When four days old, Apollo hunted down
Python and killed him with arrows (both Apollo and Artemis were
archers).[1] This story was used as imperial propaganda, particularly
by Domitian, to portray the emperor as Apollo, the son of the gods
and defeater of the chaos monster.

John has previously blended Old Testament ideas with elements
of the emperor cult, particularly in the vision of worship in

---

1. This is a summary of the version recorded by the Latin author Hyginus
   in his collection of mythology *Fabulae* (no. 140). Hyginus (*c.*64 BC –
   AD 17) was a freedman of Augustus and the superintendent of the
   library on the Palatine.

Revelation 4. Here, though, is a particular way of bringing the two together – by taking the characters from one narrative (the biblical story) and inserting them into the plotline from another narrative (the Leto myth). This is a device we continue to see today in many forms of political cartoon. To make sense of it, we need to recognize both the characters (which come from one context, the Scriptures of the Old Testament) and the plot (which comes from another context, the world of Greco-Roman mythology, particularly as appropriated in imperial propaganda). In doing this, John's vision report inverts the story, displacing imperial power from the role of Apollo by the Davidic Messiah, and instead associating the empire with the chaos monster, the dragon.

A. The woman, the dragon and the child (12:1–6)

Comment

1. John uses quite distinctive language in this part of his vision report; instead of reporting something he saw, he describes *a great sign . . . in heaven* (AT; or 'in the sky').[2] This suggests that what he reports is also visible to others, or is public knowledge, rather than his own experience alone. This is the first of seven occurrences of 'sign' (*sēmeion*), used three times with reference to things of symbolic significance in heaven (12:1, 3; 15:1) and four times in a Johannine sense, referring to apparent miracles performed to deceive people into following the beast (13:13, 14; 16:14; 19:20). Because this sign has symbolic significance, the figure of the *woman* is unlikely to refer to a particular individual (such as Mary in much Catholic interpretation); the subsequent details of the narrative rule out this possibility. The mention of *sun*, *moon* and *stars* together provide an allusion to Joseph's dream in Genesis 37:9, where the stars who bow down to him symbolize his brothers (who later give their names to the twelve tribes) and the sun and the moon perhaps symbolize his father and mother. But together they point to the people of God,

---

2. Some versions of the NIV translate it as 'a great and wondrous sign', which is incorrect; the phrase does occur with 'and wondrous' in 15:1, but not here.

whom the woman symbolizes. Within the narrative of Revelation, mention of the sun connects her to the vision of Jesus in 1:16 and of the angel in 10:1, and her association with sun and moon contrasts with their darkening in 8:12 and 9:2. The crown she wears reminds us of the victory wreath promised to the faithful in 2:10 and 3:11.

2. Although the woman is often depicted as serene in artistic portrayals, the text offers us anything but a serene portrait. She is *pregnant* (using the Greek idiom 'having in the belly') and *cried out* in *labour pains*, in the *agonies* of *giving birth* (AT). The four terms here exactly match those in Isaiah 26:17, where God's people in distress are likened to a woman giving birth, and similar language is used in Isaiah 66:7–9, where Jerusalem is the woman as a metonym for God's people. In Greek and Hebrew as well as English, the language of 'deliverance' has a double meaning in applying to both the birth of a child and the rescue of a people in distress, making the image a natural one for God's saving of his people from a time of exile or oppression. In Micah 4:8–10, the woman in labour is also characterized as either Zion or Jerusalem, again as a metonym for God's people, but the context and cause of agony are made more explicit: exile in Babylon. In the following chapter (Mic. 5:3), the woman's delivery and giving birth are identified with the return from exile of Israel 'and the rest of his brothers', an idea alluded to later in the narrative at Revelation 12:17.

3. The *dragon* is an archetypal image of primeval chaos in many cultures and is the main protagonist in the Python/Leto myth. In the Old Testament, both Leviathan and the 'monsters of the waters' are described as 'dragons' in the Greek translation of Psalms 74:13–14; 104:26, thus associating him with the 'deep' or 'abyss' and with the forces of chaos that God masters (Job 7:12; 26:13). The same word is used for the 'serpent' whom God tramples in Psalm 91:13 and which is identified with the king of Babylon in Jeremiah 51:34 and with the king of Egypt in Ezekiel 29:3; 32:2. Dragons were understood to be ferocious and combative creatures whose coming signalled the advent of war, and his *fiery red* (AT) colour here is the same as the colour of the second of the four horses (6:4) who took peace from the earth.

The dragon has *seven heads and ten horns*, which is the combination of the heads and horns of all four beasts in Daniel's vision of the beasts emerging from the sea in Daniel 7:2–7 (the third beast having four heads and the fourth beast having ten horns). These temporal, human empires actually have their origins in and owe their power to this primeval spiritual opponent of God. The *seven diadems* (that he wears, AT) signify a claim to power, though not necessarily a legitimate one; Roman emperors avoided wearing them in case this was seen as a claim to monarchy (which suggested a return to the tyrannical days before the Republic), preferring instead to wear the laurel wreath as a sign of victory. The diadems here are a counterpart to the woman's crown, and are themselves countered by the 'many diadems' on the King of kings riding on the white horse in 19:12 (AT).

4. Mythical dragons were often depicted as being of cosmic proportions, but the action of sweeping *the stars out of the sky* recalls the action of the little horn in Daniel 8:10, a reference to Antiochus IV Epiphanes who desecrated the temple sacrifices. This passage in Daniel includes the 'abomination of desolation' (AT), which Jesus anticipates will be re-enacted in the destruction of the temple in Matthew 24:15 and Mark 13:14. Within Revelation, the dragon's sweeping *a third of the stars* also connects him with the fourth trumpet, when a third of the stars turn dark; if the various plagues happen with God's permissive authority, the effects have their origin in the powers of evil.

The threatening stance of the dragon before the woman, ready to *devour her child*, reflects the general characterization of dragons and serpents as man-eating (see Jer. 51:34) as well as the aggression of Python to Leto in the mythological tale. As symbolizing Satan's opposition to Jesus and his birth and ministry, we might see it expressed in the slaughter of the innocents (Matt. 2:16), the temptations in the desert, the plotting against Jesus and even the events leading to his crucifixion. But in the narrative here the opposition is expressed in general terms dependent on the Python–Leto myth.

5. In contrast to Isaiah and Micah, the deliverance of God's people from the birth pangs of exile does not come by means of a return to the land but by means of the birth of *a son, a male*. The superfluous adjective reflects a Hebrew idiom (expressed in Jer.

20:15) which again recalls Isaiah 66:7 as well as Isaiah 7:14, which also describes a pregnant woman who gives birth to a son as a 'sign' – though the theme of 'God with you' is not developed here at all. This child fulfils the anticipation in Psalm 2:9 of one who will *rule all the nations with a rod of iron* (AT), thus identifying him unequivocally as Jesus (cf. Rev. 19:15). That the child is immediately *snatched up to God* without any reference to Jesus' life, ministry, death and resurrection seems very odd (though not entirely without parallel in the New Testament: 'he had come from God and was returning to God', John 13:3; cf. 16:28) and is the most puzzling part of the narrative. It seems to be the point where John's vision report is most clearly constrained by the Python–Leto myth into which he is locating his biblical characters. The spiritual victory won by Jesus is expounded in the next section (vv. 7–9) on heavenly warfare, and the redemptive power of Jesus' death is expounded in the second interlude in the narrative in verses 10–12, before we return to the myth narrative in verse 13. The child is snatched up to God *and to his throne* because this is the place from which he exercises his authority over the nations.

6. Just as Leto fled from the pursuing Python and was offered sanctuary by Poseidon, so the woman here flees *to a place prepared for her by God*. The language of 'preparation' (coming seven times in the text) emphasizes God's sovereign control of events, especially at 9:15 and 21:2 as well as here. Neither the chaos of how the world is, nor the remedy needed for its deliverance, nor even its final resolution, takes God by surprise. The *wilderness* of the forty-year journey was seen as a testing time for God's people, but also as a time of God's loving protection and wooing of his people (Hos. 2:14) and of refuge – the place to which Moses (Exod. 2:15), David (1 Sam. 23:25) and Elijah (1 Kgs 19:3–4) fled and in which they were provided for by God. The *1,260 days* (in the second half of the narrative described as the Danielic 'time, times and half a time', 12:14) connects this period back to the time of trampling and testimony in 11:2–3, which is now depicted as a time of nurture and protection. This symbolizes the time from Jesus' resurrection and ascension until his return, which John has characterized as a time of 'suffering and kingdom and patient endurance' (1:9).

B. War in heaven (12:7–9)

7. The register of language now changes, and John's vision report switches from drawing on the Python–Leto myth[3] to drawing on Jewish images of angelic combat. The *war in heaven* is initiated with the enthronement of the male son, which implies a clash of authorities, even though the presence of Satan in heaven has not been previously mentioned (in contrast to the scene described in Job 1:6–8). The advent of angelic warfare was taken by Jews and pagans as a sign that human warfare was about to break out, though here the heavenly conflict actually leads to conflict on earth when Satan is cast down.

Michael was one of the four or seven ruling angels ('archangel'; Jude 9) and presumably one of those who blew the trumpets (see comment on 8:2). His name (*mî-kā-'ēl*) in Hebrew means 'Who is like God?', a question parodied in the later question 'Who is like the beast?' in 13:4. Though some Jewish literature gives Michael a primordial role in confronting Satan in the creation, his main function is eschatological. He is described in Daniel 10:13, 21; 12:1 as the 'chief of princes' (AT) who assists other angels in their warfare against other angelic powers, and as 'the great prince who protects your people', thus linking him with the woman as an image of God's people. Within the narrative, it is notable that it is not the enthroned male son who fights against the dragon, but one of his angels. His authority has been delegated, and victory is certain; the struggle between the forces of good and evil is in no sense a clash of equals.

8. 'Might' or 'strength' is a quality ascribed to God (7:12) and various angels (10:1; 18:21), as well as something claimed by Babylon (18:10); Revelation could therefore be characterized as depicting an (unequal) power struggle in which (contrary to appearance) the power of the dragon (which is behind the power of human empires) is *not strong enough* to overcome the apparent weakness of the child

---

3. In a related myth, Typhon, another dragon monster, fights Zeus and is cast down to Tartarus by him. Though John's audience might have been familiar with this story, the shape of it does not appear to have been a major influence on the text.

or the slain lamb. The phrase translated *they lost their place in heaven* is grammatically very odd, literally reading 'nor was their place found any longer in heaven'. The loss of a 'place' contrasts with the 'place' prepared for the woman for her protection. But more importantly, the same phrase is found in one Greek version (Theodotion) of Daniel 2:35, describing the destruction of the statue which represents human empires by the stone 'not [made] by human hands' which symbolizes the coming kingdom of God. It is also found in the Greek of Psalm 37:36, about the wicked who 'soon passed away and were no more'. Though the psalm reads like a reflection on the wicked in general, in Qumran it was interpreted as predicting the eschatological overthrow of the Wicked Priest who opposed the Teacher of Righteousness. Michael is here enacting the rule of the promised king, now enthroned with God, whose kingdom displaces all human empires and whose rule brings wickedness to an end.

9. John here draws together the various traditions in the Old Testament about the primeval opponent of God. In the Greek Old Testament, the words for 'dragon' or 'sea monster' and 'serpent' are often the same, so this identification is natural enough, and it draws the chaotic monsters of the deep who were tamed by the ordering of God alongside the agent of evil who stands against the goodness of God. The *snake* in the Garden of Eden is not identified with Satan in the Genesis narrative, but by the first century this identification was common, for example, in Paul's encouragement that 'the God of peace will soon crush Satan under your feet' (Rom. 16:20), an allusion to Genesis 3:15. *Devil* (*diabolos*), meaning 'slanderer', is the Greek translation of the Hebrew *śāṭān*, meaning 'accuser', and the two terms are used interchangeably in the New Testament. *Satan* could refer to a human accuser (as in Ps. 71:13), but came to mean the spiritual being who was the accuser of God's people (as in Job 1:6–8). The devil was particularly associated with demons (who were understood as his malevolent *angels*) and in this capacity was called Beelzebul ('Lord of the flies', Matt. 12:24; Mark 3:22; Luke 11:15), a name derived from a Philistine god (2 Kgs 1:2–3). He is the 'evil one' from whom we pray for deliverance (Matt. 6:13) and is also Belial or Beliar, meaning 'worthless one' (2 Cor. 6:15). The devil is often depicted as deceiving people by luring them into temptation, as in Jesus' temptations in the wilderness (Matt. 4:1–11; Luke 4:1–13). In the Johannine tradition he is 'the father of lies' (John 8:44), and Paul highlights his deceptive disguise (2 Cor. 11:14).

When did Satan's fall occur when he was *thrown down* (AT)? The account of the fall of the 'morning star' (Latin *Lucifer*) in Isaiah 14:12–14 appears to refer to the king of Babylon, but has later been read as a description of Satan's primordial fall and corruption – though there is no clear connection made in this passage. When the seventy-two return from their ministry of proclamation, healing and exorcism, Jesus declares, 'I saw Satan fall like lightning from heaven' (Luke 10:18) – but this must be understood as an anticipation of Jesus' victory over evil in his cross and resurrection rather than the attainment of it. In John's Gospel, the 'hour' of 'judgment on this world' when 'Satan, the ruler of this world cast out' (John 12:31, AT) is the moment when Jesus is 'lifted up', that is, his crucifixion. In the narrative here in Revelation, Satan's fall follows Jesus' exaltation to the throne, but we are soon told that 'the accuser' has been thrown down and victory been won in the first instance 'by the blood of the Lamb' (v. 11). So there is a twin focus on Jesus' death *and* his exaltation, expressed earlier by the presence of the 'slain' lamb on the throne in Revelation 5.

Though Satan no longer has a place in heaven, he does continue to exercise power on *the earth*. John is recasting the temporal paradox of the Christian life into a spatial one. The time that the followers live in is one of testimony and victory, yet at the same time one in which they experience suffering and apparent defeat. In spatial terms, they are heaven-dwellers who are before the throne in heaven and constitute the temple of God, and so are protected from the power of Satan who has no place there. And yet they continue as members of many tribes, languages, peoples and nations, living in their various cities on earth where Satan, for a short time (12:12), wields his limited power.

C. The hymn of praise (12:10–12)

10. In the second major change of style within this chapter, John hears the authoritative declaration of a *loud voice from heaven* (AT). In the *now* we have reached the central point of the central chapter of the book – the pivot around which the whole narrative turns. John has been speaking the words of the exalted Jesus to the particular situation of the Christian communities in the province of Asia. He has shared with them his vision of worship in heaven and of the slain lamb who shares the throne. He has depicted the chaos and evil unleashed on the world under the permissive authority of God. And the repeated implicit and explicit questions have been 'How long will this last? What will God do about it?' The preliminary answers have been offered in the two interludes: that he has formed a people for himself from every nation, and that he has called John and others to exercise a ministry of prophetic witness. But now comes the fullest answer to the question, the one to which his people and their testimony point: that in Jesus' death, resurrection and exaltation *the kingdom of . . . God* and with it *the authority of his Messiah* or Christ have now come. If the first half of the book has been building up to the revelation of this, not least through its frequent anticipations of it, then the second half of the book depicts its outworking, not least in the judgment that comes to all other rival kingdoms (empires).

Salvation has been acclaimed as belonging to God by the un-countable multitude in 7:10, and will be acclaimed again at the fall of Babylon in 19:1. It represents a direct counter-claim to that of the Roman emperor, who claimed to bring salvation by subduing the empire's enemies and bringing peace and prosperity. *Power* is mentioned twelve times in the text and (like the language of strength in v. 8 above) expresses the rival claims of God and his spiritual opponents (cf. 13:2; 17:13). In the past, Satan's accusations of God's people could be countered (Job 1:8) or forgiven (Zech. 3:1–4) by God, but now the accuser himself has been expelled, and no more accusations will be heard. 'Therefore, there is now no condemnation for those who are in Christ Jesus' (Rom. 8:1).

11. The language of *triumph* (*nikaō*) connects this central passage to the exhortations in the messages to the seven assemblies in Revelation 2 – 3. Although it is the *Lamb* who has triumphed, the victory belongs too to God's people, since they now enjoy freedom from the fear of accusation and participate in the kingdom and power that have been made available to them. The victory has two parts to it, one which is *de jure* and establishes the victory, and the other which is *de facto*, in that it makes the victory real and visible. The first is the *blood of the Lamb*, which is a metonym for his death, and the second is *the word of their testimony*, that is, their faithful witness to the truth and transformative power of the death of the lamb. Without the first, there is no basis for victory over Satan and the power that he exercises; without the second, there is no reality in it. And the two are bound closely together, since true testimony means that the witnesses *did not . . . shrink from death*, which is precisely following the pattern of Jesus, the faithful witness, who 'loves us and has freed us from our sins by his blood' (1:5). To follow the crucified one means to live the cruciform life (Mark 8:34; Phil. 3:10). This kind of conquest, which involves suffering under violent oppression, is in sharp and constant contrast with the conquest of the beasts who inflict violence. This does not mean either that only the martyrs are saved, or that all God's people will die a martyr's death, but simply that this is emblematic of the kind of faith and its 'patient endurance' (1:9) to which the whole community is called.

12. The victory of the lamb is both good news and bad news – good news for those who *dwell in* the *heavens*, but bad news for *the earth and the sea*. This corresponds to John's experience of eating the scroll, which is both sweet and bitter (10:10) since his prophetic message is given both to those who receive the message of salvation and to those who reject it. The spatial distinction between heaven and earth is again about distinctions in spiritual reality, since those following the lamb are the ones who 'dwell in heaven' (13:6, AT), while those who follow the beast are described as 'inhabitants of the earth' (13:8). The earth here is bracketed with *the sea*, which in the Old Testament is the source of chaos and opposition to God. The devil's *time* (*kairos*) is short, not in terms of days and years so much as in being limited in extent by the authority of God.

Although it is not numbered by John, this is the next proclamation of *woe* following the two which corresponded to the fifth and sixth trumpets (in 9:12 and 11:14). The declaration that 'the third woe is coming soon' (11:14) is followed immediately by this narrative and this warning of woe, which suggests that John understands the present era, between Jesus' exaltation and his return, as the third 'woe'. The first two woes constitute the threats from the north and the east to the empire itself, and any other kind of threat to human peace and well-being; but the third woe is the threat that the empire itself presents as an instrument of the dragon in the oppression of the people of God. From the story of cosmic conflict in Revelation 12, we will turn in Revelation 13 to the specific expression of that manifested in Roman imperial power in the province of Asia.

D. The dragon pursues the woman (12:13–17)

13–14. The opening narrative located the biblical characters of the woman (the people of God), the male son (the expected Messiah) and the dragon (the primeval opponent of God) within a story shaped by the Python–Leto myth. The meaning of this was then explained as the victory of the angel of God's people over their accuser. The hymn of praise made it clear that the victory was established by Jesus' death and is appropriated by our faithful witness, even when we are threatened with death. John's vision report now returns to the Python–Leto narrative, with the *dragon* pursuing the *woman*; the spatial locations here are not exact,[4] in that the woman was a sign 'in heaven' and yet when she gave birth, her son was 'snatched up to God' and she is now in the same places as the dragon who has been *hurled to the earth*. The Python–Leto myth is continued in the reference to the *eagle*, since Leto is carried to safety by the north wind Aquilo (which sounds like *aquila*, the Latin for 'eagle'). But it is also an allusion to the exodus motif that we have seen in previous chapters, in that her flight is facilitated by being given *the two wings of a great eagle*, just as God carried his people from Egypt 'on eagles' wings' (Exod. 19:4, an image also used for the return from exile in Isa. 40:31). John repeats the description of her escape *to the place prepared for her in the wilderness* from verse 6, which confirms continuity of the narrative; and he repeats the time period of 1,260 days as the *time, times and half a time* from Daniel 7:25; 12:7, confirming that these different descriptions refer to the same period as they did in 11:2, 3. Though this is a time of protection from God, it is also a time when the oppressor appears to triumph, as we will

---

4. This is also why the flight of the woman need not be taken as an allusion to any particular historical event, such as the flight of Jews to Jamnia and Babylonia following the destruction of the temple in AD 70.

see in the following chapter. Once more the *dragon* is also identified as *the snake*.

15–16. The imagery here is quite unusual, in that dragons were believed to be able to dry up rivers rather than *spew* them out. The rare word *potamophoretos* is an adjective meaning 'being swept away in a torrent'; the image is used of being overwhelmed by war (Isa. 8:8; Dan. 11:10), one's enemies or even false teaching, but it is more likely a general reference to the threat of death (Ps. 18:4, 16; Isa. 43:2; Lam. 3:54; Jon. 2:5). In some key Old Testament episodes, the *earth* swallows people up in judgment (cf. Num. 16:32–34), but here it comes to the aid of the woman. This is part of the positive view throughout Revelation of the creation as serving God's purposes, represented positively in the presence of the four living creatures before the throne, and negatively in God's judgment of those who destroy the earth in 11:18.

17. The *dragon* being *enraged* runs parallel to the rage of the nations in 11:18, as both reject the actions of God in redemption and judgment. The woman enjoys protection, and the dragon can no longer contend with God or his angels, so his attention turns to *the rest of her offspring*. The phrase comes from Micah 5:3, when 'the rest of his brothers' join the one born of the woman in an eschatological return from exile to the land. But here, the fulfilment is not for the others to be 'in the land' but for them to be 'in Christ' – to *keep the commandments of God and have the testimony of Jesus* (AT). This is very close to the earlier phrase 'word of God and the testimony of Jesus' in 1:2, 9, and (as there) the testimony could be either testimony *about* Jesus or the testimony *from* Jesus – that is, the truth that Jesus speaks of – or both (see comment on 1:2, 9). John assumes here that the Old Testament commandments are broadly in line with faith in Jesus, as do other writers in the New Testament.

Theology
Even though the figure of Jesus (depicted in person or in an image) is not as central here as he is in chapters 1 and 5, in this pivotal chapter the claims of Jesus are brought most sharply into focus as rival claims to those of the Roman Empire. In the literary equivalent of a political cartoon, John's vision report takes a piece of imperial propaganda and inverts its effect. Rome is no longer the strong hero

Apollo who vanquishes the chaos monster, but is in fact allied with
the chaos monster and so is threatened with defeat. Jesus is not a
marginal figure who is the inspiration for an insignificant religious
movement, but is the Apollo figure who is the true bringer of victory
and peace. The effect of this on John's audience is to push them to
a crisis of decision; they have in different ways been affirmed and
challenged in their loyalty in the seven messages, and the seals
and trumpets have confronted them with the true source of uncertainty and the real answer to it. Now the crisis deepens: to ally
oneself with the empire is to ally oneself with the spiritual adversary
to both God and his people.

John's use of Old Testament traditions, particularly those of
Daniel, paints this crisis of decision on a wide historical canvas.
Although the particular challenge facing John's audience is one particular system of empire, his coalescing of the description of the
beasts in Daniel 7 portrays their situation as one among the many
that humanity faces from one era to the next. Inasmuch as their
claims are those that only God can make, all such human empires
ultimately derive their power from the enemy of God. Jesus' victory
by his death is not only the denial of the claims of empire, it is also
the answer to the aspirations of the people of God down the ages
to live in peace and worship God in freedom (Luke 1:69–75).

This narrative also confirms what John has already suggested
about the times we live in. The followers of the lamb live in the
in-between time which was inaugurated with Jesus' death, resurrection and ascension, and will be consummated with his return as
depicted in Revelation 19 – 22. This is the age of the 'third woe',
when Satan is at large in this world even though he has no authority
in the heavenly realm. Therefore God's people will continue to experience the presence and protection of God (because Jesus' death has
silenced the accuser and the [seven] Spirit[s] of God is [are] abroad
in the world), but they will also experience suffering (tribulation) and
opposition, because Satan continues to be at large for a 'short time'
until he is finally locked up and then destroyed in the final judgment.
This paradoxical pattern of suffering and victory for Jesus' followers
is the same thing that Jesus himself experienced; the hardships of
being a disciple are not a mistake, nor a sign of the failure of God,
but are part and parcel of what it means to be a faithful witness.

The chapters that follow now unfold this situation. In the next chapter we read in detail of the trials of John's audience living under the empire and its allies in Asia. We then read in stark contrast of the security and victory of the faithful and the certainty of God's judgment (Rev. 14). We read of the final plagues that are to come on the earth (Rev. 16), and the full disclosure of the nature of the empire (Rev. 17), before leading into the unfolding significance of the return of Jesus: the certainty of the end of evil (Rev. 18 and 19) and vindication of the saints (Rev. 20), and the sparkling vision of hope for eternity (Rev. 21).

9. THE BEASTS FROM THE SEA AND THE LAND (13:1–18)

Context

Having told the story of the cosmic conflict between God and Satan in Revelation 12, John now turns to tell the story of the local conflict that is being experienced by his readers. He does so by drawing on biblical imagery, particularly from Daniel, to describe the particular experience of those in Asia who have seen an imperial power come from across the sea and work hand in hand with a local power already in the land. But he does this in a distinctive way: on the one hand, the symbolism of empire is quite particular, and the rise and fall of the beasts is framed by the introduction and final judgment of Satan as God's cosmic enemy. In this sense, John frames his particular historical situation within the framework of the ultimate cosmic realities of salvation and judgment. On the other hand, he combines Daniel's imagery, so that the empire he faces is not simply the one that is present before him, but is in some sense the archetypal representative of all human imperial power. This is communicated by means of particularly powerful metaphorical imagery which allows subsequent readers not only to understand the challenges that John and his readers faced, but to ask for themselves: where in our world is Satan's power at work through the 'beasts' in our situation?

A. The beast from the sea (13:1–10)

Comment

1. The first sentence here is sometimes included as the last verse (v. 18) of Revelation 12, and at other times included as the first verse of Revelation 13. The concluding sense of 12:17 suggests the latter, and the beginning of the next sentence, *And I saw*, marks a new section there. It is certainly transitional, linking the narrative of the *dragon* from the previous verses to the theme of the *sea* that follows. A number of early manuscripts have the reading 'I stood on the shore', that is, John describing his own position. But John does not locate himself physically anywhere other than on Patmos, and the location here makes good narrative sense for the dragon. Physically, the sea is one part of the created order of earth, sea and sky (see comment on 5:13); but theologically the sea is the origin of evil and chaos closely related to the abyss (see comment on 4:6a and 9:1). Within the narrative we need to remember that God exercises authority over both land and sea (symbolized by the 'mighty angel' in 10:2, 5, 8), so the dragon, standing on the boundary, and the two beasts which emerge from each are all ultimately bound by God's authority. Geographically, John can see the *shore* from Patmos as he looks north and east towards the cities he is writing to; for the residents of Asia, the power of Rome has come to them across the sea, but the local leaders who enable and enforce the practices of the imperial cult come from their own land.

The first seven verses draw extensively from the language of Daniel 7. The first *beast* is *coming out of the sea* just as did Daniel's four beasts in Daniel 7:3, but where they are all 'different', this one, like the dragon, shares features of all of them. The *ten horns and seven heads* represent the sum of the four in Daniel (the third beast having four heads, and the fourth beast having ten horns), and like the dragon it has diadems (*diadēmata*, signifying total rule, rather than wreaths, *stephanoi*, which signify triumph), though they are on each of the ten horns rather than on the seven heads. Although the heads and horns of the scarlet beast in Revelation 17 are given a specific interpretation, here they simply function as the sum of the beasts in Daniel 7. Each head has a *blasphemous name* (though some manuscripts read 'names' to match 17:3), implying that every head makes the same claims to take the place of God.

2. The description continues to blend the imagery from Daniel 7, where the first beast was like *a lion*, the second like *a bear* and the third like *a leopard*; there does not appear to be any significance to the different body parts mentioned. We begin now to see that the relationship between the dragon and the beast parodies the relationship between the one seated on the throne and the lamb, as the dragon shares its *power* and *throne* and *great authority*, just as the lamb shared the throne with God and is worshipped in similar terms; 'power', glory and honour are the consistent terms in the acclamations of 4:11; 5:12, 13; 7:12 (see comment on 7:12).

3. The parody continues. Many English versions state that *one of the heads of the beast seemed to have had a fatal wound*, or something similar, but the verb used (*sphazō*) is the same as that used of the lamb in 5:6, and John sees him 'as' (*hōs*, rather than 'similar to', *homoios*) slain 'to the death'. And as the lamb is now living again, so the 'plague [or wound] of his death', that is, the blow which led to death, or *fatal wound*, was *healed*. Many commentators see in this phrase an allusion to the myth of 'Nero Redivivus', which is more clearly suggested in Revelation 17 (see comment on 9:14); it was thought that Nero did not die in AD 68 but was still alive and would lead Parthian armies to invade from the east. But the phrasing suggests that the wound to the head caused the death of the *beast* and not just the death of the head, which might then allude to the civil war and year of four emperors following Nero's suicide in AD 68. The empire itself looked as though it might come to an end, but in fact had come back to life, in some ways stronger than before.

The adulation of *the whole earth* (AT) hints at the idea of the *consensus omnium*, by which the emperor governs only with the consent of all the people since they believe that his autocratic rule is actually beneficial. The description of how they *followed the beast* uses the language of 'coming after' (*opisō*) which is used of Jesus in relation to discipleship (Mark 8:33–34).

4. John here offers the strongest possible critique of the imperial cult: when people *worship the beast*, they are in fact also *worship[ping] the dragon* because it is the dragon that gives the beast its powers. It is the primeval enemy of God who allows those who exercise the power of the empire to claim the obeisance and loyalty that are due to God alone. This fills out and sharpens the claim in 9:20 that the people are 'worshipping demons', in line with one aspect of Paul's argument about meat offerings to idols in 1 Corinthians 10:20. The parody continues with the echo of the rhetorical question 'Who is like God?' from Exodus 15:11, *Who is like the beast?* The supreme irony in the following question, *Who can make war against it?*, comes from the previous passage where the question was answered: Michael. He is the one whose very name declares the incomparability of God (see comment on 12:7) and who exercised the authority of the lamb who was slain – which overpowers not only the beast but the dragon whose authority he exercises. This heavenly conquest is made real on earth when Jesus returns as the rider on the white horse in Revelation 19.

5–8. John includes in his vision report another element from Daniel 7. The beast has a *mouth speaking proud words* (AT) in an exact parallel with the 'little horn' in Daniel 7:8, which also (in the Greek text of Daniel) 'makes war against the saints' as the beast does in verse 7. Its opposition to God, *blasphem[ing]* or slandering him and his *name* (i.e. his character and reputation), also involves slandering his *dwelling-place* (*skēnē* or 'tent'), which cannot be distinguished from God's people, who make their dwelling-place in his temple in the heavenly places (12:12; cf. Eph. 2:6) and over whom God spreads his tent (7:15). The identification of response to God with response to the people of God is a consistent theme across the New Testament writers, from Jesus saying in Matthew 10:40, 'Anyone who welcomes you welcomes me', through its parallel in John 13:20, to Paul's theology of the church as the body of Christ (1 Cor. 12:27).

Even though the heavenly war has been won already, there is a continuing conflict on the earth, and paradoxically the beast has the appearance of *conquer[ing]* God's people through violence and coercion, even as they actually conquer through faithfulness to the testimony of Jesus. Here we see the 'outer court' being trampled even while the 'inner court' is kept safe (11:1–2), the parallel being confirmed by the repetition of the time period *forty-two months*. The beast can only do so with the permissive authority of God – its power and authority are *given* – and even though it appears to have authority over *every tribe, people, language and nation* (the fifth of seven occurrences of this fourfold phrase; see comment on the first occurrence in 5:9). This challenge serves to separate humanity into *those who dwell in heaven* (AT), who refuse to follow but instead follow the lamb, and the *inhabitants of the earth*, who do follow the beast and as a consequence remain earth-bound. This difference is expressed in terms of whether or not *their names have . . . been written in the book of life*; this might sound like an expression of predetermination, especially in its next mention in 17:8, of those who are redeemed and those who are lost, except that its first occurrence in 3:5 is precisely in the context of an invitation to respond to the challenge of faithfulness. From the Greek text, it is not clear what 'from the *foundation of the world*' (AT) refers to – whether names that are written, or the *Lamb who was slain*; comparison with 17:8 could suggest the former, but the grammar here suggests the latter. The reference is not to the actual timing of the lamb's death (as the narrative of Rev. 12 has made clear), but to the plan of redemption through the blood of the lamb being in God's mind from the very beginning, an idea expressed in similar terms in Matthew 25:34; Ephesians 1:4; 1 Peter 1:20.

9–10. The sevenfold phrase which has been repeated at the end of each of the messages in Revelation 2 – 3 (and which is also found in the teaching of Jesus, Matt. 11:15; Mark 4:9; Luke 14:35) is repeated here with slight variation: *If anyone has an ear, let him hear* (AT). It serves to put the specific challenges faced by each assembly in its context into a wider narrative, that of the conflict between the dragon and beast, and God and the lamb. The proverbial saying that follows takes its rather abrupt grammar from the clear antecedent in Jeremiah 15:2, though the four destinies there (death, *sword*, starvation, *captivity*, reduced to three in the parallel saying in Jer. 43:11) have been reduced to two. In Jeremiah, the context is the certainty of the coming judgment of God on Jerusalem, but here it is the certainty of the oppression by the beast. In both cases the rhetorical impact is to discourage violent response, following the 'quietist' focus of the book of Daniel.

Some important manuscripts have an active verb: those who 'kill with the sword will be killed', bringing it into line with Jesus' saying in Matthew 26:52. But the original in Jeremiah and the parallel with the previous saying mean that the minority of manuscripts that have two passive verbs ('anyone who will be killed . . . will be killed') should actually be preferred. These fates are not specific to either those who follow the beast or those who do not, but the followers of the lamb are clearly not exempt from such ends. As John has said from the very beginning (1:9), *patient endurance* (*hypomonē*) is the essential quality of any disciple. The *faith* [*pistis*] *of God's people* (AT) can have either a subjective or an objective sense, that is, it can refer to their faith and trust in God or their own quality of faithfulness (*pistis* can mean either), and the two are closely related. John's vision report encourages his audience to continue to trust in God and remain faithful because, despite the apparent triumph of the evil empire, God is still sovereign and his judgment will come.

Theology
For John's first audience, the allusion to Roman imperial power in the beast from the sea is made clear by the continuity of the character of the dragon, which connects this chapter with the Python–Leto myth in Revelation 12. It is also confirmed by the close links between this passage and Daniel 7, where the beasts are symbolic of kingdoms (Dan. 7:23). But the symbolic description and the combining of Daniel's four beasts into one have a further effect for subsequent audiences. Rather than focus on the fourth beast alone, John draws on the characteristic of all the beast-empires, as if to say, 'This the threat of Roman imperial power – but it is actually the threat of any human empire which claims what only God can claim.' And his use of highly metaphorical language, in which the actual subject of the metaphor is not specified, allows subsequent audiences to see the same patterns of behaviour at work in later contexts.[1]

---

1. Metaphors which specify their subject (*'John* is a pig') are less transferable to new contexts than metaphors which specify only the vehicle ('That *pig* is eating lunch'). The technical term for this is *hypocatastatic* metaphor; see Introduction on 'Reading Revelation's imagery'.

John's vision report then offers a challenge for both his immediate audience and subsequent audiences. For his immediate hearers and readers, the challenge is to make decisions about their loyalty to the empire or to their faith in the light of John's claims about the nature of the empire and its source of power and authority. For later hearers and readers, the challenge is to discern where similar patterns of authority are at work and – knowing that we too are living in the forty-two months or 1,260 days or three and a half years, when we too will know both suffering and victory, when we too are in a time for testimony and patient endurance – to make hard decisions about our own loyalty and faith.

B. The beast from the land (13:11–15)

Comment

11–12. As previously, the phrase *And I saw* (AT) introduces a new character to the drama. In fact, the feel of the narrative changes at this point, primarily because the verbs change from being in the past tense in the first part of the chapter to being mostly in the present tense from here to the end of the chapter, signalling a change from historical situation to present experience. If the image of the first beast evoked the power of imperial Rome for John's audience, then the image of a beast *coming out of the land* (or 'earth', *gē*) would evoke the local power structures in Asia on which Rome depended for the exercise of its rule, and which in turn benefited from Roman rule in the consolidation of their own power. The delegation of *authority* from the *first beast* and the reciprocal coercion to *worship* it matches the social situation in Asia, where both cities and individuals vied for the right to build imperial temples and give the emperor honours in a more extravagant way than further west in the empire. But this is also a universal feature of systems that involve delegated authority; those to whom authority or power has been delegated have more to gain the more they can make people submit to the system from which they derive their power. Such submission seems all the more compelling if the system appears to be impregnable, so that it recovers even from an apparently *fatal wound*.

The *two horns* of the lamb could allude to the ram in Daniel 8:3, but neither the language nor the narrative situation matches very well. The emphasis appears to be that this beast looks harmless enough as a parody of the lamb on the throne, but in fact (like the beast from the sea) shows its real character by *speaking like a dragon* (AT). It is a 'wolf' 'in sheep's clothing' (Matt. 7:15), and like the subject of Jesus' metaphor is later referred to as 'the false prophet' (Rev. 16:13; 19:20; 20:10).

13–15. The *great signs* performed by the second beast (false prophet) stand over against the great signs offered by God (in 12:1; 15:1), and parallel the 'signs and wonders' performed by the apostles in the power of the Spirit (Acts 4:30; 5:12; 6:8) which demonstrate the fulfilling of God's purposes through the preaching about Jesus (Acts 2:19). The relationship between the second beast and the first thus offers a parody of the relationship between the Spirit and Jesus, supporting the idea that John's vision report offers us an unholy trinity of dragon, beast from the sea and beast from the land (false prophet) which is later described in threefold terms (16:13; 20:10). It was acknowledged in the Old Testament that false prophets were able to perform signs and wonders (Deut. 13:1–3), just as Pharaoh's magicians had often been able to match the miracles performed by Moses and Aaron – but that was no reason to be *deceived* by them. The deception of the second beast in causing the *inhabitants of the earth* to follow the first beast and be in awe of it follows the pattern of the dragon who 'leads the whole world astray' (12:9), and contrasts with those who follow Jesus who is the truth (3:7, 14; cf. 6:10).

Images have always been the stock-in-trade of those who make claims to power, and the greater and more absolute the claims, the larger the images. So the book of Daniel records Nebuchadnezzar making an enormous gold statue to which all must bow down (Dan. 3:1). Throughout the Roman Empire, statues of the emperor were a way of symbolically communicating the emperor's virtues and reminding people of the ubiquitous presence of his power. Nero erected a 30 m (90 ft) high statue of himself at the main entrance to his imperial residence at the head of the *Via Appia*; it was eventually moved (by Hadrian) to a place outside the amphitheatre that Vespasian and Titus (*Amphitheatrum Flavianum*) built and which became known as the 'Colosseum' after the statue. In Ephesus, the Temple of the Sebastoi was built by Domitian in the 80s and dedicated to the Flavian dynasty that comprised Domitian, his father

Vespasian and his brother Titus, who each in turn preceded Domitian as emperor. In it was a giant statue, around 8 m (26 ft) tall, often thought to be of Domitian, but in fact erected by him although depicting Titus. It would certainly have impressed all who passed it as they came down the main street of the city. Contemporary dictatorships are consistently marked by the presence of images, some of enormous size, of the dictator.

The wonder of the beast who appeared to have died and come back to life is emphasized again, though with a slightly different description as one who has *the wound of a sword and yet lived* (AT).[2] The mention of a sword and the wound belonging to the beast rather than one of its heads makes it more likely that, in relation to Roman power, John has in mind the civil war of 68 rather than the more personal reference of 'Nero Redivivus' (see comment on v. 3).

The signs mentioned, calling *fire . . . from heaven* and animating *the image of the first beast* so it could *speak*, correlate with the use of magic tricks, the development of automata and the use of ventriloquism in the ancient world as part of pagan religion and in particular as part of the imperial cult. The close association between conjuring and magic and pagan religion accounts for the wholly negative view of magic in the Old Testament (e.g. in Deut. 18:10 and Isa. 47:9), and those coming from the world of magic and sorcery saw the close relationship between this and the activity of the Spirit (so Simon Magus wants to learn his 'trick' from Peter in Acts 8:18). But these signs also continue the parody of the work of God, the fire from heaven imitating both the prophetic ministry of Elijah on Mount Carmel (1 Kgs 18:38) and the presence of God in Sinai, alluded to in the lightning and thunder from the throne (4:5; the Hebrew for 'lightning' is 'fire from heaven'). And the ability to *give breath to the image* parodies both God's breath of life that brings resurrection to the two witnesses (11:11; cf. Ezek. 37:9) and the breath of life in the creation of humanity that this draws on (Gen. 2:7). In every age, those exercising totalitarian power have wanted

---

2. There are two words for 'sword' in Revelation: *machaira* and *rhomphaia*. The occurrence of the first in 6:4 (and here) and the second in 6:8 suggests that they are interchangeable.

to impress both their subjects and other nations with the power and sophistication of their technological achievements.

C. The mark of the beast (13:16–18)

16–18. The universal nature of the beasts' domination is expressed in the 'gradable antonyms' *great and small, rich and poor, free and slave*, which were previously used to express the universal reach of God's judgment (6:15) and the universal invitation to redemption (11:18; see comment on these verses). Being branded with a *mark* (mentioned seven times in the text) was known in a variety of circumstances in the ancient world: Ptolemy IV of Egypt required all Jews to be branded with an ivy leaf; slaves could be branded, though a brand on the forehead was a sign of disgrace rather than loyalty; and soldiers might be branded on the hand as part of their oath of loyalty. The mark of the emperor (his seal) was fixed to commercial documents giving permission to trade, and the image of the emperor was on coinage, so it would be impossible to trade without handling this. The emphasis here is on the all-pervasive nature of the mark; there is no part of life where the question of loyalty to the beast can be avoided. The placing of the mark on the *right hand* or *forehead* could be interpreted as a parody of the binding of the words of God's law on the hand and forehead as commanded in Exodus 13:9, 16 and Deuteronomy 6:8; 11:18; the use of the singular 'on your hand' has been interpreted in Judaism as meaning one hand only, and for those who are right-handed this is usually the left hand.

But the primary significance of this mark (*charagma*) is not in relation to any literal marking, but as a counterpoint to the seal (*sphragis*) of protection given to the faithful people of God.[3] Within the narrative, the two (mark/seal) are mutually exclusive (see 20:4), and all of humanity has either the one or the other. Both are put on the forehead, and it turns out that both represent the name of the one that they follow. The mark is both *the name of the beast* (v. 17) and

---

3. We don't have any difficulty using the language of 'marking' without imagining any kind of literal mark. We do this in phrases like 'She's a marked woman', 'I've marked his cards' or 'He carries the mark of Cain'.

a *number* which is also the *number of a person* (AT; *anthropos* meaning 'human being' rather than necessarily a male figure). And those who have been sealed on the forehead now bear the name of the lamb and of God his Father on their forehead (14:1; 22:4).

The number *666* has a wide range of symbolic significance. Even without the Arabic number system that we now use, the triple repetition of the number 6 (in Greek *hexakosioi hexēkonta hex*) would have been clear to John and his audience. The frequency of the number 7 in the text symbolizing completeness strongly suggests that the number 6 symbolizes 'falling short' or inadequacy of some kind. Moreover, 666 is the thirty-sixth 'triangular' number, that is, one that can be formed by arranging this number of objects into an equilateral triangle of side 36.[4] This fits with John's wider numerological scheme whereby square numbers symbolize the things and people of God, this triangular number symbolizes opposition to God, and rectangular numbers like 42 and 1,260 (which look similar to square numbers but are equal to twice the corresponding triangular number) symbolize the overlap of the ages, when God's people experience the joy of the kingdom of God but also the suffering that comes from opposition (see comment on 11:3).

But in addition to this complex symbolism, does the number 666 have any sort of reference? Many commentators have suggested not, primarily in response to wild speculation about historical and contemporary references, much of which seems arbitrary, implausible or self-serving. But three factors argue in the other direction:

1. The text itself tells us that the 'number' is also a 'name', suggesting that some calculation has taken place – and it commands us to 'calculate' the number for ourselves. John is here not trying to *hide* the name, unless possibly from the prying eyes of the Roman authorities who might read this text, but for his intended audience he is *revealing* it.

---

4. For a detailed and extensive exploration of triangular numbers, their calculation and their significance, see Bauckham, *Climax of Prophecy*, ch. 11, 'Nero and the Beast', pp. 384–452.

2. The practice of *gematria* (the Hebrew term, in Greek *isopsephia*), whereby the numerical value of names and titles was calculated by adding up the values of the individual letters, was widespread, well established and entirely natural in a world which did not have a separate number system but used the value of letters for calculation. Most commonly, two different words were linked if their values were equal, and we know of many examples of this in Latin, Greek and Hebrew.

3. It is clear that such calculations were significant for at least some Christians. The third-century Christianized *Sibylline Oracles* 1:324–329 calculates the value of the name 'Jesus' in Greek as 888, correlating with Jesus being raised on the 'eighth' day of the week and inaugurating the new, eighth age of the world (the kingdom of God) following the seven ages of this world in Jewish belief. And John appears to use *gematria* elsewhere in Revelation; the method of calculation below gives the value 144 for the measuring 'angel' in Revelation 21:15–16.

The most likely solution comes from transliterating (rather than translating) the name of the Emperor Nero from Greek into Hebrew letters and then adding the values of the letters, and doing the same with the word 'beast', since the beast and the person are being identified (*the number of the beast . . . is the number of a person*), as shown in table 8.

Table 8: Calculating the number of the beast, the emperor and the angel

Term	Greek	Hebrew transliteration	Sum	Value
beast	*thērion*	TRYWN	400+200+10+6+50	666
Nero Caesar	*Nerōn Kaisar*	NRWN QSR	50+200+6+50+100+60+200	666
angel	*angelos*	ANGLS	1+50+3+30+60	144

The Hebrew alphabet does not have vowels as such (vowel sounds are indicated by 'pointing' above and below the letters), but it does have some consonants which function as vowels, and this gives rise to the transliteration above. The system of allocating values to these letters of the Hebrew alphabet is well attested, and the value of 'angel' as 144 adds confidence to this approach. Although transliterating into Hebrew might seem odd, it is clear that John is living in a multilingual world, and he makes reference to Hebrew terms and ideas in 9:11 and 16:16. The spelling of Nero with a final -n is attested in a first-century papyrus. Perhaps the most powerful argument in favour of this identification is the well-attested variant reading '616' footnoted in most English translations. If the emperor's name is spelt *without* the final -n, and the word 'beast' is taken as it is written in the text (in the genitive *theriou*), then both terms lose 50 from the calculation, but the identification of the beast with Nero remains. There is no doubt that this is what gives rise to the variant reading '616'.[5]

The identification here fits with the other allusions in the text to Nero and the legend of 'Nero Redivivus', that he had not died in AD 68 but was in hiding and would lead Parthian armies from the east to attack Rome. But John's focus here is different; the *wisdom* and *insight* here (*sophia* and *nous*) are also called for in 17:9, and in both cases they relate not to cleverness in decoding the clues, but to courage in recognizing the real nature of Roman imperial power and its demands. Whatever the other benefits of Roman rule, and whatever the virtues of individual emperors, if one wants to understand the 'spirit' of the empire, one needs to look at Nero[6] – someone who tortured and murdered the people of God. This is what Christians would experience in the coming two centuries. And this is what God's people consistently experience whenever any human leaders make the totalitarian claims to be the things that only

---

5. It is worth noting that Nero was considered a beast and the embodiment of the devil in other near-contemporary sources (Philostratus, *Life of Apollonius* 4.38; *Sibylline Oracles* 3:63; 5:343; 8:157; *Martyrdom and Ascension of Isaiah* 4:1), and so John's readers would not have been surprised by this identification.

6. John is not here trying to tell his audience at what date he is writing; they presumably already know that!

God can be, offer the things (peace and prosperity) that only God can provide, and demand the absolute loyalty that only God can require. In doing so, they set themselves up against God and therefore against God's people. This text speaks to God's people in every age, not *instead* of referring to Nero, but *through* doing so.

Theology

John is offering us the anatomy of human totalitarian rule and its defiance of the sovereignty of God, drawing, as ever, on biblical images as his symbolic vocabulary. We can see enough connection with the world of the first century to know how vivid his descriptions would have been to his first audience. But we can also feel the rhetorical power of what he says to find correspondences in subsequent generations, including our own. John is here not just heightening the significance of the decisions of loyalty that those described in the seven messages must face; he is raising the stakes for all subsequent readers who must also examine their loyalties, their compromises and the question of faithfulness.

10. THE 144,000 ON MOUNT ZION AND THE HARVEST OF THE SON OF MAN (14:1–20)

Context

In this section we are offered another form of interlude between the account of conflict in Revelation 13 and the introduction to the next judgment sequence that follows in Revelation 15. The images here are especially evocative, with the ideas of clouds, harps, and both sickles and 'grapes of wrath' as signs of judgment in the popular imagination.

This continues John's typical sense of narrative discontinuity and sudden changes of scene, and also undermines any neat sense of cosmic geography, where heaven and earth are separated or act as a kind of mirror to one another as they do in Greco-Roman mythology. The shift in scene and the introduction of a new set of symbolic vocabulary have the effect of keeping the plot moving, as did the sudden changes previously at the beginnings of chapters 4, 6, 7, 8 and 10. Together, chapters 13 and 14 offer a contrast between the outward reality and the inner truth, a dynamic set-up at the start of Revelation 11 in the contrast between the trampling of the outer court and the holy preservation of the inner sanctuary. It is the dynamic that John himself experienced in the tension between 'suffering' and 'kingdom' in Jesus (1:9).

A. The vision of the lamb and the 144,000 on Mount Zion (14:1–5)

Comment

1. After the change in style of Revelation 12 – 13, John reverts to the earlier vision report format with *And I looked* adding, in its emphatic form *behold* (AT). This has previously marked significant new elements of his vision in 4:1 and 7:9, and will recur later in verse 14 and (in a revised form) at 19:11. This episode in his vision report has significant connections with Revelation 4 – 5; he sees a *Lamb, standing* as he had in 5:6, along with the heavenly entourage of the living creatures and elders (v. 3). As had happened previously, John continues to add further detail to the scene, which is now located on *Mount Zion*, which, like previous mentions of the temple and its furniture, must be taken as the spiritual equivalent to the earthly reality. Throughout the Old Testament, Zion (as a metonym for Jerusalem) is understood to be God's dwelling-place (Ps. 74:2), and its restoration at the coming of the anointed one (Messiah) formed a key part of the hope of God's people (Ps. 102:13–17; Isa. 62:11). For John, this is fulfilled in the presence of the lamb and of those he has redeemed.

There are also clear connections with the interlude in Revelation 7, most obviously in the mention of *144,000*. John does not use the definite article, as he usually does when returning to something he has previously mentioned, but there are several reasons why this must be the same group as the one in 7:4. Both groups are marked on their foreheads, in Revelation 7 with the 'seal of the living God' (7:2–3) and here with the *name* of the lamb and *his Father's name*. The participle *written* is singular, indicating that John treats these two names as one object, just as he treats 'God and the Lamb' as well as their names as a single entity in 22:3–4. This reflects Paul's language in Philippians 2:9, where God gives Jesus 'the name that is above every name', which is the name of God (cf. Isa. 45:22–23).

2–3. As elsewhere, having seen something John then *heard* something else, and these two things mutually interpret each other (as in 1:12; 7:9, and elsewhere). The *sound . . . of many waters* (AT) had earlier described the voice of Jesus in 1:15, using the language of the voice of God from Ezekiel 1:24. But the same phrase is used, along with *the sounds of loud peals of thunder* (AT; lit. 'the sound of mighty thunder'), in 19:6 of the heavenly celebration of the fall of Babylon and the coming of the wedding of the lamb. These sounds are therefore not God's prelude to the praise of the *harpists*, but describe its sound. The harp (the *kithara* rather than the modern instrument)[1] was a common musical instrument and a favourite of David (1 Sam. 16:23), but was particularly used by the Levitical priests in their temple worship (1 Chr. 15:16; 16:5). The sound is of the 144,000 as the priestly people of God singing his praise, joining with the *elders* who have previously had this representative role (see comment on 5:8).

The *new song* they sing is mentioned only here and at 5:9, using a phrase that comes several times in the Psalms (Pss 33:3; 40:3; 96:1; 98:1; see also Isa. 42:10). The paradoxical sense is that the singer has a fresh experience of God's power, particularly his power to save, but this is an experience of the salvation that God has always effected in the past – hence the same group, described in different terms, sing the 'song of . . . Moses and of the Lamb' in 15:3. This amazing new thing that God has done in Jesus is essentially the same amazing new thing that God has always been doing, but only those who have experienced this redemption for themselves can truly sing of it. Their singing *before the four living creatures and the elders*[2] connects this scene with Revelation 5, while their being *redeemed from the earth* recalls the language of 7:9 of the multitude 'from every nation, tribe, people and language'. The sense here is not of being removed from the earth, but of being distinguished from the 'inhabitants of the earth' as those who 'dwell in heaven' (13:6, AT), even as the beast attacks them on the earth.

---

1. David is variously described as playing the 'harp' or 'lyre', and different Hebrew terms for these closely related instruments are translated variously by different Greek terms in the OT.
2. The elders and living creatures are paired together seven times in the text, at 5:6, 8, 11, 14; 7:11; 14:3; 19:4, but, as is typical of Revelation, the pairing is never described in the same way twice.

4–5. John now offers a sevenfold description of the 144,000, whose importance in this scene is emphasized by the repeated 'these ones' (*houtoi* three times in v. 4) which are not evident in English translations. First, they *did not defile themselves with women*, which is often read by feminist commentators as an androcentric and patriarchal concern that depicts the redeemed as male only. This can hardly be the case, unless Revelation alone within the New Testament thinks that salvation is for men only, and it contradicts the inclusive vision of salvation expressed in the fourfold phrase of 7:9 ('every nation, tribe, people and language'). The second description, as *virgins*, is an unusual clarification, since *parthenos* is everywhere else in the New Testament a feminine noun which (in its literal sense) is applied only to women (Matt. 1:23; 25:1; Acts 21:9; 1 Cor. 7:34) and in other literature is almost unknown as applying to men until the second century. It needs to be read here in three contexts:

1. The use of sexual imagery of adultery as a metaphor for worship of false gods and idolatry elsewhere in Revelation, drawing on customary Old Testament use (see comment on 2:22 and cf. 17:2; 18:3, 9);
2. The prohibition on those involved in (spiritual) warfare from engaging in sexual relations during the time of battle (the 144,000 being depicted as an army in Rev. 7; Deut. 23:9–11; 2 Sam. 11:8–11);
3. The nuptial imagery of the people of God as a bride, which Paul also uses when he describes the mixed community of men and women in Corinth as 'a pure virgin betrothed to one husband, Christ' (2 Cor. 11:2, AT).

So God's people are here described as devoted to God, committed to the spiritual task and purified for union with Christ. Only a wooden literalism, which pulls this verse out of its textual, canonical and theological context, could construe its meaning as androcentric.

The third description, as ones who *follow the Lamb*, uses the common term from the Gospels and Jesus' teaching for discipleship, even though it occurs in Revelation only here. The metaphor implies that disciples emulate the pattern of life of the master they follow, and accept the master's fate as their fate. The fourth description, as *purchased from humanity* (AT), draws on the metaphor of manumission from the slave market that Paul also uses (1 Cor. 6:20; 7:23) and which John has used previously in 5:9. The price is mentioned explicitly there as 'with your blood', thus connecting this idea with one of the earliest statements about Jesus in the book: that he has 'freed us from our sins by his blood' (1:5).

The fifth description, that they are *[offered as] firstfruits to God and the Lamb*, draws on the Old Testament image of the offering of the beginning of the harvest, which occurred in the Firstfruits Festival immediately after Passover (Lev. 23:10), and fifty days later as part of the feast of Weeks (Pentecost; Lev. 23:15–17). The part of the crop that has ripened first is offered to God in gratitude for the promise it represents of the whole crop eventually being ready to harvest. Paul uses the idea to describe the Spirit as the foretaste of our salvation to come (Rom. 8:23), those who first came to faith in a region as an anticipation of many more (Rom. 16:5; 1 Cor. 16:15; 2 Thess. 2:13), and Jesus as the first to be raised from the dead as an anticipation of the universal resurrection (1 Cor. 15:20, 23). But this is only one half of the meaning of 'firstfruits', and probably not the meaning here, since this group are not just the *first* who will be redeemed; they are *all* of them. The other meaning of 'firstfruits' is that they are a sacrificial offering to God, and this is also the sense of the term in Jeremiah 2:2–3 and James 1:18, and accords with Paul's language of the Gentiles who believe becoming an 'offering . . . to God' in Romans 15:16. If they do anticipate something, it is not others being saved, but the whole creation being renewed when Jesus returns.

The sixth description is that *no lie was found in their mouths*, which is an almost exact citation of Isaiah 53:9 describing the suffering servant and quoted to describe Jesus in 1 Peter 2:22. John has substituted the word 'deceit' (*dolos* in the Greek Old Testament) with the word 'lie' (*pseudos*), so that they not only follow the example of the lamb (see also Zeph. 3:13), but are a counterpoint to the 'false prophet' (*pseudoprophētēs*), as the beast from the land is called in 16:13 onwards. The parallel seventh description that *they are blameless* links this back to the nuptial imagery associated with virginity; the work of the Spirit in sanctifying God's people will one day be completed (Phil. 1:6; 2:15) so that we are presented as a holy, blameless and perfect bride (Eph. 5:27).

Theology

It is sometimes argued that this vision of the 144,000 is only of those who have been martyred, that is, who have died for their faith, rather than of the whole people of God. This is on the basis of the small actual number, the language in 13:15 of those who refuse to worship the beast 'being killed' and the language in 12:11 of 'not shrinking from death'. But the language of dying to self and carrying one's cross is elsewhere assumed to be the universal commitment of those who follow Jesus, and the sevenfold description of the group uses images that apply to all God's people. The number 144,000 is clearly symbolic, and the strong links with Revelation 7 show that this is another description of the same group, those 'redeemed' from 'every tribe, language, people and nation'. They are the saints who praise God around the throne even while they experience the suffering that comes with following the lamb in a world which mostly worships another.

B. Three angels announcing the gospel and judgment (14:6–13)

Comment

6. This new section begins with John's customary introduction *And I saw* (AT), which is not repeated again until verse 14, showing that the three angels and the voice in verse 13 belong together as part of one visionary episode. The three angels are introduced simply as *another angel*, 'another angel, a second' and 'another angel, a third'. The first flies in *mid-air* just as the eagle who announced the three woes had done in 8:13, thus being visible to all. The *eternal gospel* is a phrase occurring only here in the New Testament; 'eternal' has a sense of 'long-lasting', but it particularly refers to 'the age [to come]', so that the Johannine phrase 'eternal life' (eighteen times in John's Gospel, including John 3:16; see also Luke 18:30) is not just life that lasts, but life of the age to come and so equivalent to life in 'the kingdom of God'. A 'gospel' is an announcement of good news, used of proclamations by the emperor of a conquest, holiday or gift to the people, and the angel 'announces' the 'announcement' (*euangelizō* and *euangelion*), fulfilling the root meaning of the word 'angel' as 'messenger'. This is not a substitute for the witness and proclamation of God's people, but rather the heavenly counterpart to it, just as in Matthew 24:31 God sends his angels to gather the elect,[3] which refers to the preaching of the gospel to *every nation, tribe, language and people* and forming them as one people. This is the sixth of the seven occurrences of this fourfold phrase, on which see the comment on 5:9. The invitation is a universal one to all who (lit.) 'sit on the earth', a Hebraism using the verb *kathēmai* for people who live on earth (cf. Jer. 32:29) which John uses to refer to all people who might or might not respond, avoiding the negative phrase 'inhabitants of the earth' (which uses the verb *katoikeō*) that describes those who live a merely earthly life rather than the life of heaven (see comment on 3:10 and 6:10).

7. The angel's *loud voice* means that the invitation is heard by all; if the language of 'being afraid' and 'giving glory to God' in 11:13 was ambiguous, this triple bidding to *Fear God, give him glory* and *worship him* is an unambiguous call to repentance. The declaration that *the hour of his judgment has come* is typical Johannine realized eschatology (cf. John 3:18) in which life is to be lived in the light of the certain future, including the judgment that will not actually be fully effected until the return of Jesus. As elsewhere in Revelation, eschatology is held together with creation, and the mention of the *heavens, the earth* and *the sea* repeats the proverbial threefold description of the whole world seen earlier in 5:13 and 10:6. The *springs of water* were part of the creation subject to disaster in the third trumpet (see 8:10), but perhaps also hint at future hope since they form part of the eschatological refreshment provided by God (see comment on 7:17).

8–10. Just as the defeat of the dragon was both good news and bad news in 12:12, so following the news of salvation from the first angel comes news of judgment from the *second* and *third* angels. The second declares the general judgment of Babylon using language from Isaiah 21:9, which sets the agenda for the visions of Revelation 17 – 18. The parallel between the historical Babylon and the metaphorical Babylon (Rome) is that they were both responsible for

---

3. Note that, according to Jesus' words in Matthew, this happens in the lifetime of those listening ('this generation will not pass away', Matt. 24:34), so cannot be some distant 'end times' event.

destroying the city of Jerusalem. The fall comes because (as with the historic Babylon in Jer. 51:7–9) she made the *nations drink* her *wine*.

The third angel brings a specific warning to those who *worship the beast and its image and receive its mark*, which connects with the narrative of the previous chapter (13:15–16), while the consequences warned of (*fire and sulphur*, AT) anticipate the final judgment of the devil, beast and false prophet in 20:10. Just as those who follow the lamb will become like him and share his victory, so those who follow the beast will become like him and share his fate. To *give a drink* (AT) would normally be seen as an act of kindness and compassion (Matt. 10:42; 25:35; Rom. 12:20), but not when the cup contains the *maddening wine of her adulteries*. The phrase here is odd, literally being the 'wine of the fury [or 'passion'] of her sexual immorality'. This then links with the following phrase *the wine of the fury of God* (AT), an idea found in Old Testament texts of God's judgment, including Isaiah 51:17, 22 and Jeremiah 25:15. The two phrases linked together creates a Pauline sense of being 'delivered up' to the results of sin found in Romans 1:24, 26; those who choose to drink from the cup of fury (of Babylon) will indeed drink from the cup of fury (of God). 'Sexual immorality' could be understood literally or as a metaphor for idolatrous worship (see comment on 2:20), though the two are closely associated in the New Testament. The wine of God's fury is *poured full strength*, literally 'mixed un-mixed'; wine would normally be prepared ('mixed') by diluting it one part wine to two parts water (or a similar ratio), but here no dilution is added ('unmixed').

11. Though the rising of *smoke* has signified the prayers of God's people in 8:4 and will denote the glory of God in 15:8, here it is a sign of judgment, as it will later be for Babylon in 18:9, 18. Though the phrase *smoke of their torment rises for ever and ever* (AT) has been interpreted as indicating a continual experience of torment (which raises some particular theological problems), this is difficult to sustain in the light of the parallel at 19:3, where in an identical phrase the 'smoke from [the city Babylon] rises for ever and ever' (AT). It is impossible to imagine the city being perpetually destroyed; the image must signify the eternal *effect* of its destruction, rather than an eternal *process* of destruction (cf. the destruction of Edom in Isa. 34:10). *Rest* is a frequent description of the quality of life

for the saved in the age to come (Heb. 4:1, 11; cf. Matt. 11:28), reflecting the rest of God on the seventh day following six days of work in creation (Gen. 2:2–3). But it constantly eludes those who *worship the beast* (repeating the link with Rev. 13), despite imperial promises of peace and prosperity.

12. The call for *patient endurance*, which has been John's disposition from the beginning (1:9), echoes that in the previous chapter at 13:10, but the sense here is reversed. In 13:10, endurance is needed because of the hardship that will be faced by those who are faithful and do not bow to the pressure of the beast (a negative reason), but here it is encouraged because of the hope of salvation and judgment that are presented as certainties (a positive reason). We need patient endurance for strength to face the trials, but patient endurance will reap its reward in the end. The characterization of *the saints* (AT) as those who *keep the commands of God* (AT) parallels the description in 12:17 when the dragon sets off to wage war on them. *The faith of Jesus* (AT) can be understood in the 'objective' sense (having faith in Jesus) or the 'subjective' sense (Jesus' faithfulness to us), though the two are closely related (see comment on 13:10).

13. The non-specific *voice from heaven* has spoken twice before (in 10:4; 12:10) and is probably a circumlocution for the voice of God, who does not speak unambiguously until 21:5. John is commanded to *write* twelve times – three times in relation to the book as a whole, seven times for the messages in Revelation 2 – 3, and twice of statements here and in 19:9 – which emphasizes the importance of what is spoken. There are seven blessings in Revelation (1:3; 14:13; 16:15; 19:9; 20:6; 22:7, 14), most of which have some eschatological dimension. *Those who die in the Lord* (AT) includes all those who come to the end of life before Jesus returns, and not merely those who are martyred. *From this moment on* (AT) must refer to the period that began with Jesus' death, and the assurance is similar to Paul's assurance for the Thessalonians (1 Thess. 4:13–18) that, because of Jesus' resurrection, death is not the end but a time of awaiting the general resurrection of all humanity.

The testimony of the *Spirit* is that the followers of the lamb look forward to the *rest* that eludes those who worship the beast. The relief from *hard work* (AT) might signify an end to hardship and suffering, though Paul also uses the term for the apostolic ministry of proclaiming good news and planting new church communities (Rom. 16:12; 1 Cor. 3:8; 15:58). Their *works follow them* (AT), that is, they accompany them. This does not suggest that they have somehow attained salvation by the good deeds they have done; rather, they take with them the life of virtue which has been fashioned in them by the work of God. Works or deeds (*erga*) are mentioned twenty times in Revelation,[4] particularly in the messages to the seven assemblies, when the exalted Jesus says, 'I know your deeds.' These actions, which include love, faithfulness, service and perseverance, testify to the transforming power of faith in Jesus, which is not merely an interior attitude but also a changed way of life (see comment on 2:19).

Theology
In this passage we start to encounter some of the most challenging language about judgment in the book of Revelation. The idea of torment which lasts for ever and ever presents a problem not simply for the tender conscience but also for developing a biblical theology of evil and judgment in the context of God's description as 'gracious and compassionate, slow to anger and rich in love' and as 'good to all; [who] has compassion on all he has made' (Ps. 145:8–9; see also Exod. 34:6; Pss 86:15; 103:8). There are three contexts that we need to consider in reading the verses here:

1. Despite the two angels who pronounce judgment on Babylon and on those who worship the beast, the wider context is the proclamation of good news by the first angel. The use of the comprehensive fourfold phrase ('every nation, tribe, language and people') repeatedly emphasizes that the invitation to salvation is extended to everyone, regardless of ethnic identity or social standing.

---

4. Rev. 2:2, 5, 6, 19 (twice), 22, 23, 26; 3:1, 2, 8, 15; 9:20; 14:13; 15:3; 16:11; 18:6; 20:12, 13; 22:12. The word is always in the plural ('works', 'deeds') with the exception of the last occurrence, when it is singular. In English translations, the presence of the word is evident, though quite often it is hidden by the use of a different construction, such as 'what they have done'.

2. The language of judgment contrasts quite clearly with contemporary Jewish apocalypses, in which not only is there torment for the wicked, but the saved watch the spectacle of their suffering. Though Revelation's images have seemed extreme to many subsequent generations of readers, they are comparatively modest when read in this context.

3. We must remember that this is a text speaking to a very small, insignificant and oppressed group within a dominant system of totalitarian power. In this context, the promise that those exercising oppressive power will face justice and judgment functions to give hope and significance to the oppressed. The moment the text is appropriated by a group who are themselves in a position of oppressive power, its effect is reversed from being a text of liberation to becoming a tool of oppression, and its use in this way contradicts the core message of the text itself.

C. The harvest of the Son of Man (14:14–20)

Context

This passage is quite distinct from the surrounding passages, and this raises two main questions. First, how do the two halves (the grain harvest in vv. 14–16 and the grape harvest in vv. 17–20) relate to one another: are they two different accounts of the same event, or two distinct events; and are they both negative images of judgment, or do they offer one positive and one negative image? Second, how does this passage function within the narrative: should it really belong to the following chapter as setting the scene for the final judgment of Babylon? Careful attention to the text and to John's use of Old Testament language provide the answers to both of these questions.

Comment

14. John once again uses the emphatic *I looked and behold* (AT), marking a new section in his vision report, as he has done in 14:1. The *white cloud* signifies divine presence and authority, as it does elsewhere in Revelation; not all figures associated with clouds are divine (see the mighty angel in 10:1), but the additional mention of *one like a son of man* makes a clear connection with the vision in Daniel 7:13. This is a natural move in the narrative, since Revelation 13 drew so extensively on the earlier verses in Daniel 7 for the descriptions of the dragon and the two beasts. The exact duplication of the phrase from Revelation 1:13 makes it certain that this figure is the exalted Jesus, even though he appears to act on the order of an angelic figure in the following verse. The *crown of gold* (a *stephanos*, signifying triumph, and not yet a *diadēma* as in 19:12) confirms this, though such crowns are also worn by the elders in 4:4. The *sickle* is the usual hand tool for cutting grain for the harvest and so is almost a metonym for it. The central focus on harvest in these verses is shown by the word 'sickle' coming exactly seven times within this section.

15–16. The arrival of *another angel* does not suggest that the 'son of man' is an angelic figure rather than Jesus; the 'another' distinguishes this angel from others we have previously met. These verses on the harvest introduce us to three angels described as 'another' (vv. 15, 17, 18) and which therefore match the three described in the same way in verses 6, 8, 9. Such visual symmetry is a strong indicator that we should see Revelation 14 as a whole, rather than treating the second half as belonging to Revelation 15. As is often the case, John's heavenly geography is not entirely clear; both the cloud and *the temple* are evidently 'in heaven', but John does not specify the relation between the two. The importance of the angel's origin 'from the temple' is that he comes from the presence of God and therefore with the authority of God, sent as his messenger. The command to the Son of Man to *Take your sickle and reap* is therefore the command of God, and in doing so Jesus is executing the judgment over the earth that properly belongs to God alone.

The declaration that the *harvest of the earth is ripe* uses slightly unusual language, literally meaning that it is 'dry' (where v. 18 uses a more common term). This is closer to the idea expressed by Jesus in John 4:35 that the fields are 'white' for harvest (AT): what was green and growing has reached maturity, and has now lightened in colour as it dries out, signifying that the harvest is due. Elsewhere in the New Testament, harvest generally has a positive sense of those who are ready to respond to the proclamation of the good news (Matt. 9:37; Luke 10:2; Rom. 1:13), though it also has a clear eschatological sense (Matt. 13:39). The future kingdom has broken into the present in the ministry of Jesus, which connects the present harvest with what will take place at the end of time. The image here is therefore close to that of 'gather[ing] the grain into [God's] storehouses' (Matt. 13:30b, AT).

17–18. If the first angel brings a positive message of harvest, just as the first 'other' angel in 14:6 brought a positive message, then the second and third 'other' angels bring a negative message, as had the second and third in 14:8, 9. The *temple* again represents the presence and authority of God, indicating that the justice of judgment is God's intention, even if it brings joy to some and disaster to others. This is confirmed by the third angel who *had charge of the fire . . . from the altar*, a reference back to 8:5, where the angel takes the censer which offers the prayers of the saints and fills it with fire before hurling it on the earth. Judgment is in part the answer to the cries of the saints for justice and vindication (6:9–10). The two episodes are connected by each harvester having a *sharp sickle*, but it seems significant that this second aspect of the harvest is not undertaken by the 'one like a son of man', but by an angel. Although this comes under the sovereignty of God, there is a sense of God's distance from it by means of delegation, just as happened with the release of the four horsemen in Revelation 6. The *vine* is sometimes an image of the people of God (Isa. 5:1–7; Mark 12:1–9), but here the influence of Joel 3:13 and Isaiah 63:3 (which is also alluded to in Rev. 19:13) shows that the *earth's vine* relates to those who have opposed God and not worshipped him.

19–20. The *winepress of God's wrath* continues the metaphor of judgment from Joel 3:13 and Isaiah 63:3, and offers a gruesome image of death in sharp contrast to the images of life in the New Jerusalem ('water of life', 21:6; 'book of life', 21:27; 'river of the water of life', 22:1; 'tree of life', 22:2). The juice of grapes as they were crushed was sometimes called its *blood* (Gen. 49:11; Deut. 32:14), and this allowed wine to be a natural symbol of blood that Jesus drew on in the Last Supper. The placing of the *winepress outside the city* draws on another parallel passage of judgment in Jeremiah 51:33, where it is specified that Babylon is the one to be judged in the trampling of the harvest, thus preparing the way for the scenes of Babylon's fall in Revelation 18. The exaggerated depiction of rivers of *blood that flow* (AT) is another stock-in-trade of apocalyptic, both ancient and modern. Similar language is found in Ezekiel 32:5–6; other Jewish apocalyptic talks of horses wading up to their chests in the blood of sinners (*4 Ezra* 15:35); and Jewish leaders complained of Roman slaughter of their people by describing horses drowning in blood and the streams of blood carrying boulders far out to sea.[5]

Theology

The two harvests of grain and grapes correspond to the basic need for food and drink in bread and wine, though John's vision report does not appear to make anything of that. Rather, the grain harvest is a positive image of the one like a son of man bringing into final safety those who are faithful to God, and the text in these verses runs parallel to other New Testament images of harvest without drawing much on Old Testament ideas. By contrast, the grape harvest, delegated to an angelic harvester, draws extensively on Old Testament images of judgment of the nations who oppose God and his people. As with other episodes in Revelation where consecutive sections offer different perspectives on the same reality, John is giving us a symbolic description of two aspects of judgment. For those who have responded to the gospel, it is good news, but for those who have not, it is bad news.

This double understanding matches closely the double depiction of good news and bad news declared by the previous three angels in verses 6–12, and follows similar juxtaposition elsewhere in the New Testament. So the coming of 'God's only Son' is good news to those who believe in him (John 3:16), but spells condemnation for those who do not (John 3:18). Jesus' return will come like a thief in the night for those it catches unawares (1 Thess. 5:2), but for the people of God he will come as a friend in the day (1 Thess. 5:4–5).

---

5. In the modern era, UK politician Enoch Powell made a famous speech in 1968 predicting 'rivers of blood' flowing due to ethnic tension arising from immigration, and Saddam Hussein's claim that 'rivers of blood' would flow significantly affected Western planning in the first Gulf War in 1991.

In each of these last two sections in Revelation 14, the good news has been proclaimed before the bad news, and in the chapters that follow each is expanded but in reverse order (thus forming a chiasm), so that judgment is completed in Revelation 18 – 20 and the climax of the whole narrative is the vision of hope and life in the New Jerusalem (Rev. 21 – 22).

11. THE POURING OUT OF THE SEVEN BOWLS (15:1 – 16:21)

The third sequence of judgments – the pouring out of seven bowls, following the opening of the seven seals and the sounding of the seven trumpets – has an extended introduction which sets it apart from the previous two sequences, and its structure and shape are also distinctive.

The introduction serves to look back in the narrative and connect this episode with several that have gone before. The language of a 'sign' connects this with the 'signs' of chapter 12; seven angels have been mentioned previously in 8:2; the sea of glass is reminiscent of the sea before the throne in 4:6; the victorious who are singing are the ones we have just encountered in chapter 14, playing harps as did the elders in 5:8. The seven angels themselves appear to be dressed in a way very similar to Jesus in the opening vision of chapter 1, in white linen and with golden sashes.[1] But the sequence,

---

1. Though the angels wear the golden sashes around their 'chests' (*stēthē*), in contrast to Jesus who wore his around his 'breasts' (*mastoi*); see comment on 1:13.

together with its introduction, also looks forward to the visions of chapters 17 and 18 that follow. The song of 'Moses and of the Lamb' sung by the victorious celebrates not only God's sovereign rule and his universal acclaim, but also his justice in acting in judgment over those who have defied him and denied him. This focus on justice is repeated in the interjection of praise in the third bowl (16:5), and both these songs use language that is repeated in chapter 18.

This section also marks the end of the middle section of Revelation. Following the epistolary introduction and opening vision (chapter 1), the messages to the seven assemblies (chapters 2 and 3) and the twofold vision of the throne (chapters 4 and 5), this central section has consisted of the three sequences with visionary interludes between them as an overarching structure. In chapter 17 there is a significant shift from vision to audition – from what John sees to what he hears – which is then followed by a sequence of visions of the end in chapters 19 and 20, culminating in the final vision of the New Jerusalem in chapters 21 and 22 which is marked by another shift of language.

A. Introductory vision and the song of Moses (15:1–8)

Context

This short chapter functions to tie together the 'interlude' that we have just experienced with the bowl sequence that follows in Revelation 16. The final judgments on earth prior to the cosmic sequence of judgments that begins in Revelation 17 are dovetailed with further comment and description of the redeemed that we have just encountered. The juxtaposition of the two introduced a theme of the interrelated nature of the justice of God, and his vindication of those who have remained faithful, with the judgment of the enemies of God and his people, who will reap what they have sown. It is a theme that John returns to in the coming chapters, particular in the judgment of Babylon in Revelation 18.

Comment

1. This prelude to the last of the series of sevens begins with the usual *And I saw* (AT), but this is combined with the mention of a *great and marvellous sign*, echoing the 'signs' that appeared in 12:1 and

12:2 which were also *in heaven*. If the three (or four, including the thunders) series followed one another chronologically, then these *last plagues* cover a final period of time. But we saw in the introduction to Revelation 6 the strong parallels between the series, particularly the trumpets and the bowls, their connections with the Exodus plagues, and an anticipation of the End drawing each to a close. We should therefore understand 'last' to mean 'the last series within the narrative' and the last description of *God's wrath* and its fullest expression. The *seven . . . plagues* are mentioned here at the beginning of this section and in verse 8 at the end (forming an *inclusio*), which emphasizes their importance, but also allows John to focus on another part of his vision report before recounting the plagues.

2. We have the first of a series of allusions to the exodus in John's description of a *sea of glass glowing with fire*. This sounds similar to the 'sea of glass' before the throne in 4:6, except that John does not introduce it with the article 'the' inviting us to make the connection. Instead, the people *standing beside the sea* (or even perhaps 'upon' it; the word is *epi*) conjures up the image of the people of Israel, led by Moses, about to cross the Red Sea having left Egypt. This is also suggested by the description of them as *those who had been victorious over* [lit, 'from', *ek*] *the beast and its image and over* [again, 'from', *ek*] *the number of its name*. This will be made more explicit in the reference to the 'second exodus' from historic Babylon in 18:4; this quotes Jeremiah 51:45, which in turn is dependent on the first exodus call to fly from Egypt at the Passover. The glass *mixed with fire* (AT) recalls not just God's deliverance of his people through the sea but also his fiery judgment on Egypt, as well as his presence as a pillar of fire.

English translations generally conform the tense of *those who had been victorious* to the past tense of John's vision report ('And I saw'); but the participle is in the present tense, 'those conquering', which recalls the 'victor sayings' at the end of each of the seven messages ('to the one conquering', AT). It also recalls the language of conquest in 12:11 and its sharp contrast with the conquest by the beast in 13:7. The ones who truly conquer are those who are not cowed into conformity by the apparent power of the beast, but remain true by their non-violent resistance to the lamb who was slain. The *harps of God* (AT) might be given by God or for the praise of God; either way, they identify this group with the 144,000 of Revelation 14 ('harpists playing their harps', 14:2).

3–4. They sing *the song of . . . Moses*, that is, they sing the same kind of song that Moses sang, and are connected to him as *the servant of God* (AT), a term John consistently uses for the followers of the lamb (1:1; 7:3). There is a song of Moses in Deuteronomy 32, and its opening verses do connect with the song here (in its Greek rather than Hebrew form) by mentioning his *deeds* which are *true* and *just*, and God as *holy* (in both cases using *hosios* rather than the more common *hagios*). But in praise of God's actions, the closer overall link is with the song of Moses in Exodus 15, which he sings while standing by the sea after the waters have closed over the pursuing Egyptian troops. This is also the *song . . . of the Lamb*, though in a different sense: it is not the song that the lamb sings, but the song sung in praise of the lamb, since the redemption through his blood is another exodus which releases us from the slavery of sin and leads us to the promised land of the kingdom of God.

The words of the song itself are drawn from a whole range of Old Testament texts of praise. *Great and wonderful are your deeds* (AT) uses the language of Psalm 111:2–3, where the 'great works' of God are 'wonders' which are pondered and remembered (AT); Psalm 86:10 also describes God as 'great' and as one who does wonders. *Lord God Almighty* occurs here for the third of seven times in Revelation (see comment on 4:8). In the Old Testament, it combines the name of Israel's God ('Yahweh') with the title *ṣĕbā'ôt*, meaning 'commander of the armies [of heaven]', and here echoes the praise of God as warrior in the first part of Moses' song in Exodus 15. *Just and true are your ways* echoes Deuteronomy 32:4 and is repeated in relation to his judgments in 16:7 and 19:2. Some manuscripts read 'king of the ages' in place of *King of the nations*, and this reflects the Hebrew phrase *melek ha'ôlām*, which has the sense both of 'king of the age' (i.e. eternal king) and of 'king of this age' (i.e. king over all the nations). The title and the following rhetorical question reverse the order found in Jeremiah 10:7: 'Who should not fear you, King of the nations?'

The mentions of *all [the] nations*, *bring[ing] glory* and *worship* all come from Psalm 86:9. Most English translations render verse 4 as a pair of parallel 'cause and effect' clauses ('Who will not fear . . . For you

alone are holy/All nations will come . . . for your righteous acts . . .'),
but in fact the three following phrases are all introduced by 'for' or
'because' (*hoti*): 'for you are holy . . . for all the nations will come . . .
for your righteous deeds . . .' This makes the multinational identity
of the people of God in the new covenant a *reason* for worship and
not simply the *result* of worship; God's wonderful deeds and
righteous acts are revealed in the coming to him of all tribes,
languages, tongues and people.

5. A new subsection in John's vision report is introduced with
After this I looked, indicating once more not a chronological sequence
of events but the order of his visionary experiences. The language
here is rather abrupt, and English translations smooth this out by
including the verb *and I saw*. As has happened previously, John is
adding progressively more detail to the description of the *temple*,
now identifying it as the *tent of meeting* (AT). The phrase is difficult
to translate, because the Hebrew 'meeting' is translated by the Greek
'witness' (*martyrion* in the Greek of Exod. 27:21 and elsewhere),
which is the phrase that John also uses. In its Old Testament context,
the tent functions as a witness to God's presence with his people
and his covenant commitment (expressed on the stone tablets kept
in the tent) as they journey through the wilderness. But 'witness'
now has another whole set of meanings in the context of Revelation,
including following the example of Jesus the faithful witness even
to the point of death. Identifying the dwelling-place of the followers
of the lamb as the 'tent of witness' therefore both establishes
continuity with the first covenant and adds important new
dimensions to it. The temple being *opened* connects it with earth,
not only allowing the angels to come from it with the judgments of
God, but also allowing the saints to enter it and make it their
dwelling-place.

6. The definite article introducing *the seven angels* refers us back to
their introduction in verse 1, but no further back. These angels are
distinctive in having their apparel described for us. They wear *clean,
shining linen* (using the unusual term *linon* rather than the more
common *byssos* or *byssinos* used elsewhere), which presumably is
white, even though the colour is not specified as such. In pagan
culture, this is the assumed colour for worship, signifying purity, and
in the Old Testament is the apparel of the high priest for entering

the Holy of Holies, signifying holiness (see comment on 4:4). This provides an echo of the vision of Jesus in 1:13, who wears the full-length robe worn by priests in Exodus 28:4 and Zechariah 3:4, and like Jesus these angels wear *belts of gold* (AT), not around their waists (as the angel in Dan. 10:5) but around their *chests* (Jesus wore his around his 'breasts' in 1:13).

7–8. Two other groups are now involved, one explicitly and one implicitly. The *four living creatures*, who symbolize creation's worship of God, pass the angels *seven golden bowls* containing the plagues. This suggests that the natural world has some role in the expression of God's wrath and judgment. But the previous mention of 'golden bowls' referred to them as being 'full of incense, which are the prayers of God's people' (5:8). And we have previously seen that the angel in charge of the fire from the altar, who has just been mentioned in 14:18, mixed the incense prayers with the fire and 'hurled it to the earth' (AT) as the prelude to the trumpet judgments (8:5). So this final expression of God's wrath is in some way connected with the prayers of God's people for justice. The third mention within seven verses of the *seven angels* with either the bowls or the plagues points to their importance within this vision episode.

The prospect of the 'completion' of God's wrath contrasts with the description of God himself, who lives *for ever and ever*. This provides an echo to Old Testament contrasts between God's anger and his faithfulness like that of Psalm 30:5 ('his anger lasts only a moment, but his favour lasts a lifetime'), as well as making a counter-claim to that of Rome as the 'eternal city'. The *smoke from the glory of God* recalls the inauguration of worship in Solomon's temple, when the ark of the covenant was first placed in the Holy of Holies. All the priests had consecrated themselves, not just those on duty, and all the musicians wore fine linen. At the praise of the goodness of God by the holy people of God in unison, the cloud descended so that 'the priests could not perform their service' (2 Chr. 5:14). The full disclosure of the glory of God brings all human activity to an end.

Theology

The bowl sequence is the third of the sequences of seven (seals and then trumpets), or the fourth if you include the mention of the seven thunders in 10:3. But this sequence has a different relation to the material around it, leading to a different structure and focus within it. The first two sequences implicitly pose the questions: what is God going to do about the state of the world, and how should his people conduct themselves in it? The interludes in each of these sequences offer an answer: God is raising up a people whom he will seal and protect, who will bear costly testimony for him. God has called John to testify, and calls his people to exercise the prophetic ministry of testimony like that of Moses and Elijah.

But this sequence of seven bowls comes in quite a different context. We have now been offered the full disclosure of God's action in the world in the coming of Jesus, and the full disclosure of the opposition that God's people will face in the form of the dragon and the two beasts. Rather than contain the possibility of repentance, as the first two sequences did, this set of seven focuses more explicitly on God's response to those who refuse to accept the offer of life, and highlights the justice of God's judgments – a theme that is further developed in the judgment of the great prostitute in Revelation 18.

B. The first five bowls (16:1–11)

Context
The third and final sequence of judgments has an interesting relationship with what has gone before. Although the 'seals' and 'trumpets' were closely related in terms of structure, the 'trumpets' and 'bowls' are more closely related in terms of content, as is shown by the relation of these two sequences to the Exodus plagues in table 9 overleaf. The actual structure of the bowl judgments, grouped as 5 + 1 + 1, is notably different from the previous two sequences which were grouped as 4 + 2 + (interlude) + 1. The theme of an invitation to repentance now fades from view, as God's ultimate judgment looms on the horizon.

Comment
1. Having seen the lamb and the 144,000 on Mount Zion in Revelation 14, and the seven angels in Revelation 15, John reports that he *heard a loud voice from the temple* and (with the exception of the frog

Table 9: The plagues of Exodus and the trumpet and bowl sequence

	Exodus plagues	Trumpets	Bowls
1	*Waters to blood*	Third of earth scorched	Boils = 6th plague
2	*Frogs*	Third of sea to blood = 1st plague	Sea to blood = 1st plague = 2nd trumpet
3	Gnats	Water 1/3 bitter	Waters to blood = 1st plague = 3rd trumpet
4	Flies	Sun 1/3 darkened = 9th plague	Scorching sun = 9th plague reversed = 4th trumpet reversed
5	Death of livestock	Locust army = 8th plague	Darkness = 9th plague = 4th trumpet
6	*Boils*	Fiendish army	Euphrates dried, frogs, kings from the east = 2nd plague + 6th trumpet
7	*Hail*	The kingdom of God	Earthquake and hail = 7th plague + 6th seal
8	*Locusts*		
9	*Darkness*		
10	Death of firstborn		

spirits in v. 13) does not mention 'seeing' again until the new vision report in 17:3. This is the only episode where we hear a voice not just from heaven, but specifically from the *temple*, commissioning the angels at the outset, and forming an *inclusio* by celebrating the completion of their task in verse 17. If the 'voice from heaven' is a circumlocution for the voice of God, perhaps this is a circumlocution for the voice of God with particular emphasis on his covenant loyalty to his people (since the temple is 'the tent of [covenant] testimony', 15:5, AT). The *bowls* were first mentioned in 5:8 as holding 'incense, which is the prayers of the saints' (AT), and so there is some connection between the cries to God for justice and the judgment that is poured out (see comment on 15:7). The action of *pour[ing] out* is highly symbolic, since (in contrast to what happens when the trumpets are sounded) nothing is described as actually coming from the bowls; instead, we are simply told of the consequences of *God's wrath*.

2. The *first angel* pours out his bowl *on the land*; the Greek word *gē* is the same as that translated 'earth' in the previous verse, where it meant 'the earth' in terms of the whole world. But the contrast with the second bowl which affects 'the sea' shows that *gē* here means the 'land', following the pattern of the first trumpet in 8:7. The first three bowl judgments appear to function on the Old Testament principle of *lex talionis*, that is, the penalty should fit the crime. 'Evil and wicked' *sores* (often translated as *ugly* and *festering*) break out on those who *had the mark of the beast*. If you want to receive a mark, a mark you shall receive. This judgment affects those who reject God and not the followers of the lamb, and in that regard they are more like the plagues of Egypt, which afflicted the Egyptians but not the Hebrews, than the seals or trumpets.

3–7. The *second* and *third* bowls have a parallel action, turning the *sea* and then the *rivers and springs* to *blood*. The language of 'rivers and springs' is similar to the language of the third trumpet, and together they follow the pattern of the first Exodus plague. The description of the blood being *like that of a dead person* could be taken to mean it has coagulated, but the phrase that follows (*every living thing . . . died*) points to the simple reality that blood means death. Just as surely as people die when they lose their blood, so this blood brings death to everything. The *angel of the waters* (AT) means the angel who has spiritual charge of the waters, in line with Jewish belief that angels were given authority over different regions and domains of the world, much as pagan belief held different gods to rule over different parts of the world.

The pause in the sequence of bowls is unexpected, in that the previous two sequences have continued uninterrupted at this point. The declarations from the angel and the *altar* are framed by an *inclusio* that repeats one of the main themes of the song of Moses from 15:3: *[true and] just are your judgments* (AT). The term 'just' (*dikaios*) could have the sense of 'righteous' reflected in some English translations, but the importance of *lex talionis* in the first three bowls, and its highlighting in the middle of these declarations, makes it clear that the justice of God's actions is what is in view. It is difficult to know why the previous triple title *who is, who was [and who is to come]*

(AT; 1:4, 8; 4:8) has been truncated here; in its occurrence in 11:17 the omission of the future element makes sense because God has now 'taken [his] great power' and 'begun to reign', but that explanation does not hold here. The title *Holy One* recalls the frequent title of God in the prophets, especially Isaiah ('the Holy One of Israel', 1:4; 5:19, and so on), but the word 'holy' is *hosios* and not *hagios* as in Isaiah and most of the rest of Revelation, so the allusion is again back to the song of Moses in 15:4 which does use the same word.

The metaphor of *giv[ing] them blood to drink* is an Old Testament image of repaying in kind for bloodshed (Isa. 49:26). As with the sores, the sense here is of giving them what they ask for: if you want to spill blood, blood will be spilled. The *saints and prophets* (AT) describe respectively the whole people of God and a group within them who proclaim God's ways and message. There is no sense in Revelation that 'saints' are a distinct group, since the term is used (as in Paul) to describe all God's people; but though the people of God have a prophetic task (as expressed in the image of the two witnesses ministering like Moses and Elijah), John does not assume that every follower of the lamb is a prophet. The phrase translated *as they deserve* is odd and abrupt, literally reading 'to be worthy'. This could be taken as describing God as 'worthy' of making these judgments, but the emphasis on *lex talionis* makes it more likely that the phrase is describing those who have *shed the blood of the saints* (AT) as 'worthy', that is, deserving of the judgment they receive. The response of the *altar* again suggests the role of the prayers of the saints, since this is the altar of incense (not of sacrifice; see comment on 8:3); it repeats from the song of Moses in 15:3 the title *Lord God Almighty* emphasizing God's sovereignty, along with the affirmation that follows it there: 'just and true are your ways/judgments'.

8–11. Just as the second and third bowl judgments were closely related, so are the fourth and fifth, with closely parallel wording describing the response of those afflicted. Both the sun's *scorch[ing] . . . with fire* and the advent of *darkness* were widely seen in the ancient world as signs of divine judgment – and both things have been present in the previous series, the scorching of the earth coming after the first trumpet (8:7) and darkness coming after the fourth (8:12). It is again clear that these judgments do not afflict humanity as a whole, but only those who worship the beast rather than God. The darkness specifically afflicts the *throne of the beast*, a metonym for the beast's exercise of power, and those in darkness also have the *pains and . . . sores* which were inflicted on those worshipping the beast as part of the first bowl judgment. The scorching of the sun contrasts with the fate of the followers of the lamb, on whom 'the sun will not beat down . . . , nor any scorching heat' (7:16), and the darkness contrasts with the light of the glory of God in the holy city (21:23). The afflicted *gnaw their tongues* in the same way that Jesus describes those in 'outer darkness' (AT) or 'in the blazing furnace' as 'gnashing [their] teeth' (Matt. 8:12; 13:42).

In both bowl judgments, those afflicted *refuse to repent*, and in response to the fourth bowl they refuse to *glorify* God, a sharp contrast to the response in 11:13 to the earthquake following the ministry of the two witnesses, as well as to the sense of universal worship in the song of Moses at 15:4. There is a painful irony expressed in the two variant phrases at the end of each; God *has authority over the plagues* (AT) and is the *God of heaven* so the one who controls all things. In contrast to the prayers to God of the saints appealing to his power for protection, the people *cursed the name of God* (for which the OT penalty is death, which they are spared), instead of asking him to end their suffering.

C. The sixth and seventh bowls (16:12–21)

12. At this point, the series of bowls shows the greatest difference from the other two series. Where they were structured as 4 + 3, with a similar structure in the first four and last three items, the bowls are grouped as 5 + 2 (or perhaps 1 + 2 + 2+ 2), in that the common structure in the brief earlier judgments now gives way to two lengthier descriptions of the last two bowls. Though the theme of *drying up the river* (AT) has some connection with the first Exodus plague (in that it affects the water), the mention of the *Euphrates* connects this directly with the sixth trumpet. The Euphrates was established as the border between the Roman Empire and the Parthians by Pompey in the first century BC, and any army crossing it led by *kings from the East* (lit. 'from the rising of the sun' as in 7:2) would be interpreted as invaders (see comment on 9:14). The same kind of double causation is at work in this judgment as in the earlier series; though disaster comes through the action of agents of evil, it is God who has implicitly *prepare[d] the way*, just as was the case with the sixth trumpet (see comment on 9:15).

13. It is not clear whether the three *evil spirits* are seen as coming one each from the *mouth of the dragon, the mouth of the beast* and the *mouth of the false prophet*, or whether John somehow is envisaging all three coming out of their mouths together, since they speak, as it were, with one voice (see 13:11, 15). *Frogs* were thought of as unclean, ugly and vicious in first-century culture, and would have been included in the list of unclean animals in Leviticus 11:10, since though they live in water they do not exhibit the 'proper' features of water creatures such as fins and scales.[2] But the sense of the metaphor is clear: this evil trinity, in parody of the one on the throne, the lamb and the seven spirits (see comment on 13:14), utters deceptive speech and will be no match for the Son of Man whose true speech is like a sword (1:16; 19:15). The third member of this anti-trinity, previously described as the 'beast from the land', is now referred to as *the false prophet* (here and again in 19:20; 20:10), making the connection between this image and the local promoters of the imperial cult in Asia even clearer.

14. The *signs* performed by these *demonic spirits* refer back to the signs of 13:13–14 which 'deceived the inhabitants of the earth'. The intoxicating power of imperial might lures in *the kings of the whole world* who are prepared to rally in support of the empire but (as we see in Rev. 19) will share in its destruction.[3] The *great day of God Almighty* recalls Old Testament language of the 'day of the LORD'

---

2. Our inherent disgust at this kind of image was captured rather well in the first Harry Potter film, *Harry Potter and the Philosopher's Stone* (2001), when Ron Weasley's spell backfires and, to the horror of his friends, he starts to vomit slugs.

3. Some commentators read 'they go out' here and 'they gathered' in v. 16 as 'he [i.e. God] goes out' and 'he gathers' because both verbs are third person singular. But singular verbs are regularly used for neuter plural subjects, in this case the 'demonic spirits', so there is no need to interpret the verses in this way.

(Isa. 13:9) when God will confront sinners, 'powers in the heavens' and 'kings of the earth' (Isa. 24:21, AT).

15. There follows a short interjection in the description of the sixth bowl, just as there was an interjection earlier after the third bowl. Some commentators describe this as a shortened interlude, to match the interludes of Revelation 7 in the seal sequence and Revelation 10 – 11 in the trumpet sequence, but this is not convincing. This interjection taking the form of first-person speech (presumably of Jesus) is very brief and does not come between the sixth and seventh bowls, but within the description of the sixth bowl.[4] The idea that Jesus will *come like a thief* appears to have been well known among the early Christian communities, so that Paul can remind the Thessalonians that they 'know [it] very well' (1 Thess. 5:2). Paul's comment also explains why the interjection comes at this point, since he too links the 'thief' saying with the 'day of the Lord', transformed from its Old Testament use into meaning 'the day of the Lord Jesus'. Jesus himself coins the phrase in his eschatological teaching in Matthew 24:43; it might seem odd to liken Jesus to a thief, but, like all metaphors, it has a particular meaning in which only one aspect of the vehicle ('thief') carries over to the subject (the coming of Jesus).[5] Just as a thief's coming is sudden and entirely unexpected, so it is not possible to formulate an 'end times timetable' and count down and so predict Jesus' return – just the point Jesus makes when he says to his disciples (and not to outsiders), 'the Son of Man will come at an hour . . . you do not expect' (Matt. 24:44). John is perhaps reminding his readers that the sequence of bowl judgments is not being given to provide such a timetable!

Stay[ing] awake is a common metaphor in the New Testament for remaining watchful for Jesus' return, one he uses in relation to the

---

4. Some go on to interpret v. 16 as the second half of the interlude, thus matching the two parts of each of the previous interludes. But the language there picks up the ideas of v. 14 and brings them to completion, so it clearly belongs to the sixth bowl itself.

5. When people say they 'slept like a baby', they don't usually mean that they woke every two hours crying for attention as babies usually do!

'thief' saying (Matt. 24:42–43; 25:13) and that Paul also deploys, particularly in relation to living a holy and self-controlled life as the proper response to Jesus' coming (1 Thess. 5:6). The metaphor of being *clothed* (AT) is closely related; Paul uses it as baptismal language of new life in Christ, being 'clothed' in him (Gal. 3:27) and particularly being 'clothed' in the qualities of life that make discipleship distinctive (Col. 3:12). It is these qualities and actions, expressed as 'deeds', that the Christians in Sardis lack, since they are asleep, and Jesus will come as a thief to them (3:2–3). The failure to live a holy life in readiness to meet Jesus is likened to the cultural shame in first-century Judaism of being *naked*, the state you are naturally in when sleeping in a hot climate.[6]

16. After the brief interjection, John returns to complete his description of the sixth bowl judgment. The kings have been *gathered* as was anticipated in verse 14, and John specifies the (metaphorical) name of the place of their gathering. *Armageddon* has become a well-known metonym for apocalyptic conflict, and features widely in popular culture. The word is a Greek transliteration of the Hebrew *har mĕggidô*, meaning 'the mount of Megiddo'. Megiddo was one of the pre-Israelite cities in Canaan, one that the Canaanites held on to during the settlement of the land (Judg. 1:27), and it was associated with Deborah's victory over Israel's enemies (Judg. 5:19). It became one of Solomon's fortified cities (1 Kgs 9:15) because of its strategic location adjacent to Mount Carmel on the south side of the Jezreel Valley, a frequent site of battles because of the large open plain extending north from Megiddo and the strategic route that ran along the valley from the Jordan to the Mediterranean Sea. Solomon appears to have stabled horses there, suggesting it was used for cavalry and chariots, and the age of the city meant that it was built on an artificial *tel* or mound created by previous generations of building. Jezreel (and Megiddo with it) became proverbial for decisive battles that could destroy kingdoms (2 Kgs 9:27; 2 Chr. 35:22; Zech. 12:11) and that is its significance here.

---

6. The negative view of nakedness was one of the reasons why Jews
    disliked the Roman games, since athletes competed naked. Our word
    'gymnast' comes from the Greek *gymnos*, meaning 'naked'.

17. Instead of pouring out his bowl on some part of the earth, the *seventh* angel *poured out his bowl into the air.* The 'air' was known in Greek and Roman mythology as the lowest level of the heavens, and in the New Testament refers to the spiritual realm as it affects human life (as in 'the prince of power of the air', Eph. 2:2, AT). The *voice* comes once more from the *temple*; having first commissioned the angels to pour out the bowls in verse 1, it now declares that *It is done!*[7] The phrase is repeated in 21:6, confirming both that this is a circumlocution for the voice of God in his covenant faithfulness (see comment on 16:1) and that the end of this sequence, like the ends of the previous two, is an anticipation of the End that is more fully described in Revelation 21 – 22.

18–19. The *lightning, rumblings* [*phonē*, elsewhere translated 'sound' or 'voice'] . . . *thunder and a severe earthquake* represent the last of the four references to the appearance of God at Sinai, which increase in their drama and severity, the first occurrence in 4:5 being augmented with the earthquake in 8:5, a great hailstorm added in 11:19, and the earthquake becoming the most severe ever in this verse, indicating a sense of finality. The earthquake's incomparability (none like it *has ever occurred*) both links God's judgment with the most terrifying human experience, and shows that it surpasses it. The residents of Sardis, Laodicea, Ephesus and Philadelphia, who all experienced destruction by earthquakes, would be especially aware of their devastating power, and this earthquake destroys both the *great city* (which signifies Rome as Babylon; see comment on 11:8) and the *cities of the nations* which have colluded with her. The act of *God remember[ing]* is a metaphor for his enacting of justice, and the description of the *cup of the wine of the fury of the wrath of God* (AT) brings together the two phrases spoken by the third angel in 14:10, mentioned in passing in the interjection after the third bowl in 16:6, which indicates how closely connected these sections are.

20. In Isaiah, the *island[s]* signify the farthest reaches of the earth which, despite their distance, will see the glory of the God of Israel

---

7. Despite the similarities in English with Jesus' declaration from the cross in John 19:30, the word here is different and there is no obvious connection between the two.

and trust in him (Isa. 49:1; 51:5). But they will also see the judgment of God when he destroys the proud city of Tyre, whose king has set himself up against God (Ezek. 26:17–18). *Mountains* might be suggestive of the 'high places' where other gods were worshipped by the inhabitants of Canaan (Deut. 12:2) and which Israel reverted to when they failed to remain faithful to God (1 Kgs 11:7). Perhaps a stronger allusion is to 'every mountain [being] made low' to prepare the way for the coming of God (Isa. 40:3–4; Mark 1:3). The removal of 'every *mountain* and island' was described in the first anticipation of the End following the earthquake in the sixth seal (6:14), and the pair of phrases *fled away* and *could not be found* are repeated with reference to earth and heaven in the vision of the great white throne (20:11), the second of these phrases recalling the ejection of Satan from heaven ('there was no longer any place found for him', 12:8, AT). The awesome majesty of God is such that, in some sense, even the created world cannot stand in his presence.

21. *Hailstones* were widely understood as signs of divine judgment, and recall the seventh Exodus plague (Exod. 9:22; see also Josh. 10:11). The ludicrous size of the hailstones ('weighing a talent', translated as *about forty kilograms*) indicates that, like all the plagues, it uses proverbial images to symbolize judgment. The response of those afflicted is identical to that in the fourth and fifth bowl judgments: they *cursed God* rather than calling on him.

Theology

There is a significant shift in focus in the seven bowls compared with the seals and trumpets. The possibility of repentance is fading from view; now that God has revealed himself not only in the world and its events but also in the witness of his faithful people and, supremely, in the death, resurrection and exaltation of Jesus, humanity is 'without excuse' (Rom. 1:20). The bowl sequence shares the brevity and directness of the seals sequence and its structure has much in common with the trumpet sequence, but it is distinct from both. It is shaped more than either by the ten plagues of Exodus, directed against the unrepentant powers of Egypt as a necessary prelude to setting God's people free and enabling them to journey to the Promised Land.

John insists that this is not gleeful vindictiveness on God's part, but a reflection of his justice. Even to the end, God holds out the free offer of the gift of life (22:17) – but those who remain committed to following the beast in its opposition to the God of life will share in the beast's fate. In contrast to the previous series of seven, this sequence becomes much more developed in its eschatological focus, introducing us to ideas and images which will be expanded on in the following chapters: the final showdown between God and his opponents, the destruction of the powers of evil and the renewal of the created order. This sequence therefore makes a theological connection between the events we see in the world around us as manifestations of God's judgment and justice, his power over specific forms of human rebellion as shown in particular empires in history, and the final revelation of his sovereignty at the End.

The nature of the patient endurance and faithful witness of the saints therefore always has an eschatological character to it, as they wait for the true revelation of God and his justice at the end of time. Their suffering will be costly, but their prayers for justice, vindication and the coming of God's kingdom will be heard and answered.

12. THE GREAT PROSTITUTE AND THE SCARLET BEAST (17:1 – 19:10)

Context

The opening of Revelation 17 introduces us to a very different phase in the vision sequence from what we have encountered so far. Although John does 'see' something, what he hears becomes progressively more important, and this chapter is dominated by the explanation of an accompanying angel, something that he has rarely experienced up to this point. The auditory style continues up until 19:6, and serves to bind these chapters together. The clear identification of aspects of Roman rule, albeit done (as in Rev. 13) in ways which allow later reapplication by subsequent generations of readers, heightens the rhetorical challenge for John's audience, who are acutely aware of their political, military, economic and cultural dependence on the empire.

Chapter 17 has a chiastic structure, in that the woman is introduced first, followed by the beast, but the interpretations of these visions are given in reverse order, the beast followed by the woman. But this chapter can also be seen as sitting within a larger chiasm that stretches from Revelation 15 through to Revelation 21:

A. The vision of the saints on Zion singing the song of Moses
   and of the lamb (ch. 15)
   B. The seven plagues against the followers of the beast
      that include an anticipation of the last battle (16:1–16)
      C. The great earthquake and the destruction of
         Babylon (16:17–21)
         D. The vision of the woman and the beast (ch. 17)
      C.' The destruction of the great prostitute Babylon
         (ch. 18)
   B.' The last battle (19:11 – 20:15)
A.' The people of God as the New Jerusalem (ch. 21)

The style of Revelation 17 is dominated by participles, giving a
sense of awe and power from a more static description, just as we
saw happening in the description of God on the throne in Revelation 4. The reference to 'mystery' in 17:5 and 17:7 reminds the reader
of the 'mystery' of the seven stars and lampstands in 1:20 and
the purpose of God in 10:7. It is language used by Paul to refer to the
revelation of spiritual reality in the good news of Jesus (1 Cor. 2:7;
Eph. 1:9). But the strongest connections here are formed by the
powerful binary contrast between the city-woman Babylon and
the city-woman the New Jerusalem, both of which are shown to
John by 'one of the seven angels' of the bowls (17:1; 21:9). The first
sits in the desert, depends on the ultimately destructive power of
the beast, is adorned with luxury gained from oppression and will
meet an untimely end. The second rests on a high mountain, is
sustained by the life-giving power of God, is adorned by the gifts
of grace and will endure for ever.

John's audience is therefore presented with a powerful rhetorical
challenge: to which of these city-women will they give their allegiance? In which is found their true citizenship?

A. The vision in the wilderness (17:1–6)

Comment

1. The style of John's vision report changes markedly at the
beginning of this chapter. He was given an explanation of the uncountable multitude by one of the elders in 7:14, but for the most

part John has been unaccompanied in his visionary experiences. But now the style matches more closely other Jewish other-worldly visions, in which the seer is accompanied by an angelic guide. John's guide is *one of the . . . angels who had the seven bowls*, a description which links the following visions backwards with the previous chapter and the episodes leading up to the bowl judgments, but also forwards to the contrasting vision of the New Jerusalem, through which John is also guided by 'one of the seven angels who had the seven bowls' (21:9) – though it is unclear whether or not it is the same one.

The angel's invitation *Come! I will show you . . .* (AT) again matches the later invitation in 21:9; the word 'come' simply means 'Here!' (*deuro*) and is not used anywhere else in the book. The *punishment* of the great city Babylon has been anticipated explicitly since 14:8, but foreshadowed as long ago as 11:13 in the earthquake that strikes the 'great city'. The depiction of the city as a *great prostitute* follows the Old Testament tradition of characterizing proud cities who face God's judgment in this way (Tyre in Isa. 23:17; Nineveh in Nah. 3:4). It creates a double contrast with the vision of Revelation 21: the earthly city which is heading for destruction contrasts with the heavenly city that will endure; and the great prostitute contrasts with the 'bride prepared for her husband' (21:2, AT). She sits *upon many waters* (*epi hydatōn pollōn* [AT], not 'by' as some English translations), which alludes both to historic Babylon's geographical situation (expressed in the context of impending judgment in Jer. 51:13) and to Rome's international influence and reliance on shipping, which becomes a focus in the lament of sea captains in 18:11–19. Verse 15 below offers a further interpretation of its meaning.

2. The *kings of the earth* were first mentioned in 1:5, where Jesus is their 'ruler', and are among those who hide from the 'wrath of the Lamb' in 6:15. Three times we are told that they *committed adultery* with the great prostitute (here and in 18:3, 9), and (paradoxically in the light of 1:5) she 'rules over' them (17:18). But in Revelation's most inclusive and surprising turn, we learn that the 'kings of the earth' bring their splendour into the holy city in 21:24. By contrast, the *inhabitants of the earth* (mentioned ten times in the book) describes those who follow the beast unrepentantly, and they do not feature in the New Jerusalem.

Although it is hard to ignore the sexual elements of the language of *adultery*, we should primarily read this as a metaphor for idolatry and spiritual unfaithfulness, not least because of the close association of the term with 'eating food offered to idols' in the messages to the assemblies (see comment on 2:22). This metaphor is particularly appropriate given that it was believed that the priests of Rome (in Latin, *Roma*) knew a secret name for the city, the anagram *amor*, meaning 'love' in Latin; the distorting idolatry of Rome even corrupts the meaning of love.[1] The 'intoxicating' or 'maddening' *wine of her adulteries* has already been mentioned in the anticipation of her fall in 14:8, and is mentioned again in the same terms in 18:3. The seductive power of what Rome has to offer, in prosperity, wealth, military power and glory by association, distorts the judgment of both rulers and people just as surely as if they were drunk – as shows of imperial might always have.

3. John is now *carried... away in the Spirit* much as Ezekiel was for many of his visions (Ezek. 8:3; 11:1, 24). The phrase 'in the Spirit' has occurred at 1:10 and 4:2, signalling the beginning of his first vision and then a significant new phase in his vision experience, and it will do the same again at 21:10. The *wilderness* (AT) had positive associations of nurture and protection when mentioned in connection with the 'woman clothed with the sun' in 12:6, 14, but here has a negative connotation, providing yet another counterpoint between this female image and the female images symbolizing the people of God. That the *woman* is *sitting* suggests both leisure and power, and parallels the posture of both 'the one seated on the throne' (4:2; 5:13; 21:5, and elsewhere [AT]) and the 'one like a son of man' who is seated on a cloud (14:14). The image of the *beast* in the wilderness is a powerful archetypal symbol, and is the central idea in W. B. Yeats's famous poem *The Second Coming*.

The *scarlet* colour (*kokkinos*) of the *beast* signifies luxury and opulence, as is clear from its use in the following verse and in 18:12,

---

1. This belief is expressed in Plutarch, *Quaestiones Romanae* 61; Marcus Servius Honoratus, *Commentary on Virgil's Aeneid* 2:351; and Johannes Lydus, *De Mensibus* 4.73. See the discussion in Aune, *Apocalypticism*, p. 248.

16, and is different from the 'fiery red' (*pyrros*) of the second horse
in 6:4, the cavalry in 9:17 and the dragon in 12:3, and from the 'blood
red' (*haima*) of the moon in 6:12. John's use of imagery here has
multiple significations, not all of which are easily compatible with
others. The beast looks like both the dragon and the beast from the
sea in having *seven heads and ten horns*, though the order in which they
are mentioned matches that of the dragon (in 12:3) rather than of
the beast from the land for whom they are reversed (13:1). The
dragon had seven crowns on its heads, while the beast from the land
had ten crowns on its horns; the scarlet beast appears to combine
them both, since both its heads *and* its horns represent 'kings' (17:10,
12). The *blasphemous names*, perhaps related to the blasphemous
speech of the little horn in Daniel 7:8, are no longer on the heads
as they were for the beast from the sea (13:1), but *cover* the whole
beast. It is not just the rulers of human empires but all the people
who collude with them that are guilty of blasphemy. Inasmuch as
this beast looks more and more like the dragon, John is implying
that Rome (and with it all totalitarian imperial power) looks like Satan
incarnate.

4. In terms of the imagery John is using, the woman is depicted
as a high-class courtesan (*hetaira*), but in his language John describes
her as a common prostitute (*pornē*). Rome's excessive wealth
and indulgence are debasing and corrupting it. The Tyrian *purple*
(*porphyra*) that she wears uses a dye made from tens of thousands
of murex rock snails; the process was highly labour-intensive, which
made the dye very expensive and a valuable trading commodity (the
trade of Lydia from Thyatira in Acts 16:14). Its use was highly
regulated in the Roman Empire, with only the elite of the wealthy
political aristocracy allowed to wear cloth dyed with it. *Scarlet* was
also an expensive dye, usually made from the dried bodies of
cochineal beetles.

The woman's ornamentation matches the actual goods traded by
Rome as they are listed in Revelation 18, with *gold, precious stones and
pearls* among the twenty-eight cargoes that the merchants can no
longer trade when Babylon falls (18:12). But they also adorn the
New Jerusalem, and in much more extravagant terms: the city itself
is not simply decorated with gold but actually made 'of pure
gold' (21:18); the appearance of the whole city is 'like that of *very*

precious stones' (21:11, AT), and it has foundations decorated with precious stones as well (21:19); and the twelve gates consist of single pearls of enormous size (21:21). Between this image and the depiction of the city in Revelation 21, John is setting before us two alternative ways to be wealthy and to enjoy wealth: the human way, by oppression and corruption, and the spiritual way of enjoying what is given by God, a challenge he previously set before the Christians in Laodicea (3:17–18). The *cup* that she holds perfectly illustrates the contradiction of imperial power; on the outside it looks precious and valuable, made of *gold*, but on the inside it is filled with the *detestable* and the *filthy* (AT). It is a visual illustration of the saying of Jesus in Luke 16:15: 'What people value highly is detestable in God's sight', which immediately follows on from his warning about wealth: we 'cannot serve both God and Money'.

5. As with both the servants of God who are sealed on their foreheads (7:3) and the followers of the beast who receive his mark (13:16), the woman's true identity is visible to all by means of a *title* written *on her forehead*. It is not clear whether the term *mystery* is descriptive of the title or is the first part of it. In either case, the sense is neither that this is something hidden, nor that it is something to be decoded, but that the true identity of the woman is revealed and that it takes discernment to acknowledge the reality that is described. The epithet of *Babylon* as *the great* is both a recognition of its real economic, military and cultural power and the influence it exercises over humanity, and also an ironic claim in the light of its coming destruction which has already been anticipated. The phrase *mother of prostitutes* and *abominations* could be either comparative or causal; it is either the greatest example of idolatry compared with all others, or it is the source, in the sense of representing the essential corruption and compromise that arise from the lure of power.

6. In the declarations following the third bowl (16:6), being given blood to drink is a punishment for shedding the 'blood of the saints and the prophets' (AT), but here the metaphor of drinking refers to the act of shedding their blood itself. The *saints* and the *witnesses* [*martyrōn*] *of Jesus* (AT) are not two different groups; rather, the second phrase should be understood as epexegetical (i.e. explanatory) of the first: 'the blood of the saints, that is, the blood of the witnesses of Jesus'. Ironically, the witness to Jesus which has led to the

woman consuming their blood was also identified in 12:11 as the
key to their victory. This victory is not about avoiding death, but
about staying faithful to God and to the lamb, and not allowing the
threat of death to corrupt them and deflect them from that call.
John's grammar suggests that the expression of his astonishment
belongs to this section, and that the start of the angel's explanation
begins the next section. John is not amazed in a positive sense, but
(in a typical Hebraism) *wonders with a great wonder* (AT) at the shocking
nature of the vision he is reporting.

B. The interpretation of the beast (17:7-11)

7-8. The angel's soothing of John's astonishment and his
extended narrative explanation are quite unlike any other part of
John's vision report, and have the effect of reminding John's audience
of the visions of Daniel. In Daniel 7:17-18, 23-27 an angel offers
a precise explanation of the beasts and the horns, and these match
historical figures because the narrative setting is around four
centuries earlier than the events it refers to, and the credibility of
the visions depends on their accuracy. But John's situation is different,
since he is writing to people whose situation he knows and whose
context he shares, and he has no need to demonstrate the correlation
between the different aspects of his vision and the world in which
he and his audience live. Since he has freely adapted Daniel's
numerical schemes to make a theological point, we might not be
surprised if he exercises similar freedom with his use of Daniel's
beast symbolism.

The *beast* is described with the triple title of the one *[who] was, . . .
is not, and will come up*, as a sort of bizarre parody of God 'who is,
and who was, and who is to come' (1:4). The parallels between this
beast and the beast from the sea in Revelation 13 have suggested
that this too symbolizes Roman imperial power – but the middle
term 'is not' suggests that the beast also symbolizes one who wielded
the power of the empire, the Emperor Nero who, in the myth of
'Nero Redivivus', was believed to be about to return to lead an army
against Rome itself. The origin of his return, *out of the Abyss*, links
the beast to the source of the locust army in 9:1, a natural connection
given the identification in the Old Testament of the 'abyss' with the

'deep' or the sea, from which the first beast came. It is not clear that, in his vision report, John is identifying this beast with the 'angel of the Abyss' in 9:11, but he continues the pun on the name of Apollo. Where the angel is called Apollyon, meaning 'destroyer', this beast will experience *destruction, apoleia*.

The *inhabitants of the earth* were identified in 13:8 as those who 'worship the beast' and 'whose names have not been written in the Lamb's book of life', but here the next phrase from that verse has been shortened, so that instead of the lamb being slain, it is the writing of the names that is *from the creation of the world*. Revelation's focus on repentance and decision makes it impossible to understand this as predetermining who will be saved; the point is the security of salvation for those whose names *are* written in the book, which will be opened at the End (20:12; 21:27). The amazement of these people at the beast parallels the amazement of the 'whole world' at the beast from the sea in 13:3, using the same verb (*thaumazō*), suggesting that the phrase 'was, ... is not, and will come up' is parallel to the earlier beast having a fatal wound that had healed.

9. The call for a *mind with wisdom* uses the same two terms (*nous*, mind or understanding, and *sophia*, wisdom) as the similar call at 13:18 in relation to the number of the beast. It also echoes the language of Daniel 9:22 ('I have ... come to give you insight and understanding'), though using slightly different terms. The wisdom and understanding here, as with 13:18, are not in order to 'decode' the obscure symbolism, since in both places John is making clear that identification (the most unambiguous expression comes in 17:18). Rather, wisdom lies in having the discernment to recognize the truth of the identification that John's vision report is making. Many cities have claimed, and continue to claim, that they are built on *seven hills* because of the universal symbolism of 'seven'. But for John's audience, this phrase is an unambiguous reference to Rome, with the seven hills forming the heart of the ancient city within the city walls to the east of the Tiber and overlooking the Field of Mars.

10–11. These verses have been the source of endless speculation, within a number of different interpretative approaches to the book, but all based on the idea that there is a one-to-one correspondence between the *seven kings* and the *eighth king* and specific historical figures or empires. But there are many good reasons to believe that

John does not intend his vision report (or rather, report of the angelical explanation) to be interpreted in this way:

1. Throughout the book, John uses numbers in symbolic ways, and there is no reason to think he is changing his usage now. There is little more point in asking who these seven kings are than in asking for the names of the 144,000 in Revelation 7. And this symbolic way of speaking collectively of Rome's rulers was found elsewhere; contemporary writers summarized Rome's early history as the time of seven kings (even though there were many more), and John appears to be doing the same for its time as an empire.

2. John is working with a given symbol – the beast with seven heads and ten horns – from Daniel, and adapting it to describe his own situation. Unlike Daniel's own use, where the numbers of beasts, heads and horns appear in his narrative to have a correspondence with particular historical periods, John has already merged Daniel's images together to form a generic, composite image of human imperial rule.

3. Because the narrative of Daniel is set many centuries before the time it refers to, the correspondences need to work within the narrative in order for the visions to have their rhetorical force. John has no similar need, since he is writing to his contemporaries about their shared context; the challenge is not one of chronology, but of theology, recognizing the true nature of their situation. (For the difference with Daniel in this regard, see comment on 22:10: 'do not seal the words of this book' [AT].) John does not need to identify to his audience when he was writing, and if we use the text to do this, we are doing something John had not intended.

4. The use of symbolism here is actually contradictory if taken as referring to particular emperors. The seven kings are the seven heads of the beast,[2] but the seven heads are also seven

---

2. Some commentators assume that there is a natural correlation between 'heads' and 'kings', but the correlation was not so evident in first-century

hills – and the beast itself is also one of the kings. It is not possible for a beast to be its own head! The fluidity of imagery here is similar to that found in political cartoons; in the UK in the Second World War, Churchill was sometimes depicted as leading the bulldog, representing the country, but at other times was himself the bulldog, embodying both the nation and its defiance. Leaders at times serve their nations or empires, and at other times are served by them; leaders also destroy empires and are destroyed by them.

5. Most significantly for the history of interpretation, none of the suggested correspondences between the 'seven kings' and Roman emperors actually works. The counting must either begin in an unconvincing place or end in one, or unaccountably miss out certain emperors. To date the writing of Revelation to Nero's reign, we must start counting with Julius Caesar, who is never considered an emperor. To date it to Domitian's reign (the other major alternative), we need to start with Nero, or omit the three emperors who reigned in 69 – but nothing in the text suggests we should do either of these things (see comment on dating in the introduction).

Instead, we need to note the characteristics that John describes in human empires, including the one he is facing. *Five have fallen* suggests a violent end to their reign; human empires often treat their rulers with ruthless violence which betrays their true nature. Of the twelve first rulers of the empire, eight met violent ends: Julius Caesar, Caligula, Galba and Domitian were stabbed to death; Claudius was poisoned; Nero and Otto committed suicide; and Vespasian was beaten to death. There are *seven kings*, but the one who is to come *must remain for a little while*. Imperial power might look complete and never-ending, yet all human empires last but a brief

---

(note 2 *cont.*) vocabulary. The metaphor of 'head' primarily suggested prominence and life, rather than leadership and control, so that in the Greek OT the Hebrew metaphor of 'head' (*rō'š*) for 'leader' (e.g. of a clan or tribe) was almost never translated by the Greek for 'head' (*kephalē*), literal terms being used instead.

time in the context of eternity. This gives the lie to Rome's claim to be 'eternal', and contrasts with the lamb and those who follow him who 'will reign for ever and ever' (11:15; 22:5). The empire might defy all expectations, and even though it seems to have come to an end (it *is not*) and then makes a miraculous recovery, lasting longer than expected (*an eighth king*), the final end of its destructive power will bring about its own *destruction*.

C. The interpretation of the horns and the woman (17:12–18)

12–13. The angel's interpretation of the *ten horns* as *ten kings* follows the angel's interpretation to Daniel in Daniel 7:24, but then changes it in two regards. First, in Daniel's vision report the kings 'arise from this kingdom' (AT), that is, they are rulers in it, whereas in John's vision report the kings *give their power and authority to the beast*. For John's audience, this would remind them of the rulers of client kingdoms who collaborate with the empire and share their power, not least because they *have not yet received a kingdom*, that is, they do not rule independently. Second, for Daniel the horns represent specific individuals, with the 'little horn' representing Antiochus IV Epiphanes (see comment on 12:4), whereas for John these appear to be generic since the number 10 is a natural number, suggesting various kings of the known world. They receive authority for *one hour*, which is the proverbial phrase meaning 'a short, limited time' (cf. 18:10, 17, 19).

14. The kings who share their power with the beast will make war as the beast has, though not just against the saints (13:7), but ultimately *against the Lamb* himself, a phrase anticipating the conflict that will be described in 19:11–21. The lamb *will conquer them* (AT), but there is no suggestion that it will be in any other way than by the truth, faithfulness and sacrifice that have always been his 'weapons'. He will triumph because, in the end, he is the true *Lord of lords and King of kings*, a title that others have usurped (Ezek. 26:7) and (among the Parthians) continue to claim – but his final victory will show that the title belongs to him alone. The phrases can be understood either relationally – that Jesus is the Lord over all other lords – or in a superlative sense – that he is the greatest of all lords.

Those who accompany the lamb in the spiritual battle recall the vision in Revelation 7 of God's people being counted off as a spiritual army. They are *called* in the sense that they are the ones who have responded to the invitation of the 'eternal gospel' (14:6) from 'every nation, tribe, people and language' (7:9; 14:6); they are *chosen* in the sense that they are God's distinctive people on whom he has set his love (John 15:16); and they are *faithful* in that they have kept faith with the faithfulness of Jesus, the 'faithful and true' (3:14; 19:11; cf. 2 Tim. 2:11–13). They participate in the victory through their faithfulness, though the victory ultimately belongs to the lamb and is theirs only by association (12:11).

15–18. The angel's interpretation of *the waters* confirms that the prostitute was sitting 'on' rather than 'next to' them in verse 1. Her situation parallels the description of the first beast which (like the beasts in Dan. 7) emerges from the sea (see comment on 13:1); the sea in the Old Testament can signify the 'abyss' as a source of chaos and evil, but also the nations of the world, 'churn[ed] up' (Dan. 7:2) in agitation and conflict. This is the seventh and final mention of the fourfold phrase *peoples, multitudes* [in place of 'tribes'], *nations and languages* (see comment on 5:9). In the light of the kings previously having 'one mind' (v. 13, AT) and sharing their power, it comes as a surprise that they and the *beast . . . will hate the prostitute* – and yet it is often true of political partnerships that friendship can quickly turn to enmity, especially when the alliance has been based on the advantages of power. The language of devouring her (*eat[ing] her flesh*) is a metaphor of complete destruction which is deployed in more detail in 19:18 and 21, while *burning by fire* (AT) was the normal fate of conquered cities in the ancient world (see e.g. Josh. 6:24; 8:28).

We now hear of the paradoxical interplay of human freedom and God's sovereignty which has been behind much of the judgment material in the book, particularly in the sequence of seals and trumpets in Revelation 6, 8 – 9, but is stated explicitly here. The destructive tendencies of the beast and kings/horns which lead to the *ruin* of the prostitute and expose her true nature (*leave her naked*) function in some strange way to *accomplish [God's] purpose*. Just as God's wrath is 'being revealed from heaven' against the wickedness of human beings by God '[giving] them over' to the consequences of their sin (Rom. 1:18, 24, 26, 28), so here God's wrath is expressed in allowing the destruction and violence at the heart of imperial power to do its full work in bringing self-destruction. The angel passes on to John the unambiguous identification of the woman as *the great city*, which for John's audience could only have been understood to be Rome (see comment on 11:8). For a while she has *rule[d] over the kings of the earth*, but with her destruction she must give way to their true and lasting ruler, Jesus (1:5).

D. The judgment of Babylon (18:1–8)

Context

In the previous chapter, John has recounted his vision of the woman riding the beast in the desert, and the extended interpretation of this vision by the accompanying bowl angel. But now there is quite a distinct change of style and focus. We hear a series of different voices (and John 'sees' very little) who by turn celebrate and mourn the judgment and destruction of 'Babylon', starting with the angel who has great authority and splendour declaring 'Fallen is Babylon the Great!' (18:2).

Much of John's language and vocabulary here is adapted from Old Testament judgment texts, particularly relating to the (anticipated) fall of Tyre in Ezekiel 27 and the fall of Babylon in Jeremiah 25. But John revises the language in several ways. First, he embeds it in a distinctive poetic structure, so this chapter is one of the most carefully poetic of any section in the book, marked by repetition, rhythm and parallelism throughout. Second, he includes elements which connect with other language that he has used earlier and which he will revisit later, so that the splendour of 'Babylon' and its destruction offer a constant contrast to the life of the people of God so far described and the New Jerusalem that will be revealed in the final chapters. Third, as elsewhere in the text, his language reflects actual concerns of life in the first century. So the list of twenty-eight cargoes in verses 12–13 feels a little like a tour round a grand house of one of the wealthy elite in Rome itself.

The most striking aspect of this section is the centrality of the economic critique of Rome. The forty cargoes of Tyre listed in Ezekiel 27 have become a list of twenty-eight, to fit in with John's numerology. The grief of the kings of the earth and that of the seafarers top and tail the central and more extended grief of the merchants, making it central, and the text suggests that the principal idolatry of Rome was not so much the adulation of the emperor as the adulation of the wealth and prosperity that come from international trade and the consumption that drives it.

Comment

1. Some commentators suggest that the verses that follow really belong to the previous section and that the chapter division here is therefore mistaken. But in fact John gives us a clear indication that this is a new stage in his vision report by starting with *After this I saw* as he has done previously in 4:1; 7:1, 9; 15:5. He sees *another angel*, not described as 'mighty' as at 5:2 and 10:1, but who nevertheless has *great authority*. He will need this for the announcement he is about to make; it is perhaps difficult for modern readers who have the benefit of hindsight to grasp what an astonishing claim John is about to make in reporting this part of his vision. The Roman Empire was the dominant – in some senses the only – political, military and economic system known by the inhabitants of the ancient western world. It was seen by both admirers and enemies as invincible, and was yet to persist for hundreds of years; it is difficult to think of a system of rule so extensive and enduring in all of history. Yet John sees its demise as so certain that he reports it in the past tense. It is an astonishing claim, and 'apocalyptic' in every sense in its vision. Although many feel they have benefited from the rule of the empire, and therefore have much to lose, *the earth was illuminated* by the angel's *splendour* or 'glory', suggesting that the news he brings is ultimately good news for humanity – though of course bad new for those who have allied themselves to the prostitute and the beast.

2. The angel shouts *with a mighty voice*, implying that all can hear what he proclaims – or perhaps that all should listen. The title of *Babylon the Great* goes all the way back to the claim of Nebuchadnezzar in Daniel 4:30 that he had built 'Babylon the great' (AT), and his hubris and the pride in his claim lead in Daniel's narrative to his immediate fall and humiliation. The double proclamation *Fallen! Fallen . . . !* functions as a prophetic past tense, reporting a future event as though it has already happened, just like the prophetic text of Isaiah 21:9 from which it borrows its language. In this section there is a distinctive mix of past, present and future tenses, as if in his vision report John is inviting his audience to live their present lives in the light of the prophetic future − which is the call to all disciples of Jesus.

Becoming a *dwelling-place for demons* (AT) is little more than the fulfilment of what she already is on the basis of John's claim in 9:20 that idolatry is tantamount to worshipping demons. The threefold claim that the city will become *a haunt* for *unclean spirit[s]*, *unclean bird[s]* and *unclean and detestable animal[s]* appears to be adapted from the description of (historic) Babylon on the 'day of the LORD' in Isaiah 13:19−22, a judgment that arises from God's 'compassion on Jacob' (Isa. 14:1).[3]

3. The reason for her fall is expressed emphatically by the phrase translated *the maddening wine of her adulteries* coming first in the Greek text and being set out as a series of genitives: 'the wine of the fury/passion of the adulteries of her'.[4] This is the third time John has recorded this phrase: the first was in 14:8, using exactly the same words, and the second was in 17:2, using a slight variation of wording, but paired as here with *the kings of the earth committed adultery with her* (on the phrase 'kings of the earth', see the comment on 1:5a; 6:15; 17:2). It seemed previously that the language of 'adultery' wasn't primarily a reference to literal sexual immorality (though it might include that), but drew on Old Testament sexual metaphors for idolatry and unfaithfulness to God (see comment on 2:22 and 14:8). Weight is added by the third of the three parallel phrases explaining

---

3. Many reliable manuscripts omit the third of the three statements about 'unclean and detestable animal[s]'. But such an omission is easy to explain on the basis of 'haplography', an error arising because the words on consecutive lines of a manuscript are the same, and the threefold structure of the saying makes most poetic sense.

4. Some reliable manuscripts have the variant reading 'the nations have fallen' instead of 'the nations have drunk', using the verb *piptō*, 'to fall', in place of *pinō*, 'to drink'. Although this creates a parallel with the fall of Babylon, the similar phrases in 14:8 and 17:2 and the threefold phrases in this verse make the variant reading unlikely to be original.

Babylon's fall, which in Greek are in one sentence simply separated by 'and'. That *the merchants of the earth grew rich* puts the economic critique of Rome (which will be focused on in detail throughout this chapter) 'front and centre' of John's prophetic judgment. Their wealth came from the appetite for consumption of the Roman Empire and of the city of Rome itself, which, as the biggest population centre in the western world, was the hub of a vast trading network that sucked commodities and resources from every land that it had conquered. The *excessive luxuries* are literally 'the power of her sensuality', the second term (*strenos*, found only in this chapter in the New Testament) meaning the indulgence and satisfaction of every appetite.

4–5. For the seventh and last time, John hears a *voice from heaven*, continuing the primary theme of this chapter which is all that John *hears* in contrast to the other parts of the revelation where he is primarily *seeing* things. The judgment on a fallen world is one thing; how God's people should respond is another, and hence John hears *another* voice, different from that of the angel. Our earlier suspicion that such a voice is that of God is confirmed by the appeal to *my people*, a possessive that is reiterated in 21:3. The call in Jeremiah 51:45 to *Come out of her* in a literal sense, by physically fleeing the city that is under judgment, becomes here a call to ethical distinctiveness, not least in the light of the issues that were identified in the seven messages to the assemblies. Most English translations express the reasons for 'coming out' as parallels, but John has actually written in a chiasm:

> So that
> > you will not share
> > > in her sins
> > and
> > > from her plagues
> > you will not receive.

This emphasizes the connection between the sins committed and the plagues experienced in line with the principle of *lex talionis* which was evident in the seven bowls (see comments on 16:2, 3–7). The present command (*Come out*) is expressed in future terms (*will not share ... will not receive*) in the light of the judgment to come which has been expressed in the past tense ('Fallen ...'), and the *plagues* must refer back to the earlier narrative, either just the bowls (which are particularly directed at Babylon and the beast and their followers), or perhaps even to all three series, going back as far as Revelation 6. This illustrates the cyclical nature of Revelation's narrative and the complex nature of its chronology.

It was said of Rome that its seven hills 'reached to the heavens', and the tower of Babel was also intended to 'reach to the heavens' (using a different phrase from the one used in this verse) in Genesis 11:4, while in Jeremiah 51:9 the judgment of historic Babylon 'reaches to heaven' (AT). God *remembered* people by answering their prayer (Noah in Gen. 8:1; Sarah in Gen. 21:1; Rachel in Gen. 30:22; Hannah in 1 Sam. 1:19; David in Ps. 132:1), but in Psalm 109:14 and Hosea 9:9 God's remembering brings judgment for sin.

6–8. Many commentators follow the majority of English translations in understanding verse 6 as saying *pay her back* double *for what she has done* and *pour her a* double *portion*. There is an immediate narrative problem with this, as it contradicts both the statement immediately before (*give back to her as she has given*) and the one that follows (*give her as much ... as ... she gave herself*), which emphasize the proportionality of her punishment and not the disproportionality. There is also a wider problem in the contradiction to the repeated emphasis on *lex talionis* in the bowl judgments, reiterated subsequently, as well as in the focus on punishment as a manifestation of the justice of God articulated in the praise of 15:3 and 16:4–7. In fact, though the verb *diploō* and its cognate noun *diplous* can mean 'double' (as in Matt. 23:15; 1 Tim. 5:17), they can also mean 'duplicate', that is, 'create a double' of something, and this must be the sense here. A better English way of expressing this would be to translate: 'Pay her back a match for what she has done; pour a matching portion from her own cup.'

The measure of her judgment matches not only the suffering she has inflicted on others, but also the *glory and luxury she gave herself.* Her own indulgence has led to deprivation for others, and her own glory has meant a denial of the glory of God. Her threefold boast that she *sit[s] ... as queen* (suggesting power and wealth as in 17:3), is *not a widow* and *knows not grief* (AT) summarizes the empty boasts of historic Babylon in Isaiah 47:7–8, and is matched by the threefold plagues of *death, mourning and famine*, an echo of that brought by the four horsemen in Revelation 6. Once more, the fate she meets at the hands of the ten kings and beast in 17:16, being *burned by fire* (AT), turns out to be the just punishment from God. All this will happen in *one day* (cf. Isa. 47:9), signifying a short time, as does 'one hour' in 17:12; 18:10, 17, 19. The final phrase, *mighty is the Lord God*, could read 'God is a mighty Lord', but the parallels with Jeremiah 50:34 and Zephaniah 3:17 suggest the former is the right reading. This is the only place where God is described as 'mighty', countering the claim of Babylon in verse 10, and suggesting that he is the source of power for the 'mighty angels' of 5:2; 10:1; 18:21.

Theology
If Revelation 17 set out the full description of the woman riding the beast as the climax of earlier descriptions and bringing them to completion, this section is the beginning of the final response to that vision in the description of God's judgment, which unfolds through the next three chapters. John's language is distinctive here in moving between the past, present and future and back again, as with prophetic certainty the fall of 'Babylon' is anticipated using the past tense, the actual judgments are described in the future tense, but the response of God's people is urged in the present tense.

The repeated emphasis is on God's justice in judgment, so that 'Babylon' receives not only a punishment that matches how she has dealt with others, but also a fall from grace whose depth reflects the height of her own self-exaltation in defiance of God. John continues to connect this distinct section with what has come earlier by redeploying words and phrases from earlier in the text, ensuring that we read this in the light of what has gone before.

E. The mourning of the kings, merchants and seafarers (18:9–20)

Context
This section is highly structured, with the laments of the kings of the earth and seafarers first and third being the shortest, and the lament of the merchants in the middle the longest and most

developed. They each sing a dirge, all three beginning with 'Woe! Woe to you, great city!' and each ending with a saying 'In one hour . . .', emphasizing the suddenness and swiftness of her fall.

Comment

9–10. These two verses are one sentence in the Greek, which begins with the pair of lament verbs *[They] will weep and wail over her* (AT), emphasizing them by placing them first. The *kings of the earth* have already been mentioned as those who *committed adultery with her* in 17:2 and 18:3 (see comment on those verses). The two actions of 'committing adultery' and *shar[ing] her luxury* match the two actions of lament, and (as in the parallelism of v. 3) the second illuminates the first, confirming our understanding of 'adultery' as a metaphor for the worship of the false god of material wealth and pleasure. The *smoke of her burning* suggests the finality of her destruction, rather than the destruction as a continuing process (see comment on 14:11). There is a supreme irony in the observation that *they . . . stand far off*; despite the apparent intimacy and shared commitment suggested by the metaphor of 'adultery', ultimately the kings are merely self-interested and concerned about their own gain and self-preservation.

The double cry of *Woe! Woe . . . !* is the first of three such cries, which add to the seven mentions of 'woe' announced by the high-flying eagle in 8:13; 9:12; 11:14 and the 'woe' of the devil's fall in 12:12 to make fourteen occurrences in all. Once again, there is an ironic juxtaposition of the acclaim of Babylon as a *great city* (AT) and the lament of its *judgment* (AT; or 'doom', *krisis*).

11–13. The *merchants* are mentioned four times in this chapter, and nowhere else in the New Testament other than in Jesus' parable of the pearl of great price in Matthew 13:45. The phrase *merchants of the earth* puts them in parallel with the 'kings of the earth', showing the close relationship between the two groups. Just as in the role of the East India Company in the British Empire and the 'industrial military complex' in the modern USA, in the Roman Empire trade and conquest went hand in hand. Where conquest has been made, there is trade to be done; where the conqueror is undone, the trade comes to an end. The merchants *weep and mourn* over her, just as the kings will 'weep and wail' (AT); their action is in the present tense rather than the future, but there is the same sense of anticipation of their reaction to the predicted fall of Babylon.

The list of *cargoes* is grouped into sub-collections separated by semi-colons in many English translations, but in the Greek text it consists of a single list with each item separated by 'and'. The only structural difference is in items nine, ten and eleven in the list, which are described as *every sort of citron wood and every vessel of ivory and every vessel of costly wood* (AT); the other terms are simply in the genitive referring back to the word 'cargo' at the head of the list – that is, 'cargo of gold and of silver and of . . .', and so on. The list naturally falls into six groups by type of cargo listed:

1. *Precious metals and jewels: gold* and *silver* were mostly mined in Spain, while *precious stones* and *pearls* were imported from India, though lower-quality pearls came from the Red Sea. Military expansion was frequently motivated by access to metal deposits. Claudius's invasion of Britannia was largely motivated by access to the deposits of copper, tin and Welsh gold. Roman society was obsessed with pearls, which were valued only a little less than diamonds. Wealthy women wore huge numbers of pearls, and others were known to dissolve pearls in vinegar and drink them, just for the thrill of consuming something so expensive in a single gulp.

2. *Cloth and textiles:* the province of Asia, the location of the seven assemblies, was the main source of *fine linen, purple* (meaning cloth dyed with Tyrian purple; see comment on 17:4) and *scarlet* cloth, though Egypt was also a major supplier of linen. *Silk* was imported from China at great expense.

3. *Materials of wood and metal: citron* is a fragrant variety of cypress. *Ivory* came from the Syrian elephant, which was driven to extinction by the demand, and from Africa; *costly wood* is probably a reference to ebony, also from Africa. *Bronze* from Corinth and *iron* from Spain and the province of Pontus (north of the province of Asia) were needed for building and for military equipment. *Marble* from Africa, Egypt and Greece became a sought-after building material, not just for temples and civic buildings but also for the homes of the wealthy. Augustus boasted, 'I came to Rome in brick; I left it in marble.'

4. *Spices and perfumes: cinnamon* came from India and Ceylon (Sri Lanka), and the aromatic *spice amomum* (AT) was from south India. *Incense* came from all over the east, *myrrh* from the Near East and *frankincense* from southern Arabia.

5. *Foods: wine* came from grapes grown all over the empire, including Asia, and at times was in over-supply at the expense of the production of bread, hence Domitian's abortive order to uproot vines (see the introductory comment on the message to Philadelphia and the comment on 6:6). *Olive oil* was produced all over the empire, but over time was particularly imported by Rome from Africa and Spain. *Fine flour* refers to the best and most expensive grades; it and *wheat* were imported from Africa, with the region along its north coast acting as the bread basket for Rome. *Cattle and sheep* were raised in all regions.

6. *Horses, carriages and slaves: horses* were used in warfare, for travel for the wealthy and in the circuses as part of entertainment. The word for *carriages* (*rhedai*) refers to four-wheeled carriages used by the wealthy. There are two terms in the list to describe *slaves*: 'bodies' (*somata*) is the common term for those being bought and sold in the slave market, but John adds to that (as an explanation) 'human lives' (*psychas anthrōpōn*), taken from Ezekiel 27:13. In doing so, John is offering a critique of the slave trade; these are not mere commodities to be bought and sold, but human lives made in the image of God.

The list has similarities to the list of cargoes traded with Tyre in Ezekiel 27, where there is a similar lament from merchants at God's judgment of the city, and it demonstrates John's sophisticated understanding of the workings of imperial trade. Where Ezekiel's list comprises forty cargoes, John's includes twenty-eight, which is 4×7, thus signifying Rome's total dominance (7 being the number of completion) of world trade (4 being a natural number). The list is striking in that it mostly focuses on the indulgent consumption of the wealthy elite, and in that respect agrees with many Roman critics of their society's opulence and ostentatious show, many of whom wanted to return to the earlier days of simplicity of life. But by including slaves at the end of the list, John is emphasizing both ends of the chain of consumption: luxury and prosperity for the few has created poverty and oppression for the many. The slaves who worked in gold and silver mines, for example, had an extremely short life expectancy, and provinces could be impoverished by the export of goods and materials since the resources were often requisitioned by the emperor.

14. Some English translations introduce this verse with *They will say* in order to continue the previous speech of the merchants in verse 11 which is resumed again in verse 16. But the form of address here is striking, speaking to Babylon in the second-person singular, which makes it look like John's own interjection. Having recited the list of cargoes, and thinking of both the indulgence and the oppression they represent, he cannot suppress his anger and dismay. The *fruit* must be a metaphor for all the wealth listed above, since other foods are not mentioned; *longed for* translates 'the desire (or 'lust', *epithymia*, always a strongly negative term in the NT) of your soul'. The loss of *luxury* and *splendour* completes the threefold critique of consumption, indulgence and ostentatious display; their loss is described using the language of the expulsion of Satan from heaven in 12:8 by saying 'they will no longer be found' (translated as *never to be recovered*).

15–17a. The narrative of the merchants' lament continues, emphasizing as with the kings both their self-interest (they *gained their wealth from her*) and their distancing of themselves from her judgment (they *will stand far off*). After the exposition of the list of cargoes, John reiterates their response from verse 11 that they *weep and mourn*. Their dirge of lament has the same structure as that of the kings, beginning and ending with the ironic contrast of the *great city* which is now *in one hour . . . brought to ruin*. This uses the verb *eremoō*, 'to make a desert, wilderness', which matches both John's vision of the woman and beast 'in the wilderness' (17:3, AT) and the criticism of Rome by its contemporaries: 'where they make a desert they call it "peace"' (Tacitus, *Agricola* 30; see comment on 6:4). Where Babylon has visited desolation on others, she has now become desolate herself.

Their description of her as *dressed in fine linen, purple and scarlet* and *glittering* with her ornamentation is (with the exception of 'fine linen') word for word the same description that John uses in 17:4. But where John holds up the image as condemnation of her indulgence, the merchants still see this as part of her glory, whose loss they mourn. The key issue is not what you see, but how you interpret its significance: for the merchants, it was glory they admired and the source of their own gain; for John, it was an affront to God and to the poor whom she oppressed.

17b–19. The third lament is shorter in length, matching that of the kings of the earth. The four groups of *captains* (*kybernētēs*, used as a metaphor for leadership in 1 Cor. 12:28), *seafarers, sailors* and those who *work on the sea* (AT) illustrate the range of people who are affected by sea trade, demonstrating the importance of sea trade in the Roman Empire. Because of the reliance of the population of Rome on imports, communication by road and sea was vital; the ancient port for the city at Ostia, on the south bank of the Tiber at its mouth, eventually grew to a population of 100,000, making it one of the largest cities in the empire in its own right. It was supplemented by the building of the enormous artificial harbour at Portus, on the north bank of the Tiber, together with a canal to return traffic to Rome. In a similar way, European empires up to the modern era have depended on their dominance of sea traffic (often obtained through naval combat), and the rapid increase in sea traffic using container vessels has been key to the growth of global capitalism.

Like the kings of the earth, the seafarers lament when they see *the smoke of her burning* (cf. v. 9), like the merchants they *weep and mourn* (cf. v. 15), and like both they too *stand far off*; their lament thus connects the merchants whose cargoes they carry and the kings from whose kingdoms they carry them. In addition, they *throw dust on their heads* as a traditional sign of mourning (Josh. 7:6; Ezek. 27:30; Lam. 2:10), though out of grief at their own loss, rather than as a sign of repentance (Job 42:6). Again, there is the ironic contrast between the acclaim of the *great city* and her desolation (*ruin*) – this time enclosing the most explicit expression of self-interest of all those who *became rich through her wealth*.

20. It is not quite clear whether this invitation to *rejoice* belongs with the previous section of the threefold woes, or (speaking from the perspective of those who welcome rather than mourn the destruction of Babylon) with the angelic voice that follows. Neither is it clear who is speaking. It cannot be the 'voice of heaven' from 18:4 (AT), since it refers to God in the third person; nor can it be the angelic voice that follows, which is distinguished from it. The best reading is that it is John himself, responding to what he has seen, just as he interjected in verse 14. Some English translations include a threefold 'rejoice' which counterbalances the three woes that have been proclaimed, but in fact there is only one verb here. The word 'rejoice' (*euphrainō*) suggests an exceptional celebration marking a special event (as used in Luke 15:23); such a celebration in 12:12 marked the defeat of evil in the victory of the lamb, and it is completed here in the anticipation of final judgment. It is the counterpart to the celebration and gloating over the two witnesses in 11:10, and to the indulgent life of Babylon (cf. 17:4 and 18:16 with Luke 16:19, where the rich man 'feasts sumptuously' [AT], *euphrainō* and *lampros*, daily).

After the invitation to *heaven* (plural in many English translations, but singular in the Greek text here and everywhere except in the parallel of 12:12), John invites the threefold *saints* (AT), *apostles* and *prophets* to join the celebration, a natural succession since God's people are both described and pictured as those dwelling in heaven or before the throne (7:15; 13:6; 14:1). Although apostles and prophets are paired elsewhere in the New Testament (Luke 11:49; Eph. 2:20; 3:5), the pairing occurs only here in Revelation. These are not three separate groups, since 'saints' is a consistent designation for the whole people of God, so that 'apostles' and 'prophets' designate specific groups within the larger group. Once again there is an emphasis on God's justice expressed in the *lex talionis* of Babylon receiving what she has dealt to others, here specifically how she has treated God's people and their leaders. But it is important to note that this justice sits within the wider context of God's invitation to all to receive forgiveness and his free offer of life, something reiterated in the final vision of the holy city and the climax of the book ('the free gift of the water of life', 22:17). The symmetrical and proportionate judgment of God comes only on those who refuse the offer of the asymmetrical and disproportionate invitation of the grace of God.

Theology

The threefold 'woe' here matches the eagle's declaration of three woes on the earth in 8:13. But where those woes came upon the earth in the time prior to the End, these woes are the final judgment of God over the principal rival power to God in John's day. The seven mentions of 'woe' in 8:13; 9:12; 11:14, together with these three pairs of 'woe', add to the central (unnumbered) third woe of 12:12 to make fourteen woes in total, 2 x 7, signifying the true testimony of the fate of those who refuse God's free offer of life.

The vividness of the imagery and the power of the poetic expression draw the reader in, inviting self-involvement rather than offering a detached description. This is emphasized by what appear to be John's two personal interjections in verses 14 and 20, directed negatively at the mourning merchants and positively at the people of God in turn. Although John reports his vision in terms that make clear connections with first-century life, the result is a curiously contemporary critique of power and wealth in human empires of every age. And of course it was ever thus. The Old Testament prophet Amos regularly criticizes the exploitation and dehumanization of others for the sake of personal gain when he rebukes those who '[buy] the poor with silver and the needy for a pair of sandals' (Amos 8:6). John's vision report looks backwards to such Old Testament judgments, through the realities of his own world, and (by means of his poetic metaphors of justice and judgment) continues forwards to speak into our contemporary world.

F. The declaration of the mighty angel (18:21-24)

Comment

21. This is the third *mighty angel* that John has mentioned (5:2; 10:1), though there does not appear to be any particular connection between the three; this is simply John's reporting of the numerous and varied cast involved in his vision narrative. The action of the angel in *pick[ing] up a boulder* and *[throwing] it into the sea* does not suggest any specific symbolic significance – though a boulder signifying destruction has a slight echo of Daniel 2:34 (the rock which destroys the statue of empires in Nebuchadnezzar's dream), and its being cast into the sea is reminiscent of the blazing mountain in Revelation 8:8.[5] Just as we feel the power of waves crashing against a rocky shore, so the rhetorical impact here is of the power, suddenness and decisiveness of the destruction of the ironically described *great city.*

22–23a. What follows is a kind of funeral dirge, offered with a relentless poetic rhythm set off by the proclamation of judgment ('thrown down') in verse 21. Although the sense is future (which is reflected in English translations), the dirge is structured around six alternating past (aorist) passive verbs with emphatic negatives that communicate the finality and certainty of the judgment:

21   never more found
22   never more heard in you
         never more found in you
            never more heard in you
23   never more shine in you
         never more heard in you

Of the five activities listed, four match the description of God's judgment through (historic) Babylon in Jeremiah 25:10: *music* ('sounds of joy'), *the sound of a millstone, the light of a lamp* and the *voice of the bride and bridegroom* (AT). The repetition of these terms again emphasizes the principle of *lex talionis* in the judgment of meta-phorical Babylon (Rome) which is repaid with the judgment meted out by literal Babylon on God's people. The additional activity, done by *any craftsman of any craft* (AT), is pertinent because of the power of craft guilds in Roman cities which incorporated elements of pagan worship in their membership and so put pressure on any Christian craft workers. We can see early signs of this conflict in the protests of the Ephesian metalworkers against Paul in Acts 19:23–31 when they see that the growth of 'the Way' threatens their businesses. The phrase 'never more found' (AT) echoes the judgment language going back to 12:8 when the devil's place was 'never more found'

---

5. There is also a slight echo of Jeremiah's scroll being attached to a stone so that it sinks in the Euphrates as a warning of Babylon's judgment, but the point of the symbolism seems different here.

(AT) in heaven, and the deathly hush as the sounds of life fall silent contrasts with the great sound of rejoicing in heaven that follows. The whole picture of loss of light and life is a counterpoint to the vision of the New Jerusalem, the whole city a bride united with her bridegroom, filled with the light of God and of the lamb (21:23), and to the people of God who rejoice with the music of harps (5:8; 14:2; 15:2).

23b–24. The economic critique of Rome reaches its pinnacle in the observation that *your merchants were the world's most important people* (AT); trade together with the wealth and power that come from it were the most highly exalted aspects of imperial life. The negative assessment of *magic* is not very prominent in Revelation, though where it is mentioned (9:21; 21:8; 22:15, as well as here) it is in line with the negative assessment of the Old Testament (such as Deut. 18:10). But the parallelism with the previous line ('Your merchants . . . by your magic . . .') suggests that the real subject of criticism is the almost magical ability of the imperial system to create wealth and prosperity for its citizens.

In contrast to the previous signs of life and joy that 'were not found', what is *found* are signs of violence and death, *blood* standing as a metonym for the deaths not just of *prophets and saints* (AT), that is, of God's people and particularly those who proclaimed God's truth, but of *all who have been slaughtered on the earth*. Here is a double irony: the woman Babylon appears to be clothed in scarlet (17:4), but in fact she is drenched in the blood of the innocent. And the inhabitants of the earth who have followed the beast (13:12) and drunk from the woman's cup (17:2) find in her not life, but death and violence. At times Revelation's critique of empire is focused on the exaltation of the emperor, who is given the adulation that belongs to God alone (Rev. 4), but here we see equally trenchant critiques of the empire's obsession with wealth and violence.

Theology

This final section of the lament for fallen Babylon completes the process of unveiling which has revealed her true nature in contrast to how she has been seen by others. The life of the city appeared to involve the ordinary activities of human life – music and marriage, craftsmanship and trade. But it was built on an insatiable appetite for luxury which created a ruthless and exploitative system of international trade. And it depended on violent conquest that went hand in hand with the desire for control of trade systems.

By drawing on the language used of Tyre and Babylon in the Old Testament, John links the anticipated fall of Babylon/Rome with the judgment that befell the historic enemies of God's people. Rome's acquisitiveness and violence expressed a sense of self-aggrandizement which made her claim for herself things that were true only of God and demand the allegiance that only God could command. But by expressing these things in terms of universal human activity, John is allowing his later readers to see here a rebuke of all forms of human imperial pretension which echo the failings of Rome.

G. Celebration in heaven (19:1–10)

Comment

1–2. There is some question as to whether the opening verses of Revelation 19 really belong with the previous verses in Revelation 18 rather than with the verses that follow in the rest of chapter 19. The poetic structure continues as previously, and John continues to 'hear' rather than 'see', which he does again in verse 11. But the section is introduced with *After these [things]* (*meta tauta*, AT), which often marks a new vision, or a significant new section of a vision (see 4:1; 7:1; 7:9; 15:5; 18:1), and the cause for rejoicing quickly moves *from* the defeat and destruction of 'Babylon' *to* the celebration of God's reign and victory which have now come. This then sets the stage for the sequence of visions of victory which follows in the rest of the chapter and into Revelation 20. This praise section, with some links to Revelation 18 but stronger ones back to the praise of God in Revelation 4, therefore functions as a transition from Revelation 18 into 19 and 20.

John hears the *roar* (lit. 'great voice' or 'sound') of an enormous multitude *in heaven*, which presumably includes not only the myriads of angels of 5:11 but also the uncountable multitude of the redeemed in 7:9. The Roman emperor claimed legitimacy in the exercise of power because he ruled with the *consensus omnium*, the agreement of all, since (in theory) he reigned for the benefit of all. But in fact it is God who rules with the consent and recognition of all creation, and John's readers, though appearing to be in the minority in their cultural context, are on the side of the majority – even if this majority is, for the time being, hidden from sight (cf. Elisha's revelation to his servant in 2 Kgs 6:17).

The term *Hallelujah* is a transliteration into Greek of the Hebrew phrase meaning 'Praise the Lord'. It occurs frequently in the Psalms, especially in the 'Hallel' psalms (Pss 113 – 118), where the Greek Old Testament transliterates it almost as a heading rather than translating it into the equivalent Greek phrase (which in fact comes in v. 5, 'Praise our God'). Because of this, it is correct to transliterate once again into English, rather than translating the term, just as we also should transliterate 'Amen' in verse 4 and elsewhere in the New Testament, since this is also a transliteration of a Hebrew phrase. It is a testimony to the remarkable influence of this passage on Christian worship that the term 'hallelujah' (which comes four times in these verses) occurs only here in the New Testament and yet has become such a dominant term within Christian hymnody.

The acclamation that *salvation and glory and power* belong to God connects this praise to the hymns we have previously heard, especially the sequence of acclamations in 4:11; 5:12, 13; 7:12 (see comment on 7:11–12). It takes the three terms that are present in each of the four earlier lists (glory, honour and power) and substitutes 'salvation' for 'honour' in line with the language of the 'Hallel' psalm 118:25. The work of God in bringing to his people salvation which was effected by the blood of the lamb (12:10) is now being fully revealed as the enemies of God come under judgment and finally lose their power. The reason for the praise of God is found in the affirmation of his *true and just . . . judgments,* in a phrase repeated from the song of Moses in 15:3 and celebration in 16:7. In both instances, the focus is the fairness of God's judgments in repaying in kind what the agents of evil have themselves meted out to others, echoing the song of Moses in Deuteronomy 32, and enacted in the bowl judgments (see comment on 15:3; 16:7).

Although the word here for *corrupted* (*phtheirō*) comes nowhere else in Revelation, the closely related compound *diaphtheirō* does occur in 11:18: 'The time has come . . . for *destroying* those who *destroy* the earth' (emphasis added). The sense here is that, just as the *great prostitute* has brought the world to ruin, so God will now bring her to ruin, a further expression of the principle of *lex talionis*, very close to the one that Paul articulates using the same vocabulary in 1 Corinthians 3:17 ('if anyone brings to ruin God's temple, God will bring that person to ruin', AT). The *aveng[ing] . . . the blood of his servants* reiterates the central accusation of the *inclusio* of 16:5–7 and offers the fullest answer to the question first posed in 6:10: 'How long, O Lord, until you avenge our blood?' (AT).

3–5. Some commentators see either the repetition of *Hallelujah* in verse 3 or the instance in verse 4 as somehow 'secondary', and then point to the remaining three as offering a triple response to the triple 'woes' of Revelation 18. But John is very careful in his use of words and the frequency with which they occur, so this is unlikely. In fact, this section has two major hymns introduced by 'Hallelujah' – in verses 1–2, 6b–8 – with the two minor acclamations (and their own 'Hallelujah's) here in verses 3 and 4. The emphasis here is on the unity of the acclamation, coming as it does from the great multitude in verses 1 and 6, with agreement echoed by the *elders* and *the four living creatures* in verse 4, supported by the *voice . . . from the throne* in verse 5. Here is a picture of the whole creation in harmony and celebration.

Smoke in Revelation is mentioned twelve times, sometimes signifying the holy presence of God (as in 15:8), but at others pointing to evil and the judgment of God (see comment on 9:2). As with the similar phrase in 14:11, the significance of the smoke rising *for ever and ever* cannot signify some kind of eternal torment or continual destruction, but points to the finality and eternal effect of the destruction of the city by God (cf. the language about Edom in Isa. 34:10). Despite the beast earlier having a fatal wound which appeared to have healed in imitation of the lamb (13:3), there will be no resurrection for the great prostitute who rides the beast once God's final judgment is enacted.

The *twenty-four elders* and the *four living creatures* are mentioned here for the last time, the seventh of seven occurrences of this pairing, never described twice in exactly the same way (5:6, 8, 11, 14; 7:11; 14:3, and here). The throne scene is displaced by the arrival of the New Jerusalem coming from heaven to earth. The elders are no longer needed to function as representative of God's people since the people fill the holy city, and the living creatures are no longer needed to represent God's creation since the city includes a redeemed Eden. In the meantime, they *bow* (AT) before the throne, just as they had done in 5:8, thus connecting this scene with the worship of the lamb in Revelation 5, and linking the judgment of 'Babylon' with the victory won by the lamb in being slain (12:10–11).

The *voice . . . from the throne* has spoken previously, anticipating the completion of the work of redemption in 16:17, and will speak again when it is fully enacted in 21:3; in both cases this looks like a circumlocution for the voice of God. That is less clear here, since the voice makes reference to *our God*, but it nonetheless speaks with the authority of God as King. The term for *servant* (or slave, *doulos*) is mentioned fourteen times in the text, three times with reference to actual slaves (6:15; 13:16; 19:18), but elsewhere as a metaphor for those who serve God and are obedient to him (1:1; 11:18), just as Paul uses it as a favourite self-designation ('slave of Christ', Rom. 1:1; Gal. 1:10, AT). The word for *fear* is the usual one for reverence and submission to God deployed elsewhere in Revelation (14:7; 15:4), and its combination with the term 'servants' and the 'gradable antonyms' *great and small* (functioning as a merism meaning 'everyone'; see comment on 6:15; 13:16) makes this phrase a very close parallel to the earlier anticipation of the End in 11:18.

6–8. Once again, John *hear[s]* rather than 'sees', continuing the distinctive style of this section from the beginning of Revelation 18. He repeats the phrase from 19:1 but with some variation; instead of hearing 'the great sound of a large crowd' (AT), he simply hears *the sound of a large crowd* and adds that it was also like the *sound of many waters* and the *sound of mighty thunder* (AT). The sound of 'many waters' had at first designated the voice of Jesus in 1:15 (AT), using a metaphor from Ezekiel 1:24 for the voice of God. But this sound of divine speech, along with the sound of thunder signalling the divine presence at Sinai (see comment on 4:5), was already merged in the praises of 144,000 on Mount Zion in 14:2. It seems as though the people of God are in harmony not only with the creation of God, but also with the voice of God in the presence of God.

This is the sixth of seven occurrences of the title *Lord God Almighty*, beginning in 1:8 and ending in 21:22 where it also marks the close association between God and the lamb. The roots of the phrase are in the Old Testament, translating the expression of Israel's God Yahweh as the commander of the heavenly armies (*yhwh ṣěbā'ôt*; see comment on 4:8). Once again, the anticipation of God's reign in 11:15–17 and its inception in 12:10–11 are being unfolded in reality as God's opponents lose their power. The acclamation of the reign of *our* Lord God has echoes of the joyful anticipation of the return from exile in Isaiah 52:7, and is a powerful counter-claim to the power and reign of Caesar. The realization of God's reign is tied in with the welfare and rejoicing of his people, just as we frequently see in the Psalms, most characteristically in Psalms 95 and 100. Throughout Revelation, the ruling power of God is never detached from the fate of his people, and the reign of God here is expressed precisely in the unhindered union of Jesus with his people as *the wedding of the Lamb* for which *his bride has made herself ready* (cf. Paul's language in 2 Cor. 11:2), which will be more fully explicated in Revelation 21.

The description of the *fine linen, bright and clean* expresses a fascinating theology of the relationship between faith and works. Throughout the text, works (or 'deeds', *ergoi*, mentioned twenty times) have been the indicator of true allegiance. The exalted Jesus sees the works of those in the assemblies in Revelation 2 – 3, and as a result either rebukes or commends them. The failure of those on earth to respond to judgment is expressed in the refusal to 'repent of the works of their hands' (9:20, AT), and judgment of the dead is on the basis of 'their works' (20:13, AT). John now uses a different term for *righteous acts* (*dikaiomata*), which parallel the actions of God (15:4) but contrast with the unrighteous acts (*adikēmata*) of 'Babylon' (18:5). And where 'Babylon' has gained her fine garments by violence and oppression, and worn them for her own glorification, the garment of the bride has been *given [to] her* (the passive implying by God) and in order to please her bridegroom, the lamb. The righteous deeds which demonstrate faithfulness and patient endurance on the part of the saints remain a gift from God.[6]

---

6. Some commentators, noting the parallel in 15:4, argue that these 'righteous acts' are the acts that God does, rather than those the people do. But this interpretation does not fit the grammar or the sense of the text here.

9. Most English translations specify that *the angel* is now speaking to John, but the text simply says 'he said to me'. The 'he' is unlikely to be the 'voice . . . from the throne' of verse 5, and could be referring back to the 'mighty angel' of 18:21, the splendid angel of 18:1 or the bowl angel of 17:1. This last option is the most likely, since we are now at the end of the long section dominated by voices (rather than visions as such) that has run from 17:1 through to 19:10. John is commanded to *Write* twelve times – three times in relation to the book as a whole (1:11, 19; 21:5), seven times in the messages in Revelation 2 – 3 and twice of statements here and in 14:13 – which emphasizes the importance of what is spoken. There are seven blessings in Revelation (1:3; 14:13; 16:15; 19:9; 20:6; 22:7, 14), most of which have some eschatological dimension to them, and the pairing here of the command to write and a proclamation of blessing matches that in 14:13.

The metaphor of the invitation to a *wedding banquet* (AT) is one that Jesus also draws on in his parable in Matthew 22. In first-century Jewish culture, the betrothal and exchange of vows would happen early, and only at a later date would the bride leave and go to the groom's home, at which point the celebration would take place. Within John's use of this metaphor, the present time is the period when the vows and commitments have been made, but the wedding will be consummated only at the End. It is a highly mixed metaphor, since followers of the lamb constitute both the bride and also the guests at the banquet. In Isaiah 25:6–8, it is at the banquet he has prepared on Mount Zion that God will 'wipe every tear from their faces' (AT) and 'swallow up death for ever', aspects that are made explicit in Revelation 21.

The question of who is *invited* is also ambiguous, in that this refers to those who have resisted the mark of the beast and have received the seal of the living God (7:2; 14:1, 9), which in some of the language of Revelation has a sense of predetermination (22:11). Yet it is also clear that the invitation remains open, at least at the time at which John is writing, so that all who wish to can receive the gift of life (22:17). This divide between the invitation offered to all but received by only a few parallels Jesus' other banquet parable in Luke 14:16–24. It is not clear what *these . . . true words* refers to – whether the immediately preceding saying, or the preceding section from

17:1, or the whole of what John has written. This last option is less likely, in contrast to the parallel phrase in 22:6 which does appear to refer to everything John has heard (and seen). The sense of future promise there also applies here, so it should best be read as referring to the promises of hope that will allow John's readers to live with committed confidence.

10. Verses 9 and 10, with their future promise, pronouncement of blessing and declaration of truth followed by John's temptation to worship the angelic messenger, have a close parallel in 22:7–8. In terms of John's own human experience, the action of *[falling] at his feet to worship him* seems natural enough, since John has seen and heard some remarkable things, including the dazzling splendour of the angel in 18:1. In terms of the narrative, this episode serves to close off the extended (and relatively untypical) description of the guidance from the interpreting bowl angel and the long report of what has been spoken by the range of characters. In terms of theology, the angel's rebuke that *I am a fellow-servant with you* serves two important purposes. The first is to bring angelic beings onto a level with human servants and messengers of God, which functions as an important correction to tendencies towards angelic devotion in the area (such as nearby Colossae; see Col. 2:18). The second is to offer a narrative contrast with John's opening encounter in Revelation 1 with Jesus, who is described using angelic imagery from Daniel 10 (see comment on 1:13). When John falls down before the angel, he is rebuked for his action, but when he falls down before the angelic Jesus, he is simply told not to be afraid (1:17). The theme of falling before an angel and being told not to worship since the angel is not God occurs elsewhere in Jewish apocalyptic (see *Apocalypse of Zephaniah* 6:11–15; *Martyrdom and Ascension of Isaiah* 7:21). In this narrative contrast between Jesus and the angel, John is incorporating the identity of Jesus into the identity of the one true God, just as Paul does propositionally in his reworking of the *Shema* from Deuteronomy 6:4 in 1 Corinthians 8:6.

The *testimony of Jesus* (AT) can have an 'objective' sense (the testimony about Jesus) or a 'subjective' sense (the testimony that Jesus gives). Some commentators argue that it must be the former, since the followers of the lamb 'have' the testimony of Jesus in 12:17, but that is not a necessary conclusion (see comment on that verse). The occurrence of the phrase in 1:2 suggests that it is possible for it to have the double sense of being both *about* Jesus and also imparted *by* Jesus, so that the true testimony aligns with what Jesus reliably claims and truly reveals about himself. The word for *Spirit* (*pneuma*) comes twenty-four times in the text, and fourteen (2 x 7) of these are a reference in the singular to the Spirit of God: seven times at the end of the messages in Revelation 2 – 3; four times in the phrase 'in the Spirit' (1:10; 4:2; 17:3; 21:10); and three times in relation to the Spirit's speech (14:13; here; 22:17). From these occurrences, it is clear that the Spirit is the animating power behind John's visions and his reporting of them, and the close relationship between the words given by the Spirit and the speech of Jesus has already been made clear in the seven messages, since Jesus' royal pronouncements to his people constitute 'what the Spirit is saying to the assemblies' (2:7, 11, and the rest, AT).

The whole of John's message, as a record of what he has seen and heard, as well as being a revelation and a testimony, is in letter form a *prophecy* (1:3; 22:18–19), that is, a message from God giving his perspective on the world which is quite different from what the human eye can see unaided. This key theological statement thus binds together not only the person of Jesus with the person of the Spirit, but also the testimony of who Jesus is and what he does with the prophetic activity of the Spirit. Testimony to Jesus can happen only when animated by the Spirit (cf. 1 Cor. 12:3); and the prophetic word that the Spirit brings cannot be separated from the truth about Jesus.

Theology

It is commonly said that praise is the language of heaven, and that the worship that we practise now is a rehearsal for spending eternity with God. It is, therefore, surprising to note the absence of any hymns of praise in the vision of the New Jerusalem, and to realize that this is the last hymn-like section of material in the book. This reflects the consistent emphasis in Revelation that praise is not simply for what God has done or is doing, but for what he is going to do when his justice is fully revealed at the End. The praise here, though expressed in the past tense since in the narrative it follows the account of Babylon's fall, is for John's readers still anticipating something in the future.

All through the Scriptures, God's justice in his judgments is something for which he is praised. Indeed, it is core to his character and closely related to the idea that God is 'true'; he is not fickle, changing his mind from one time to another, but is the dependable constant in an inconstant and changing world. Trusting in the justice of God is essential for John's audience as providing the sure ground for their remaining faithful, with 'patient endurance' (1:9), in the face of, at times, ferocious opposition. If God is to vindicate his people, it will mean the defeat of his people's foes, and bringing to an end all systems of power that oppose and oppress them. As elsewhere in Scripture, rejoicing over their fall is not an expression of revenge or glee, but the delight and relief of those who have been oppressed seeing their oppressors brought to justice.

The description of the cosmic opponent of God, Satan, in chapter 12 was followed by the introduction of the temporal opponents of God's people, the beasts from the sea and the land, in chapter 13, representing Roman imperial power and its reception in the east of the empire. We now see God's justice exercised over them in reverse order: here we have seen Rome itself falling to ruin, and in the next section the beast (from the sea) and the false prophet (the beast from the land) will face destruction. Following that, God's cosmic opponent will face defeat and destruction in chapter 20.

It is fascinating to see how John here portrays himself. On the one hand, he is a model of the patient endurance that he exhorts in his audience. But in this part of the narrative, he is only a near-perfect model, rather than an unqualified success. He, too, is tempted to fall short, just as his audience might be, and he, like them, needs to maintain vigilance in his commitment to worshipping God alone.

13. SEVEN UNNUMBERED VISIONS OF THE END (19:11 – 20:15)

Following the long section from 17:1 to 19:10, which is mostly styled as a record of what John has *heard* (from various angels, the voice from the throne and the great multitude in heaven), we now return to the more common style of the text from Revelation 4, recording episodically what John has *seen*. Just as the previous section was unified by the form of the revelation, so the remainder of Revelation 19, the whole of Revelation 20 and the beginning of Revelation 21 are unified by seven occurrences of 'And I saw' (*kai eidon*), creating a sequence of seven unnumbered visions:

1. 19:11 And I saw heaven [standing] open . . .
2. 19:17 And I saw an angel standing in the sun . . .
3. 19:19 And I saw the beast and the kings of the earth . . .
4. 20:1 And I saw an angel coming down from heaven . . .
5. 20:4 And I saw thrones . . .
6. 20:11 And I saw a great white throne . . .
7. 21:1 And I saw a new heaven and a new earth . . .

The phrase also occurs in 20:12, 'And I saw the dead . . .', but this is clearly part of the vision section begun in the previous verse. By contrast, after the opening of the final vision in 21:1, the phrase is entirely absent, with the elements of that vision being introduced by a variety of phrases, such as 'he showed me' (22:1, AT). The repetition of the phrase thus creates a distinct section, into which the beginning of the final section is tied before moving into a different style of writing.

It has been common to read these seven visions as sequential, offering a complex chronology of events connected with the End, but such an approach faces some major problems. Given that the main arena of the events is the earth, it suggests that Jesus returns multiple times, which contradicts everything else the New Testament says about the End. And throughout Revelation, we have frequently been offered a report of visions which appear to describe the same thing (the situation of the world, the people of God, the nature of God's judgment, the End) from different perspectives with different theological emphases – though often linked and interconnected. It therefore makes better narrative and theological sense to see these seven visions as offering seven perspectives on what the future of God's relationship with the world, as expressed in the return of Jesus, means for humanity and the people of God. Here, at last, is revealed in these different visions what it means for God to be the one 'who is, and who was, and who *is to come*' (1:4).

A. The rider on the white horse (19:11–16)

Context
The first of these seven unnumbered visions offers us a striking new image of Jesus as the rider on the white horse. Though the image itself is quite new in Revelation, the description includes numerous references to words and ideas from earlier in the text. We encountered riders on horses in chapter 6, including a white horse as the first of the four; Jesus was 'faithful and true' in the message to Laodicea (3:14); the language of justice echoes the praise of God in 16:7 and 19:2; his blazing eyes and sword coming from his mouth recall the opening vision of chapter 1; a name that 'no-one knows' formed part of the promise to those in Pergamum (2:17); the robe dipped

in blood as he treads the 'winepress of God's wrath' (AT) recalls the harvest of grapes in 14:19–20.

As with other sections of Revelation, we are therefore presented with both continuity and discontinuity – a new vision, but one which is connected with a series of episodes that has gone before. This one is particularly striking, in that (like the description of the one on the throne in chapter 4) John writes in the present tense, often using present participles, as if he were describing to us a work of art that he is admiring and wants to communicate to his audience the impact of what he sees.

Comment

11. The phrase *I saw heaven [standing] open* marks the beginning of a new section of John's vision report, but has strong echoes of an earlier new beginning in 4:1: 'I saw a door [standing] open in heaven' (AT). The difference is that, where in the first instance it was something that gave access to heavenly realities for John alone, here heaven itself has opened, and the heavenly figure is about to come from heaven to earth, beginning the movement which reaches its climax in the coming of the heavenly city to earth in 21:1. The six verses 11–16 are all marked by present and perfect tense verbs, which keeps our focus on the central character whom John describes and his attributes; the subsequent action in verses 19–21 is described much more briefly and without any real detail.

The description that follows does not, in contrast to other passages, introduce any new references to the Old Testament, but instead interweaves a complex series of allusions to images and ideas from earlier in the text. The colour of the *white horse* here does not suggest purity so much as the power of the elite, since white horses were considered to be the best and so often selected for rulers. The white horse here and its rider offer a counterpoint to the white horse and rider in 6:2, which symbolized either the deception of pagan religion or the threat of Parthians bringing war and conquest (see comment on 6:2).[1] The rider of the horse *is [called] Faithful and True.*

---

1. It is worth noting here that Revelation's symbolism of colour is quite complex, and the use (for example) of black and white, particularly in

There is significant disagreement among the best manuscripts on the inclusion of the word 'called', but it is clear that this title recalls Jesus' title in the message to the assembly in 3:14, thus linking this vision to the vision of Jesus in the early chapters. The phrase will also be repeated in relation to John's own writing of his vision report in 21:5 and 22:6; the character of Jesus is intimately linked to the true testimony to Jesus that John offers. Jesus is not like other kings, ruling with fickleness or out of self-interest, but remains faithful and self-giving.

The word for *justice* (*dikaiosynē*) is mentioned elsewhere only in 22:11, where it refers to 'doing right', but the phrase *judging in justice* (AT) is closely related to the celebration of God's just judgments in the interjection within the bowls in 16:5 and their repetition in the praise of 19:2. The just judgments of God are executed by the person of Jesus, offering another interweaving of the roles and actions of Jesus and God. The addition of *making war* (AT) does not refer to the single action of the coming conflict; both verbs are in the present tense, suggesting that this is something he habitually does. Warfare has previously been engaged between Michael and his angels and the devil and his, as Michael has enacted the victory won by the male son (12:7), and in return the beast has made war on God's people. But Jesus has earlier talked of 'making war with the sword of my mouth' (AT) on those in Pergamum who do not repent – clearly a metaphor for correction by the truth of his word (see comment on 2:16).

12. John's description continues by noting *his eyes blazing like fire* (AT), suggesting divine vision and understanding, and offering a direct connection between this vision and his opening encounter with the exalted Jesus in 1:14 (where the wording is identical). It is significant that *on his head are many crowns*, using the word *diadēma* rather than the previous term 'wreath', *stephanos* (e.g. in 14:14). The wreath signifies victory (as in 2:10; 3:11; 4:4) whereas the diadem signifies the power to rule. Jesus' victory through his faithful sacrifice is now translated into his actual reign, realizing the anticipation that

---

(note 1 *cont.*) relation to the colour of horses throughout the book, is not (to coin a phrase) black and white!

'the kingdom of the world has become the kingdom of our Lord and of his Messiah' (11:15), and displacing the usurping rule of the dragon and the first beast (who wore diadems rather than wreaths in 12:3 and 13:1).

It seems odd within the narrative for John to tell us that he has a *name written . . . that no-one knows but he himself,* since he has already given us one of his names and will give us two more in the following verses. Some commentators suggest that there is a progressive revelation, so that this unknown name is revealed in verse 16 (since it is not specified here where the name is written), and they suggest that the 'mystery' of Babylon that is then revealed in 17:5 is a parallel. The difficulty with this view is that the text does not suggest this progression, either here or in 17:5. So perhaps instead this phrase reflects the connection that was thought to exist between knowing someone's name and having mastery over that person, just as Jesus asks the name of the demons who possess the man of the Gerasenes in Mark 5:9 before driving them out. By offering us three names which communicate who this rider is, but also mentioning one other secret name, John is telling us that he is known by all but mastered by none.

13. The description of the rider continues using present participles (vv. 12–13 are one sentence in Greek). The image of the *robe dipped in blood* is not a parallel to the robes of the great multitude washed and made white in the blood of the lamb (7:14), since the language is quite different, including the term for 'robe' (here *himation,* but *stolē* in 7:14). Rather, it is language borrowed from Isaiah 63:1–4, where God tramples the nations in the winepress of his wrath and their blood spatters his garments, drawing on the double meaning of 'blood' as the juice of grapes (see comment on 14:19–20). It is of no consequence that the mention of the winepress does not come until verse 15, since this whole section is present and perfect tense description, and the narrative action does not begin until verse 19.

The *word[s] of God* is mentioned seven times in Revelation (including 'the true words of God' in 19:9), and on four of these occasions it is closely associated with 'testimony of Jesus' (1:2, 9; 6:9; 20:4). Both phrases can have an 'objective' as well as a 'subjective' sense, so the word of God is both a word from God and a word about God (see comment on 1:2 and 19:10 in relation to 'testimony of Jesus'). In 17:17 and 19:9, it is clear that the word(s) of God have content as communication, but the identification here of the word of God with the person of the rider on the white horse has a clear theological resonance with the prologue of John's Gospel. Elsewhere in the New Testament, the phrase can refer to the Old Testament Scriptures (Matt. 15:6; John 10:35), Jesus' preaching of the kingdom (Luke 5:1; 8:21) and the subsequent preaching of the good news (Acts 6:7; 1 Thess. 2:13; Heb. 13:7). This phrase therefore connects the person of Jesus not only with the past revelation of God to his people (Heb. 1:1–2) and the preaching of the kingdom as expressed in the rest of the New Testament, but also with John's own testimony to the revelation he has recorded.

14. *The armies of heaven* share with the rider the elite status of *riding on white horses*. This army could consist of the redeemed who *follow* the lamb (14:4), are implicitly described as an army in their numbering 144,000 (see comment on 7:5), and as the bride of the lamb are dressed in *fine linen, white and clean* earlier in 19:8. It could consist of the angels, who are also dressed in white linen and are involved in the war which effects the victory of the male son in 12:7 – or it could consist of both together, since they are identified implicitly by their shared devotion to God in worship (5:11; and see comment on 7:11) and explicitly by the angel's rebuke of John in 19:10. This army is in striking contrast both to the armies of the fifth and sixth seals (9:1–19), with the detailed description of their armour and weapons, and to armies in the real world of the first century. The armies of heaven need no armour, since their protection comes solely from their purity and righteous deeds; and they have no need of weapons, since the victory in which they participate is won by Jesus alone (see comment on v. 19 below).

15. The *sharp sword* coming *out of his mouth* links this description back to the vision of Revelation 1 (1:16 and its repetition in the message to Pergamum in 2:12), although here John omits the mention of the sword being 'two-edged', in line with his usual practice of repeating phrases with variation. Although the vehicle of the metaphor ('sword') is a violent one, the tenor of the metaphor is not; it contrasts with both the actual violence of the horsemen in Revelation 6 and the right of *ius gladii* of the emperor to execute his opponents.

Jesus' weapons in the spiritual war he wages are faithfulness, sacrifice and truth (see comment on 2:12). The citation again of Psalm 2:9, *He will rule them with an iron rod* (AT), links this vision back to the narrative of the male son in 12:5 and its anticipation in 2:27, and emphasizes the authority to rule and to judge that is given by God.

This authority to act on God's behalf is also expressed in the next phrase, which is a sequence of five genitives emphatically piled up on one another, literally 'he treads the *winepress* of the wine of the *fury of the wrath of God* [of] the *almighty*', turning the previous passive expression in 14:19 into an active one and making clear who is exercising the judgment. It is striking that, in the source passage in Isaiah 63, the text emphasizes God's sole right to exercise judgment, since he alone is just ('I . . . alone . . . no-one was with me', Isa. 63:3). Jesus exercises the judgment that is God's sole prerogative, since he shares the attributes of justice that belong to God ('with justice he judges', v. 11; cf. 16:5 and 19:2).

16. The third title John recounts (following 'Faithful and True' and 'Word of God') is also *written*, as is the unknown name of verse 12. But the unknown name is written in an unspecified place (possibly on the rider's diadems), while the name here is on his *robe and on his thigh*. The title KING OF KINGS AND LORD OF LORDS was previously attributed to the lamb in 17:14, though with characteristic variation – in this case, a reversal of the order of the titles. (The mention of warfare and of the followers of the lamb/rider on the white horse indicates the close links between the angelic exposition of John's vision in Revelation 17 and the vision he sees now.) The title has been usurped by others before (Ezek. 26:7) and continues to be claimed in John's first-century world (particularly among the Parthians) and by successive rulers with imperial aspirations through history. But the final victory of the lamb/rider on the white horse shows that the title belongs to him alone. The phrases can be understood either relationally – that Jesus is the King and Lord over all other kings and lords – or in a superlative sense – that he is the greatest of all kings and lords.

Theology
This final image completes a remarkable composite picture of Jesus, which by its multiple references to other parts of the text integrates

the quite distinct earlier visions: the angel-like figure of Revelation 1 which drew on imagery from Daniel, the lamb who was slain but is now alive and shares the throne of God in Revelation 5, and the son of man who swings his sickle in Revelation 14 and (it turns out) is the one who treads the winepress of the grape harvest. There is a similar linking of the different images of the people of God, the 144,000 from Revelation 7 and 14 who are also the great multitude in praise and the bride of the lamb earlier in this chapter, and who now constitute the 'armies of heaven'. In making these connections, John is urging us to read these different images in relation to one another. In particular, the apparent violence in the vehicles of the metaphors ('swords' and 'making war') cannot be detached from the clarity of earlier images, where the conflict is won by the speaking of truth and not by the violence of power, and the victory of the lamb has come from the unexpected sacrifice resulting from his faithfulness to the truth of God.

B. The beast and the kings of the earth, and the last battle (19:17–21)

Context
The next two, quite short, visions in the series of seven belong with the first, but include additional links to earlier passages in Revelation. The opponents of the rider on the white horse are described using the language of the sixth seal in 6:15; we meet again the beast from the sea of chapter 13 and the beast from the land who became the false prophet in 16:13; we are again referred to the mark of the beast from 13:18; and the battle itself was anticipated in 16:16. But there are new images here, most notably the fiery lake, which becomes the most memorable image of the finality of judgment. And, in contrast to the first vision, John here draws on important Old Testament passages in his description of the last battle.

Comment
17–18. For a second time in this section, John states *And I saw*, shifting the focus from the description of the rider on the white horse and introducing new characters and action. *Angels* have previously been *standing* at the four corners of the earth (7:1), around the

throne or before God and the altar (7:11; 8:2, 3), or on the sea and land (10:5). The *sun* has previously been both subject to and part of the judgments of God, darkening in 6:12 and 8:12, and in 16:8 scorching people who do not know the protection of God and the lamb (7:16). As in 12:1, it here signifies illumination and glorification, giving this angel a splendid appearance somewhat similar to that of the mighty angel of 18:1. The angel's *loud voice* means that it is widely heard, and the *birds . . . in mid-air* can be seen by all (cf. the eagle in 8:13 and the angel in 14:6).

The invitation to the birds to *Come . . . eat the flesh of kings* draws on the defeat of Gog, the eschatological enemy of God, in Ezekiel 39:17–20. This is in the context of the completion of the redemption and ingathering of God's people, the time when their exile finally comes to an end. John makes no mention of the 'beasts' (Ezek. 39:17, AT), presumably because in his narrative the beast is one of those consumed along with the kings, princes and others. This event is not a sacrifice (since the self-sacrifice of the lamb has been sufficient), but is now *the great supper of God*, in parallel to the 'wedding supper of the Lamb' (19:9); the destruction of evil is continually the counterpoint to the redemption of the saints throughout Revelation. John's use of the same section of Ezekiel in the battle that follows the thousand years of 20:2 (Ezek. 38:2–3, 8 in Rev. 20:8) shows that he views this whole process of judgment and the defeat of evil as part of the same dynamic, which confirms the view mentioned in the introduction to 19:11–12 that these visions offer different perspectives on God's final victory, rather than a chronological sequence of events.

John's final adaptation to the Ezekiel tradition here is to extend the feast to include not just the powerful but also *all people, free and slave, great and small*, extending judgment to all those who fled from the wrath of the lamb in 6:15 and who were deceived by the beast and received its mark in 13:16.

19–21. Following the descriptive vision of the rider on the white horse, and the transitional vision of the angel in the sun, John introduces this next vision section with another *And I saw* (AT). The *beast* here is the first beast from the sea in 13:1, and the *kings of the earth* are those who are rightfully ruled by Jesus (1:5), but who have allied themselves with the great prostitute (17:2) and mourned her demise (18:9; see comment on 6:15; 17:2). The 'great battle' has already been anticipated in the sixth bowl (16:12–16), which also mentions the deceptive *signs*, performed here by the *false prophet*. The alliance of the beast and the kings was also anticipated in the angel's explanatory narrative in 17:12–14, which confirms the interpretation of the ten horns as the rulers of client kingdoms in the empire.

The account of this great eschatological battle is very striking – in that there is no account of it whatever! In particular, the armies of heaven appear to play no role in the battle victory, simply accompanying the rider on the white horse in his conquest. This offers a clear parallel to the initial defeat of the dragon by the male son in 12:7, where there is no climactic struggle, but the victory has been won so clearly that its execution is delegated to the angel Michael (see comment on 12:7) and God's people participate in the lamb's victory through their faithful testimony (12:11). There is no dualism here between the forces of good and evil; a 'divine passive' declares the beast to be *captured* and with him the false prophet, the name given from 16:13 to the beast from the land of 13:11. It had *performed signs before the beast* (AT), that is, with its authority and on its behalf, as explained in 13:12–13, sharing in the deception of the dragon (12:9; 20:3) and the great city 'Babylon' (18:23). The *mark of the beast* continues to function as the thing which delineates those who fell into the idolatry of *worshipping the beast* (AT; the two things being paired in 14:9, 11; 16:2; 20:4); the call to patient endurance in the light of future redemption and judgment for John's readers is nothing less than a call to worship God in Spirit and in truth.

To be *thrown alive* into the underworld was thought to be the most painful torture in Greco-Roman literature, and *fire* and *burning sulphur* symbolized the ultimate punishment as far back as the account of Sodom and Gomorrah in Genesis 19:24. The image of a *lake of fire* (AT) is unique to Revelation; this place of final destruction is distinct from other subterranean realms in the text, including the domain 'under the earth' (5:3, 13), 'Hades', which is the temporary realm of the dead in Greco-Roman mythology (1:18; 6:8; 20:13, 14), and the 'abyss', which is the origin of chaotic and demonic forces corresponding to 'the deep' in the Old Testament (see comment on the abyss in 9:1). Elsewhere in the Bible and Jewish apocalyptic literature, these realms are often conflated (so e.g. Gehenna in

Matt. 10:28 and Mark 9:43 has some correspondence with Hades but includes torment by fire), but they are kept distinct in the narrative of Revelation.[2]

It is striking that *the rest*, which refers to the human participants of the kings and their armies, do not suffer the destruction that is meted out on the imperial system symbolized by the beast or on the structures of local power symbolized by the beast from the land/ false prophet. Though they are *killed with the sword coming out of the mouth of the rider*, this cannot refer to actual death, since the kings of the earth return in 21:24 to bring their splendour into the holy city, and the nations who were deceived by the beast 'will walk by its light'. As with the false teachers in Pergamum (2:16), this war is a polemical battle for truth in which the one who is Faithful and True will always triumph. To be left unburied with the *birds* consuming one's mortal remains was thought to be the ultimate indignity (Deut. 28:26; Jer. 7:33), but this too must be symbolic. The false beliefs into which the nations were deceived will not be afforded even the dignity of a decent burial.

Theology

In chapter 18, the lament and praise anticipate the demise of the prostitute-city Babylon, and this is attributed to God's just judgment – but God's agency in the city's fall is not made explicit. Now, for the first time, we see the judgment of Jesus against the enemies of God enacted. There is a clear connection made between the victory of Jesus over those who oppose him and the rest enjoyed by the redeemed in the New Jerusalem – both are the 'wedding supper' of God and the lamb (19:17, 19:9/21:2), with judgment and redemption as two sides of the same coin. The connection is maintained in the vision of the holy city by repeated reminders of the impure who are prohibited from entering, alongside the glory and purity of the

---

2. It is worth noting that the end-state of God's enemies is elsewhere in the NT described as 'darkness' rather than fire – see Matt. 8:12; 22:13; 25:30; 2 Pet. 2:17; and Jude 13. The contrast between darkness and fire confirms the symbolic (metaphorical) nature of these images, and suggests that the focus of both images is on extinction.

city itself. The earlier anticipations of the End, in the messages and in the series of 'sevens', included the possibility of repentance and change, but that possibility has now come to an end, and the delineation between those with allegiance to the beast and those with allegiance to the lamb becomes decisive.

The divine warrior is accompanied by angelic and human escorts, but they play no part in the battle; the victory belongs to Jesus alone, even though they share in its benefits. And this is no kind of cosmic struggle; as in Revelation 12, the battle is one-sided, and victory is so swift and decisive that John has no time to describe it. There is no comparison between the opponents who have been ranged against one another. The beast (the system of imperial power) and the false prophet (the local power structures that welcomed the beast) share the same fate as the city from which they both got their power, so that their destruction is final. The introduction of the dragon and the beasts forms a chiasm with their judgment:

Chapter 12	Introduction of dragon/Satan
Chapter 13	Introduction of beast from the sea, beast from the land
Chapter 19	Defeat of the beast and the false prophet
Chapter 20	Defeat of Satan

The victory is won not by reciprocating the literal violence that the beast and prophet have inflicted on the people of God, but by the faithfulness of the rider, found in the truth of his speech represented by the sword from his mouth. The promise of the end of the 'destroyers of the earth' (11:18) has been fulfilled.

C. Satan chained for a thousand years (20:1–3)

Context
Chapter 20 contains three further sections of the seven unnumbered series, continuing the sequence from 19:11 until the beginning of Revelation 21. The first short section introduces quite abruptly the incarceration of Satan for a thousand years, the 'millennium'. It is remarkable to see the influence that these few verses have had on Christian theology through history. Different interpretations of this

idea delineate major divisions within Protestant Christianity in the contemporary world. For an overview of the main views on the millennium, see the Introduction.

As with every other part of Revelation, key to our reading needs to be understanding the individual texts in the context of the whole book, and it is evident that the use of Ezekiel 38 – 39 here and in the previous chapter points to these sections in John's vision report as being closely bound together, part of his theological vision of the destruction of the forces of evil that has been anticipated throughout the text. We also need to pay attention to John's use of other biblical and contemporary cultural images and ideas, and take seriously the symbolic nature of the text and the rhetorical impact it would have had on his first audiences. The great mistake here (as with other parts of the book) is to detach these episodes from what has gone before in Revelation or what follows after, and dislocate the text from its first-century world.

Comment

1. John begins the fourth section of this vision sequence once again with *And I saw* and typically introduces yet another *angel.* The lack of connection with previous angelic figures turns the focus from the individual character onto his origin and purpose. Like the angels in 10:1 and 18:1, he is *coming down from heaven* (AT), sent with God's authority to execute his will on earth. There is no reason to identify this angel with the 'star that had fallen' in 9:1 who is neutral and acting under the authority of God, rather than an agent of malevolence (see comment on 9:1), even though both have *the key to the Abyss.* The common feature is that they are both acting with the authority of God. Two (or three) keys have been mentioned previously: Jesus holds the 'key to death and Hades' in 1:18 (AT) as well as the 'key of David' which gives access to the presence of God in 3:7, and the star has used a key (the same one?) to unlock the abyss in 9:1. On the relation of the abyss to other subterranean domains in Revelation, see the comment on 9:1. In contemporary Western culture, where most things are locked and need keys to open them, we associate keys with access; in the ancient world, keys and locks were much more expensive and less common, and so would naturally be associated more with locking and securing than with giving access.

2. There are close parallels here with the events of Revelation 12. Just as the enacting of the victory that the male son wins over Satan is delegated to Michael and his angels, so here it is the angel who *seize[s] the dragon*, using the language (*krateō*) describing Jesus' firm hold of the assemblies (see comment on 2:1) and related to the description of God as 'Almighty' (*pantokratōr*; cf. 1:8; 4:8; 19:6, 15; 21:22, and others). Once again John draws together a wide range of biblical traditions about the primeval opponent of God by heaping up the four major titles one upon the other – *dragon, snake, devil* and *Satan* – just as he did in 12:9. The snake in the Garden of Eden is not identified with Satan in the Genesis narrative, but had come to be so by the first century. 'Devil', meaning 'slanderer', is the Greek translation of the Hebrew *śāṭān*, meaning accuser, and is particularly associated with demons, understood as malevolent angelic beings. For fuller details, see comment on 12:9.

The 'binding' of spirits or evil angels features in a number of Jewish apocalyptic texts, to restrain them for a period of time, possibly for later punishment (see *Jubilees* 5:6, 10; 10:11; *1 Enoch* 10:4–5, 11), and this tradition has found its way into the New Testament (see 2 Pet. 2:4; Jude 6). In the Gospels, Jesus binds evil spirits (Matt. 12:29) in anticipation of their final binding and judgment (Matt. 22:13). The idea of an intermediate messianic age prior to final judgment appears frequently in Jewish literature (see the examples in *2 Baruch* 40:3; *Sibylline Oracles* 3:741–759; *Testament of Abraham* 13A), but Revelation is unique in describing it as lasting for *one thousand years* (AT). This round number suggests a long period of time, hence its common use by rulers or dictators who want to impress their subjects with the permanence of their regime, and as such it offers another counter-motif to Rome's claim to be an 'eternal' city. But it also fits with John's use of numerology, 1,000 being the cube of 10 (a natural number) and so expressing the holy presence of God on the earth mediated by the reign of the martyrs with Christ (v. 4). It also provides a contrast to the 'three and a half years' of the present age, and reverses the features of this age, so Satan is imprisoned rather than wielding authority, and the faithful are raised to life instead of being slain with the sword. The age of glory far outweighs the passing age of suffering. The term 'a thousand years' is mentioned six times (here and in vv. 3, 4, 5, 6, 7), three times in relation to Satan's binding and three times in relation to the reign of the martyrs. As elsewhere in Revelation, the defeat of evil and the vindication of God's people are inextricably connected, a theme found throughout the New Testament.

3. The *Abyss* was previously the bottomless pit (corresponding in many ways to 'the deep' in the OT) which was the origin of evil powers. In 'throwing' the dragon into the abyss, there is a sense in which the angel is casting him back whence he came – though the correspondence is not exact unless we think that Satan is the 'angel of the Abyss' in 9:11 (which offers a nice symmetry though there is little textual connection). The abyss is treated as a prison, since Satan is *locked* in it, and this is made explicit in verse 7. The *seal[ing]* which has previously suggested God's protection of his people from evil and judgment in 7:3 now protects *the nations* from being *deceiv[ed]*. As with the sealing of Jesus' tomb in the Gospel accounts, the seal shows by whose authority something has been closed up, and means that it can be opened only with that person's permission. In contrast to modern ideas about prison, in the ancient world the purpose of prison was less for punishment (which would follow later) or for the rehabilitation of offenders, and more to subdue them, protect others from harm, and force the offenders to recognize the power of the authorities as they awaited their trial and punishment which would follow the period of incarceration.

The idea that Satan will be *set free for a short time* after the interim messianic reign is also unique to John among Jewish apocalyptic. It is unclear how this functions in relation to any chronological considerations within the rest of the book, and looks more like 'theology done through narrative chronology' in the same way as we saw happening in the vision of the two witnesses in Revelation 11. There the witnesses were struck down dead and then raised to life, symbolizing the apparent defeat but spiritual life that is the paradoxical reality of the people of God, expressed spatially in the image of the temple whose outer courts were trampled while the inner sanctuary was kept safe. In this vision, the victorious work of Christ keeps Satan bound, and what influence he does have is brief and passing, and within the constraints of the sovereignty of God. If his return after imprisonment looks like a parody of Jesus' return, then it is temporary and short-lived, whereas Jesus' return is permanent and everlasting.

Theology

In drawing such close correspondences between Revelation 12 and this episode, John is connecting the decisive victory of Jesus in his death, resurrection and exaltation with the final destruction of the forces of evil. The defeat of Satan and all who align with him has been shown to be implicitly present in Jesus' ministry (see John 12:31) and the outpouring of the Spirit; the actual defeat of Satan visible to the world is only (as it were) a matter of time.

D. The reign of the martyrs and the destruction of Satan (20:4–10)

Comment

4–6. The fifth vision section is marked again by *And I saw* (AT). *Thrones* feature prominently through Revelation, being mentioned in almost every stage in the narrative and the most prominent being the throne of God and of the lamb introduced in Revelation 4 – 5. It is striking that thrones, as a sign of authority to rule, are never mentioned in relation to Satan and his allies, with the single exception of Pergamum as the place 'where Satan has his throne' (2:13). God alone sits on the throne with the lamb, but he shares his throne of authority with his people, as promised in 3:21 and symbolized by the thrones of the twenty-four elders as the representatives of God's people (see comment on 4:4). It is characteristic of John to mention the thrones first and then those *seated on them* (AT), which emphasizes their majesty and authority. The mention of the *souls of those who had been beheaded* is a close parallel to the vision at the breaking of the fifth seal in 6:9 of the souls under the altar who have also been slain *because of the testimony of Jesus and the word of God* (AT). Being *given authority to judge* (by God, expressed as a 'divine passive') is the clearest answer yet to their cry for vindication in 6:10, though we have already seen a response in the repeated acclamation of God's just judgments in 15:3; 16:5; 19:2. The word used for soul (*psychē*) should not be understood as a reference to a distinct, immortal part of the human being, separate from, or even trapped in, the physical body – not least because the martyrs are described as *[coming] to life*, which is further explained as the *first resurrection*, and resurrection is universally (in the New Testament and in Judaism in the first century) understood as bodily.[3]

Although this group clearly does not comprise all the people of God, since *the rest of the dead did not come to life* until the end of the millennium, they are typical of them, in that they *did not worship the beast or his image* (AT; 13:12; 14:9–11; 15:2) or *receive his mark* (AT). They become a kingdom of *priests* for God and Christ, the destiny of all God's people because of Jesus' death for their sins (1:6), and they share in his *reign*, something promised to those 'from every tribe and language and people and nation' who have been purchased by his blood (5:9–10). The singular reference to *his* reign (AT) could refer back to 'Christ', but more likely is a singular pronoun for God and Christ together, pointing to their single identity in parallel with 11:15. Those who follow an 'amillennialist' approach and interpret the thousand years as another description of the time between Jesus' first coming and his return see the 'first resurrection' as a reference to the spiritual reign with Christ of those who died in faith. But that cannot be the case, since this first resurrection is the preserve of the martyrs alone, and not of the whole people of God; and their reign appears to take place 'on the earth' (5:10), since it happens once Satan can no longer deceive the nations, and it comes to a temporary end on his release before its restoration in the holy city in 22:5. Rather, the emphasis here is their pre-eminence within God's people because of their exemplary faithfulness after the example of Jesus, so that they are counted as *blessed and holy* in contrast to their treatment by their executioners. Their description as *beheaded* rather than simply 'slain' (cf. 6:9) also suggests a sense of dignity, since this was the most noble way to die in contrast to crucifixion, garrotting, being burnt alive or being thrown in a sack into a river, all common methods of execution in the empire.

7–8. The close connection between the vindication and reign of the saints and the binding and defeat of Satan is continued by the

3. See the discussion of 'soul' in the comment on 6:9, and note the description of slaves as 'human souls' in 18:13 (AT).

release of Satan at the end of their reign. The 'completion' of the thousand years and the 'divine passive' (Satan plays no part in his own release) continue the emphasis on God's sovereignty. The *four corners of the earth* deploys the proverbial phrase for the whole world, as previously used in 7:1. In Ezekiel 38, *Gog* appears to be the ruler of the country of *Magog*, but here *Gog and Magog* as a pair represent all the *nations* ranged against the people of God in eschatological battle, as is found commonly in Jewish texts of this period (in both the Dead Sea Scrolls and rabbinical texts). The *sand on the seashore* is a hyperbolic expression signifying a great number – most often in the Old Testament used for the promised flourishing of the people of God (Gen. 22:17; Isa. 10:22; Hos. 1:10; Rom. 9:27; Heb. 11:12), but here echoing the vast numbers of the 'manticore' army of the sixth trumpet (9:16). Though the enemies of God and the people of God might seem to be overwhelming and without number, God's victory is still assured: 'Not by might nor by power, but by my Spirit' (Zech. 4:6).

9. The *camp of God's people* alludes to the encampment of Israel during their wilderness journey (Exod. 17:1), which symbolizes the vulnerability of God's people and their dependence on God for guidance, sustenance and security. This camp is inhabited by those who are citizens of the heavenly *city* (cf. Phil. 3:20; Heb. 12:22) which God *loves* and also dwells in, and which will be fully revealed in the next chapter. The *fire . . . from heaven* expresses a repeated motif of judgment from God (see Luke 9:54 and parallels) which has been deployed by the two witnesses after the example of Elijah (11:5; 1 Kgs 18:38). In this instance, the fire consumes the nations who have come against God's people, echoing the destruction of Sodom and Gomorrah (Gen. 19:24) and following the pattern of God's dealing with Magog (Ezek. 39:6) which will both bring God glory and assure his people of protection (Ezek. 38:14–16). As with the fire from the mouths of the two witnesses (11:5), this must be a symbolic destruction, since the nations will in the end bring their glory into the holy city in 21:24–26.

10. The character of the devil as *deceiver of the nations* (AT) continues the description previously found in 12:9 and 20:3, also characteristic of the devil's allies the beast from the land (the false prophet, 13:14;

19:20) and the great prostitute 'Babylon' (18:23) – because he is 'the father of lies' (John 8:44). The *lake of fire and sulphur* (AT) was previously mentioned in 19:20 as the destiny of the *beast and the false prophet*, and will be mentioned again in 20:14 and 21:8 as the destiny of all those who refuse God's invitation of life.[4] The dragon and then the beast from the sea and beast from the land were introduced in that order in Revelation 12 – 13, and now the destruction of the beast and false prophet has preceded the destruction of the dragon in Revelation 19 – 20, thus forming an overarching chiastic frame for the second half of the text.

In interpreting the language of *torment . . . for ever and ever*, we need to consider at least three things. First, the dragon, beast and false prophet are metaphors for spiritual agents and systems opposed to God, rather than human agents. Second, the theme throughout these judgment chapters (from Rev. 17 onwards) has been the principle of *lex talionis* and the justice of God's judgments, so the punishment is more severe for the agencies of deception than for those who were deceived. Third, the primary significance of the lake of fire and sulphur, going right back to its origins in the Old Testament, is destruction rather than continual torture (see comment on 14:11). The most remarkable thing about the destruction of Satan is that John goes on to offer us a vision of a new world not only where there is no sin or evil, but where even the possibility of evil is eradicated.

Theology

Given the pervasive symbolism of John's use of numbers, there is no reason to take the thousand years of the millennium as designating a literal time span, particularly given the significance of cubed numbers elsewhere. There is a strong connection between the events of the millennium and the initial victory of Christ as it is depicted in Revelation 12. But key details of the reign of the martyrs do not

---

4. Characteristically of John, each mention takes a slightly different form: 'lake of fire and burning sulphur', 19:20; 'lake of fire and sulphur', 20:10; 'lake of fire', 20:14, 15; 'lake of burning fire and sulphur', 21:8 (AT).

match the time between Jesus' exaltation and his return, which in Revelation 13 is characterized as a time of the power of the dragon and the beast (as well as of protection from God of his people), and not as a time of the binding of Satan's power, even if that is experienced in anticipation of the eventual triumph of God and the lamb over the forces of evil. The beginning of the millennium is also depicted as decisive, and in the narrative sequence follows Jesus' return to defeat the beast and the false prophet, which in turn follows the fall of 'Babylon', so it cannot easily relate to any period within history. The use of the eschatological visions of Ezekiel 38 – 39 in Revelation 19 – 20 holds the whole sequence together, pointing to each dimension of God's victory being rooted in the faithful sacrifice of Jesus as the lamb who was slain. Just as the primeval and cosmic opponent of God (Rev. 12) finds temporal allies in particular imperial systems in history (Rev. 13), so such temporal systems will be shown for what they are and dismantled (Rev. 19) within the wider story of God's defeat of the source of all evil (Rev. 20).

What does the particular vision of the millennium communicate to John's audience and to us as later readers? First, that those who were publicly humiliated in their martyrdom will be publicly vindicated. This goes even further than Jesus' saying in Matthew 10:32 and Luke 12:8, 'Whoever publicly acknowledges me I will also acknowledge before my Father in heaven', by adding acknowledgment before those on the earth. Second, such martyrs will have pride of place among the people of God in the resurrection; those who are persecuted for the sake of the kingdom will indeed receive great reward (Matt. 5:11–12). Third, the reign of the martyrs appears to take place on the earth, anticipating the fuller vision unfolded in the seventh section of this vision sequence in Revelation 21, and confirming God's commitment to the restoration of creation already expressed in the rainbow around the throne (4:3) and the 'destroying of the destroyers of the earth' (11:18, AT). Fourth, there is a clear connection between the overthrow of the forces of evil, both temporal and cosmic, and the vindication of God's people, so that the call to 'patient endurance' (1:9) and the repeated challenge to be victorious (in Rev. 2 – 3) by means of faithful witness will be worth it.

E. The final judgment before the great white throne (20:11–15)

Context

We now come to the sixth and last judgment scene of the section that begins at 19:11; the completion of this final judgment clears the way for the (re)new(al) of heaven and earth, and the descent of the New Jerusalem, in 21:1. Like the battle scene in the third vision of this sequence, it draws together and brings to completion earlier ideas, such as elements of creation fleeing from God's presence in 20:11 (cf. 6:14 and 16:20), and the importance of deeds which were first mentioned in chapters 2 and 3.

Comment

11. The sixth section of the sevenfold vision of 19:11 – 21:1 is introduced again with *And I saw* (AT). As previously, John first mentions the *great white throne* and only second the *one seated on it* (AT), emphasizing the throne as a consistent symbol of authority and power attributed to God (see comment on 20:4). It is not clear whether John understands this to be the same throne as the one in Revelation 4, which was then shared with the lamb. Although Jesus has shared in the task of judgment previously (19:11) in parallel with God, it is notable that he is not mentioned in this scene, though the shared throne is mentioned again in 22:1, 3. *White* has been the colour of purity throughout the text, but has also been used to describe a sense of radiance (cf. 19:8, 'fine linen, bright and clean', with 19:14, 'fine linen, white and clean'). The response of *earth and heaven* (AT; 'heaven' is singular in the Greek text) as they *fled from his presence* has been anticipated in two earlier sketches of the end; in 6:14, on the opening of the sixth seal, 'heaven receded like a scroll . . . and every mountain and island was removed' (AT), and in 16:20 this is developed as 'every island fled away and the mountains could not be found'. This language draws on the vision of Isaiah 34:4, but here in Revelation it makes way for the establishment of a 'new heaven and a new earth' in 21:1 following the vision of Isaiah 65:17–24. The phrase *no place was found for them* (AT) communicates their total absence, and has previously been deployed in the context of God's total victory and judgment, first describing the ejection of

Satan from heaven ('there was no longer any place found for him', 12:8, AT) and then the desolation of 'Babylon' ('never more found in you', 18:22, 23, AT), drawing on the phrase in Daniel 2:35. The awesome majesty of God is such that, in some sense, even the created world cannot stand in his presence.

12–13. The narrative here is, strictly, speaking, out of order, since John says, *And I saw the dead* in verse 12, before explaining in verse 13 that this is a result of *the sea* and *death and Hades* giving up *the dead that were in them.* The imagery here owes more to Greco-Roman ideas of death than to Old Testament notions, where Hades was the abode of all the dead and there was a general anxiety about those lost at sea who could not be properly buried.[5] For the last time, John deploys a single pair of 'gradable antonyms' in *great and small* as a merism to denote all of humanity (cf. 6:15; 11:18; 13:16; 19:5); in this climactic scene, *standing before the throne* no longer denotes enjoying the presence of, and intimacy with, God as it did earlier, but rather being accountable before his universal judgment.

The opening of *books* in which the deeds of each person were *recorded* follows the tradition of Daniel 7:10, which is also found in Jewish apocalyptic literature (*1 Enoch* 81:1–4), in some cases with separate books recording righteous acts and sins (*Apocalypse of Zephaniah* 7:1–11). This is in line with Revelation's repeated emphasis on the importance of 'deeds', in relation to both the messages to the assemblies (see particularly 2:23; 3:15) and the anticipations of future judgment (see comment on 14:13). But John reports another dynamic alongside this in the form of the *book of life*, which lists the names of all those who receive the gift of life from God. Some of the previous mentions of this book suggest a sense of pre-determination as to who will be named here ('from the foundation of the world' in 17:8, AT), but its first mention is in the context of the appeal to remain faithful (3:5), and it is twice described as the 'Lamb's book of life' (13:8; 21:27), connecting it with the costly redemption purchased by Jesus' death (see comment on 3:5; 13:8).

---

5. Note that both righteous and unrighteous are raised here, in line with Dan. 12:2, since only those martyred were raised in the 'first resurrection' of 20:5 rather than all those who have died in faith.

When mentioned on its own, it emphasizes the importance of the judgment of God as opposed to the judgment rendered by others claiming authority over our lives, and also the security of salvation, since 'I will never blot out their names' (3:5). But in this context, there is a further dynamic: the choice to face judgment based on one's own deeds, which leads to death in the 'lake of fire' (v. 15), since 'no-one living is righteous before you' (Ps. 143:2, quoted in Rom. 3:20), or to follow the lamb and have one's name in the book of life, which gives entry by God's grace to the New Jerusalem (21:27).

14–15. The remaking of the world in the removal of the old heaven and earth and the coming of the (re)new(ed) cosmos is accompanied by another radical change. *Death and Hades*, now empty of those who had died and have been raised for judgment, continue to be personified as in their mention in 6:8 and are now themselves destroyed in the *lake of fire*. This is celebrated in the following vision of a world where 'there will be no more death' (21:4), since the victory of the lamb in his sacrifice and exaltation has swallowed up death (1 Cor. 15:54, citing Isa. 25:8 which is behind the vision of 21:4). Here we see the 'death of death, and hell's destruction' which will, for those who accept the invitation to the New Jerusalem, 'land me safe on Canaan's side'.[6]

The *second death* is a term used in both Jewish and Greco-Roman literature, but with important differences. In Greco-Roman thought, the first and second deaths affect different parts of the human life, so that the first death separates the body from the mind and soul, while the second death separates the soul from the mind and offers a kind of release (Plutarch, *Moralia* 942F). But in Jewish and Christian thought, both deaths affect the whole person, since belief in bodily resurrection does not allow for separation of mind or soul from the body. The refusal to accept the offer of life leads to the finality of death, symbolized by the destructive power of fire here just as in the teaching of Jesus (Matt. 13:40, 50; Mark 9:48).

Theology
The scene of the great white throne completes the series of visions describing the final coming of Jesus from different perspectives: as

---

6. William Williams (1717–91), 'Guide Me, O Thou Great Jehovah'.

the rider on the white horse, the victor in the final great battle, the ruler with the martyrs in the messianic kingdom, and the one whose victory leads to the final destruction not only of the spiritual power of evil but even of death itself. God takes his throne to enact judgment over all the world, and through the two (sets of) books (the books of the deeds of all and the lamb's book of life) there is a double focus on grace amidst judgment, on the free offer of life in the midst of accountability for how we have lived our lives. And judgment does not have the last word, since the final vision section in Revelation 21, connected by the seventh and last 'And I saw . . .' (AT), pulls back the veil on a whole new world, described by John in a quite distinct style.

14. THE NEW JERUSALEM (21:1 – 22:5)

We are now approaching the pinnacle of the book, and that towards which the rhetorical dynamic of conflict and contrast has been leading. This passage is very often studied and preached on in isolation, but there are multiple allusions to, and repetitions of, what has gone before, so we cannot read this in isolation from the preceding chapters. Although in its appeal to the imagination it has extraordinary rhetorical power in its own right which has permanently shaped the Christian imagination over the centuries (think 'pearly gates'), it cannot be fully understood without the context of the previous chapters. The brightness of the city contrasts with the darkness of Babylon; every facet of it represents a fulfilment of earlier promises; the peace of the city contrasts with the earlier visions of suffering; and the vision as a whole sets out the rhetorical goal of the exhortations in the messages to Christians in the seven cities.

Despite the continuing emphasis on the different destinies of those who are faithful to the lamb and those who have been lured away by the deception of Satan and the beast, the primary focus is on the triumph of hope and the repeated message of grace and invitation – there is no gloating over the fate of the lost as we find in contemporary Jewish apocalypses. It is possible simply to be caught up in the splendour of the vision – and it is important that we give the language here its full symbolic seriousness, as there are numerous elements that simply do not make literal sense, just as there were in the opening visions of both Jesus and the heavenly throne room in Revelation 1 and 4. Are the walls of the city made of jasper or of gold (21:11, 18)? Does the angel measure the wall's width, or some other feature (21:17)? It is notable that earlier allusions to cultural realities are muted here; the only thing that can communicate effectively God's purpose for the world is the vocabulary of the story of his dealings with his people.

Once more, John's style changes from all that has gone before. Rather than recounting a vision sequence (using the previously frequent 'And I saw . . .'), John is now 'shown' different aspects of the heavenly city. It is almost as if the nature of time itself has been renewed along with the (re)new(ed) heaven and earth. As John pulls back the curtain on the climax of hope, there is a timeless quality to the symbolic description, similar to the language that Tolkien uses in *The Lord of the Rings*: 'The grey rain curtain of this world is pulled back, and all turns to silver glass. And then you see it – white shores, and beyond them a far green country under a swift sunrise.'[1]

In reading this kind of metaphorical poetry, we need to continue to focus on understanding the tenor carried by these metaphorical terms – what they *evoke* rather than what they *refer* to.

A. The appearance of the holy city (21:1–8)

Context
The first five verses of the opening of this new, final vision have a chiastic structure to them, and are followed by the first declarations in the whole book from God himself:

---

1. In Peter Jackson's film trilogy, these words are spoken by Gandalf to Pippin during the final siege of Minas Tirith. But in the book, they form part of a dream that Frodo has (Book 1, ch. 8) while in the house of Tom Bombadil, and which he then recalls on the last page of the book as he sails with Gandalf and the elves away from the Grey Havens to the Undying Lands.

A. *New* heaven and new earth (v. 1a)
   B. *No longer* any sea (v. 1b)
      C. The holy *city* (v. 2a)
      C.' God's *dwelling-place* (v. 3)
   B.' *No longer* death or mourning or crying or pain (v. 4)
A.' I make all thing *new* (v. 5)

This makes the city itself the central focus of these opening verses, leading into its detailed description in the next section.

Comment

1. John introduces this final section of his vision report with his last use of *And I saw* (AT). This makes this section the last of the series of seven that began in 19:11, but also signals a change of style as he does not use the term again as a marker of the sections within this vision (the word order is different in v. 2 so the phrase is not repeated). The coming of a *new heaven and a new earth* fulfils the expectation of Isaiah 65:17, itself an expression of the longing that God will deliver his people not just from sin and oppression but from the very possibility of these things. Within the narrative of Revelation, though, this occurs because *the first heaven and the first earth had passed away*, having fled from the presence of the one seated on the great white throne. We will find in these two chapters a drawing together of narrative ideas in Revelation and theological themes from across the Old Testament. The *sea* is sometimes seen in neutral terms as part of God's creation (as in 5:13 and 7:1), but at other times in Revelation draws on negative Old Testament understandings of the sea as a threatening and unruly realm, characterized as 'the deep' (so connected to 'the Abyss'), and the source of evil forces. It is used in this sense in Daniel 7:2–3, probably symbolizing the peoples of the world, and this is taken up in 13:1 when the first beast emerges 'from the sea' (AT). In the new creation there is *no longer* any sea; there are no parts of the renewed cosmos which defy and resist God's rule and which can be the sources of evil and opposition to him or to his people.

2. In contrast to his language elsewhere, John starts his sentence with the thing he sees, emphasizing that and avoiding the use of his introductory phrase 'And I saw'. The *Holy City* is a standard phrase

for the city of Jerusalem (Matt. 4:5; 27:53, drawing on Isa. 52:1) as
a reflection of the presence of the temple, the dwelling-place of
God on earth. But it has been used earlier in Revelation to signify
the people of God (the 'saints' or 'holy ones') as they experience
oppression in the forty-two months of their wilderness wanderings
between the exaltation of Jesus and his return ('The Gentiles will
trample it . . .', 11:2, AT). Different features of the report that follows
will emphasize both aspects, of the city as the dwelling-place of
God and the dwelling-place of God's people. The direction of travel,
with the city *coming down out of heaven*, is in line with the rest of Revelation (see comment on 11:15) and with other expressions of New
Testament eschatology, which does not envisage the saved leaving
the earth to be with God in heaven, so much as sleeping in death
and awaiting the bodily resurrection at the return of Jesus, and it
matches the desire expressed in the Lord's Prayer: 'your kingdom
come . . . on earth as it is in heaven'. Descriptions of the dead in
the presence of God (as in 6:9–11) need to be read in the light of the
understanding that all those following the lamb are, in some sense,
already citizens of heaven (see comment on 14:4), expressed by Paul
in Ephesians 2:6 as being already 'seated with Christ in the heavenly
realms' (AT).[2] That the city comes down *from God* reiterates the claim
that the kingdom comes by God's sovereignty and is something 'not
made by human hands' (Dan. 2:34, AT).

In the anticipation of this vision in 19:7, it is the *bride* who has
prepared herself, though elsewhere preparation is something that is
accomplished by God (12:6). The bride is *beautifully adorned* (AT;
using the word *kosmeō* from which we get 'cosmetics'), which is
expounded in two directions. As the vision report unfolds, using the

---

2. Even the 'rapture' proof text 1 Thess. 4:13–17 clearly envisages the
   bodily resurrection of the dead ('those who have fallen asleep') prior
   to those still alive 'meet[ing] the Lord in the air'. Jesus is coming to the
   earth, and Paul's assumption is that it is we, not Jesus, who will change
   direction so that we accompany him as he assumes his earthly throne,
   drawing on the metaphor of the emperor returning to visit one of his
   cities, with the city elders coming out to greet him and accompany him
   into the city as he takes up his rightful authority.

metaphor of the people of God as the city, John describes the dazzling adornment of gold and precious jewels. But previous use of the personal metaphor of the people of God as the bride in 19:7–8 identifies the adornment of her fine clothing as 'the righteous acts of God's people', which connects this vision to the earlier, less-developed nuptial imagery of 14:4–5. The personal adornment and the jewels of the city are neatly connected by the background text of Isaiah 61:10, where the 'bride adorns herself with . . . jewels'. This kind of nuptial imagery, with the Messiah as bridegroom and the people of God as his bride, is present in the Gospels (Matt. 9:15; 25:1–2; Luke 5:34; John 3:29) as well as in Paul (2 Cor. 11:2).

3. For the last time in Revelation, what John sees is complemented by what he *hear[s]*, just as he has previously seen and heard things that mutually interpret one another (as in 1:12; 7:4, 9) or at other times records an extended account of what he hears without seeing anything (as in Rev. 17 – 18). John has twice before heard *a [loud] voice from the throne*, at 16:17 and 19:5, and on both occasions it has been in relation to the End and made its pronouncement with authority. This voice (as with the 'voice from heaven') is closely related to the voice of God himself (see comment on 18:4), and in verse 5 the 'one seated on the throne' (AT) speaks for the first time, and does so in parallel with this voice.

John has previously used the interjection *Behold!* (AT) to draw attention to the importance of what follows. The *dwelling of God* (AT) is the *skēnē* (meaning 'tent', from which we get 'scene', referring to the painted backdrop of tent material used in theatres), which is loaded with theological significance. It alludes to the 'tent of meeting' where God's presence dwelt with his people as they journeyed through the wilderness (Exod. 27:21; see comment on 15:5), as well as to John's use of this term at the beginning of his Gospel to express the significance of the coming of Jesus in his incarnation ('The Word became flesh, and dwelt [*skēnoō*] among us', John 1:14, AT). Within Revelation, the term (together with its cognate *skēnoō*, 'to dwell') describes God's protective presence over those who are faithful to him (7:15), as well as the people of God who (spiritually speaking) reside before the throne (12:12; 13:6). The coming of God's dwelling-place to earth means the end of the separation between the earthly and the heavenly (expressed in the binary of

12:12 between the two realms) following the elimination of all that is unholy by means of the victory, judgment and destruction of evil described in Revelation 18 – 20.

God's close presence with his people is emphasized by the phrase *God himself will be with them*, later expanded as 'see[ing] his face' in 22:4. But this interjects between two halves of the Old Testament covenant formula: 'they will be my peoples ... and I will be their God'.[3] The formula summarizes God's covenant relationship with his people from the time of the exodus, but is expressed by the later prophets as their hope for the renewal of the covenant in the future (Jer. 32:38; Ezek. 37:27) when the people are purified and live in holy obedience, are restored to their homeland, and God's dwelling-place is established with them for ever. It is striking that, whereas the Old Testament uses the singular 'people', John uses the plural 'peoples', signifying the overflow of grace in the inclusion of those from 'every nation, tribe, people and language' (7:9) in the renewed covenant community. This fulfils the (sometimes muted) note in Old Testament prophetic expectation that sees all the nations coming to worship God in Zion (see Ps. 86:9; Isa. 2:3; 66:20; Mic. 4:2). The coming of the New Jerusalem is the final fulfilment of the Old Testament longings of God's people, though sometimes in surprising ways.

4. The close presence of God with his people continues in the affirmation that *he will wipe away every tear* (AT), an idea that derives from the vision of the eschatological banquet in Isaiah 25:8. John reverses Isaiah's order by following his second affirmation with the previous one, that *death* (the shroud that enfolds all peoples in Isa. 25:7) *will be no longer* (AT), or will be 'swallowed up in victory' as Paul notes in 1 Corinthians 15:54, following Isaiah 25:8 more closely.

---

3. There is ambiguity about the final clause 'I will be their God' in the manuscript evidence, with good witnesses both including and excluding it. Against its originality is the possibility that it might have been added by a scribe in order to complete the allusion to the covenant formula; in favour of inclusion is the fact that the phrase is written in a style uncharacteristic of John (with 'God' coming after 'their' uniquely in the book) which makes it the harder reading, which is to be preferred.

John then expands the banishment of death to include the hope, expressed in Isaiah 35:10 and 51:11, that *mourning and crying and pain* (AT) will also be no more. Despite the continuities between the first creation and what is now coming into being, there is also radical discontinuity, since *the first things have passed away* (AT). This echoes the experience of those who have passed from the kingdom of darkness to the kingdom of light, in whom there is 'new creation – the old has gone and the new has come' (2 Cor. 5:17, AT), and completes what they have begun to know as a foretaste of what is to come.

5. *The one seated on the throne* (AT) is God. Remarkably, this is the first direct speech from God since 1:8, where he declared his title as the 'Alpha and the Omega'. In all the intervening chapters, in the confusion and complexity of the world and the shadow of judgment as well as deliverance, God's voice and actions have been communicated by circumlocution and the use of intermediary agents. But the full revelation of the final redemption of the world calls forth God's direct speech in unambiguous terms. God's *making everything new* is entirely consistent with his character as Creator, making the world new *ex nihilo* in the beginning, and continually seeking to do a new thing in the redemption of his people, whether that is forming his people anew in the exodus or doing 'a new thing' in their return and restoration from exile (Isa. 43:19). The new thing God will do is the same new thing he has been continually doing since the beginning of time.

The command to *write* is introduced with a change of tense ('the one seated on the throne *said* . . . Then he *says* . . .', AT), suggesting that this is a parenthetical comment before God's speech continues in the next verse. This is the last of twelve times that John is commanded to write – in relation to the book as a whole in 1:11 and 1:19, seven times in the messages in Revelation 2 – 3, and twice of statements in 14:13 and 19:9. Since God's speech continues, the command here is similar to those in Revelation 1, referring to the whole of the message rather than to the specific saying alone, but mention of the command draws attention to it. Old Testament prophets are usually commanded to 'Go and say . . .' (Isa. 6:9; Jer. 2:2; Ezek. 3:4), suggesting that the message given at a particular time and place has wider relevance only later; the command for John to 'write' adds wider significance from the beginning, so that John is adding to 'what it written', that is, the Scriptures. The words John is given are *trustworthy* [or 'faithful', *pistos*] *and true* here and in 22:6 (cf. 19:9) and match the one with whom they originate, both Jesus (the faithful and true witness, 3:14; 19:11) and God ('holy and true', 6:10; 'just and true', 15:3; 16:7).

6. The declaration *It is done!* (AT) fulfils the anticipation of the End in the seventh bowl of 16:17. Although there is a general sense of echoing the triumphant cry of Jesus on the cross in John 19:30, the vocabulary is different here and matches the Greek of the creation account in Genesis 1, when God speaks the creation into existence and 'it was so' (Gen. 1:6–7, 9, and elsewhere). The two titles *Alpha and O* (AT; the first is spelt out, but the second is just the letter in the text) and *Beginning and the End* express similar ideas drawn from Greco-Roman texts and the Old Testament. The Greek translation of God's name YHWH (the Tetragrammaton) was spelt IAO (see comment on 1:8), and this was of interest because the Greek chief of gods, Zeus, was said to hold the beginning, middle and end of all things (in Plato and Plutarch). God is the 'first and the last' in Isaiah 41:4; 44:6; 48:12 in contrast to other powers, and has been speaking and acting 'from the beginning' (Isa. 40:21; 41:26). This double title is part of the convergence of the identity of God with that of Jesus, who is the 'ruler' or 'beginning' (the same word *archē*) of creation in 3:14, and who also claims the similar triple title in 22:13.

The offer to *the thirsty* to drink *freely* (AT) echoes both the invitation of God in Isaiah 55:1–3 and that of Jesus in John 7:37 (and cf. John 4:15; 6:35), as well as the anticipation in Revelation 7:17. In these contexts it particularly relates to those among the people of God who long for spiritual refreshing, but as a metaphor it naturally extends to all who are weary of life, not least in the light of Revelation's vision of cosmic rather than national salvation for God's people. The nature of this offer both as a free gift of grace and a universal invitation is emphasized in its repetition in 22:17; Old Testament use suggests that this living water is not merely something God gives (such as wise teaching, the 'spring [or 'fountain'] of life' in Prov. 10:11 and elsewhere) but the gift of God himself (Jer. 2:13; 17:13). In the foretaste of the new creation for believers, the Spirit is that 'living water' (John 7:38) as the presence of God which is now realized in all its fullness.

7. The invitation is freely given, but it needs to be received, and that reception is marked by the patient endurance (1:9) and faithfulness which are part of the *conquering* (AT) or 'being victorious' which was the repeated challenge and invitation at the end of each of the seven messages in Revelation 2 − 3. The offer of grace always needs a response of obedience. The language of *inherit[ing]* is common in the New Testament in relation to the kingdom of God (Matt. 25:34; 1 Cor. 6:9; Gal. 5:21), usually with a strong eschatological focus (1 Cor. 15:50; 1 Pet. 1:4), though it is not used other than here in Revelation. For those who do effectively receive this inheritance, the promise made in general terms is now expressed directly and personally: *I will be his [or her] God* (AT). Although the explicit term 'Father' is reserved in Revelation for the relationship of God to Jesus (1:6; 2:27; 3:5, 21; 14:1), other parts of the New Testament see this relationship as applying to all those who are in Christ, and Jesus teaches us to address God as 'Father' (Matt. 6:9), something the Spirit nurtures in us (Rom. 8:15). This is clearly implied here by those who conquer becoming *my sons* (AT); the more common English translations of 'my children' or 'my sons and daughters' miss the cultural significance by which it is sons who inherit, so believers of either sex are inheriting 'sons' (Rom. 8:17).

8. If John's vision report holds in tension the free offer and the need to respond, it also constantly holds in tension the acceptance of the offer with the consequences of rejecting the 'free gift of the offer of [the water of] life' (22:17, AT) which is the *second death* in the *lake of burning fire and sulphur* (AT). Without the gift from God, life itself is extinguished; there is no sense here that human beings (or their 'souls') are inherently immortal. The repetition of this term from 20:14−15 indicates how this first section of Revelation 21 functions as a completion of the previous section as well as the introduction to the detailed description of the New Jerusalem. Those rejecting life are characterized in the second 'vice list' of the three in the book, the first coming at the end of the series of trumpets describing those who did not repent, there listed as nouns describing the vice, while in 21:8 and 22:15 it is kinds of people who are named (see table 10 overleaf).

Table 10: The vice lists of chapters 9, 21 and 22

9:20–21	21:8	22:15
	cowardice	
	faithlessness	
	abominations	
idolatry	idolatry	idolatry
murder	murder	murder
magic	magic	magic
sexual immorality	sexual immorality	sexual immorality
theft		
	liars	liars

The second half of the list is close to the other two, and like them includes things forbidden in the Ten Commandments (see comment on 9:20–21), continuing John's emphasis on the importance of keeping 'the commandments of God' (AT; 12:17; 14:12). Together they offer a critique of the failings of the empire, with its false worship, violence and superstition, sexual immorality (probably in a literal rather than metaphorical sense; see comment on 2:20) and deceit, the last of these betraying the influence of Satan, the 'deceiver of the nations' (see comment on 12:9; 20:10). But the first half of this list emphasizes the particular issues that were at stake for John's audience. Cowardice was generally thought to be a moral failing, but here the connotation is the lack of courage to stand up against the social pressures to conform to contemporary culture and loyalties. In a similar way, lack of *faith* (AT; *pistos*) was seen as a general moral failing, but here contrasts with the 'faith of Jesus' and the faith exemplified in 'my faithful witness Antipas' (2:13, AT). In Old Testament context, *abominations* (AT) includes both sexual immorality (Lev. 18:22–29) and idolatry.

Theology

The opening of this extraordinary vision is already drawing many of the themes from earlier in the book to their (theo)logical conclusion. The binaries of good and evil are drawing to a close, and the distance between God and humanity, opened up by the disobedience in the Garden of Eden, is finally being ended by the promise of God's intimate and infinite presence. Yet key themes from earlier in the book cannot be left behind: the often costly response that is needed to accept the invitation to receive the free and gracious gift of life, and the greater ultimate cost of rejecting it altogether. The vision will eventually complete the urgent rhetorical challenge that John has set out from the very beginning to those in the assemblies of the seven cities (and with them, all Christians contemporary with John and then all those sharing with him the in-between times until Jesus' return): the decision to choose between life and death.

B. The description of the holy city (21:9–21)

Context
The second part of this grand final vision involves a shift in focus; from the sequence of sweeping statements that John hears in the opening verses, we zoom in on the details of the city itself that John is shown by an accompanying angel. The dimensions and decorations of the city pick up on ideas from earlier in the book, but the main impact of John's descriptions is to create the striking contrast between the gracious glory of this city and the sordid spectacle of Babylon in chapters 17 and 18.

Comment
9. John continues to avoid his previous language of 'and I saw' and instead is accompanied by an angelic guide, *one of the seven angels who had the seven bowls*. The opening wording is identical to that of 17:1 (though it is not clear whether or not this is the same one of the seven), thus making the vision of the city as the pure bride a contrasting parallel to the city of 'Babylon' as a great prostitute. Characteristically, John includes the variation giving the detail of the bowls as *full of the seven last plagues*, thus continuing the connection between the judgment of evil and the redemption of the saints as two sides of the same coin – God's plan to make all things new. The invitation to *Come!* (AT) has echoes of the first invitation John received to enter through the door into heaven (4:1), though in fact the wording is different. But the parallel with 17:1 continues, so this angel shows John the *bride*, not the prostitute, who is the *wife of the Lamb*, not the one committing adultery with the nations (the 'many waters').

10. In terms of the narrative geography, John does not need to be *carried . . . away* since he has already seen the *Holy City, Jerusalem, coming down out of heaven from God* in verse 2. It is striking how, in a compact text packed with such a dazzling variety of theological and cultural ideas, John still finds space for such repetition, making the city itself the emphatic centre of his vision, though again with slight variation, omitting the adjective 'new' included previously. Being carried away offers a strong parallel to the experience of Ezekiel (Ezek. 8:3; 11:1, 24), whose visions have already extensively shaped John's vision report over the last three chapters, and will continue to do so in the contrast of the city with Ezekiel's vision of the restored temple (see comment on 21:22). The parallel with the vision of 'Babylon' continues with John being carried away *in the Spirit* (cf. 17:3), a phrase that has already marked the beginning of new vision experiences at 1:10 and 4:2. The *mountain great and high* fulfils the hope that 'the mountain of the LORD's temple will be . . . highest of the mountains' (Isa. 2:2; cf. Ps. 48:2), which is what draws the nations to it (see comment on 21:3) – and it contrasts with the claim of Rome (like the planned tower of Babel) that its hills 'reached to the heavens' (see comment on 18:5).

11. That the city *shone* immediately contrasts it with the darkness of the desolate 'Babylon' in 18:23 ('The light of a lamp will never shine in you again'). The light of the *glory of God* is developed more fully in the next section at 21:23, and is in fulfilment of the hope of Zechariah 2:1–5, a vision which clearly shapes John's language here, that God 'will be [the] glory within' the restored Jerusalem. That the dwelling-place of God's people should be radiant with the glory of God reflects the convergence of the character of God with the character of his people, so that (for example) Jesus is the light of the world (John 8:12), but his people are also the light of the world (Matt. 5:14). Up until now, *very precious jewel[s]* have been mentioned only in relation to the adornment of 'Babylon' (17:4), which she has by virtue of the international commerce she commands (18:12) but which symbolize the indulgence that brings judgment (18:16). Here, by contrast, they symbolize the value and permanence of the presence of God. *Jasper* had characterized the appearance of God in the opening vision of heavenly worship (4:3), and the clarity of *crystal* is a reminder of the sea of glass before the throne. The previous detail of the earthly temple in its heavenly counterpart is now displaced as the heavenly presence of God is established on earth.

12–14. Just as John had earlier given the key features of the heavenly throne room/temple and then added further detail as his vision report unfolded, so he now continues to describe the key features of the city, to which he then adds greater detail in the following verses. The walls of a city in the ancient world both defined its boundaries and provided security, so that cities in the Roman Empire were commonly overcrowded and unsanitary, and local farmers would also come inside the walls for protection at times of threat. The new Jerusalem has *great, high wall[s]* (whose height is as yet unspecified) offering complete security and protection. Large cities sometimes had *three gates* in one wall, the gates being the key points of entry for citizens, visitors and trade, but the holy city has three on every side, *twelve* in all. Where the empire had been threatened by Parthians from the east (see comment on 6:2; 9:14; 16:12) and barbarians from the north (see comment on 9:7), no such anxiety now exists since all the forces of evil have been destroyed. The presence of *angels* at the twelve gates is usually overlooked in artistic renditions of John's vision report; angels have often acted as messengers in the text, but their primary function has been to exercise God's will with his authority, and here it is presumably to guard the gates.

The *names of the twelve tribes of Israel* on the gates appear to designate who may enter, following the vision of Ezekiel 48:30–35 (though with the sides listed in a different order); the gates are open to welcome the people of God as they have been described in 7:4, which we know from 7:9 to be those without number from 'every nation, tribe, people and language'. The *twelve foundations* have inscribed on them the *names of the twelve apostles*, which cannot simply designate the individuals concerned, not least because 'no-one can lay any foundation other than the one already laid, which is Jesus Christ' (1 Cor. 3:11, though cf. Eph. 2:20). They stand instead for the apostolic message of Jesus as the fulfilment of his people's longings and the one who 'has freed us from our sins by his blood' (1:5), which is made clear by their designation as apostles *of the*

Lamb.[4] It is often suggested that the names of the tribes and the names of the apostles represent the first-covenant and the second-covenant peoples of God respectively, or Jews and Gentiles, but this cannot be the case, not least because Gentiles are clearly included in the 'twelve tribes' of 7:4, and because the apostles are themselves Jewish. Rather, the names together simply designate the fullness of God's covenant people won through the death and exaltation of Jesus.

15–17. The *angel* (the same one mentioned in 21:9) has a *measuring rod* and measures the city as John himself had been instructed to do in 11:1, both following the pattern of Ezekiel's extended vision of the restored temple (particularly Ezek. 40:5 – 42:20; see also Zech. 2:1–2). But where John has measured a temple whose outer courts were being trampled while the inner court was safe – the people of God outwardly suffering pressure and opposition though guarded by God – now the angel measures the whole city, which turns out to be composed entirely of the Holy of Holies. He measures with a *rod of gold* to signify how precious is the city he is measuring. Like the temple in Ezekiel's vision (Ezek. 48:35), the city is *laid out like a square*, but is of enormous proportions – just under 1,400 miles (2,250 km) in each direction, compared with Ezekiel's 1.25 miles (2 km) for the temple. If this city were centred in Patmos, from where John is writing, it would extend all the way to Jerusalem in the east and to Rome in the west, covering the central and eastern Mediterranean; its northern edge would go beyond the Roman Empire's northern border, and its southern edge reach down into Egypt and the empire's border in the south. It would easily be large enough to accommodate the population of the Roman world in John's day with room to spare.

---

4. We should note that the language of the church being 'apostolic' refers to the sense of both apostle as messenger and apostle as the bearer of a particular message. We are apostolic when we are sent to proclaim the message of the good news of Jesus, but also when we are faithful to the message that the apostles shared, which is now inscribed in the NT documents, both Gospels and letters.

The area is 144,000,000 stadia, which is 1,000 x 144,000, the latter being the number of the saints counted in Revelation 7 and mentioned again on Zion in Revelation 14. The figure *144* occurs again in the *measurement* of the *wall*. John does not specify whether this is the height or the thickness of the wall, but it must be the latter, since the height of the wall is presumably the height of the city, that is, 12,000 stadia. This city truly reaches to the heavens, in a way that Rome (as 'Babylon') and the tower of Babel (Gen. 11:1–9) could never do. What human effort could never achieve, God gives as a gift to his people. It being *as wide and high as it is long* makes it a perfect cube, the shape of the Holy of Holies in the earthly temple (1 Kgs 6:20) – the place of God's holy presence, as John explores in verse 22. The enormous size of the city suggests holiness on a cosmic scale. John explains that the *cubit* is the *measure of a human, which is the measure of an angel* (AT). Using the same *gematria* calculation as for the number of the beast in 666 (transliterating the Greek term into Hebrew letters and adding their value), the word 'angel' does indeed come to 144 (see comment on 13:18). Where the measure of humanity under the tyranny of the beast's rule had been debased, now it has been lifted to that of the angels.

18–21. Exactly which part of the city is made of what is not always clear in John's vision report, but this matters less than the symbolic significance of the different elements. *Jasper* has already been mentioned (v. 11), and will feature again as decorating the foundations; it characterized the appearance of God in 4:3 (along with carnelian, another of the foundation gems), and though there are different varieties, John is probably referring to one that is fiery red in colour (see comment on 4:3). *Glass* was difficult to make well before the advent of modern methods where it is floated on molten metal, and was hard to make pure – even the slightest impurity was visible, so clear glass was rare and expensive. Despite the walls being of jasper, the city as a whole is made of *gold*. This is the material of the seven lampstands, and is consistently used in Revelation as the colour of spiritual power and majesty, as well as of the heavenly realm. As a *gold* cube, the city matches even more closely the Holy of Holies, whose walls were lined with gold.

John at first reports that the *foundations . . . were decorated with every kind of precious stone*, using the language of adornment of the bride

in the nuptial imagery of verse 2, and fulfilling the promise of Isaiah
54:11–12. Decoration of buildings would usually be applied to the
upper, more visible portions; it is adornment of quite a different
order when even the foundations have precious stones. But John
then describes the foundations as if they are each a giant gemstone.
The list of gems closely matches two lists of gems in the Old
Testament.[5] The first is the list of gems which represent the twelve
tribes on the 'ephod' or breastplate of Aaron as high priest and have
their names inscribed on them (Exod. 28:15–21), which functions
as a way of bringing the people of God into his presence (Exod.
28:29). The city is the home of the priestly people of God, fulfilling
the achievement of Jesus' death to make for God a 'kingdom and
priests to serve him for ever' (1:6, AT). The connection between
the names of the tribes and the gems which have the names of the
apostles (v. 14) confirms the observation that we should not see
them as representing two parts of the people of God, but one
people identified in two related ways (see comment on v. 14). The
second list of gems comes in Ezekiel 28:13, part of the oracle
against the king of Tyre which has already been alluded to in 16:20
(where the islands flee) and in 18:12–13 (the list of cargoes). Ezekiel
lists the king of Tyre's adornment 'in the garden of Eden' (AT),
which includes nine of the twelve gems from the ephod and
mysteriously also has them 'mounted in gold' (AT). So, in addition
to the bridal imagery and the connections with priesthood, the list
of gems connects the city with the splendour of creation at the very
beginning.

The mention of *pearls* as gates completes the contrast of the
bride/city with the threefold depiction of 'Babylon' as 'glittering
with gold, precious stones and pearls' in 17:4. Pearls were judged to
be more precious than gold in Roman society and valued only a little
less than diamonds (see comment on 18:12). Popular appropriation

---

5. Where there are slight differences between the lists, it is not clear whether
these are of significance; since there are difficulties in translating from
the Hebrew terms to Greek, it is not always clear exactly which gem
(in modern classifications) is being referred to. The importance of the
list is more in its overall impact than in its detail.

of the idea of 'pearly gates' often imagines actual gates adorned with pearls, but in John's vision report it is the gateways (rather than the gates themselves) which are giant pearls; holes were bored in pearls in order to use them in jewellery, and it is through such a hole in the pearl-gate that people can enter the city.[6] Roman cities were often laid out on a foursquare plan, based on the plan of army camps, and usually had one *great street* running down the centre (possibly with another running at right angles to it). The street was often muddy through frequent use, though in wealthy cities it would be *paved* (AT). The magnificence of this holy city is such that it uses the most precious material, *gold*, for the most mundane of tasks: to pave its streets. John does not appear to be interested in the practical detail here (what about the other streets?), but the image of a city 'whose streets are paved with gold' must have gripped the imagination of John's audience, just as it has done for every generation of readers up till the present day.

Theology
As John's report of what he has seen unfolds, the contrasts and connections with earlier parts of his vision report become more muted, especially those connected with judgment, but continue to be present. The details of the bride-city offer a clear contrast with the depiction of 'Babylon' earlier, but John is content to allow us to notice these for ourselves, rather than draw attention to them.

He does his theology through numbers, structures and lists as he has done at key points earlier in the text, especially in Revelation 7 − 13. This extraordinary (and, literally speaking, impossible) giant cube-city is a new Holy of Holies, not one that is a single part of a single temple in a single city in a single country in the world, but encompassing the world itself of John's day. This is the holy presence of God on a truly cosmic scale. As with his first vision of heavenly worship in Revelation 4, the exact details of what John sees are impossible to make sense of − but their multiple significance is to be found in his reuse of Old Testament imagery. This city is not just

---

6. John does not appear to make any connection here with the parable
   of the kingdom as a priceless pearl in Matt. 13:45−46.

the counterpoint to all failed human aspiration to transcendence and significance (to 'make a name for ourselves', Gen. 11:4), but fulfils the specific hope of the people of God as they longed to see themselves returned home from exile and to see God's name glorified once more.

The city that shines with the glory of God is (with its walls reaching to the skies) the ultimate place of security and peace. Its splendour and magnificence are without compare, dwarfing all human measures of extravagance. It is the home for the beautifully adorned bride of the lamb; it is the home of the priestly people of God; it is the place where the created order is restored to its original splendour.

C. The glory of the holy city (21:22–27)

Context
The opening section of chapter 21 functioned both to close off the previous judgment visions as well as to introduce the city as the subject of this new vision section, and the next set of verses offered an exercise in 'theology through architectural detail'. In this last section of Revelation 21, the style and tone shift significantly, focusing on the function and importance of the city and the place in it of God and the lamb. As with other sections in Revelation, the tenses of verbs here are mixed ('I did not see . . . , God . . . and the Lamb are . . .'). This has the effect on the reader or hearer of giving a sense of immediacy to the vision, and in this sense makes it a future reality that shapes present decisions – though mostly the tenses simply reflect John's vivid description.

Comment
22. Given the dependence of John's vision report on Old Testament texts of hope for the restoration of Israel and Jerusalem, and in particular his progressive dependence on Ezekiel's series of visions which culminated in an extended depiction of the restored temple, what John says here comes as a shock, emphasized by his word order: *And a temple I did not see in it* (AT). Here, John comes close to using his favourite 'And I saw' formula, and it serves to highlight the central importance of what is missing. There is no need

for one special place of encounter with God through a mediatorial priestly caste, because *the Lord God Almighty and the Lamb is its temple* (AT). The verb here is singular; on some occasions this could prioritize the first of the two subjects, but here it functions to identify the two as one, just as the lamb has shared the throne with the one seated on it in Revelation 5, and just as the kingdom and the reign of God and the lamb are treated as singular in 11:15 (see comment there). This is the last of the seven occurrences of the phrase 'Lord God Almighty' (including 1:8), which is used nowhere else in the New Testament as a title for God and emphasizes God's sole sovereignty. Jesus is identified as the *temple*, the tabernacling presence of God, within the Johannine tradition (John 1:14; 2:19–21), but it is highly unusual to talk of God himself as the temple, and again shows the close identification that John makes between God and the lamb.

23. John continues his central focus on *the city* by again bringing it to the beginning of the sentence. He does not precisely say that in this (re)new(ed) cosmos there is no *sun or . . . moon*, simply that the city *does not need* them, because it has an alternative source of illumination. The *glory of God* which John mentioned earlier (21:11) is in a chiastic parallel with the *Lamb* as its *lamp* (the shape is lost in most English translations that rearrange the word order):

> the glory of God
>   is its light
>   and its lamp
> is the lamb

This puts the lamb in a direct parallel with the glory of God; his holiness, grace and invitation of forgiveness and new life are made manifest in the sacrifice and exaltation of Jesus. The term for *lamp* (*lychnos*) is closely related to the term for 'lampstand' (*lychnia*) which comes seven times in the book, suggesting a close relationship between Jesus and his people, whether historically as the seven assemblies of Revelation 1 – 3, or theologically as the two witnesses exercising their prophetic priestly testimony like Moses and Elijah (11:4).

24–27. John's next statement offers one of the most important and challenging statements in the whole of the text. In the narrative so far, *the nations* have participated to an extent in the faithful people of God, in that they feature in every one of the seven occurrences of the fourfold phrase 'people, tribe, nation and language' (or similar) coming at 5:9; 7:9; 10:11; 11:9; 13:7; 14:6; 17:15, which describes the diversity of those redeemed by the blood of the lamb (see comment on 5:9; 7:9). And yet, taken as a whole, the nations seem to be constantly opposed to God and his people. They trample the holy city (11:2); they are angry with God (11:18); they were seduced by the great prostitute (14:8; 18:3) and deceived by the magical spells of her prosperity (18:23); they are deceived by Satan and make war with the lamb in the final battle (19:15; 20:8). Nevertheless, from the beginning, Jesus is the rightful Lord over them (1:5; 12:5) and shares his authority with his followers (2:26), and God is 'King of the nations' (15:3). The same is true of the *kings of the earth*. They hide from the wrath of the lamb (6:15); they are ruled by the prostitute who is the great city (17:18) and 'commit adultery' with her (17:2; 18:3); and they also make war on the rider on the white horse (19:19). Yet they too are subject to the rule of Jesus from the beginning (1:5), and the vision of the holy city makes true *de facto* on the earth what has always been true *de jure* in the economy of God.

The meaning of *there [being] no night there* needs to be read in the context of the Pauline and (in particular) Johannine symbolic significance given to 'night'. Though we might think that night is a positive image, associated with rest and relaxation, for John and Paul 'night' signifies the time of darkness and sin, when wicked people can perpetrate their evil plans (see especially John 13:30; cf. Rom. 13:12; 1 Thess. 5:5). More generally in first-century culture, night was a time of danger; travellers would need to ensure that they were inside the city they were aiming to reach, so that the *gates* would be *shut* behind them, protecting them from brigands. In the holy city there is neither sin nor danger – no night-time when the gates must be shut for protection and security. The presence of God and the lamb is security enough.

Contrary to what we might be tempted to think by the language of the clear distinction between the faithful and the faithless, between those sealed with the mark of God and those who receive the mark of the beast, God in Jesus wins his victory not simply by disposing of those who oppose him, but in some mysterious way by winning them over. The nations *walk by [the] light* of the city, the kings of the earth *bring their splendour into it* and (repeated for emphasis) the nations also bring their *glory and honour* into it. John is once again reminding us to take his vision report with its full symbolic seriousness; in the light of the outcome of the last battle in Revelation 19, this does not make 'literal' sense, even within the narrative world of the text. Lest we are drawn to think that Revelation has some kind of universalist vision of salvation, John emphasizes the purity of the city in the very next verse. *Nothing impure will ever enter it* since the city *is* the Holy of Holies, and just as the high priest who entered the most holy space in the tabernacle and temple had to be without blemish, so the city cannot be entered by *anyone who does what is shameful or deceitful*. It seems not simply that the holiness of God and the lamb demands holiness, but that, through the sacrifice of the lamb, God effects it. As with every aspect of Revelation and its theology, it constantly and surprisingly resists any simplistic binaries that we try to impose on it in any direction; there is a clear binary between good and evil, salvation and destruction, and life and death – but how that maps onto human life prior to the final judgment and the return of Jesus is much less clear.

D. The river of the water of life and the tree of life (22:1–5)

John has described the appearing of the holy city, with its significance explained by a series of pronouncements by God. Then he has been shown the details of the city by the interpreting angel who measures its features. Next, he has expounded the glory of the city. In this fourth and last section of his concluding vision (all held within the 'And I saw' of 21:1, AT) he is shown a final set of features of the city, and draws out their significance. Although we have a chapter division at the beginning of this section, it is clearly part of the previous narrative and should be read with it; the final change (from vision to epistolary conclusion) happens at 22:6.

Comment

1. John continues to avoid his earlier 'And I saw' formula, and again refers to the actions of the guiding angel who *showed me* as he had in 21:10. (The Greek does not mention the angel, and simply says, 'And he showed me', but the angel is the only possible subject.) The *river of the water of life* provides the means by which God fulfils the offer made in 21:6, giving to all who thirst to drink from the 'spring of the water of life', signifying not just the life-giving things God provides for us, but the life of God himself (see comment on 21:6). An eschatological river flowing from or within a restored city or temple is a common feature of prophetic hope (Isa. 33:20–21), sometimes suggesting purification (Zech. 13:1) but more often suggesting the giving of life, which must be the meaning here. In a warm Mediterranean climate, where many rivers flowed only in the winter, this was a natural symbol – the rivers in Joel 3:18 contrasting with the barren deserts of surrounding countries – but the most dramatic is that of Ezekiel 47:1–12, where the river brings life to the Dead Sea so that it is full of fish like the Mediterranean.

In the Johannine tradition, this water of life is closely associated with both the outpouring of the Spirit (John 7:38) and the life springing from Jesus' death (John 19:34). John describes the river as *clear as crystal*, indicating its purity, and as closely associated with *God and . . . the Lamb* by flowing from the single *throne* that they share. Although most of the previous detail from the early visions of heaven (the altar, incense, rainbow, thrones) has been displaced by the simplicity of the holy city, the throne remains, less as an item of furniture and more as an indication of the authority of God and the lamb to reign.

2. There is some debate about whether the phrase *in the midst of the main street* (or 'square', *plateia* [AT]; see comment on 11:8) belongs with the previous sentence, so that the river flows down the street, or with the following sentence, so that it is the *tree of life* that is in the main street or square. Manuscript evidence supports the latter of these, and this provides an echo of the creation account where the tree of life is 'in the midst of the garden' (Gen. 2:9, AT). But it makes the grammar very awkward, and means that the sentence begins with 'in', which never happens elsewhere in Revelation (and sentences rarely begin with prepositions). It is more likely, then, that it is the river that flows down the main street, which is striking enough; in Roman cities, such a central river would be an open sewer – but here the river is clean and pure, and by flowing here it is accessible to all those in the city.

As noted above, the *tree of life* was planted in the middle of the Garden of Eden (Gen. 2:9–10), and access to it was lost when Adam and Eve were banished. Within the biblical tradition, the term is used as a metaphor for wisdom (Prov. 3:18) which in later Jewish tradition is found in Torah, or more generally simply as things that give life (Prov. 11:30; 13:12; 15:4). In Ezekiel's vision of the temple and its river, fruitful trees of every kind grow on both banks (Ezek. 47:7, 12), and John appears to be combining Genesis's description of (a restored) Eden with Ezekiel's vision of the restored temple by having a singular tree which is growing on *each side of the river*. It might be possible to envisage such a tree planted over the river with its roots on each bank, but John seems more concerned that we recognize the symbolism from the Old Testament than that we try to reconstruct his literal vision.[7] The trees in Ezekiel 47:12 bear fruit of 'every kind' (AT), something the tree of life does not seem to do. But like them it does *yield its fruit every month*, something highly unusual in a pre-supermarket age when most foods are only seasonally available. In the holy city, God's provision for his people is constant and endless. It was common to use *leaves* for *healing* in the ancient world; where the leaves of Ezekiel's trees were for 'healing' (presumably for the elect only), John once again expresses a more universal scope by adding *for the nations* (AT).

3–4. In this last section of John's actual vision report, there is a striking shift of tense from past and present to future; it is almost as though John has stepped out of the narrative and is addressing his audience directly about the future reality that he has seen: 'This is what it will be like.' Although the word for *curse* here (*katathema*) occurs nowhere else in the New Testament, two related words do:

---

7. I am not persuaded by commentators who suggest that the singular tree derives from the singular term in Ezekiel's vision; the phrase 'every tree' does not look very singular to me, even if it includes the word 'tree' rather than 'trees'.

anathema in Romans 9:3; 1 Corinthians 12:3; and *katara* in Galatians 3:10, 13: 'Christ redeemed us from the curse of the law by becoming a curse for us, for it is written: "Cursed is everyone who is hung on a pole."' The triple curse of Genesis 3:14–19, of enmity with nature, dominance in relationships and, in the end, death, is now banished, having been dealt with decisively by the sacrifice of the lamb, and freedom from the curse is fully realized in the holy city. There is no more death, and all have free access to the tree of life. John might also have had in mind Zechariah 14:11, which uses the language of 'curse' in relation to destruction by warfare. The holy city is at peace because all her enemies have been vanquished.

It is typical of John's narrative style for him to assume the existence of something which he then later introduces. We already knew that the *throne of God and of the Lamb* was at the centre of the city, because the river of the water of life flows from it (in v. 1), but now he tells us of it explicitly. As previously, from Revelation 5 onwards, the two persons occupy the one throne, but once again John goes further and the two are so much of a unity that he can use a singular pronoun: *his servants will serve him*. 'Servants' (or 'slaves', *douloi*) is John's regular word for the people of God as they live faithfully for him, the word occurring fourteen times in the text. John identifies himself as one (1:1), and they exercise a prophetic ministry after the pattern of Moses (10:7; 11:18; 15:3). In particular, they are sealed with the seal of God, protecting them from judgment even though they experience suffering and opposition (7:3). But here, in three assertions made in a continuous sentence (vv. 3b–4), they have a priestly role. Whereas previously the assembled company of heaven 'worship' God (*proskyneō*), here John describes God's servants as 'serv[ing]' him (*latreuō*), using the language of worship and practical service associated with the sanctuary (Exod. 3:12; Deut. 6:13) which is distinctively the role of priests (Heb. 8:5). Paul uses such language of priestly service to describe the offering of our whole lives to God (Rom. 12:1); anticipated earlier in Revelation of those who have 'washed their robes . . . in the blood of the Lamb' (7:15; see comment there), it finds its fulfilment in the holy city.

The (high) priestly images continue with the promise that *they will see his face*. Although occasional, privileged individuals are said to have seen God's face (Jacob in Gen. 32:30; the elders of Israel in

Exod. 24:11; Moses in Exod. 33:11), the most widespread conviction in Scripture is that 'no-one may see God and live'. This is in part because of sin which distances us from God's presence (Gen. 3:8; cf. Isa. 6:5 and Heb. 12:14), but also because of the majesty of God which sets God apart from humanity (Exod. 33:20–23). Yet the unmediated communion of seeing God's face remains an eschatological hope (Matt. 5:8; 1 Cor. 13:12), and in the Johannine tradition it is what Jesus effects in the atonement (John 1:18; 1 John 3:2). In the tabernacle and temple, encounter with God in the Holy of Holies was reserved for the high priest (who risked death by entering God's presence, Exod. 28:35), and the priestly prayer for God's blessing and favour is expressed in the face of God 'shin[ing]' on us and 'turn[ing] towards us' (Num. 6:24–26).

The final priestly element is expressed in their having *his name . . . on their foreheads*. Within the narrative, humanity has been divided between those who received the seal of God on their foreheads in 7:3 and those receiving the mark of the beast, which is a number of a name (13:18). It then transpires that the seal of God is also a name, but the (single) name of 'the Lamb and his Father' (14:1, AT), which signifies ownership and allegiance as well as protection. But here, as they stand before God and the lamb face to face, the name alludes to the attire of Aaron as high priest who wore, along with the ephod holding the twelve gems of the twelve tribes, a plate of gold on his turban with the name of God inscribed on it (Exod. 28:15–21, 36).

5. John repeats the observation that *there will be no more night* from 21:25. The significance there was the gates of the city (which would normally close at night) remaining open; there is nothing to fear, and all are invited to enter. The significance of the repetition here seems to be slightly different; throughout the text, night and darkness have been times of threat and judgment (6:12; 8:12; 9:2; 16:10), but these, like death, mourning, sadness and pain, have passed away. Together with the complementary emphasis that *they will not need the light of a lamp or the light of the sun*, the phrase is drawing on the hope expressed in Isaiah 60:19 for the restored city of Jerusalem – but the metaphorical nature of the language is made clear by the parallel comment: 'Your sun will never set again, and your moon will wane no more' (Isa. 60:20). This metaphor of day and night is used by Jesus in John 11:9–10, as well as by Paul in 1 Thessalonians 5:5;

Ephesians 5:8 and by Peter in 1 Peter 2:9, where moving from
darkness to light is connected with becoming the royal priesthood.
As with all metaphors, we need to take the particular sense of the
metaphor, rather than all possible meanings of 'night'; unlike in real
life, the absence of night does not mean the absence of rest, since
those dying in the Lord enjoy rest (14:13).

Theology
John's vision of the holy city and its architectural features had the
effect of deconstructing the differentiated *space* of country, city,
temple and sanctuary so that almost the whole world becomes the
sanctuary of God's presence (see the 'Theology' section following
21:21). In describing the people of God and their experience in the
holy city before the presence of God, John effects a parallel
deconstruction of differentiated *status*. Where previously there were
nations, a holy people, a priestly caste and a high priest, now all who
enter the city from 'every tribe, language, people and nation' attain
the status of the high priest, seeing God and the lamb face to face
and enjoying unmediated communion, having access to the waters
of life and the tree of life. This undifferentiated priestly people of
God, functioning as a temple and with the water of life (expressing
the presence of the Spirit) poured out on them all, is exactly how
Paul and the other New Testament writers characterize the early
Christian community. We are God's temple (1 Cor. 3:16–17; Eph.
2:21), which is the place of his dwelling; we have had the Spirit
poured out on and in us (Rom. 5:5); we are the priestly people of
God, mediating between God and the world, and offering up to God
those who come to know him through our testimony (Rom. 15:16;
1 Pet. 2:5, 9). All this is true because we are beginning to live out the
future in the present: we are living in the (partly realized) vision of
the heavenly city in our day-to-day earthly lives (1 Cor. 10:11).

15. EPILOGUE TO THE VISION REPORT AND THE LETTER (22:6–21)

Context

Although the chapter division falls five verses earlier, it is clear that the first five verses of Revelation 22 belong to the vision that formed the bulk of Revelation 21, not least because of the repetition of 'And he showed me' in 22:1 (AT). The final words of 22:5 draw this final vision together with a series of affirmations and negations ('No longer . . . they will see him . . . no more night . . .'), reaching a climax in the promise that 'they will reign for ever and ever'.

The focus now turns from the content of what John has seen and heard to what he has written to communicate this to others. There is a fascinating shift of emphasis: what matters is not John's revelatory experience, nor the content of his visions and auditions themselves, but the words he has used to describe them. It is these very words that are the prophetic gift from Jesus, suggesting to John's audience that it is to the words themselves that they must attend. Repeated focus on the importance of these words is interwoven with repeated promises and warnings – warnings to those who tamper with these words, and to those who fail to heed the call to repentance, and promises to those who keep (i.e. both preserve and act on) the words John has written, and to those who accept the invitation of the free offer of life. In this way, John is closely identifying what he has written with the very words of Jesus himself; to receive this book (rightly understood) is to receive the good news.

Comment

6. Once more, it is not entirely clear who is speaking to John – whether Christ, the angel mentioned in 1:1 (who is never clearly identified) or the angel who is one of the seven who had the bowls and who showed John the holy city in 21:9 (which is not necessarily the same angel as in 17:1; see comment on 21:9). This last option is the most likely (notwithstanding the change in the following verse), since the narrative does not suggest any change of subject by its content. The claim that *these words are [trustworthy] and true* has been made twice before (19:9; 21:5; see also Dan. 2:45), each time in relation to a specific saying and attached to the command to 'write'. The quality of the sayings in each case relates to the quality of the one with whom they originate, whether Jesus (the faithful and true witness, 3:14; 19:11) or God ('holy and true', 6:10; 'just and true', 15:3; 16:7; see comment on 21:5). But here, no specific command has been given, and the comment that follows connects 'these words' with the whole of the revelation given to John from the beginning. Rather than referring to something *within* John's vision report, then, John's record of the angel's words refers to *all* that he has written, and is thus a claim for the divine inspiration of the whole book, such that (as a testimony to Jesus) it is to be on a par with other eyewitness apostolic testimony to Jesus in the Gospels.[1] It also emphasizes that John has not written a report of a divinely inspired vision, but is giving us a divinely inspired vision report.

John's claim for what he writes as being 'the words of this prophecy' (1:3; 22:18) is confirmed by the angel's words that this message has come from *the Lord, the God of the spirits of the prophets*

---

1. In a similar way, John's Gospel records Jesus saying that his teaching is God's sanctifying word and that he has passed it on to the disciples, and John claims to have made a faithful record of it (John 17:14, 17; 20:31).

(AT). This unique title for God (elsewhere 'Lord God', *kyrios ho theos*, but here *ho kyrios ho theos*) comes in a saying very similar to that of 19:10: 'The testimony of Jesus is the Spirit of prophecy.' It is the Spirit of God who guides the prophets, such that the words of true prophets need to be taken seriously as the words of God and the testimony of Jesus. The cascade of transmission (God/Jesus, angel, John, servants) matches that in 1:1, and is one of many parallels between this epilogue and the opening epistolary prologue in the first half of Revelation 1.

7. Although that language of 'what must soon take place [*en tachei*]' in 1:1 had a connotation of swiftness rather than immediacy (see comment on 1:1), the phrase *I am coming soon [tachys]* (which must now be the unannounced words of Jesus) does have this sense of immediacy of relevance. This need not suggest that all the events of the vision report will happen straight away, but rather that John's message is to be heard by his audience and is not about some far-off future (see comment on v. 10 below). This is the sixth of the seven blessings in the text, the first one (1:3) and this one related to *the words of the prophecy in this book* (AT), while the others (14:13; 16:15; 19:9; 20:6; 22:14) are related to those who receive the eschatological promises described. *Keep[ing]* is typical Old Testament language for obeying the commandments; the purpose of this prophecy (like all others) is not to entertain or to invite speculation, but to call the audience to faithful, joyful and hopeful obedience to God.

8–9. *John* had not mentioned himself by name since the epistolary opening in Revelation 1 (1:1, 4, 9), and this change of style makes some commentators see this point as the beginning of the epilogue proper, with the previous two verses belonging to the end of the final vision. As we have seen, what John has *heard* has been as important as what he has *seen*, with some extended sections recording speech only. This is characteristic Johannine language of testimony ('what we have seen and heard', 1 John 1:3) which even finds its way into Peter and John's confession before their accusers in Acts 4:20. It echoes Daniel's first-person declaration in Daniel 12:5, and is typical of the statements of first-century witnesses in official documents.

It is unlikely that the repetition of the scene in 19:10, where John similarly *fell down to worship at the feet of the angel*, is the result of a secondary editor making a clumsy mistake, since we have seen how often John repeats and reiterates things, even within a single vision episode. Rather, it creates a parallel ending of the vision of the holy city with the ending of the vision of the unholy city, 'Babylon'. It also has the effect at the end of the letter of depicting John as close to his audience's world, making mistakes just as they do, to complement the way he has identified with their situation at the beginning ('I, John, your brother and companion', 1:9). Just like the episode in 19:10, it also identifies the angels as *fellow-servant[s]* so that those who *keep the words of this scroll* (repeated from v. 7 for emphasis) are indeed on the side of the angels. This sets Jesus quite apart as someone who shares the worship of God in a way that no-one else, human or spiritual, is permitted to do.

10. The angel's next command, *Do not seal up the words of the prophecy of this book* (AT), is a direct parallel to the contrary command to Daniel during his visions: 'seal up the vision, for it concerns the distant future'; 'close up and seal the words of the scroll until the time of the end' (Dan. 8:26; 12:4). The visions of Daniel, who lived in the sixth century BC, related to events in the second century, which in comparison was 'the distant future'. This command tells John and his audience that what he has seen, heard and written down is quite clearly *not* about some distant time in the future, but relates to their immediate context. This does not exhaust the meaning of the final visions, since the historical challenges that John's audience face are located within a larger, cosmic vision. In terms of the timescale of Revelation as a whole, as modern readers we will sit between Jesus' exaltation and his return, and John remains our 'brother and companion in the suffering and kingdom and patient endurance . . . in Jesus'.

11. The following saying is structured as a poetic parallel:

Let those who are wrong . . . let those who are vile . . .
Let those who are right . . . let those who are holy . . .

In making the parallel, John coins the verb 'to be vile' or 'filthy' (*rhypainō*, based on the preceding noun *rhyparos*) which is otherwise unknown in Greek literature. The saying is close to both Daniel

12:10, 'Many will be purified, made spotless and refined, but the wicked will continue to be wicked', and Ezekiel 3:27, 'Whoever will listen let them listen, and whoever will refuse let them refuse', which in turn comes close to Isaiah's saying about those who will hear that Jesus quotes in relation to the mystery of his parables (Isa. 6:9–10; Mark 4:12). The point here is not that destiny is fixed, which would nullify the primary rhetorical point of the whole book – which is to urge steadfastness and (where necessary) repentance – but that our present actions will have eternal consequences.

12–13. Jesus says seven times in Revelation, *I am coming!* Despite the clearly future sense of the phrase here (and at 16:15; 22:7, 20; and probably 3:11), and the future orientation of Revelation's eschatology, in the first two occurrences of the phrase (2:5 and 2:16) the sense is clearly a local one. Moreover, Jesus is from the beginning depicted as coming among the assemblies by being the one like a son of man who is in the midst of the lampstands (1:13), and is also depicted as having a presence in the world through the seven spirits who are the 'seven eyes' of the lamb which are 'sent out into all the earth' (5:6). Jesus' final return should be seen in continuity with the other ways in which he 'comes', and as the completion and fulfilment of them.

The statement that he brings his *reward* with him continues a tradition that goes all the way back to God's encounter with Abraham in Genesis 15:1, 'I am ... your very great reward', and continues throughout the prophetic tradition (Isa. 40:10; 62:11). The repayment according to *their deeds* (AT) is a consistent theme of both Revelation and the wider New Testament, and does not stand in opposition to the free offer of the gift of life (see comment on 14:13: 'their deeds go with them', AT). But in both Old and New Testaments, it is God who repays according to deeds (Ps. 62:12; Jer. 17:10; Rom. 2:6), and here Jesus takes up the role that was previously God's.

This merging of the roles and identities of Jesus and God is decisively confirmed in his claiming the titles that were distinctly attributed to God in 1:8 (*Alpha and O*, AT) and 21:6 ('the Alpha and the Omega', *the Beginning and the End*), and combining it with his claim to be *the First and the Last* from 1:17, to make a total of seven occurrences of this idea.

God	1:8	I am the Alpha and the O.
Jesus	1:17	I am the First and the Last.
God	21:6	I am the Alpha and the O,
		the Beginning and the End.
Jesus	22:13	I am the Alpha and the O,
		the First and the Last,
		the Beginning and the End.

The fullness of God is found in our encountering him in the person and redemption of Jesus.

14–15. The speech of Jesus, which began (unannounced) in verse 12, appears to continue here, since it is clearly continued in verse 16. These two verses again hold together the double emphasis carried throughout the book on the gracious invitation to the free gift of redemption, and warning of the consequences of judgment for those who refuse this offer – an emphasis which would have had a significant rhetorical impact on John's audience in the assemblies. Here we have the last of seven blessings in the book which began with those who read it aloud in the assemblies (1:3). The *wash[ing]* of *robes* is not a direct reference to baptism (which involves the washing of a person, not what the person wears), but is a close parallel to the washing 'in the blood of the Lamb' from 7:14, where it symbolizes the forgiveness of sins and the redemption that have been won by Jesus' death. The result of accepting this gift of grace is the *right to the tree of life*, which was denied Adam and Eve when they were expelled from the garden and means an end to death, and entry *through the gates of the city* (AT). It was made clear that 'nothing impure will ever enter it' (21:27), and so those who accept the gift of life are assumed also to become obedient to the holy commands of God (12:17; 14:12); on entering the city, they are admitted to the holy presence of God with his people.

The list of those prohibited is a close match to the other two lists of 'vice-committers' in 9:20–21; 21:8 (see comment on 21:8), though substituting the term *dogs* (not domestic pets as in some cultures, but wild, aggressive and unclean animals)[2] for the opening three

---

2. See the negative use of the term in Matt. 7:6; 15:26; and Phil. 3:2.

terms in 21:27. From a narrative point of view, the statement does not make sense, since the immoral have died in the lake of fire, the second death, in 20:15. The statement here contributes less to a universalist perspective on future destiny, and more to the rhetorical impact of the differentiation between the two groups: those who enter the city in response to the universal invitation, and those who choose to remain outside the always-open gates.

16–21. The shape of these final verses bears a remarkable resemblance to the final verses in Paul's first letter to Corinth, where he appears to take the pen from his amanuensis to add final greetings in his own hand (which seems to have been his habit) in 1 Corinthians 16:21–23 (AT):

I, Paul write this greeting	I, Jesus . . . bear witness . . .
Let anyone be accursed . . .	If anyone adds . . . God will add to the plagues . . .
Our Lord, come!	Come, Lord Jesus!
The grace of the Lord Jesus be with you	The grace of the Lord Jesus be with all

In terms of the narrative form of the text, John is claiming that Jesus is the real author, not just of the visions that John has seen, but of his prophetic testimony to all he has 'heard and seen'. It is not just the visions and auditions themselves, but John's record of them which have the apostolic authority that comes from being an eyewitness to Jesus. The solemn warnings in verses 18–19 confirm the importance of the exact words which John has written.

The articulation of Jesus' name, his affirmation of his testimony and the confirmation of his titles all conform to the usual practice of witnesses establishing the reliability of the account they are authenticating. The *you* to whom the message is sent is plural; this is unlikely to be the 'angel[s] of the assemblies' in Revelation 2 – 3, since they do not feature again, nor the members of the assemblies themselves, since the message is to be passed on to them. It perhaps refers to John's 'fellow-prophets' alluded to in 11:18; 16:6; 22:6, and those who 'read aloud' the message (1:3). The title *Root . . . of David*, repeated from 5:5, affirms his identity as the Davidic Messiah, and his being the *Morning Star* suggests both Jewish messianic hope and Roman ideas of a divine ruler (see comment on 2:28).

John's prophetic, visionary letter concludes with multiple affirmations which echo the rhetorical effect of the pattern of the praise and acclamation of all creation. John's audience are not a small and insignificant group surviving within the crushing power of a human empire, but are joined by *the Spirit* of God in their longing to see Jesus *come* and take up his just and holy rule. Despite the seriousness of the consequences for those outside the city, the generous invitation remains open for all *who are thirsty* to come and *take the free gift of the water of life*. Whatever else the book of Revelation says, it remains essentially a book that communicates a message of *grace* for those who will receive it. Amen.

Theology

And so John ends where he has begun – signing off using epistolary features that match the epistolary features in chapter 1. His emphasis is not on his own revelatory experience, but on the very words he has used to describe them – and, surprisingly, it is not just his visions that come from Jesus, but the words themselves. John is claiming that it is Jesus himself – the origin and the subject of this 'revelation' in 1:1 – who is the real author of this message, and that John is merely his visionary-prophetic amanuensis, passing on to others what has been passed on to him.

What more can we add as we reach the end of this extraordinary prophetic-revelatory letter? The vividness of its images, the power of its rhetoric, the depth of its theological reflection and the continued relevance of its message have made it the most influential text in all human history.

Like the tracks coming into a central railway station in a capital city, all the lines of theological thought from earlier in the book converge in these last chapters and in the climactic vision of the eschatological presence of God with his people. Because John has been drawing on the whole range of the Old Testament canon, there is a powerful sense in which the end of Revelation also draws together all the hopes and aspirations of the people of God from the long history of his dealings with his people – and in doing so, all the hopes and aspirations of humanity itself. It is a fitting end to the canon of Scripture. Here we find the rediscovery of the idyll of Eden, though transformed from a garden into a city; here are realized both the promise to Noah for the renewal of the earth and the promise to Abraham that his offspring will be beyond counting. We enter here the final freedom from the slavery of sin, a city that fulfils every promise of the Promised Land. It is occupied by a holy people under the rule of a just and holy God, free from threat and danger. The exile of sin and rebellion which led to estrangement from God has finally come to an end, and all God's people have found their home. All this has come about because of the sacrifice of the lamb on the throne – the faithful witness of the man Jesus in whom the fullness of the Godhead dwelt bodily (Col. 2:9).

Yet the final verses remind us of the beginning: that this message does not float free from human history, but was given to a particular person, at a particular time and in a particular place, and was given to transform the particular lives of those who first read it and heard it read. And we need to read it, the message of Jesus to the assemblies in Asia conveyed through John, knowing something about their own particular circumstances, so that we can understand how this transcendent vision of hope and faith might transform the particulars of our time, place and culture as we wait with them for God's promises finally to be fulfilled.